Ending

Reviewing the Process

Final Evaluating

Sharing Ending Feelings and Saying Goodbye

Recording the Closing Summary

Working and Evaluating

Rehearsing Action Steps

Reviewing Action Steps

Evaluating

Focusing

Educating

Advising

Representing

Responding with Immediacy

Reframing

Confronting

Pointing Out Endings

Progress Recording

Contracting

Reflecting an Issue

Identifying an Issue

Clarifying Issues for Work

Establishing Goals

Developing an Action Plan

Identifying Action Steps

Planning for Evaluation

Summarizing the Contract

GENERIC SOCIAL WORK SKILLS
(apply throughout all phases and processes)

Professionalism

Integrity

Professional Knowledge and Self-Efficacy

Critical Thinking and Lifelong Learning

Self-Understanding and Self-Control

Cultural Competence and Acceptance of Others

Social Support

Ethical Decision Making

Identify Applicable Legal Duties and Professional Ethics

Explore Motives, Means, Ends, and Effects

Decide and Plan Ethical Action; Record

Implement Plan; Record

Monitor Effects and Outcomes; Record

The Basic Interpersonal Skills: Talking and Listening

Talking: Using Speech, Language, and Body Language

Listening: Hearing, Observing, Encouraging, and Remembering

Active Listening: Combining Talking and Listening to Promote Understanding

THE SOCIAL WORK SKILLS WORKBOOK

Fourth Edition

Barry Cournoyer
Indiana University

THOMSON
BROOKS/COLE

Australia • Canada • Mexico • Singapore • Spain
United Kingdom • United States

Editor: Lisa Gebo
Assistant Editor: Alma Dea Michelena
Editorial Assistant: Sheila Walsh
Technology Project Manager: Barry Connolly
Marketing Manager: Caroline Concilla
Marketing Assistant: Mary Ho
Advertising Project Manager: Tami Strang
Project Manager, Editorial Production:
    Candace Chen

Print Buyer: Doreen Suruki
Permissions Editor: Sarah Harkrader
Production Service: Robin Gold,
    Forbes Mill Press
Cover Designer: Roger Knox
Cover Image: © 2003 Roger Knox
Cover Printer: The Lehigh Press, Inc.
Compositor: Linda Weidemann, Wolf Creek Press
Printer: Quebecor World/Dubuque

Printed in the United States
1 2 3 4 5 6 7 07 06 05 04

For more information about our products, contact us at:
**Thomson Learning
Academic Resource Center
1-800-423-0563**
For permission to use material from this text, contact us by: **Phone:** 1-800-730-2214
Fax: 1-800-730-2215
Web: http://www.thomsonrights.com

Library of Congress Control Number: 2003114701

ISBN 0-534-53413-9

**Thomson Brooks/Cole
10 Davis Drive
Belmont, CA 94002-3098
USA**

Asia
Thomson Learning
5 Shenton Way #01-01
UIC Building
Singapore 068808

Australia/New Zealand
Thomson Learning
102 Dodds Street
Southbank, Victoria 3006
Australia

Canada
Nelson
1120 Birchmount Road
Toronto, Ontario M1K 5G4
Canada

Europe/Middle East/Africa
Thomson Learning
High Holborn House
50/51 Bedford Row
London WC1R 4LR
United Kingdom

Latin America
Thomson Learning
Seneca, 53
Colonia Polanco
11560 Mexico D.F.
Mexico

Spain/Portugal
Paraninfo
Calle Magallanes, 25
28015 Madrid, Spain

Contents

CHAPTER 3   Ethical Decision Making   81

CHAPTER 4   Talking and Listening: The Basic Interpersonal Skills   125

CHAPTER 5   Preparing   159

CHAPTER 6   Beginning   187

CHAPTER 7 Exploring 215

CHAPTER 8 Assessing 267

CHAPTER 9 Contracting 313

CHAPTER 10   Working and Evaluating   363

CHAPTER 11   Ending   419

Preface

The impetus for developing this workbook originated with the observations and, yes, complaints from students that social work professors and their textbooks tend to "talk *about* practice rather than help us learn what to do and how to do it." This was a typical comment: "In the classroom, the professors talk at such abstract levels that when I'm with clients, I don't really know what I'm supposed to do." Clearly, we needed more practical and applied learning materials. *The Social Work Skills Workbook* addresses this need and provides opportunities for learners to gain proficiency in the essential social work skills using simulated case situations and various learning exercises.

This workbook is designed for use in the following contexts: (1) as the primary text or source book for social work skills laboratory courses (which might be entitled "interviewing skills," "interpersonal skills," "professional skills," "interactional skills," "interpersonal communication skills," or "helping skills" labs); (2) as a secondary text and workbook for social work practice courses; (3) by social work students and field instructors during practicum experiences; and (4) by professional social workers interested in refreshing their proficiency with essential social work skills. Social workers and social work students currently providing service to actual clients may alter some of the workbook exercises, particularly the summary exercises, for use in agency settings.

Purpose

The overall purpose for *The Social Work Skills Workbook* is to enable learners to develop proficiency in skills needed for ethical and effective social work practice.

Goals

Following completion of this workbook, learners should be able to demonstrate the following:

- Understanding of the essential facilitative qualities and the characteristics of professionalism
- Proficiency in the basic interpersonal skills of talking and listening
- Knowledge of the core values, ethics, and legal obligations of professional social workers
- Proficiency in ethical decision making
- Knowledge of the phases and processes of social work practice
- Proficiency in skills associated with the preparing, beginning, exploring, assessing, contracting, working and evaluating, and ending phases of social work practice
- Ability to assess proficiency in the social work skills
- Ability to integrate and synthesize learning through the preparation of a Social Work Skills Learning Portfolio

The Social Work Skills Workbook provides opportunities for students to understand and practice the essential skills of social work practice. All the various skills that might potentially have some relevance for some social workers on some occasions are not presented. Rather, the workbook addresses those skills that are (1) most applicable to the purposes and phases or processes of contemporary social work practice; (2) supported by social work knowledge, values, ethics, and obligations; (3) consistent with the essential facilitative qualities; and (4) reflective of the characteristics of professionalism.

The social work skills are organized and presented to coincide with the phases, processes, or "waves"[1] of contemporary social work practice. Of course, any phase-to-phase or step-by-step approach runs the risk of suggesting that service to all clients follows the same linear sequence and that the characteristics and skills relevant to one phase are distinctly different from those of another. This is not the case. Sometimes the work usually undertaken in one phase may occur in another or the phases themselves may be reordered to address urgent circumstances. Indeed, many of the dynamics, tasks, functions, and skills applicable to one phase may, in work with a particular client system, be evident in other phases as well. Some skills may be used repeatedly throughout the course of a social worker's efforts with and for the people served.

The fourth edition of *The Social Work Skills Workbook* maintains the general organizational structure of earlier editions. However, a number of changes enhance its congruence with contemporary social work practice and emerging research findings. For example, recent meta-analytic studies concerning the significance of the "core facilitative conditions" are summarized to provide a solid scientific basis for the social work

---

[1] The term "wave" has been used by certain theorists to suggest that a metaphor of ocean waves coming into and receding from a beach might more aptly describe individual growth and development than does the term "stage" or "phase."

skills. Court decisions and policies such as the Americans with Disabilities Act (ADA) and the Health Insurance Portability and Accountability Act (HIPAA) that affect professional practice receive increased attention. Cultural competence and strengths perspectives are incorporated as integral dimensions of all aspects of social work practice. The ethical decision-making chapter has been substantially revised. In addition, information technology resources are recognized as increasingly important for contemporary practice. Indeed, accompanying this book is a password that entitles you to a four-month subscription to InfoTrac® College Edition, an invaluable resource that permits access to bibliographic databases and full-text materials. Several exercises in the workbook afford students opportunities to read pertinent journal articles through InfoTrac College Edition and to review relevant materials via the World Wide Web.

Several features of earlier editions are maintained. Students prepare a Social Work Skills Learning Portfolio to facilitate learning and document progress. The learning portfolios may be used for individual or group formative and summative assessment as well as for the purposes of program and outcomes evaluation.

Professionalism continues to receive substantial attention. Integrity, professional knowledge, critical thinking and lifelong learning, self-efficacy, cultural competence, and certain other individual characteristics are recognized as fundamental aspects of professionalism. They are essential for developing and maintaining competence as a social worker. Ecological factors such as social support and social networks receive attention, as do strengths, resources, resiliencies, and assets within clients and their social systems. Goals, rather than problems, are featured as the guiding foci for social work practice. The ethical decision-making chapter incorporates changes in the code of ethics, the impact of recent court decisions, and the enactment of laws that affect social work practice. In addition, several exercises have been updated to reflect emerging social problems and service contexts.

The book is arranged in the following manner:

Chapter 1 provides overall perspective concerning the nature of social work practice, populations served, social problems addressed, and settings where social service occurs. The first chapter includes a definition of *social work skill* and outlines the conceptual framework used to select skills addressed in the book. The chapter also introduces you to the essential facilitative qualities and the characteristics of professionalism that ethical, effective social workers consistently reflect in their work with and on behalf of clients.

Chapter 2 explores the topic of professionalism in greater depth. In that chapter, you will explore aspects of integrity and complete an instrument to stimulate further consideration of the issue in relation to professional practice. The dimensions of the contemporary social work knowledge base are outlined. Critical thinking, lifelong learning, and self-efficacy are explored in recognition of the increasingly important need for social workers to engage actively and continuously in self-directed lifelong learning in order to maintain currency during this ever-advancing information age.

Several exercises yield self-assessment information related to the characteristics of social work professionalism. For example, you will complete activities designed to further your self-understanding of factors such as family of origin, ecological context, critical events, and social support. You will also attempt to identify your own prejudicial attitudes and discriminatory behaviors, determine the degree to which you accept others, and assess the extent of your self-control. Finally, you will complete a practice test and conduct a preliminary self-assessment of proficiency in the social work skills, assess your own readiness for the profession of social work, and begin to incorporate materials into your Social Work Skills Learning Portfolio.

Chapter 3 reviews the processes of ethical decision making in social work practice. You will learn about fundamental legal duties and obligations that apply to all helping professionals and review the core values and ethical principles that apply specifically to social workers. You will consider the issue of malpractice, the implications of recent court decisions, and the passage of relevant laws. You will explore decision-making processes by which ethical conflicts and dilemmas may be addressed. Finally, you will complete several exercises to strengthen development of the ethical decision making skills.

Chapter 4 reviews the fundamental interpersonal skills of talking and listening, and writing. Included in this chapter are talking skills associated with voice, speech, and language; body language; and listening skills related to hearing, observing, encouraging, and remembering. The talking and listening skills are then combined in the form of active listening—through which social workers invite, listen, remember, and reflect what other people express. Because of the rich racial and cultural diversity throughout North America, considerable attention is paid to the significance of language, choice of words, and nonverbal behavior within the context of cultural competence.

Chapters 5 through 11 address the skills associated with the following phases or processes of social work practice: preparing, beginning, exploring, assessing, contracting, working and evaluating, and ending. Each chapter includes a general introduction to the purpose and tasks associated with that particular phase. Following the introduction, the social work skills commonly used during the phase are identified and illustrated. Exercises intended to help you learn to apply each skill are provided after each section and at the end of each chapter. Completion of the learning exercises leads to the preparation of two "case records." Based on self-understanding gained earlier, you will prepare the description and assessment sections of your own "Personal Case Record." In addition, you will develop a more complete "Practice Case Record" in the course of conducting five interviews with a colleague who agrees to serve as a "practice client." The five interviews provide an opportunity for you to simulate all phases of the working relationship (preparing, beginning, exploring, assessing, contracting, working and evaluating, and ending). In addition to the description, assessment, and contract sections, you will also prepare progress notes and a closing summary as you engage your colleague in this intensive practice exercise. Both "case records" represent important written products for inclusion in the Social Work Skills Learning Portfolio.

Cases and situations selected as illustrative examples and for use within learning exercise sections have been drawn from a variety of agency settings and circumstances. Although many of the case vignettes involve interaction with individuals, the significance of environmental factors is consistently reflected. Several examples of multi-person client systems (e.g., dyads, families, groups) and nonclient systems (e.g., referral sources, community resources, or related social systems) are included. The case vignettes have been selected with a view toward diversity of age, gender, sexual orientation, and racial, ethnic, and socioeconomic status.

Professors who employ the workbook in their social work courses may use the exercises in a variety of ways. As part of a homework or in-class assignment, learners may be asked to respond to certain exercises. Instructors may then call on class members to share their responses and discuss the characteristics that account for proficient applications of the skills. Alternately, instructors may assign certain exercises as written homework to be submitted for evaluation. The pages of the workbook are perforated to allow for easy removal. Numerous self-assessment opportunities stimulate evaluation processes of various kinds: self-evaluation and peer-assessment as well as evaluation by instructors. Indeed, instructors may use aggregated assessment data to highlight skill areas that need further collective attention or to move more quickly through those where proficiency has been achieved. Similarly, the Social Work Skills Learning Portfolios may be reviewed periodically and used for process or summative assessment purposes.

During classroom meetings, learners may be asked to form pairs, triads, or small groups to carry out selected learning exercises. Role-plays in which learners alternately assume the part of client and social worker can be especially effective learning experiences—particularly when there is timely constructive feedback from others. In general, instructors should recognize that the social work skills are ultimately used in the context of helping people. Therefore, learning processes that approximate the actual *doing* with opportunities for evaluative feedback are preferred.

This edition contains several appendices to support learning. Appendix 1 introduces the Social Work Skills Learning Portfolio and contains a checklist of products that may be included. Appendix 2 contains a Social Work Skills Practice Test that learners may use as a pretest and again as a posttest indicator. The practice test may also serve as a useful study guide, or as an overall gauge of knowledge and proficiency in a wide range of social work skills. Appendix 3 presents the Social Work Skills Self-Appraisal Questionnaire, another tool for assessing proficiency in the skills addressed in the workbook. Subscales of the questionnaire are duplicated at the end of most of the chapters enabling learners to track changes in their proficiency ratings over time.

Appendix 4 presents an alphabetized vocabulary of Standard English "feeling words" that learners may find useful for developing their empathic reflection skills. Appendix 5 consists of a rating form that may be used to assess the quality of performance of the social work skills during interviews with simulated or actual clients.

Acknowledgments

The fourth edition of *The Social Work Skills Workbook* reflects the experience of some 30 years of social work practice and 25 years of teaching experience. Over the years, clients and students have consistently been my most important teachers. For this edition, I am most appreciative of my physically challenged students and clients. Time and time again, they forgave my mistakes and guided me toward reverence.

I am especially indebted to those clients who allowed me a glimpse into their worlds. Their life stories are remarkable. I feel privileged to participate with them in their heroic journeys. Likewise, students in my social work courses have been my most gifted teachers. They have taught me a great deal. If they have learned half of what I have learned from them, I will feel satisfied. I also appreciate the letters and email messages I have received from social work students and professors. I treasure their suggestions for improving the book.

I would also like to recognize those social workers whose teachings and writings have affected me professionally and contributed to the approach taken in this workbook. Dr. Eldon Marshall, my former professor and current colleague, was the first to introduce me to the *interpersonal helping skills* (Marshall, Kurtz, & Associates, 1982). I shall never forget his class or the impact of my first videotaped interview. Dr. Dean Hepworth, both through his teaching and his writing, furthered the skills emphasis begun during my master's education. My former colleague, the late Dr. Beulah Compton, also deserves much credit. Her clear conception of fundamental social work processes has served me well indeed. I shall long remember our sometimes heated but always stimulating conversations about social work practice.

Thanks are due to manuscript reviewers, who offered valuable suggestions: Michael Berghoef, Ferris State University; Cynthia Bishop, Meredith College; Krishna Guadalupe, California State University, Sacramento; Lee Hipple, Texas Women's University; and Tammy Linseisen, University of Texas, Austin.

Much credit is due the extraordinary editorial staff at Brooks/Cole and Thomson Learning. Lisa Gebo, Alma Dea Michelena, and Caroline Concilla are precious! Their professionalism, dedication, enthusiasm, understanding, and friendship have remained constant for many, many years.

I also wish to thank my mother, Marjorie Murphy Cournoyer, for her love and compassion for others, and Catherine's parents, Grant and Karma Hughes for their unflagging support. And, finally, to my loving partner, Catherine Hughes Cournoyer, and our children, John Paul and Michael, I can only express enormous gratitude. Catherine is the most generous person I have ever met and, without question, the best social worker. Each day, she and the boys continue to make me more and better than I could possibly be without them.

Barry Cournoyer

Chapter 1

Introduction

Welcome to the exciting and challenging profession of social work! As a social worker, you will serve people in all walks of life and in all kinds of situations. The range of settings in which you might serve is wide and varied. The contexts for social work practice are often complex, usually demanding, and always challenging. To serve competently in such circumstances, social workers today need to be knowledgeable, ethical, accountable, and proficient. This chapter (see Box 1.1) introduces the social work skills, qualities, and characteristics needed for ethical, effective social work practice in contemporary society.

BOX 1.1

Chapter Purpose

The purpose of this chapter is to introduce learners to the social work skills, qualities, and characteristics needed for ethical, effective social work practice in contemporary society.

Goals

Following completion of this chapter, learners should be able to

◆ Understand the breadth and complexity of contemporary social work practice
◆ Define social work skill

(continued)

BOX 1.1 *continued*

- ◆ Identify the phases or processes of social work practice
- ◆ Discuss the significance of the essential facilitative qualities for professional relationships
- ◆ Discuss the characteristics of professionalism
- ◆ Understand the purposes and functions of the Social Work Skills Learning Portfolio
- ◆ Discuss the qualities and characteristics needed by ethical, effective social workers

At some point in your career as a social worker, you might serve in a child-protection capacity, responding to indications that a child may be at risk of abuse or neglect. You may help families improve their child-caring capabilities or serve in the emergency room of a hospital, intervening with persons and families in crises. You may lead therapy groups for children who have been sexually victimized or provide education and counseling to abusive adults.

You may aid couples whose relationships are faltering or help single parents who seek guidance and support in rearing their children. You may serve persons who abuse alcohol and drugs or help family members who have been affected by the substance abuse of a parent, child, spouse, or sibling. You might work in a residential setting for youthful offenders, a prison for adults, or a psychiatric institution. You might serve in a University counseling center, working with college students, faculty members, and other campus employees. You could help people who are in some way physically or mentally challenged. You might serve in a school system or perhaps as a consultant to a police department. You could work in a mayor's office, serve on the staff of a state legislator, or perhaps even become a member of Congress yourself.

You may function in a crisis intervention capacity for a suicide prevention service. You could work for a health maintenance organization (HMO), a managed health care system, or an employee assistance program (EAP). As a social worker, you might act as an advocate for persons who have experienced discrimination, oppression, or exploitation, perhaps because of racism, sexism, or ageism. You might work with homeless persons, runaway youth, or with street people struggling to survive through panhandling or prostitution. You might work with people victimized by crime, or perhaps with those who engaged in criminal activity. You might serve in a domestic violence program, providing social services to people affected by child abuse, spouse abuse, or elder abuse. You could provide psychosocial services to persons dealing with a physical illness, such as cancer, kidney failure, Alzheimer's disease, or AIDS, and help their families cope with the myriad psychosocial effects of such an illness. You might work in a hospice, helping people prepare for their own deaths or that of a family member from a terminal illness. You could help persons locate needed services or resources by providing information and arranging referrals. You might serve immigrants, refugees, transients, or migrant workers. You might counsel individuals suffering from a serious mental illness, such as schizophrenia or bipolar disorder, and provide support and education to their families. You could work in an assisted-care facility for aged persons, leading groups or counseling family members. You might serve in a halfway house, work with foster parents, or perhaps provide information and support to teenage parents. Or, as an increasing number of social workers do, you might serve in industry, consulting with employers and employees about problems and issues that affect their well-being and productivity.

The range of settings in which you could practice your profession and the variety of functions that you could serve as a social worker are immense indeed. Such breadth, diversity, and complexity can be overwhelming. You may ask yourself, "Can I possibly learn what I need to so that I can serve competently as a social worker in all those places, serving such different people, and helping them to address such complex issues?" The answer to that question is certainly No! You could never become truly competent in all the arenas where social workers practice because it would require a greater breadth and depth of knowledge and expertise than any one person could ever acquire. Indeed, a specialized body of knowledge and skill is needed for each practice setting, each special population group, and each psychosocial issue. You cannot know everything, do everything, or be competent in helping people struggling with every one of the enormous array of social problems. However, you can acquire expertise in those skills that are common to social work practice with all population groups and all psychosocial issues in all settings. These common social work skills bring coherence to the profession, despite its extraordinary variety.

In addition to applying certain common skills, social workers tend to approach clients from a similar perspective—one that is reflected in a distinct professional language. For example, when referring to the people they serve, most social workers prefer the term *client, person,* or *consumer,* rather than *patient, subject,* or *case.* Social workers also favor the word *assessment* rather than *diagnosis, study, examination,* or *investigation.* Furthermore, they tend to look for *strengths, assets, resources, resiliencies, competencies,* and *abilities* rather than attending exclusively to *problems, obstacles, deficiencies,* or *pathologies.* Reflected by this distinctive use of professional language, such a common perspective is characteristic of most contemporary social workers, regardless of their particular practice settings.

Professional social workers have earned a baccalaureate, master's, or doctoral degree in social work. They are licensed or certified to practice social work in their locale. They adopt certain common professional values that pervade all aspects of their helping activities, pledge adherence to a social work code of ethics, and usually view social work in a manner similar to that reflected in the International Federation of Social Workers' (IFSW) definition of social work:

> The social work profession promotes social change, problem solving in human relationships and the empowerment and liberation of people to enhance well-being. Utilising theories of human behaviour and social systems, social work intervenes at the points where people interact with their environments. Principles of human rights and social justice are fundamental to social work. (IFSW, 2000, Definition section, para. 1)

Social workers, regardless of setting or function, tend to view the *person-and-situation* (PAS), *person-in-environment* (PIE), or *person-issue-situation* as the basic unit of attention. In addition, they consider the enhancement of social functioning and the promotion or restoration of "a mutually beneficial interaction between individuals and society to improve the quality of life for everyone" (National Association of Social Workers, 1981c) as the overriding purpose of practice. This dual focus on people and society leads social workers to consider multiple systems—even when an individual person is formally the "client." Indeed, most social workers always consider and regularly involve other people or other social systems in the helping process.

Social workers tend to conceive of people and situations as continually changing and as having the potential for planned change. They view professional practice as predominantly *for* clients, the community, and society. Whatever personal benefits might accrue to them personally are secondary; the notion of service to others is foremost. The primacy of service in social work is reflected through a special sensitivity to those living in poverty and other at-risk individuals, vulnerable populations, and oppressed peoples. Indeed, people with the lowest status and the least power constitute social work's primary constituency.

Social workers recognize that professional service to others often involves powerful interpersonal processes that have considerable potential for harm as well as for good. They realize that competent practice requires exceptional personal and professional integrity. Each social worker needs a highly developed understanding of oneself and extraordinary personal discipline and self-control. A great deal more than good intentions, admirable personal qualities, and compassionate feelings are required. Social workers' words and actions should be based on professional knowledge, informed by critical thought, and guided by social work values, ethics, and obligations.

Social Work Skills

The term *skill* has become extremely popular in social work and other helping professions during the past half-century. Several social work textbooks incorporate *skill* or *skills* in their titles (Freeman, 1998; Henry, 1981, 1992; Hepworth, Rooney, & Larsen, 2002; Middleman & Goldberg, 1990; Phillips, 1957; Shulman, 1999; Vass, 1996; Yuen, 2002). The term *skill*, however, is not always used in exactly the same way. It means different things to different authors.

For example, *skill* has been described as "the practice component that brings knowledge and values together and converts them to action as a response to concern and need" (Johnson, 1995, p. 55), "a complex organization of behavior directed toward a particular goal or activity" (Johnson, 1995, p. 431), and a "social worker's capacity to *use* a method in order to *further* a process directed toward the accomplishment of a social work purpose as that purpose finds expression in a specific program or service" (Smalley, 1967, p. 17). And *skill* has also been described as "the production of specific behaviors under the precise conditions designated for their use" (Middleman & Goldberg, 1990, p. 12).

Henry (1981, p. vii) suggested that skills are "finite and discrete sets of behaviors or tasks employed by a worker at a given time, for a given purpose, in a given manner."

She (Henry, 1992, p. 20) also cited Phillips (1957), who characterized *skill* as "knowledge in action." Morales and Sheafor described *skills* as the "ability to use knowledge and intervention techniques effectively" (Morales & Sheafor, 1998, p. 140).

These various definitions are extremely useful. They provide context for the way skills have been selected and addressed here. The following definition has been adopted for use in this workbook:

> A social work skill is a circumscribed set of discrete cognitive and behavioral actions that (1) derive from social work knowledge and from social work values, ethics, and obligations, (2) are consistent with the essential facilitative qualities, (3) reflect the characteristics of professionalism, and (4) comport with a social work purpose within the context of a phase or process of practice.

Although they are usually associated with particular phases or processes of practice, social work skills should never be viewed as technical activities to be carried out, robot-like, at the same relative time and in the same way with all clients and all situations. Rather, the social worker selects, combines, and adapts specific social work skills to suit the particular needs and characteristics of the person-and-situation.

The range and scope of skills that effective social workers might use in the context of their service are wide and varied. A "social worker's skills include being proficient in communication, assessing problems and client workability, matching needs with resources, developing resources, and changing social structures" (Barker, 1995). More than 20 years ago, the National Association of Social Workers (NASW) outlined 12 skills (1981b, pp. 17–18, used with permission):

1. Listen to others with understanding and purpose.
2. Elicit information and assemble relevant facts to prepare a social history, assessment, and report.
3. Create and maintain professional helping relationships.
4. Observe and interpret verbal and nonverbal behavior and use knowledge of personality theory and diagnostic methods.
5. Engage clients (including individuals, families, groups, and communities) in efforts to resolve their own problems and to gain trust.
6. Discuss sensitive emotional subjects supportively and without being threatening.
7. Create innovative solutions to clients' needs.
8. Determine the need to terminate the therapeutic relationship.
9. Conduct research, or interpret the findings of research and professional literature.
10. Mediate and negotiate between conflicting parties.
11. Provide inter-organizational liaison services.
12. Interpret and communicate social needs to funding sources, the public, or legislators.

The Council on Social Work Education (CSWE, 2001) also identified 12 abilities that professional social workers should reflect. Several refer specifically to selected skills. Among other abilities, graduates of CSWE accredited social work programs are expected to be able to "apply critical thinking skills," practice according to "the value base of the profession and its ethical standards and principles," "practice without discrimination and with respect, knowledge, and skills related to clients' age, class, color, culture, disability, ethnicity, family structure, gender, marital status, national origin, race, religion, sex, and sexual orientation," "apply the knowledge and skills of generalist social work practice with systems of all sizes," "evaluate their own practice interventions," and "use communication skills differentially across client populations, colleagues, and communities" (CSWE, 2001).

The skills chosen for inclusion in this workbook are compatible with those identified by the NASW and the abilities described in the Educational Policy and Accreditation Standards (EPAS) of the CSWE. More specifically, however, the skills addressed here are derived from the tasks associated with commonly identified phases or processes of social work practice, the essential facilitative qualities exhibited by most effective professional helpers, and the fundamental characteristics of professionalism. In this context, the *phases or processes of social work practice* include the following:

- Preparing
- Beginning
- Exploring
- Assessing
- Contracting
- Working and evaluating
- Ending

Effective social workers consistently demonstrate the following *essential facilitative qualities* in their work with clients:

- Empathy
- Respect
- Authenticity

Finally, competent social workers integrate the following characteristics of *professionalism* throughout all aspects of their service:

- Integrity
- Professional knowledge
- Critical thinking and lifelong learning
- Ethical decision making
- Self-understanding and self-control
- Cultural competence and acceptance of others
- Social support and self-efficacy

The tasks associated with each phase are organized into small, manageable units of thought and action that are consistent with the essential facilitative qualities and compatible with the central characteristics of professionalism. Integrated and synthesized in this fashion, they form *the social work skills*.

Common Factors and Essential Facilitative Qualities

During the second half of the 20th century, findings from research studies (Carkhuff, 1969; Carkhuff & Anthony, 1979; Lambert, 1976, 1982, 1983; Lambert & Bergin, 1994; Lambert, Christensen, & DeJulio, 1983; Rogers, 1951, 1957; Truax & Carkhuff, 1967; Weinberger, 1993) suggested that certain common conditions present in most counseling and psychotherapeutic approaches accounted for much of the beneficial outcomes.

As early as the 1930s, helping professionals (Rosenzweig, 1936) discussed the presence of implicit common factors in diverse therapeutic approaches. Recent analyses of the research yielded four general categories of common nonspecific factors associated with client outcomes in counseling and psychotherapy (Asay & Lambert, 1999; Lambert, 1992, 2003; Lambert & Bergin, 1994; Lambert & Cattani-Thompson, 1996):

1. *Client and Situational Factors:* Strengths, assets, resources, challenges, and limitations within the client and client's external situation. These extratherapeutic factors—what clients bring with them to the relationship with the helping professional—may have the most powerful impact on client outcomes (Lambert, 1992). Social work's emphasis on the person-and-situation corresponds to this finding.

2. *Relationship Factors:* Qualities of the helping professional and the resulting relationship between the client and helper. The nature of the client-worker relationship may have the second most significant effect on client outcomes (Lambert, 1992). Social workers have long recognized the importance of the relationship. Proficiency in the social work skills addressed in this book will help you establish and maintain positive working relationships with clients and others with whom you interact as part of your professional activities.

3. *Expectancy Factors:* Hopefulness, optimism, and expectations that the helping encounter will be beneficial are important dimensions. Such "placebo effects" significantly affect client outcomes (Lambert, 1992). Social workers commonly encourage hope and serve as examples to others through their positive attitudes and enthusiasm.

4. *Model and Technique Factors:* The models, strategies, techniques, and protocols adopted in the process of helping also affect outcomes. When combined, expectancy and model/technique factors may account for about the same amount of client outcome impact as do relationship factors (Lambert, 1992).

Other scholars reached similar conclusions about categories of common factors. In addition to the important dimensions of the nature and quality of the working relationship and client expectancies, one researcher also included (1) exposure to and exploration of problem issues, (2) practice in coping with or mastering aspects of the problematic issues, and (3) a conceptual means to understand and explain why and how the problems occur and how they can be managed (Weinberger, 1993, 1995, 2003).

Recognition of the importance of relationship factors encouraged researchers to explore qualities exhibited by helpers that might be associated with better client outcomes. Qualities such as empathy, caring, nonpossessive warmth, acceptance, affirmation, sincerity, and encouragement are frequently included among the characteristics of effective helpers (Hubble, Duncan, & Miller, 1999). When professionals reflect these qualities, they "result in a cooperative working endeavor in which the client's increased sense of trust, security, and safety, along with decreases in tension, threat, and anxiety, lead to changes in conceptualizing his or her problems and ultimately in acting differently by reframing fears, taking risks, and working through problems in interpersonal relationships (i.e., clients confront and cope with reality in more effective ways)" (Lambert & Cattani-Thompson, 1996, p. 603).

Identifying and measuring all the potential factors that affect the outcome of helping processes are enormously complicated undertakings. The picture is especially complex for social workers who fulfill disparate professional functions in extremely varied settings with a wide range of populations and extremely challenging psychosocial issues. Different social workers in different contexts assume quite different roles and responsibilities. Indeed, a single social worker may emphasize certain characteristics at various times. The social worker serving parents and siblings of babies in neonatal care in a children's hospital emphasizes different qualities than does one serving persons addicted to heroin or crack cocaine. Similarly the social worker "engaged in advocacy may need a more aggressive, directive, dominant approach to the interview" (Kadushin, 1983, p. 84).

Despite the breadth and diversity inherent in social work and the evolutionary nature of the relevant research findings, certain aspects of the worker-client experience are clearly related to client satisfaction and effective outcomes. Krill (1986, p. xi) suggested that the relationship between a social worker and a client is more likely to be productive if

◆ The participants like and respect each other.
◆ The client is clearly told what to expect and how to contribute to the helping process.
◆ The worker is warm, genuine, and sincere and regularly expresses empathy about the client's experience.
◆ The worker and client engage in goal-directed activities such as practice, in-session tasks, or between-session action steps.
◆ The social worker actively seeks to involve significant persons in the client's life in the helping process.

The characteristics of effective helpers are often called the *facilitative qualities* or *the core conditions* (Carkhuff, 1969; Carkhuff & Truax, 1965; Ivey, 1971; Ivey & Authier, 1978; Ivey & Simek-Downing, 1980; Marshall, Charping, & Bell, 1979; Marshall et al., 1982; Rogers, 1951, 1957, 1961, 1975; Truax & Carkhuff, 1967) These qualities, when consistently demonstrated by professionals, aid in developing and maintaining a special rapport with their clients. This rapport is sometimes called *the helping relationship*, *the working relationship*, *professional rapport*, or *the therapeutic alliance*. Perlman suggested that the professional working relationship between social worker and client is distinguished from other relationships by the following characteristics (Perlman, 1979, pp. 48–77):

- It is formed for a recognized and agreed-upon purpose.
- It is time-bound.
- It is *for* the client.
- It carries authority.
- It is a controlled relationship.

Within the context of this special relationship, the *essential facilitative qualities* become critical. When social workers consistently reflect these qualities, the risk of harming the person-and-situation tends to decrease and the probability of helping usually increases. However, demonstrating these qualities alone is rarely enough to enable clients to reach their goals. Social workers nearly always need to add expert knowledge and skills to help clients progress toward goal attainment. Furthermore, the qualities must be applied differentially according to the individual and cultural characteristics of each client. Some clients feel quite uneasy when the worker is frequently and intensively empathic. They might prefer a formal encounter in which the worker provides direct advice and guidance in a business-like fashion. Others seem to benefit from an emotionally charged, close relationship where intimate thoughts and feelings are shared by both the client and the worker. Finally, client characteristics also play a very powerful role in both the process and outcomes of the working relationship. Motivated clients who expect favorable results and participate actively generally benefit more than do unmotivated, pessimistic, and inactive clients. Of course, the qualities of both social workers and clients may change, sometimes from moment to moment. A caring, involved, and encouraging worker may help increase a client's hope and optimism, and a motivated, energetic, hard-working client may encourage a social worker to become more understanding and supportive.

Regardless of theoretical orientation and choice of intervention approach, effective helpers tend to reflect common characteristics in their service to others. Helping professionals express those qualities differentially according to the individual client, the unique circumstances of the person-and-situation, the nature of the social worker's role, and the phase of service. Nonetheless, as a general guide, social workers should reflect the following essential qualities in relationships with others: (1) *empathy*, (2) *regard*, and (3) *authenticity*, and (4) *professionalism*.

Empathy

The term *empathy* (Altmann, 1973; Bohart & Greenberg, 1997; Bozarth, 1997; Keefe, 1976; Pinderhughes, 1979; Rogers, 1975) is widely used in social work and other helping professions. Derived from the Greek word *empatheia*, empathy may be described as a process of joining in the feelings of another, of feeling how and what another person experiences. Empathy is a process of *feeling with* another person. It is an understanding and appreciation of the thoughts, feelings, experiences, and circumstances of another human being.

Stotland and colleagues (Stotland, Mathews, Sherman, Hansson, & Richardson, 1978) concluded, "that the key antecedent condition for empathy appears to be the empathizer's imagining himself or herself as having the same experience as the other—thus imaginatively taking the role of the other" (Stotland, 2003). In effect, empathy involves the proverbial "putting oneself in another's shoes."

However, empathy is not an expression of *feeling for* or *feeling toward*, as in pity or romantic love. Nor is it a "diagnostic or evaluative understanding *of* the client" (Hammond, Hepworth, & Smith, 1977, p. 3). Rather, it is a conscious and intentional joining with others in their subjective experience.

Of course, there are limits to anyone's ability and willingness to feel with and feel as another does. In fact, as a professional social worker, you must always retain a portion of yourself for your professional responsibilities. Be careful not to over-identify with clients by adopting their feelings as your own. After you feel clients' feelings, you need to be able to let them go. They remain the clients'. These feelings are not yours to be taken or assumed.

Empathy helps you, the social worker, gain an understanding of, appreciation for, and sensitivity to the people you serve. Through empathic connection with your clients, you increase the probability of developing rapport and maintaining productive working relationships.

Regard

The facilitative quality of *regard* or *respect* (Hammond et al., 1977, pp. 170–203) suggests an attitude of noncontrolling, warm, caring, nonpossessive acceptance of other persons. It involves demonstrating *unconditional positive regard* (Rogers, 1957, 1961). In cross- or inter-cultural contexts, regard also includes the genuine acceptance of difference. Respect of this nature goes well beyond basic tolerance to include appreciation of the value of diversity in human communities.

There are very few relationships in which people are truly accepted as unique human beings with full rights, privileges, and responsibilities—without regard to their views, actions, and circumstances. In most social contexts, people tend to spend time with people like themselves who live and work in similar circumstances, hold views that resemble their own, and are friendly toward them. Conversely, people are often less affectionate toward persons unlike themselves who live and work in different circumstances, who espouse views that differ from their own, or who are unfriendly or disinterested in them.

During your professional career, you are likely to work with many people who differ from you in numerous ways. You may find that you do not personally like some you serve and some clients will undoubtedly dislike you. Nonetheless, as a social worker, you should maintain regard for and caring acceptance of all the clients you serve. View each human being you meet as unique and inherently valuable. As a social worker, you convey regard by prizing and cherishing the personhood of all clients, regardless of the nature of their racial or ethnic backgrounds, gender, age, ability, appearance, status, views, actions, or circumstances. Although you may personally disagree with and perhaps even disapprove of a particular client's words or actions, you nonetheless continue to care about and accept that person as a unique individual of dignity and worth. Furthermore, you recognize the fundamental right of clients to make their own decisions. This ability to respect clients neither because of nor in spite of their attributes, behaviors, or circumstances is an essential facilitative condition in social work practice.

Caring for clients as valuable human beings does not, however, preclude you from making professional judgments or from offering suggestions and advice. Respect for clients does not mean that you neglect other persons or groups as you attend to clients. Indeed, a person-and-situation perspective suggests that you always consider persons and social systems affecting and affected by the clients you serve.

Authenticity

Authenticity refers to the genuineness and sincerity of a person's manner of relating. Reflecting fundamental honesty, an authentic social worker is natural, real, and personable. The presentation is congruent so that verbal, nonverbal, and behavioral expressions reflect synchronicity. Words and deeds match. The genuine social worker is nondefensive, open to the ideas of others, and forthright in sharing thoughts and feelings. "An authentic person relates to others personally, so that expressions do not seem rehearsed or contrived" (Hammond et al., 1977, p. 7). Genuineness, congruence, transparency, or authenticity (Rogers, 1961) may sometimes seem contrary to the notion of the professional social worker as cool, calm, and collected. However, professionalism in social work does not mean adopting a stiffly formal or overly controlled attitude. As a social worker, you need not and should not present yourself as an unfeeling, detached, computer-like technician. People seeking social services almost always prefer to talk with a knowledgeable and competent professional who comes across as a living, breathing, feeling human being—not as someone playing a canned role, spouting clichés, or repeating the same phrases again and again.

This emphasis on authenticity or genuineness in the working relationship, however, does not grant you license to say or do whatever you think or feel at the moment. Remember that the helping relationship is fundamentally for the client—not primarily for you, the social worker. Expression of your own thoughts and feelings for any purpose other than serving the client and working toward mutually agreed-upon goals is, at best, inefficient and, at worst, harmful.

Professionalism

Integral to the values and ethics of social work, and inherent in several aspects of the essential facilitative qualities, professionalism is so important to social workers individually and collectively that it requires special attention. Professionalism includes several characteristics: (1) integrity, (2) professional knowledge and self-efficacy, (3) ethical decision making, (4) critical thinking and lifelong learning, (5) self-understanding and self-control, (6) cultural competence and acceptance of others, and (7) social support. These will be explored in the next two chapters.

Summary

Effective social workers reflect empathy, regard, and authenticity as well as professionalism as they provide services to others. These characteristics and qualities are reflected throughout the entire helping process—from preparing for and beginning with clients through the conclusion of work. They are also apparent in your exchanges with friends, family members, colleagues, and others whom you encounter in your day-to-day lives.

◆ CHAPTER 1 SUMMARY EXERCISES

Following completion of this first chapter, use the spaces provided to outline brief one-to-two paragraph responses to these questions:

1. As you reflect thoughtfully about the content and implications of this chapter, what are your initial reactions to the wide range of challenging roles, responsibilities, and functions undertaken by professional social workers?

2. Consider the lengthy array of knowledge, values, attitudes, qualities, and abilities identified as essential for effective social workers. Identify which of these will be the most challenging for you and explain why.

3. Anticipate that you will need to commit several hours of focused study and practice each week to learn the skills addressed in this book. What will you need to do to ensure that you have the necessary time and motivation?

◆ CHAPTER 1 WORLD WIDE WEB EXERCISES

1. Log on to the World Wide Web and electronically visit each of the following Web sites. In the space that follows, record a few notations regarding the nature and value of each Web site to you as a student and as a practicing social worker.

   ◆ www.socialworkers.org

   ◆ www.cswe.org

   ◆ www.aswb.org

   ◆ www.loc.gov

   ◆ www.firstgov.gov

- www.fedstats.gov

- www.bls.gov/oco/ocos060.htm

- www.nlm.nih.gov

- www.os.dhhs.gov

- www.sc.edu/swan

- http://users.erols.com/jonwill/freebooks.htm

- http://www.socialworksearch.com

- http://www.nyu.edu/socialwork/wwwrsw

Chapter 1 Self-Appraisal

As you conclude this chapter, please reflect on your current level of understanding by completing the following self-appraisal exercise.

SELF-APPRAISAL

Please respond to the following items to help you reflect on aspects of professional social work presented in this chapter. Read each statement carefully. Then, use the following four-point rating scale to indicate the degree to which you agree or disagree with each statement. Record your numerical response in the space provided:

4 = Strongly Agree

3 = Agree

2 = Disagree

1 = Strongly Disagree

_____ 1. I can discuss the breadth and complexity of contemporary social work practice presented in this chapter.

_____ 2. I can discuss the significance of social work skills for professional practice.

_____ 3. I can describe and discuss the phases or processes of social work practice.

_____ 4. I can describe and discuss the significance of the essential facilitative qualities for professional relationships.

_____ 5. I can discuss the qualities and characteristics needed by ethical, effective social workers.

_____ Subtotal

Reflect on the dimensions of professional social work addressed in this chapter and the results of your self-appraisal. Based on your analysis, write a short essay entitled "Initial Reflections about the Qualities and Characteristics of Ethical and Effective Social Workers." Limit yourself to 500 words (i.e., two double-spaced, typed pages) or less. Focus on the more important ideas, questions, and issues that occurred while you reflected on the introductory chapter.

This short essay will become a part of your Social Work Skills Learning Portfolio. Described more specifically in Appendix 1, the learning portfolio is essentially a container (e.g., an expandable folder, a three-ring binder, or space in an electronic storage medium such as a hard drive or floppy disk) of selected products that you prepare while completing _The Social Work Skills Workbook_. The learning portfolio provides ready access to documentary evidence of your progress in developing proficiency in the social work skills. The Social Work Skills Learning Portfolio may be used for self-assessment, by others for the purposes of evaluating your individual learning, or when combined with the portfolios of other learners for the purpose of evaluating the effectiveness of a course or educational program. The assessments and evaluations may be used _formatively_ to suggest where additional individual or group learning may be needed, or _summatively_ to determine a rank, status, or grade.

Chapter 2

Professionalism

Membership in the community of professional helpers includes considerable status, power, and prestige. Society entrusts social workers in particular with authority and responsibility associated with service to vulnerable people. In this chapter (see Box 2.1), you will explore the following characteristics of professionalism: (1) integrity, (2) professional knowledge and self-efficacy, (3) critical thinking and lifelong learning, (4) self-understanding and self-control, (5) cultural competence and acceptance of others, and (6) social support. You will consider the relevance of professionalism for social work practice and complete a preliminary self-appraisal. You will prepare a family genogram, an eco-map, and a critical-events timeline. You will complete exercises to help you explore several aspects of professionalism. Importantly, you will integrate these various learning experiences in an assessment of your own readiness for the profession of social work. Finally, you will contribute additional materials to your Social Work Skills Learning Portfolio.

Knowledge of relevant laws and regulations, social work values and ethics, and the skills associated with ethical decision making are, of course, absolutely critical to professionalism. They will be addressed separately in Chapter 3.

Individuals, families, groups, organizations, communities, and the society as a whole depend on the social work profession to fulfill vital psychosocial functions and address pressing social problems. Each year, enormous amounts of public and private monies are invested in health and human services of all kinds. In the United States alone, considerably more than one trillion dollars of public and private funds are allocated annually to health and social welfare services (Morales & Sheafor, 1998, p. 15). In 1996, some 2,403,00 people worked in the nonhealth and non-education social services sector alone (Franklin, 1997, Table 4, p. 48).

Approximately 585,000 college educated (baccalaureate level or higher) social workers were employed in the United States in 1996. By 2006, the number of employed social workers is expected to rise to 772,000. In 1996, there were more social workers than psychologists (143,000) or dentists (162,000). Indeed, more social workers were employed than medical doctors (560,000). Furthermore, employment opportunities for social workers are increasing at a more rapid rate than for most professions and occupations (Silvestri, 1997, Table 4, p. 78). Clearly, social workers constitute a significant proportion of the entire United States labor force and fulfill important societal functions.

Social workers affect people in profound ways—usually for better, sometimes for worse. Given the large number of social workers, and the nature and scope of the services they provide, the topic of professionalism cannot be overemphasized. When social workers are competent and trustworthy, their clients feel satisfied and society as a whole benefits. The profession grows and the overall reputation of social work improves. When, however, social workers lack professionalism, many people suffer. Clients may be harmed. Employers may become reluctant to hire social workers. The stature of the profession may decline and funding sources may become less inclined to support social services in general.

Because the stakes are so high, social workers are obligated—personally, morally, ethically, and legally—to reflect high standards of professionalism in all aspects of their professional activities. Fortunately, most social workers are committed to providing effective services to their clients and to promoting a better quality of life for all people. Most social workers are knowledgeable in their areas of practice, and honest and trustworthy in their relations with others. Most social workers sincerely try to demonstrate understanding, respect, compassion, and competence in their efforts to provide ethical and effective service to others. Most social workers try to keep current with advances in professional knowledge. Most social workers recognize that personal behavior in their private lives may affect the quality of their professional performance. Indeed, most social workers are well aware that their reputation among colleagues and constituents is maintained primarily through conscientious attention and consistent adherence to high standards of professionalism.

Integrity

Fundamental to the facilitative qualities of authenticity and respect, integrity is also an essential aspect of professionalism. Within the context of social work service, integrity suggests honesty, truthfulness, and sincerity. In its Code of Ethics, the National Association of Social Workers (NASW) states, "Social workers should not participate in, condone, or be associated with dishonesty, fraud, or deception" (1999, Section 4.04). Keeping promises and following through on commitments are additional aspects of integrity.

As a social worker, you demonstrate integrity when you share information that is supported by valid and reliable evidence. You reflect integrity when you acknowledge publicly the contributions of others and credit sources of information used to support your own statements and positions. You demonstrate integrity when you openly state that you are sharing a personal opinion rather than a professional recommendation. You display integrity when you willingly acknowledge mistakes and errors in your own thoughts, words, and deeds. You exemplify integrity when you resist temptations to cheat, lie, or misrepresent facts. You manifest integrity when you report a friend and colleague who defrauded or exploited a client, cheated on an exam, or plagiarized a report. In sum, you demonstrate integrity as a social worker when you behave in an honorable manner and hold yourself accountable to high professional standards.

The Code of Ethics of the NASW includes *integrity* as one of its core values and describes the ethical principle as follows:

Value: *Integrity*

Ethical Principle: *Social workers behave in a trustworthy manner.*

Social workers are continually aware of the profession's mission, values, ethical principles, and ethical standards and practice in a manner consistent with them. Social workers act honestly and responsibly and promote ethical practices on the part of the organizations with which they are affiliated. (1999)

As you consider various aspects of professionalism, none will be more essential than integrity. Adherence to the values and ethics of the profession and to fundamental moral principles such as sincerity, fairness, truthfulness, reliability, dedication, and loyalty is central to professional integrity. However, integrity goes beyond the sum of these virtues to include a general sense of coherence, wholeness, and harmony with social work roles, responsibilities, and expectations. Involving the essential facilitative quality of authenticity as well as personal honor, professional integrity relates to virtually all facets of professional social work. Consider, for example, the issues of trust and credibility. Clients tend to seek the services of social workers and other helping professionals because they assume that they will be treated honestly, fairly, responsibly, and competently. First meetings are often characterized by an initial trust that may continue throughout the relationship. However, when the professional's words or actions suggest dishonesty, irresponsibility, unfairness, or incompetence, trust and credibility may be damaged—sometimes permanently. Relationships with colleagues, employers, and community members are quite similar in this regard.

Perhaps because integrity is so often associated with honesty, trustworthiness, and one's personal character, once damaged it is extremely difficult to recover. The *New York Times* recently discovered that one of its reporters had committed journalistic fraud through numerous instances of falsification, fabrication, and plagiarism. Recognizing the potential impact on its reputation for accuracy and integrity, the *New York Times* assigned an investigative team to study the trail of deceptive reporting. The results of that investigation were summarized in lengthy reports prominently published in the *New York Times* itself (Staff, 2003a, 2003b).

The reporter will probably never work in journalism again. Publishers and editors simply cannot trust him. He is no longer credible. The damage to his personal and professional reputation is so severe that association with any newspaper or magazine would tarnish its image as well. However, the effects go well beyond the individual reporter and even the *New York Times*. His actions raise questions about the profession of journalism itself. After all, if he could falsify and plagiarize in dozens of reports over several months or years, might there be other reporters doing the same? Can readers trust any reporters or any newspapers to be honest and accurate?

Some social workers and social service organizations have also violated basic principles of integrity. Some have neglected to fulfill fundamental responsibilities such as regularly checking on the welfare of abused or neglected children under their supervision (Kaufman & Jones, 2003). Others have committed fraud by falsifying documents and reports to suggest that they completed work or provided services that they actually did not. When violations such as these occur, the consequences may be profound. Children may die or suffer severe injuries, and citizens may fail to report suspicions of abuse for fear that children will be worse off if placed in custodial care than they would be if left alone.

Integrity is an essential aspect of professionalism and crucial to ethical and effective social work. Clients accept services on the basis of implicit trust that social workers are trustworthy, honest, dependable professionals. Lapses of integrity jeopardize that faith and may leave disappointed clients unwilling to trust other social work professionals in the future.

As a social worker, you benefit from a general presumption of integrity because you have professional status. What an extraordinary gift! Involving exceptional power and influence, it carries enormous moral responsibility. Cherish it and consider your personal and professional integrity among your most valuable assets! Keep your promises. Sincerely acknowledge your mistakes. Be forthcoming about your level of knowledge, skills, and areas of competence. Tell your clients the truth. And most important, be brutally honest with yourself. Adopt an extreme attitude in this regard. Among helping professionals, self-deception is a most dangerous conceit.

◆ EXERCISE 2-1: INTEGRITY

Use the spaces provided to write one-to-two paragraph responses to each of the following items:

1. What does professional integrity mean to you and how does personal integrity relate to professional integrity?

2. Would a social work student ever be justified in lying to a professor? Would a social worker ever be justified in lying to a supervisor? A client? A judge?

3. As a social work student, you certainly sometimes experience feelings of stress and pressure when faced with the numerous demands and deadlines. You may occasionally be tempted to cheat in some fashion, perhaps by plagiarizing a paper or lying to a professor to obtain an extension. How do you deal with such temptations?

4. Suppose you served on a peer-review jury for a fellow social work student who was caught cheating on an exam. The evidence is overwhelming. There is no doubt that the cheating was intentional. What should happen to that student (e.g., expulsion from the university or the social work program, a failing grade on the exam or the course, opportunity to re-do the exam)?

5. Suppose you serve as the supervisor of a social worker who is responsible for overseeing the welfare of abused and neglected children placed in foster care homes. What would you do if you discovered that the social worker fraudulently reports making twice-weekly visits with each child when the truth is that most children receive visits about once every two or three months and some children have not been visited in more than four months? How would your decision about what to do be affected if (a) the children were all safe and healthy or (b) one of the unvisited children died as a result of abuse by members of the foster care family?

Professional Knowledge and Self-Efficacy

Advanced professional knowledge is, of course, essential for ethical and effective social work practice. In social work, the particular knowledge required varies considerably according to the characteristics of the setting, the issues for work, the populations served, and the roles assumed. However, a common base of knowledge exists for all social workers. The Council on Social Work Education (CSWE), for instance, requires that all accredited programs include the following content areas within their curricula (CSWE, 2001):

- Values and ethics
- Diversity
- Populations-at-risk and social and economic justice
- Human behavior and the social environment
- Social welfare policy and services
- Social work practice
- Research

The Council also requires all social work students to complete field practicum experiences where they learn to apply professional knowledge in carefully supervised practice contexts. In such settings, students learn through doing and acquire knowledge that is, quite simply, impossible to gain in any other way.

Although they may vary in specific information and emphasis, all CSWE accredited social work programs include content in these curriculum areas, contributing to a common knowledge base. These content areas are consistent with a more expansive array suggested by the NASW (1981b, p. 17). They are also congruent with the content areas addressed in the nationally standardized social work licensing examinations used throughout most of the 50 United States, the District of Columbia, Puerto Rico, the U.S. Virgin Islands, and some Canadian provinces. The content areas addressed in the Association of Social Work Board (ASWB) sponsored Basic Examination (ASWB, 2002) include the following:

- Human development and behavior
- Effects of diversity
- Assessment in social work practice
- Social work practice with individuals, couples, families, groups, and communities
- Interpersonal communication
- Professional social worker/client relationship
- Professional values and ethics
- Supervision in social work
- Practice evaluation and the utilization of research
- Service delivery
- Social work administration

The national social work licensing examinations ensure that reasonably equivalent standards exist throughout much of the United States. They, along with the policies of NASW and CSWE, contribute to the maintenance of a common social work knowledge base.[1]

In addition, social workers must believe they can make a difference. Supported by knowledge and expertise, attitudes of optimism and confidence are required. For social workers, self-efficacy is "confidence in their ability to execute specific skills in a particular set of circumstances and thereby achieve a successful outcome" (Holden, Meenaghan, Anastas, & Metrey, 2002, p. 116). Without knowledge-based self-efficacy, social workers would likely be relatively inactive, passive observers rather than energetic, collaborative agents of change.

During the early part of the 21st century, extraordinary challenges face most social workers and the social work profession as a whole (Austin, 1997). A broad and deep base of current, valid, and reliable knowledge and corresponding self-efficacy are required for competent social work practice.

The NASW (1981b), the CSWE (2001), the ASWB (2002), and eminent social workers (Bartlett, 1970) have identified the general parameters of a common social work knowledge base. In actual practice, of course, social workers need a great deal of specialized knowledge that applies to the unique characteristics of the clientele and community they serve. Suppose, for example, that you were employed to provide social work services to women who have been physically abused in domestic violence circumstances. Just imagine how much you would need to know to serve your clients and community effectively! You would you need to be well acquainted with the current theoretical and research literature concerning the nature and outcome of services to domestically abused women. You would need to know the factors that contribute to domestic violence as well as those that tend to reduce its likelihood. You would need to understand the range of risks facing women in such circumstances and know how to assess the risk of injury or death. You would need to know what to do when risk is high, moderate, or low. You would have to know how to help clients consider the risk-benefit ratio of various courses of action.

In approaching service from a person-and-situation perspective you would, of course, need to know how to identify, assess, and intervene with primary and secondary social systems. You would need to know about the racial and ethnic cultures of your community. You would need to know how to determine the psychosocial needs of children who might be affected by the domestic violence directed against their mothers and older sisters and how to assess the strengths and potentials of all members of the primary social system—including persons suspected of initiating violence. You would need to know the laws and regulations of the locale where you serve and the professional values and ethics that might apply. You would need to know the actual and potential resources—locally, nationally, and sometimes internationally—that might become needed at various times in the process. In sum, competent social work service in such a setting would require a truly enormous amount of professional knowledge and expertise.

---

[1] You may access Web sites of the Association of Social Work Boards at www.aswb.org; the Council on Social Work Education at www.cswe.org; and the National Association of Social Workers at www.socialworkers.org.

This workbook focuses on fundamental social work skills. It is not intended to address the general knowledge base or the specific expertise needed in particular service contexts. There are several extremely rich sources of information in these areas. Recently published textbooks in human behavior and social environment, social policy, research, and social work practice cover the common base extraordinarily well. The most recent edition of *Social Work Encyclopedia* (Edwards, 1995) and its *Supplements* (Edwards, 1997; English, 2003) contain a wealth of highly relevant information for social workers at all levels of practice and in many contexts. Numerous high-quality professional journals that address specific aspects, dimensions, approaches, and areas of social service also help inform social workers.

In this workbook, you explore an important part of the common social work knowledge base—but it is only a part. You focus on the skills needed for ethical, effective social work practice throughout the preparing, beginning, exploring, assessing, contracting, working and evaluating, and ending phases of practice. The following exercise should help you to formulate a preliminary self-assessment of your current level of proficiency in the social work skills addressed in the workbook.

◆ EXERCISE 2-2: SOCIAL WORK SKILLS PROFICIENCY

1. Please turn to Appendix 2 and complete the Social Work Skills Practice Test. Recognize that you have just begun the learning process. Unless you have previously addressed this material, your proficiency in these skill areas may well be quite limited. You may be unable to respond to many items. Do not despair! With study and practice, you will improve.

2. After finishing the Social Work Skills Practice Test, turn to Appendix 3 and complete the Social Work Skills Self-Appraisal Questionnaire. Base your proficiency estimates on your performance on the Practice Test. Your assessment ratings in certain areas may be low. View them as baseline or pre-test ratings. As you progress in your readings, complete the learning exercises, and engage with colleagues in practice sessions, you should become more proficient in using and assessing the social work skills. Your responses to the Practice Test items will probably improve and your ratings on the Self-Appraisal Questionnaire will increase. At this time, your self-appraisal will be imprecise. Nevertheless, you may use the results as a general but preliminary indication of your initial proficiency.

3. Using the results of the Practice Test and the Self-Appraisal Questionnaire as a guide, please use the spaces provided to identify in outline fashion those skill areas where you think you are most and least proficient, respectively.

Most Proficient

Least Proficient

Critical Thinking and Lifelong Learning

The intellectual challenges and the breadth and depth of knowledge you will need in your social work career are daunting. To process the massive amount of emerging information and to provide service to people facing difficult challenges, you need highly developed critical thinking skills. "Critical thinking involves the careful examination and evaluation of beliefs and actions" (Gibbs & Gambrill, 1996, p. 3). As noted earlier, the CSWE requires that both undergraduate and graduate students in social work acquire critical thinking abilities. Indeed, CSWE expects graduates of accredited programs to "apply critical thinking skills" (CSWE, 2001, p. 9) in their service as professional social workers.

You need to think clearly, logically, and creatively to adapt effectively to the wide range of people, issues, and contexts you will face. Especially when you feel frustrated, overwhelmed, and ineffectual in the face of obstacles, you may be tempted to "just try something." You may feel an impulse to respond to a client solely on the basis of strong emotion or perhaps an intuitive hunch. Occasionally, you might be tempted to react to a client as you might to one of your own family members—perhaps as a parent might react to a child. Critical thinking skills are needed to provide balance, rationality, and sometimes restraint in such contexts.

Similarly, you may find yourself attracted to information presented on television, in popular magazines, or the World Wide Web. You might think, "I could try this with my clients who are dealing with the same issue." Be very careful. Think critically and reflectively before taking action based on such information. Although some may be accurate, pertinent, and useful, much of the information published and distributed widely may be untested, unexamined, or even false. Critical thinking skills are essential in determining the relative validity, reliability, and relevance of new information for professional social work service.

Knowledge is expanding and changing at a speed never before known in human history. Some of what was taken as fact 10 years ago has since been disproved. Other information rapidly becomes obsolete as researchers continuously advance the professional knowledge base. You will find it difficult indeed to stay abreast of the most recent research studies. At the same time, you will probably yearn for additional information to help you help others. In your efforts to serve, you will soon become aware that you personally, and social workers collectively, need to know more—despite the ever-expanding knowledge explosion.

The most effective social workers find themselves engaged in an ongoing search for valid and relevant knowledge on which to base their helping efforts. In effect, they dedicate themselves to lifelong learning. You should do the same. Adopt an attitude of insatiable but purposeful curiosity and a fundamental humility. Keep reading and learning, but realize that you will almost certainly never ever know enough!

Critical thinking is "the propensity and skill to use reflective skepticism when engaged in some specific activity" (McPeck, 1990, p. 3) involving "the careful examination and evaluation of beliefs and actions" (Gibbs & Gambrill, 1996, p. 3). Critical thinking is "the art of thinking about your thinking while you are thinking in order to make your thinking better: more clear, more accurate, or more defensible" (Paul, 1993, p. 462). All professional social workers should be good critical thinkers because the quality of their analysis and the nature of their judgments affect people.

The CSWE tries to ensure this by requiring both baccalaureate and master's students in social work to learn critical thinking skills (CSWE, 2001). The Council recognizes that knowledge alone does not necessarily lead to good decisions. Even highly informed social workers need to think carefully and critically before making decisions and taking actions that affect the lives and well-being of others. They ask questions about the validity, reliability, and relevance of all information that might influence the nature and quality of their service. They carefully consider factors such as risk of harm, efficiency, probability of success, and sometimes even cost-effectiveness.

In considering the value of information, critical thinkers tend to be adept at these skills:

- Distinguishing between verifiable facts and value statements;
- Distinguishing relevant from irrelevant observations or reasons;
- Determining the factual accuracy of a statement;
- Determining the credibility of a source;
- Identifying ambiguous statements;
- Identifying unstated assumptions;
- Detecting bias;
- Identifying logical fallacies;
- Recognizing logical inconsistencies in a line of reasoning;
- Determining the overall strength of an argument or conclusion. (Beyer, 1988, p. 57, as cited by Duplass & Ziedler, 2002, p. 116)

Following careful analysis of the value of selected information, critically thinking social workers proceed to consider its relevance and applicability. In doing so, you might ask yourself questions such as these:

- In what aspects or arenas of social work practice, if any, might this information be relevant and useful?
- How compatible is the information with the values and ethics of the profession and the laws that regulate social work practice?
- What psychosocial issues might be better understood or addressed with this information?
- What clientele (e.g., population groups), if any, might benefit from the application of the information?
- If the information were used in service to clients, what might be the risks to them or to others who might be affected? What might be the benefits? Are there safer approaches? Are there more time-efficient or more cost-effective approaches?
- If the information were applied, how effective in addressing issues and achieving goals might it be? Are there more effective approaches and applications?

Thoughtful reflection and analysis are necessary throughout all phases, aspects, and forms of professional social work. Particularly because social workers address "unstructured" issues that do not have easy "right" or "wrong," "true" or "false," or "multiple-choice" solutions, they need to be adept at several critical thinking skills. In particularly, social workers require the abilities to

- Identify and frame the nature of issues accurately.
- Formulate useful, relevant, and appropriate questions to guide data collection.
- Collect relevant, valid, reliable, and useful information.
- Select or formulate relevant, valid, reliable, and useful thinking processes by which to reach decisions or make judgments based on relevant, valid, reliable, and useful information.

- Use relevant, valid, reliable, and useful thinking processes to reach and support professional decisions and judgments.
- Base their actions on sound professional decisions and judgments.
- Evaluate the effects of their decisions, judgments, and actions.
- Reconsider and revise judgments and actions based on relevant, valid, reliable, and useful information.

Proficiency in these abilities requires considerable intellectual prowess. In human terms, the stakes are extremely high. Social work practice is complex, multidimensional, multisystemic, and certainly challenging. There are few simple issues and fewer simple solutions. Social workers proficient in critical thinking skills are better able to address complex issues and more likely to help than to harm. Those who do not think critically represent a genuine risk to themselves, their clients, and their colleagues.

Thinking critically is increasingly necessary because of the information and technology revolution and the ongoing knowledge explosion. Much of the world and most of North American society has entered the "third wave" (Toffler, 1983) when knowledge and learning attain extraordinary value. As are most forms of wealth, they will probably be unevenly distributed. Information "haves" will likely be distinguished from "have nots" by the ease and extent to which they can access current, relevant, and accurate knowledge and the facility with which they can adapt and improve based on it. As Toffler suggests, "the illiterate of the 21st century will not be those who cannot read and write, but those who cannot learn, unlearn, and relearn."

According to some authorities, the total knowledge in the world, on average, doubles about every seven years (Davis & Botkin, 1994). In some subject areas, knowledge doubling occurs even more rapidly. As many social workers realize from the rapid obsolescence of their personal computers, the rate of change in the technological sciences is simply astonishing. However, the knowledge explosion is hardly limited to high technology. The helping professions are affected as well. As a social worker, you might wonder how much of what you now believe to be true is actually false. You might ask how much of what you learned one or two years ago has since become obsolete. We may reasonably anticipate that more and more of what you now "know" will become less and less relevant, valid, and applicable with each passing year. Unless you as a social worker continuously and aggressively pursue additional learning, you will inexorably fall further and further behind the knowledge curve. If you do not continue to learn throughout your social work career, clients could suffer because of your ignorance. You need to find a way to keep current during this never-ending, always expanding, knowledge explosion. Up-to-date, valid, and reliable knowledge and expertise is vital so you can serve your clients effectively. Try to become a "learning person" within the context of "learning organizations," "learning communities," and "learning societies." As Hoffer suggested, "In a time of drastic change, it is the learners who inherit the future. The learned usually find themselves equipped to live in a world that no longer exists" (Hoffer, 1973, p. 22).

In its Code of Ethics, the NASW outlines several ethical principles that refer to the obligation of professional social workers to regularly improve their knowledge and skills throughout their career. Consider these excerpts (NASW, 1999):

- Social workers should provide services and represent themselves as competent only within the boundaries of their education, training, license, certification, consultation received, supervised experience, or other relevant professional experience. (Section 1.04.a)
- Social workers should provide services in substantive areas or use intervention techniques or approaches that are new to them only after engaging in appropriate study, training, consultation, and supervision from people who are competent in those interventions or techniques. (Section 1.04.b)
- When generally recognized standards do not exist with respect to an emerging area of practice, social workers should exercise careful judgment and take responsible steps (including appropriate education, research, training, consultation, and supervision) to ensure the competence of their work and to protect clients from harm. (Section 1.04.c)
- Social workers should accept responsibility or employment only on the basis of existing competence or the intention to acquire the necessary competence. (Section 4.01.a)
- Social workers should strive to become and remain proficient in professional practice and the performance of professional functions. Social workers should critically examine and keep current with emerging knowledge relevant to social work. Social workers should routinely review the professional literature and participate in continuing education relevant to social work practice and social work ethics. (Section 4.01.b)
- Social workers should base practice on recognized knowledge, including empirically based knowledge, relevant to social work and social work ethics. (Section 4.01.c)

The ongoing knowledge explosion and the related changes in information and technology are dramatically affecting social workers and their clients. Critical thinking and continuous lifelong learning help social workers respond effectively and serve clients competently during a professional career.

◆ EXERCISE 2-3: CRITICAL THINKING AND LIFELONG LEARNING

Please complete the following questionnaire. This instrument is designed to help you assess selected aspects of critical thinking and lifelong learning. It is not a graded test. You cannot pass or fail. Furthermore, the instrument is still under development. Its validity and reliability have not yet been fully established. Please be cautious in interpreting the results.

Please read each of the statements contained in the following questionnaire.[2] Rate the degree of agreement or disagreement by circling

---

[2] The Evidence-Based Social Work Questionnaire (EBSWQ) copyright © 2000 by Barry R. Cournoyer

the number that most closely reflects your view. Please use the following rating system:

1 = Strongly Agree

2 = Agree

3 = Disagree

4 = Strongly Disagree

1.	1 2 3 4	I rarely make judgments based solely upon intuition or emotion.
2.	1 2 3 4	I almost always think before I speak or act.
3.	1 2 3 4	I almost never express opinions as if they were facts.
4.	1 2 3 4	I always identify the assumptions underlying an argument.
5.	1 2 3 4	I carefully consider the source of information in determining validity.
6.	1 2 3 4	I rarely reach conclusions without considering the evidence.
7.	1 2 3 4	I regularly think in terms of probabilities.
8.	1 2 3 4	I rarely think in terms of absolutes.
9.	1 2 3 4	I always question the validity of arguments and conclusions.
10.	1 2 3 4	I rarely assume that something is valid or true.
11.	1 2 3 4	I regularly identify my own biases and preferences.
12.	1 2 3 4	I regularly think about issues of reliability.
13.	1 2 3 4	I routinely identify my own logical fallacies.
14.	1 2 3 4	I rarely say that something is true unless I have supporting evidence.
15.	1 2 3 4	I regularly use a thinking process routine to reach decisions.
16.	1 2 3 4	I regularly read professional journals in my field.
17.	1 2 3 4	I genuinely enjoy learning.
18.	1 2 3 4	I always do more than the minimum requirements in courses, seminars or workshop.
19.	1 2 3 4	I regularly pursue opportunities to advance my knowledge and expertise.
20.	1 2 3 4	I never become defensive when someone offers feedback that could improve my skill.
21.	1 2 3 4	I like to study.
22.	1 2 3 4	I know my personal learning style.
23.	1 2 3 4	I am actively involved in learning experiences.
24.	1 2 3 4	I take personal responsibility for my own learning.
25.	1 2 3 4	I view examinations as a way to learn.
26.	1 2 3 4	I know how to conduct a professional literature review.

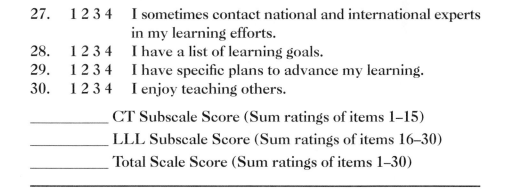

27. 1 2 3 4   I sometimes contact national and international experts in my learning efforts.
28. 1 2 3 4   I have a list of learning goals.
29. 1 2 3 4   I have specific plans to advance my learning.
30. 1 2 3 4   I enjoy teaching others.

_____ CT Subscale Score (Sum ratings of items 1–15)

_____ LLL Subscale Score (Sum ratings of items 16–30)

_____ Total Scale Score (Sum ratings of items 1–30)

To score the questionnaire, simply sum the total of your ratings to the 30 items. Your score should range somewhere between 30 and 120. There are two subscales. Items 1–15 involve critical thinking and 16–30 relate to lifelong learning. Lower scores suggest greater levels of critical thinking and lifelong learning. Remember, however, that the questionnaire is still under development. At this point, it has not been fully tested. Validity and reliability have not been established. View the results with caution. However, as a tentative reflection of the potential relevance of your score, note that a convenience sample of 21 members of a foundation-year master of social work (MSW) social work practice class obtained an average score of 32.38 (range 20–42; SD 6.26) on the critical thinking and 33.10 (range 20–43; SD 7.44) on the lifelong learning subscales (Cournoyer, 1999). Another sample of more than 90 foundation and concentration-year MSW students combined reflected an average score of 31.79 (n = 95; range 20–51; SD 4.51) on the critical thinking, 29.12 (n = 97; range 16–41; SD 5.44) on the lifelong learning subscales, and 60.97 (n = 92; range 40–91; SD 8.555) on the total (Cournoyer, 2003).

When you have completed the questionnaire and calculated your subscale and total scores, consider the implications of your responses by addressing the following questions. Record one-to-two paragraph responses in the spaces provided.

1. How much and what kind of a critical thinker and lifelong learner are you?

2. Why might critical thinking and lifelong learning be especially important for social workers during the 21st century?

3. Suppose you decided to become a more proficient critical thinker, what steps might you take to do so? What steps might you take to become a more effective lifelong learner?

Self-Understanding and Self-Control

In addition to integrity, knowledge and self-efficacy, and critical thinking and continuous lifelong learning, professionalism also involves a sophisticated level of self-understanding and self-control. Because social work practice involves the conscious and deliberate use of self, *you* become the medium through which knowledge, attitudes, and skill are conveyed. You need a truly extraordinary depth of self-awareness and a refined ability to selectively access various aspects of yourself in your efforts to serve others. Without these qualities and abilities, you could—indeed most likely would—act out your unresolved personal issues with clients or colleagues. You might have the most noble and idealistic of motives, intending only to help others. Nonetheless, if you lack self-awareness or self-control, you may unwittingly enact emotional or behavioral patterns that harm the very people you hope to help (Caplan & Caplan, 2001; Keith-Lucas, 1972).

Self-understanding and self-control are not products or outcomes that can be completed and then set aside. Rather, they reflect ongoing processes through which you continuously grow personally and professionally. Self-understanding and self-control tend to reduce the risk of harm to others that can occur if you are unaware of or unable to manage your own habits, patterns, and issues. To be effective, you need to know how you present yourself, how you appear to others, and what mannerisms you commonly exhibit. You need to know which issues cause you anxiety or uneasiness, which topics trigger emotional responses, what kinds of people or events elicit fear or anger, and which patterns of personal interaction you tend to prefer. Of course, such a level of self-understanding does not occur through a single set of exercises, a course, or even a complete program of university study. It is certainly not awarded along with a bachelor of social work (BSW), an MSW, or a doctoral degree. Rather, sophisticated self-understanding is a never-ending process that is never truly finished.

At a minimum, social workers should develop substantial understanding of how their families and cultures affected their development and influence their psychosocial functioning and relationship patterns. Recognize the potential impact of significant life events and learn about your preferred relational styles including how you typically seek, receive, and give social support. You should be aware of your own biases, stereotypes, prejudices, and tendencies to discriminate against others as well as the ways you might express genuine acceptance of others. You should recognize and personally manage maladaptive patterns of thinking, feeling, and behaving that might interfere with your ability to provide high quality social work services.

As is the case with most worthwhile endeavors, engaging in self-awareness activities involves certain risks. You may discover aspects of yourself that you have not previously recognized or considered—especially as they might affect your service as a social worker. For example, you may learn that you have a strong need for power, control, and predictability in relationships. You may find that you relate to women with less interest, energy, or attention than you do to men. You may realize that you have not fully examined the potential implications of a physical challenge that you personally face (e.g., vision or hearing loss) for clients you will serve. You may become aware of fixed racial or ethnic stereotypes that interfere with an objective assessment of individual members of certain groups. You might become aware of unmet childhood needs for acceptance and approval that lead you to avoid confrontation or withdraw from conflict. You may find that you experience heightened anxiety when in the presence of authority figures. You may discover that you have an alcohol or drug problem; that you suffer from occasional periods of depression, carry substantial unresolved rage, or even that you are unsuited for a career in the profession of social work.

This process of self-exploration and self-discovery may give rise to disturbing thoughts and feelings. You may even find yourself reconsidering significant life choices. Indeed, numerous risks are inherent in any serious process of self-examination. However, as a social worker, the pursuit of self-understanding is usually well worth the costs. Failure to do so may put yourself and the people you serve at risk of being harmed by the very process you hope will help.

As you grow in self-understanding, you will inevitably recognize a parallel need for self-control. Professional social workers need to be able to manage their thoughts, feelings, words, gestures, and behavior. Under conditions where other people might well be overwhelmed by powerful emotions and impulses, you must maturely choose your words and actions in accord with professional purpose, knowledge, values, ethics, and agreed-upon goals for service.

Social workers must manage their emotions and "restrict impulses or behaviors to appropriate circumstances in the environment" (Barker, 1995). In work with and on behalf of clients, carefully select your verbal and as well as your nonverbal expressions. Manage both your overt and covert behavior by skillfully choosing the words you say; monitoring your body movements, gestures, and facial expressions; and modulating your voice and speech. Doing all these things simultaneously requires an extraordinary degree of self-control.

At times, it may even be necessary to control your internal thoughts to better serve clients and advocate on their behalf. Self-control is one of the true hallmarks of professionalism. It distinguishes a professional social worker from a friendly person with good intentions.

Furthermore, you must manage maladaptive patterns of behavior that might affect your professional judgment and performance. Alcohol or cocaine use, for example, could impair your capacities. Identify and try to manage all your potentially problematic traits and behaviors. Address your anxieties, phobias, depression, and similar personal issues that might affect the nature and quality of your service. Excessive eating, dieting, exercising, and television viewing may indirectly interfere with effective social work practice. Procrastination may be a problem, as might issues with authority, a quick temper, or impulsiveness. Similarly, some interpersonal or interactional social patterns may become compulsive and interfere with your professional functioning. One example is sexual addiction or perhaps a powerful need to be liked. Another is the relational pattern of *rescuing*. In professional practice, this may be evident when a social worker tends to view clients as victims in need of rescue or salvation. The "social worker-as-savior" often assumes disproportionate control over and responsibility for clients. Rather than empowering clients, rescuing behavior often diminishes others' sense of competence, autonomy, and self-efficacy. Of course, sometimes people actually need to be rescued. A child in danger of freezing to death, because she lives under a bridge during wintertime, should be provided with warmth and shelter. This would not be *rescuing* in the compulsive sense, as it would be if you took responsibility for the decisions of fully competent adults.

Self-understanding and self-control are continuous processes that may be furthered by personal counseling, individual or group psychotherapy, consultation or supervision by experienced social workers, and participation in professional workshops and training institutes. If you are open to it, self-awareness and self-discipline may also improve as a natural outgrowth of interaction with peers, clients, friends, and family members. This section contains a series of exercises intended to help you develop greater awareness, self-understanding, and perhaps additional self-control. In particular, you will examine the influences of your family and social systems through the preparation of a genogram, an eco-map, a timeline, and completion of a self-control scale.

The Family: Context for Development of Self

Social workers (Hartman & Laird, 1983) have long recognized that families powerfully influence the course of social, psychological, and even biological development. Family and childhood experiences significantly affect people's attitudes, beliefs, values, personality characteristics, and behavioral patterns. Families tend to be the primary means of cultural socialization. Unless you are keenly aware of the influence of your family experiences, you may inadvertently or unconsciously play out a family role or pattern in your work with clients and colleagues. Among the common family roles (Satir, 1972; Wegscheider-Cruse, 1985) that people may assume include *rescuer, peacemaker, hero,* and *parental child.* Of course, sometimes it is entirely proper to use a part of your family-based self in social work practice. In all such cases, however, it should be for a clearly identified social work purpose, and you should be fully aware that you are doing so.

The intergenerational family genogram is one way to become more aware of how your family[3] influenced you. A genogram is a graphic representation of one's family tree. It provides a picture of the parties involved and a chronology of significant events or themes. In addition, a genogram may be used as "a subjective interpretive tool" (McGoldrick & Gerson, 1985, p. 2), to develop hypotheses about a person's psychosocial characteristics or a family's interactional patterns.

Certain symbols are commonly used in preparing family genograms (McGoldrick, Gerson, & Shellenberger, 1999). For instance, males are usually characterized by squares, females by circles. Bracket lines represent spousal relationships. A solid bracket line (|_____|) reflects a committed couple (e.g., marriage or its equivalent); a dashed bracket line (|_ _ _|) reflects a relationship of somewhat lesser commitment; and a dotted bracket line (|. . . . |) suggests a relatively uncommitted relationship (e.g., a short-term affair). A line extended downward from a relationship bracket line may be used to indicate a pregnancy, biological child, or adopted child from that relationship. Separations and break-ups or divorces are indicated by one and two slash marks (/ and //) respectively, cutting across the relationship bracket line. Pregnancies and children from each relationship are placed in order from earliest to latest, proceeding from left

---

[3] Not all people have biological or adopted families of origin. Many children grow up in foster care settings, children's institutions, or hospitals. In such circumstances, some adaptation of the genogram may be necessary to identify significant persons in the individual's life. Sometimes creation of an eco-map (see the next section) may be more applicable than a genogram.

to right. Deaths are indicated by an X symbol placed within the pertinent circle or square. If known, names of persons and dates of birth, adoption, marriage, separation, divorce, and death are written alongside the symbols. For example, just above or beneath a bracket line indicating a marriage relationship might be written "m. 3/18/1987." This reflects the date of marriage as March 18, 1987. If this relationship leads to a birth or adoption, such events might be recorded by "b. 4/21/1989" or "a. 4/21/1989." If the couple later separates, that event could be indicated by "s. 4/23/1994." A subsequent divorce could be shown by "div. 5/7/1995."

You may add descriptions of individual persons and relationships with brief notations. For example, one family member may have served in the military during a war, and perhaps another suffered from diabetes. Significant events, such as major accidents, injuries, crimes, and changes in residence or occupation, may also be recorded. Additional symbols or notations may be used to characterize the nature of selected relationships (McGoldrick & Gerson, 1985; McGoldrick et al., 1999). Very close relationships, those that are emotionally cool, those that are strained, and those that involve conflict may be identified. The sources of information should be placed at the bottom of the genogram along with the date and name of the person who prepared the genogram.

A family genogram may be as brief or as extensive as the person organizing the information desires. Some people pursue its creation with great zeal, spending hours interviewing parents, aunts and uncles, and grandparents. They may even contact distant relatives and former neighbors. Others base their genograms solely on information they personally recall. Usually, the amount of energy expended in collecting data and preparing genograms varies according to the purposes for which they are created. Genograms may be prepared in the present—the family as it is now—or the past tense—how it existed at some earlier point. It is even possible to prepare a genogram based on predictions of the future—how the family may appear five or ten years hence. Many people find it useful to take "genogrammatic" snapshots of the family as they remember it at significant points in their development (e.g., beginning and graduating from school, leaving home, entering military service or college, marrying, or giving birth to or adopting children).

As an illustrative example, consider the case of Mrs. Lynn Chase. Later, additional information about her situation will be presented, but at this point we are primarily concerned with displaying a typical genogram, as shown in Figure 2.1. Susan Holder, the social worker who prepared the genogram from Mrs. Chase's perspective, put together a considerable amount of information in readily accessible form. There are concise notes regarding some major intergenerational family themes and patterns. This genogram will be an important reference in Susan's service to Mrs. Chase.

Although social workers are most familiar with family genograms, other forms may be created as well. For example, you may sometimes find it useful to collaborate with clients in the preparation of cultural genograms (Congress, 1994; Hardy & Laszloffy, 1995; Keiley et al., 2002) or spiritual genograms (Frame, 2000; Hodge, 2001). In child welfare service, the development of a household or placement genogram (Altshuler, 1999; McMillen & Groze, 1994) may be particularly helpful.

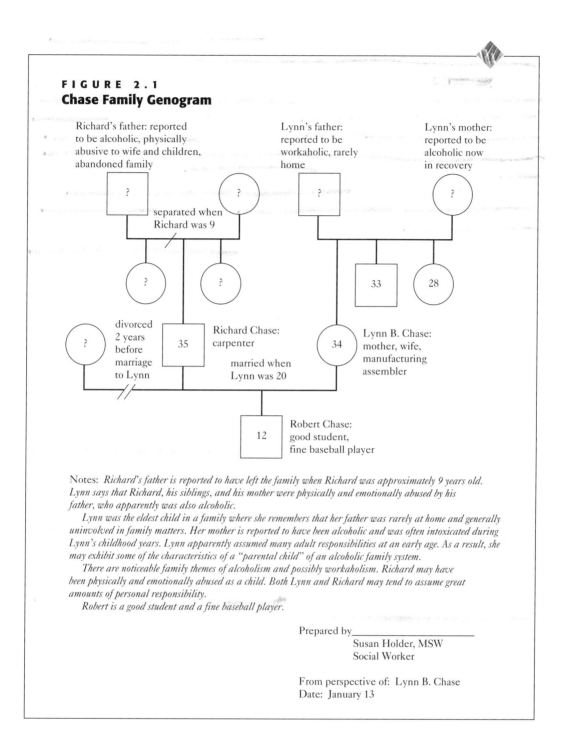

FIGURE 2.1
Chase Family Genogram

Richard's father: reported to be alcoholic, physically abusive to wife and children, abandoned family

Lynn's father: reported to be workaholic, rarely home

Lynn's mother: reported to be alcoholic now in recovery

separated when Richard was 9

divorced 2 years before marriage to Lynn

Richard Chase: carpenter

married when Lynn was 20

Lynn B. Chase: mother, wife, manufacturing assembler

Robert Chase: good student, fine baseball player

Notes: *Richard's father is reported to have left the family when Richard was approximately 9 years old. Lynn says that Richard, his siblings, and his mother were physically and emotionally abused by his father, who apparently was also alcoholic.*

Lynn was the eldest child in a family where she remembers that her father was rarely at home and generally uninvolved in family matters. Her mother is reported to have been alcoholic and was often intoxicated during Lynn's childhood years. Lynn apparently assumed many adult responsibilities at an early age. As a result, she may exhibit some of the characteristics of a "parental child" of an alcoholic family system.

There are noticeable family themes of alcoholism and possibly workaholism. Richard may have been physically and emotionally abused as a child. Both Lynn and Richard may tend to assume great amounts of personal responsibility.

Robert is a good student and a fine baseball player.

Prepared by_____
Susan Holder, MSW
Social Worker

From perspective of: Lynn B. Chase
Date: January 13

Ecological Assessment

In addition to their family experiences, people are also affected by the broader ecological context in which they live. They are influenced by past and present social and
environmental circumstances, and by expectations for their future. As a social worker,
you are affected by these factors as well. They influence various aspects of both your

personal and your professional lives. Indeed, your social ecology is likely to affect your professional experience and performance as a social worker.

An eco-map (Hartman & Laird, 1983; Hartman & Wickey, 1978) is an extremely useful tool for portraying the ecological context because it provides a diagrammatic representation of a person's social world. In addition to presenting an overview of a person, family, or household in context, the eco-map readily identifies the energy-enhancing and energy-depleting relationships between members of a primary social system (e.g., family or household) and the outside world (Mattaini, 1995). The graphic nature of the eco-map highlights social strengths and social deficiencies and helps identify areas of conflict and compatibility. It often indicates areas where change may be needed. There are various forms and purposes for eco-maps (Fieldhouse & Bunkowsky, 2002; Hodge, 2000) that naturally complement genograms (Mattaini, 1990).

Squares or circles are used to represent members of the primary social system (e.g., household). These are drawn in the middle of a sheet of paper and placed in a large circle. Other significant social systems with which the person, family, or household members interact are also identified and encircled. Lines characterize the interactions and relationships among the identified social systems. A solid line (———) reflects a strong (generally positive) relationship; a dotted line (- - - - -) reflects a tenuous relationship; and a hatched line (+++++) reflects a stressful or conflicted relationship. Arrows (→ → →) are used to indicate the direction of the flow of energy or resources between systems. These relationship lines may also be used to characterize the exchange of energy among family members. Plus (+), minus (–), and plus minus (±) signs may be placed adjacent to relationship lines as a supplement, indicating that the relationship is energy enhancing, energy-depleting, or evenly balanced in terms of energy investment and return.

As an illustrative example, an eco-map of Lynn Chase's family is shown in Figure 2.2. Using information provided by Mrs. Chase, the social worker depicted important social systems with which the Chase family members interact. The relationships among the systems are characterized. When used in the context of providing social work services, the eco-map provides the worker and client with a great deal of information in graphic form. As you can easily observe, Mrs. Chase appears to expend much more energy than she receives from most of her interactions with other people and social systems.

Timelines

Human beings are affected by events and experiences in the past and the present, and even by their expectations concerning their future. One way to organize information in the temporal dimension is through timelines. A timeline is a simple table that reflects, in shorthand fashion, important events or experiences in chronological order during a designated period. At least two kinds of timelines may be especially useful. A "Critical Events Timeline" provides an opportunity to outline significant or meaningful experiences in a person's life. An "Issue (or Problem) Timeline" provides a means

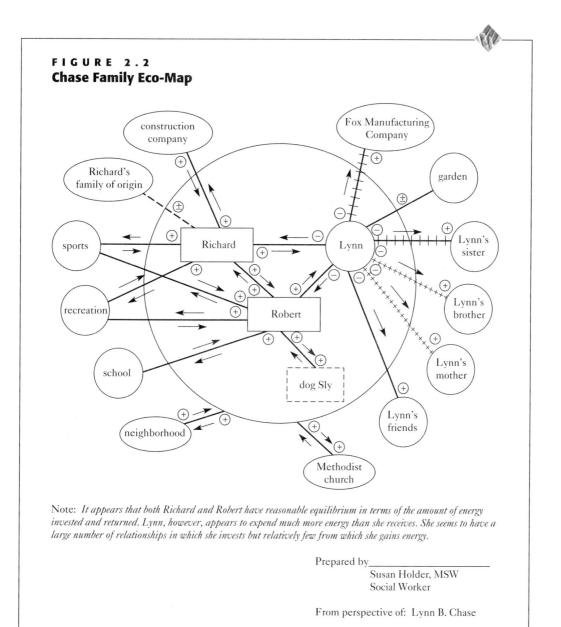

FIGURE 2.2
Chase Family Eco-Map

Note: *It appears that both Richard and Robert have reasonable equilibrium in terms of the amount of energy invested and returned. Lynn, however, appears to expend much more energy than she receives. She seems to have a large number of relationships in which she invests but relatively few from which she gains energy.*

Prepared by_____
Susan Holder, MSW
Social Worker

From perspective of: Lynn B. Chase

to trace the origin and development of a particular issue or problem. Other timelines may be helpful as well. For example, a "Relationship Timeline" could provide a graphic temporal representation of key moments in a personal, family, or professional relationship. A "Successes Timeline" can help in the process of looking for strengths by recording dates of accomplishments, achievements, and other successful experiences. All sorts of timelines are conceivable. You can even extend timelines into the future by imagining or forecasting significant events, moments, or experiences that might occur and could have an impact later on in life.

FIGURE 2.3

Lynn Chase
Critical-Events Timeline

1965 (October)	Lynn Shaughnessy is born
	Unhappy childhood
	Father often away; mother drinks
	Good student
1977	Boy calls her "fat"—very upsetting
1978	Maternal uncle approaches her sexually
1980	Feels intense shame during adolescent confession to priest
1983	First dates; first sexual experiences as H.S. senior
1984	Drinks heavily; parties; several sex partners
	Meets Richard
1985	Marries Richard; stops heavy drinking
1987	Robert is born
1991	Cyst discovered and removed; unable to have more children
1998 (July)	Goes to work at Fox Manufacturing; headaches, weight loss; irritability begins; starts smoking again
1999 (January)	First visit to agency

Creating your own timelines tends to produce considerable self-understanding—because you must actively reflect on important lifetime events. Many clients could also benefit from the experience of constructing their own timelines. Sometimes, however, someone else may need to help. For example, a parent might generate a timeline for a child or a social worker might create a timeline to record critical events in the life of a support group.

The guidelines for creating timelines are quite simple and highly flexible. Feel free to be creative. The basic components are (1) a fairly long, continuous, horizontal or vertical line representing a period of time, (2) several perpendicular, intersecting, or angled lines of shorter length to indicate the dates of selected events, and (3) short descriptions of the events or experiences adjacent to the shorter lines. Additional codes or symbols may be used for other purposes. For example, events of a positive nature may be indicated with a plus sign (+) whereas those of a negative nature could be accompanied by a (−) sign. You could accomplish the same purpose by placing positive events above a horizontal timeline (or to the left of a vertical timeline) and those of a negative nature below (or to the right) the line.

As an illustrative example, a "Critical Events Timeline" of Lynn Chase is shown in Figure 2.3. In this instance, the social worker prepared a preliminary timeline based on information provided by Mrs. Chase. Later, she gave the working draft to Mrs. Chase who edited the timeline and returned a copy of the updated version.

As you notice, the Critical Events Timeline yields a temporal outline of important experiences in Mrs. Chase's life. When used in the context of serving clients, timelines provide both parties ready access to significant information. Both Mrs. Chase and her social worker could use the timeline for easy reference throughout the course of their work together.

◆ EXERCISE 2-4: SELF-UNDERSTANDING AND SELF-CONTROL

1. As a part of an effort to enhance your understanding of self, prepare a genogram of three generations of your own family. You may draw the genogram on one or more letter-size pieces of paper or use a software program to create the graphic. Several word-processing packages allow for creation of squares, circles, triangles, and ways to draw lines to link them. You could also use one of the "family genogram" programs that are available commercially or as shareware. You may download a free copy of GenoPro® at http://www.genopro.com. In creating the genogram, include your grandparents and parents, if possible, as well as your siblings and yourself. If you have children or grandchildren, you may include them as the fourth and fifth generations, respectively. For this exercise, rely on your own memory, rather than seeking a lot of information from other family members. Try to include the approximate dates and categories of significant family events such as births, deaths, marriages, divorces, separations, graduations, military service, hospitalizations, relocations, injuries, and traumatic experiences. Include pleasant as well as unpleasant events. If you do not remember details, enter question marks instead of facts. Develop a succinct, few-word synopsis of the personal characteristics of the more significant family members in your experience. In addition, briefly

summarize the nature of the various relationships within your family—from your perspective.

When you have completed the genogram, reflect on your childhood and family experiences by addressing the following questions. Record your one-to-two paragraph responses in the spaces provided.

a. What role or roles (e.g., family hero, scapegoat, peacemaker, rescuer, or parental child) did you play in your family? What role or roles do you currently tend to play in family or family-like relationships?

b. How was affection expressed in your family? How do you tend to express affection now?

c. How were feelings such as anger, fear, and joy expressed in your family? At this point in your life, how do you express of these feelings?

d. How were people (especially children) educated, guided, and disciplined in your family? Who performed these socialization functions? Today, how do you attempt to educate or influence others?

e. How did your family reflect its ethnic and cultural identity and heritage? How do you?

f. What is your conception of the ideal family? How does it compare with your actual family experience?

2. As a part of the ongoing effort to enhance your self-understanding, prepare an eco-map of your current social ecology. You may draw the eco-map on one or more letter-size pieces of paper or use a software program to create the graphic. Several word processing packages allow for creation of assorted graphic symbols and means to draw lines to link them. You could also use an eco-map computer program such as Ecotivity™ (http://www.interpersonal universe.net/wware.html). You may view an eco-map created with the program at http://www.interpersonaluniverse.net/ecomap.html.

   Using the guidelines just described, identify and characterize the significant social systems with which you interact. Identify sources of stress or conflict as well as sources of support and nurturance. Indicate the direction of energy or resource flow between yourself and other people and systems; use plus (+), minus (–), or plus minus (±) signs to indicate energy use.

When you have completed the eco-map, reflect on your current social situation and address the following questions. Record your responses in the spaces provided.

a. Which relationships in your current situation enhance your energy level? Which deplete energy?

b. How does your social situation affect the physical, intellectual, and emotional energy you have available for use in critical thinking and lifelong learning activities, service to clients, and other aspects of your social work roles?

c. What would you consider the ideal social situation? How does it compare with your current situation?

d. Given the nature of your present social situation, what kinds of clients and what issues would be likely to elicit strong emotional reactions?

e. What changes in your current social situation might enhance the psychological, emotional, physical, cultural, spiritual, and social resources needed to provide high quality social work services to clients?

3. As a part of the ongoing effort to enhance your self-understanding, prepare a personal critical-events timeline. Draw the timeline on one or more letter-size pieces of paper or use a word-processing or drawing software program to create the simple, linear table.

Using the basic guidelines described earlier, identify the approximate dates of events and experiences that you believe have significantly affected your life. When you have completed the timeline, think about its implications, and address the following questions. Record your responses in the spaces provided.

a. What events or experiences in your life were "turning points" that led you to change directions or alter the course of your lifetime path?

b. Look ahead 10 or 15 years. Assume that you continue along in your current life path. What significant events or experiences do you anticipate? How might those affect you?

c. Consider your critical-events timeline in relation to the roles and responsibilities of social workers. What do you see as the implications for you and your career as a social worker?

4. Complete the following measure of self-control. This questionnaire is intended to help you assess your current level of self- control. It is not an examination. You cannot "fail" this exercise!

SELF-CONTROL SCHEDULE[4]

Please read the following statements. Indicate how characteristic or descriptive each of the following statements is by using the code given below.

+3 = Very characteristic of me

+2 = Rather characteristic of me

+1 = Somewhat characteristic of me

–1 = Somewhat uncharacteristic of me

–2 = Rather uncharacteristic of me

–3 = Very uncharacteristic of me

Thank you for your cooperation.

_____ 1. When I do a boring job, I think about the less boring parts of the job and about the reward I will receive when I finish.

_____ 2. When I have to do something that makes me anxious, I try to visualize how I will overcome my anxiety while doing it.

_____ 3. By changing my way of thinking, I am often able to change my feelings about almost anything.

_____ 4. I often find it difficult to overcome my feelings of nervousness and tension without outside help.

_____ 5. When I am feeling depressed, I try to think about pleasant events.

_____ 6. I cannot help thinking about mistakes I made.

_____ 7. When I am faced with a difficult problem, I try to approach it in a systematic way.

_____ 8. I usually do what I am supposed to do more quickly when someone is pressuring me.

_____ 9. When I am faced with a difficult decision, I prefer to postpone it even if I have all the facts.

_____ 10. When I have difficulty concentrating on my reading, I look for ways to increase my concentration.

_____ 11. When I plan to work, I remove everything that is not relevant to my work.

_____ 12. When I try to get rid of a bad habit, I first try to find out all the reasons why I have the habit.

---

[4] From "A Schedule for Assessing Self-control Behaviors: Preliminary Findings," by M. Rosenbaum, 1980, *Behavior Therapy, 11*, 109–121. Copyright © 1980 by the Association for Advancement of Behavior Therapy. Reprinted by permission of the author and publisher.

_____ 13. When an unpleasant thought is bothering me, I try to think about something pleasant.

_____ 14. If I smoked two packs of cigarettes a day, I would need outside help to stop smoking.

_____ 15. When I feel down, I try to act cheerful so that my mood will change.

_____ 16. If I had tranquilizers with me, I would take one whenever I feel tense and nervous.

_____ 17. When I am depressed, I try to keep myself busy with things I like.

_____ 18. I tend to postpone unpleasant tasks even if I could perform them immediately.

_____ 19. I need outside help to get rid of some of my bad habits.

_____ 20. When I find it difficult to settle down and do a task, I look for ways to help me settle down.

_____ 21. Although it makes me feel bad, I cannot help thinking about all sorts of possible catastrophes.

_____ 22. I prefer to finish a job that I have to do before I start doing things I really like.

_____ 23. When I feel physical pain, I try not to think about it.

_____ 24. My self-esteem increases when I am able to overcome a bad habit.

_____ 25. To overcome bad feelings that accompany failure, I often tell myself that it is not catastrophic and I can do anything.

_____ 26. When I feel that I am too impulsive, I tell myself to stop and think before I do something about it.

_____ 27. Even when I am terribly angry with someone, I consider my actions very carefully.

_____ 28. Facing the need to make a decision, I usually look for different alternatives instead of deciding quickly and spontaneously.

_____ 29. Usually, I first do the thing I really like to do even if there are more urgent things to do.

_____ 30. When I realize that I am going to be unavoidably late for an important meeting, I tell myself to keep calm.

_____ 31. When I feel pain in my body, I try to divert my thoughts from it.

_____ 32. When I am faced with a number of things to do, I usually plan my work.

_____ 33. When I am short of money, I decide to record all my expenses in order to budget more carefully in the future.

_____ 34. If I find it difficult to concentrate on a task, I divide it into small segments.

_____ 35. Quite often, I cannot overcome unpleasant thoughts that bother me.

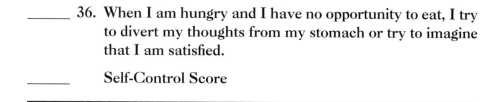

_____ 36. When I am hungry and I have no opportunity to eat, I try to divert my thoughts from my stomach or try to imagine that I am satisfied.

_____ Self-Control Score

The Self-Control Schedule is scored in the following manner. First, reverse score items 4, 6, 8, 9, 14, 16, 18, 19, 21, 29, and 35. On this scale, reverse score means to change a positive number to its negative or a negative number to its positive (e.g., a +3 would become –3; +2 would become –2; +1 would become –1). Then, sum the ratings for the 36 items. The total represents your self-control score.

As with other self-report measures, view the results of this inventory with a degree of caution. In assessing your capacity for self-control, consider information from other sources as well. In reviewing your score on the Self-Control Schedule, recognize that the scores could possibly range from –108 to +108. Most samples taking this schedule yield mean scores in the 23 to 27 range. The average score of nonclinical populations tends to be approximately 25 (SD = 20) (Rosenbaum, 1980). A sample (Cournoyer, 1994) of 24 beginning MSW students scored an average of 36.46 (SD = 20.60) on the Self-Control Schedule. A higher score represents a greater degree or level of self-control. If your score is substantially less than these average scores, it may be helpful to institute a program designed to increase your level of self-control. If your score is +5 or lower, you should probably consult a professional concerning development of a self-control enhancement program. If the score is an accurate reflection, such a low level of self-control could be problematic in your role as a professional social worker.

When you have completed and scored the Self-Control Schedule, reflect on its implications by addressing the following questions. Record your responses in the spaces provided.

a. How would you know if someone truly possessed a well-developed capacity for _self-control?_

b. In what life-areas have you exhibited strong self-control? In what areas have you shown insufficient self-control?

c. Repetitive patterns of maladaptive behavior, sometimes called *bad habits*, *compulsions*, or *addictive behaviors*, can significantly interfere with your degree of self-control and the quality of your social work service to others. Identify those repetitive maladaptive behaviors in your own life that could impair your functioning as a social worker.

d. Discuss those aspects of social work practice that are likely to require you to exercise the greatest amount of self-control.

e. Outline a plan to strengthen your self-control in those areas that might adversely affect your performance as a professional social worker.

_____

Cultural Competence and Acceptance of Others

"Culture is a learned worldview or paradigm shared by a population or group and transmitted socially that influences values, beliefs, customs, and behaviors, and is reflected in the language, dress, food, materials, and social institutions of a group" (Burchum, 2002, p. 7). Competence refers to the ability to complete a task or activity, or to fulfill a responsibility correctly, effectively, or proficiently. In the context of professional social work practice, then, cultural competence refers to the awareness, knowledge, understanding, sensitivity, and skill needed to effectively conduct and complete professional activities with persons of diverse cultural backgrounds and affiliations. The notion of cultural competence should not be misinterpreted to mean that anyone ever becomes fully or completely culturally competent—even in regard to one's own culture (Dean, 2001). Rather, cultural competence is an ongoing developmental process that is "never ending and ever expanding" (Burchum, 2002, p. 14).

The NASW (1999) recognizes the importance of cultural competence by including in its Code of Ethics a discrete section entitled Ethical Responsibilities to Clients: Cultural Competence and Social Diversity. That section includes the following passages:

◆ Social workers should understand culture and its function in human behavior and society, recognizing the strengths that exist in all cultures. (Section 1.05.a)
◆ Social workers should have a knowledge base of their clients' cultures and be able to demonstrate competence in the provision of services that are sensitive to clients' cultures and to differences among people and cultural groups. (Section 1.05.b)
◆ Social workers should obtain education about and seek to understand the nature of social diversity and oppression with respect to race, ethnicity, national origin, color, sex, sexual orientation, age, marital status, political belief, religion, and mental or physical disability. (Section 1.05.c)

In its Standards of Cultural Competence, the NASW suggested,

Cultural competence refers to the process by which individuals and systems respond respectfully and effectively to people of all cultures, languages, classes, races, ethnic backgrounds, religions, and other diversity factors in a manner that recognizes, affirms, and values the worth of individuals, families, and communities and protects and preserves the dignity of each. (NASW National Committee on Racial and Ethnic Diversity, 2001, p. 11)

Cultural competence requires respect for and acceptance of others. Acceptance of others involves the process of self-understanding, cross-cultural understanding, valuing, and joining with people regardless of the degree of similarity or difference from oneself. As a social worker providing needed services to sometimes highly vulnerable people and to widely diverse communities, you attempt to transcend those powerful psychological and social forces that maintain patterns of prejudice, ethnocentrism, xenophobia, rankism (Fuller, 2002), and discrimination. Social workers require a capacity to accept people who differ as well as those who resemble themselves in appearance, background, attitudes, abilities, and behavior. Each person, family, group, community, and society deserves genuine acceptance from the social workers who serve them.

In the context of cultural competence and acceptance of others, the term *reverence* seems especially meaningful (Woodruff, 2001). Reverence involves an attitude of deep respect or awe and humility in the presence of another. Although reflecting a religious or spiritual connotation, as in reverence toward a higher being, it aptly captures the special attitude social workers manifest as they evolve toward cultural competence and acceptance of others.

In a highly competitive and evaluative society, it is exceedingly difficult to develop genuine reverence for and acceptance of others. Nonetheless, for the practice of social work, acceptance of others is crucial. The capacity for such acceptance, however, is inevitably affected by the nature of one's prejudices. *Prejudice* is "an opinion about an individual, group, or phenomenon that is developed without proof or systematic evidence. This prejudgment may be favorable but is more often unfavorable and may become institutionalized in the form of a society's laws or customs" (Barker, 1995). *Discrimination* is, of course, closely related to prejudice. Discrimination involves the "the prejudgment and negative treatment of people based on identifiable characteristics such as race, gender, religion, or ethnicity" (Barker, 1995). As a social worker, you must learn to transcend the powerful psychological and social forces that maintain prejudiced attitudes and discriminatory behaviors. This is necessary so that you can genuinely accept others who are similar and those who are different in appearance, background, attitudes, abilities, and behavior. You must be able to tolerate and value both similarity and diversity and to accept others on their own terms.

Such acceptance does not come easily in a heterogeneous society in which people are highly diverse in economic resources, race and ethnicity, religion, culture, and education. If you are similar to most North Americans who aspire to become professional social workers, you have been exposed to prejudiced attitudes and to both covert and overt forms of discrimination. In all likelihood, you have had prejudiced thoughts and discriminated against (or for) others. You have probably experienced some of the effects of others' prejudiced attitudes and discriminatory behaviors against (or for) you.

You may even have experienced prejudice for or against yourself and those similar to yourself. Some persons of color and other members of minority groups, for example, have negative prejudices about themselves, judging themselves critically because of a perceived majority standard. Conversely, some white males show positive prejudices about themselves. They may consider themselves deserving or entitled because of their own sex and skin color. This "tendency to consider one's own group, usually national or ethnic, superior to other groups using one's own group or groups as the frame of reference against which other groups are judged" (Wolman, 1973, p. 129) is called *ethnocentrism*. Of course, such prejudices can also occur in reverse. For example, some white males hold negatively prejudiced attitudes about themselves, and some minority group members view themselves as specially entitled or privileged. The forms of prejudice and discrimination are myriad and insidious. As a member of North

American society, you have probably adopted some prejudiced attitudes and discriminatory behaviors in your own life. As a step toward transcending these and genuinely accepting other human beings, please undertake the following exercise.

◆ EXERCISE 2-5: CULTURAL COMPETENCE AND ACCEPTANCE OF OTHERS

Using what you learned from the preparation of your family genogram and eco-map, reflect on your own personal background and socialization experiences as they pertain to the acceptance and appreciation of diversity and difference. Explore the psychological and social factors associated with the development of your own prejudiced attitudes and discriminatory behaviors. Consider how you personally manifest aspects of racism, sexism, ageism, rankism, xenophobia, homophobia, able-ism (prejudice or discrimination based on physical or mental ability), look-ism (prejudice or discrimination based on appearance or attractiveness), and class-ism (prejudice or discrimination based on socioeconomic status). Also, consider the phenomenon of ideological chauvinism—prejudice based on a difference in beliefs—as it might occur in your relations with others.

When you have seriously thought about these issues, respond to the following in the spaces provided:

1. Make note of at least one occasion when you personally adopted a prejudicial attitude against or engaged in discriminatory behavior toward:

   a. Someone of the other sex

   b. Someone of your own sex

   c. Someone of another ethnic group

d. Someone of your own ethnic group

e. Someone older than yourself

f. Someone younger than yourself

g. Someone about your own age

h. Someone of a homosexual orientation

i. Someone of a heterosexual orientation

j.   Someone of a "higher" economic group

k.   Someone of a "lower" economic group

l.   Someone of your own economic group

m.   Someone you think is better educated

n.   Someone you think is less well educated

o.   Someone who looks different from you (e.g., height, weight, skin color, facial characteristics, or attractiveness)

p.   Someone who looks similar to you

q.   Someone more physically able-bodied than yourself

r.   Someone less physically able-bodied than yourself

s.   Someone you consider more intelligent than yourself

t.   Someone you consider less intelligent than yourself

u.   Someone with different beliefs (e.g., religious, philosophical, or political)

  v. Someone who has a similar belief system

2. Carefully read each of the following items (Leigh, 1998). Based on a frank and objective assessment of your own attitudes and behavior, rate the degree to which you agree or disagree with each item. Use a scale where 1 = Strongly Agree, 2 = Agree, 3 = Disagree, 4 = Strongly Disagree. Record your ratings in the spaces provided.

  a. _____ I accept the fact that I have much to learn about others.

  b. _____ I have an appreciation of the regional and geographical factors related to people of color and contrasting cultures, how the individual may vary from the generalizations about their regional and geographical group, and how regional groups vary from the total cultural group.

  c. _____ I follow the standard that knowledge is obtained from the person in the situation and add to my learning about the situation from that person before generalizing about the group-specific person.

  d. _____ I have the capacity to form relationships with people from contrasting cultures in social, work, and professional relationships.

  e. _____ I can engage in a process characterized by mutual respect and conscious effort to reduce power disparities between myself and persons of minority status.

  f. _____ I have the ability to obtain culturally relevant information in the professional encounter.

  g. _____ I have the ability to enter into a process of mutual exploration, assessment, and treatment with people of contrasting culture and minority status in society. (Leigh, 1998, pp. 173–174)

Leigh (1998) developed these statements to help professionals interested in developing cultural communication competence. Review your ratings to each item. Use the following space to discuss what the ratings mean to you about your developing competence in cultural communications.

3. In the space provided, please discuss how prejudiced attitudes and discriminatory behavior might influence your personal life. Then address how such attitudes and behavior might affect your effectiveness as a social worker.

4. If you can transcend the powerful forces of prejudice and discrimination and come to accept others, you are more likely to conform to the values and ethics of the profession and to be effective in your practice. Unless you can develop the capacity for sincere acceptance of other people, regardless of their similarities or differences, you will be incapable of fulfilling the tasks, functions, and obligations of professional social work practice. To help you further the process of self-understanding in this critical area, please complete the following instrument.

ACCEPTANCE OF OTHERS SCALE[5]

This questionnaire is designed to assess your relative acceptance of others. It is not a test, so there are no right or wrong answers. Please answer each item as carefully and accurately as you can by placing a number by each one as follows:

1 = Almost always true

2 = Usually true

3 = True half of the time

4 = Only occasionally true

5 = Very rarely true

---

[5] From "Acceptance by others and its relation to acceptance of self and others: A revaluation," by W. F. Fey, 1955, *Journal of Abnormal and Social Psychology, 30,* 274–276.

Please begin.

Score   Statement of Present Condition or Action

_____ 1. People are too easily led.

_____ 2. I like people I get to know.

_____ 3. People these days have pretty low moral standards.

_____ 4. Most people are pretty smug about themselves, never really facing their bad points.

_____ 5. I can be comfortable with nearly all kinds of people.

_____ 6. All people can talk about these days, it seems, is movies, TV, and foolishness like that.

_____ 7. People get ahead by using "pull," and not because of what they know.

_____ 8. Once you start doing favors for people, they'll just walk all over you.

_____ 9. People are too self-centered.

_____ 10. People are always dissatisfied and hunting for something new.

_____ 11. With many people you don't know how you stand.

_____ 12. You've probably got to hurt someone if you're going to make something out of yourself.

_____ 13. People really need a strong, smart leader.

_____ 14. I enjoy myself most when I am alone, away from people.

_____ 15. I wish people would be more honest with me.

_____ 16. I enjoy going with a crowd.

_____ 17. In my experience, people are pretty stubborn and unreasonable.

_____ 18. I can enjoy being with people whose values are very different from mine.

_____ 19. Everybody tries to be nice.

_____ 20. The average person is not very well satisfied with himself (or herself).

_____   **Acceptance of Others Score**

The Acceptance of Others Scale is scored in the following manner: First, reverse score items 2, 5, 16, 18, and 19. *(Reverse score* means to change an answer of 1 to 5; 2 to 4; 3 remains 3; 4 to 2; and 5 to 1.)* Now add the answers for all 20 items to find your total score. As with other scales, interpret the results of this questionnaire with some caution. Use the results to formulate hypotheses to test by examining evidence from other sources. The guidelines that follow will help you evaluate your results (Fey, 1955).

Persons who score in the 85–100 range generally tend to accept other people, to experience others as accepting of them, and to be accepted by others. The 66–84 range includes the average scores of the majority of people. Approximately two-thirds of all people taking the scale score in this medium range. A sample (Cournoyer, 1994) of 20 beginning MSW students, reflected an average score of 78.4 (SD = 7.61) on the Acceptance of Others Scale. Such midrange scores show a mixture of caution about and acceptance of people. Although less accepting of certain persons, individuals scoring in this range clearly have the capacity to accept others fully. Persons scoring in the 0–65 range may be very cautious about and intolerant of others. This hesitancy about other people could be a consequence of significant social, emotional, or physical pain caused by others at some point in the past.

When you have scored the scale, consider its implications by addressing the following questions. Record your responses in the spaces provided.

a. How would you know when someone truly accepts another human being? How would the form of acceptance vary if he or she differed in some identifiable way (e.g., race, gender, religion, or ethnicity) from the accepted person?

b. Have you ever been truly and completely accepted by someone who differed from you (e.g., race, gender, religion, or ethnicity)? If so, what did it feel like? How did this acceptance affect your beliefs, attitudes, and behavior?

c. Have you ever truly and completely accepted someone who differed from you (e.g., race, gender, religion, or ethnicity)? If so, what do you think enabled you to do so? If not, what prevented you?

d. How do you think people acquire intolerant attitudes about other people? How do you think people develop the capacity to accept others who differ from themselves?

e. To transcend those powerful internal and external forces that tend to perpetuate prejudice, intolerance, and discrimination, outline the key points of a plan by which you might strengthen your capacity to accept others, especially those who differ from yourself?

Social Support

Social work is not a solitary endeavor. Rather, it is social profession. Grounded in a person-and-situation perspective and motivated by a mission to serve individuals and the society as a whole, social workers are deeply involved with others. The nature of the work requires regular collaboration with others, ongoing supervision or consultation, and a great deal of social support. In the absence of energy enhancing and reality testing social support, social workers would quickly deplete their personal resources and increase the likelihood of meeting some of their psychosocial needs and wants through their relationships with clients. In many ways, solitary social workers who lack strong, positive personal and professional social networks are quite vulnerable to acting out temptations.

Genograms and eco-maps graphically represent family and social relationships. Timelines reflect the temporal dimension. Scales regarding self-control and acceptance of others provide information about personal beliefs, behaviors, and attitudes. All these exercises promote self-understanding. They may also reveal something about the sources of and contexts within which social support is given and accepted, or withheld and rejected. Social support may be vital for human well-being (Lang, 2002; Sinha, Nayyar, & Sinha, 2002; Turner & Marino, 1994; Whitfield & Wiggins, 2003) and represents an especially relevant theme for social workers—personally as well as professionally. Social support includes those "formal and informal activities and relationships that provide for the needs of humans in their efforts to live in society. These needs include . . . a network of other individuals and groups who offer encouragement, access, empathy, role models, and social identity" (Barker, 1995).

The genogram and eco-map that you prepared should provide excellent graphic representations of the primary and secondary social systems with which you interact. Maps such as these help people identify key relationships and social systems. They may not, however, fully reflect the nature of the feelings and experiences of social support that occur within various systems and interactions. For this purpose, another kind of assessment may be used.

Recognize that social support involves several dimensions. As a social worker, you and your clients sometimes identify sources of social support that they find most satisfying. Frequently, you and clients take steps to increase or enhance their social networks and relationships. Often you encourage key family members and friends to join you and your client in meetings intended to further such goals. At other times, you and a client may determine that certain people are unlikely to become sources of support. In such contexts, you and your client may reconfigure or restructure your client's social networks. Efforts such as these may help clients enhance their social functioning and overall quality of life.

Social relationships and networks also influence social workers. Indeed, the nature and extent of your social supports are likely to affect the quality of your professional work as well as the satisfaction you experience in providing service. The interpersonal and emotional demands of professional social work practice can be substantial. Social workers who feel personally and professionally supported in their social networks and relationships may be better prepared to cope effectively with the stress. What's more, social workers who lack adequate social involvement and support may be tempted to use relationships with clients to meet some of their social and emotional needs. For example, suppose you are a social worker who does not feel supported in your relationships with family members and friends. Might you be tempted to seek such support from some of your clients? Might you be tempted to judge harshly a client who does not appear to be supportive of his own spouse or children?

Especially when faced with multiple demands of a highly stressful nature, social workers might be influenced by their own social circumstances. As a social worker steeped in the person-and-situation perspective, you recognize the importance of the social world for your clients' well being. Do not underestimate its importance for your own.

◆ EXERCISE 2-6: SOCIAL SUPPORT

As a supplement to the genogram and eco-map, complete the Social Support Appraisals Scale (SS-A). This questionnaire is designed to assess your personal experience of social support. It is not a test. You can neither pass nor fail.

THE SOCIAL SUPPORT APPRAISALS SCALE[6]

Please respond to each item as carefully and accurately as you can by choosing the response that best reflects your opinion. Please use the following four-point rating system to record your responses.

1 = Strongly Agree

2 = Agree

3 = Disagree

4 = Strongly Disagree

_____ 1. My friends respect me.
_____ 2. My family cares for me very much.
_____ 3. I am not important to others.
_____ 4. My family holds me in high esteem.
_____ 5. I am well liked.
_____ 6. I can rely on my friends.
_____ 7. I am really admired by my family.
_____ 8. I am respected by other people.
_____ 9. I am loved dearly by my family.
_____ 10. My friends don't care about my welfare.
_____ 11. Members of my family rely on me.
_____ 12. I am held in high esteem.
_____ 13. I can't rely on my family for support.
_____ 14. People admire me.
_____ 15. I feel a strong bond with my friends.
_____ 16. My friends look out for me.
_____ 17. I feel valued by other people.
_____ 18. My family really respects me.
_____ 19. My friends and I are really important to each other.
_____ 20. I feel like I belong.
_____ 21. If I died tomorrow, very few people would miss me.
_____ 22. I don't feel close to members of my family.
_____ 23. My friends and I have done a lot for one another.

_____ Overall Social Support Score
_____ SS-A Family Subscale Score
_____ SS-A Friends Subscale Score

---

[6] Vaux, A., Phillips, J., Holly, L., Thompson, B., Williams, D., & Stewart, D. (1986). The Social Support Appraisals (SSA) Scale: Studies of reliability and validity. *American Journal of Community Psychology*. Vol. 14, pp. 195–219. Copyright © 1986. Reprinted by permission of the lead author and Kluwer Academic/Plenum Publishers.

To calculate your overall score on the Social Support Appraisals Scale, first reverse score Items 3, 10, 13, 21, and 22. Then add the ratings for the 23 items. Your overall SS-A score should range somewhere between 23 and 92.

This instrument also contains family and friends subscales. To determine your family subscale score, sum the ratings for items 2, 4, 7, 9, 11, 13, 18, and 22. Find your friends subscale score by adding the ratings for items 1, 6, 10, 15, 16, 19, and 23. Your family social support appraisal subscale score should range between 8 and 32. Your friends subscale score should range between 7 and 28.

As you reflect on the significance of these scores, please consider that a *lower* score indicates a greater level of appraised social support. The SS-A Scale has been used in numerous studies. The instrument appears to have acceptable validity and reliability characteristics. Various studies have yielded average overall SS-A Scale scores that tend to range from the mid-to-high-sixties (Miller & Lago, 1990; O'Reilly, 1995), average family subscale scores in the low-to-mid-twenties, and average friend subscale scores in the low-twenties. Consider your results in light of these average ranges.

When you have scored the scale, think about its implications by addressing the following questions. Record your responses in the spaces provided.

1. Where and from whom do you experience the greatest, and the least, social support?

2. What kinds or forms of social support do you most like to give, and to receive?

3. In what ways would you like to change your social support systems? Why? What steps might you take to make those changes?

Summary

Social workers come from all sorts of backgrounds. They reflect a wide range of personality profiles and social lifestyles. They are attracted to the profession for many different reasons. Their motivations for service vary. Some social workers have a strong sense of altruism—a desire to give of themselves to others. Others have a philosophical commitment to social justice or to a better world. Some are proponents of a particular cause they can appropriately pursue through a career in social work. Others follow in the footsteps of a relative or other significant person who is or was a social worker. Some see social work as a way to continue in a family role, such as caretaker, with which they are personally familiar, while others see social work as a way to become a counselor or psychotherapist.

Some choose educational programs in social work because they believe admissions requirements are lower, course work less challenging, and professors less rigorous than in certain other schools or departments. Still others have personal or social problems that they believe might be resolved through schooling in social work and through service to others, or perhaps they have been clients themselves and identified with the social workers who served them.

You may have thought about some of your own motives for choosing social work as you read this chapter and completed the exercises. You have considered the characteristics of professionalism. At this point, you should have a preliminary sense about your level of proficiency in the social work skills; a recognition of the significance of integrity, critical thinking, and lifelong learning for practice; and a developing awareness of several aspects of yourself and your social world. You should be able to prepare genograms, eco-maps, and timelines and appreciate the importance of self-understanding and self-control, cultural competence and acceptance of others, and social support as they pertain to professionalism in social work practice.

In effect, you have adopted a person-and-situation perspective as you completed the exercises in this chapter. We hope that you have gained some awareness of the relationships among your attributes as a person, your family and social environments, and the characteristics needed for effective service as a professional social worker in contemporary society.

Of all the issues that pertain to professionalism, none is more important than the issue of one's suitability, motivation, and readiness for the profession. At some point, you honestly need to address the questions, "Am I personally suited for this profession? Are my beliefs, motives, attributes, and characteristics congruent with those needed by social workers? Am I ready for the challenges and sacrifices this work entails?" These questions are fundamental to the consideration of personal and professional integrity. As a way to address them, please complete the following summary exercise. It will help you explore your motives for selecting social work and evaluate your overall readiness to pursue it as a profession.

◆ CHAPTER 2 SUMMARY EXERCISES

1. Reflect on and integrate the results of the earlier exercises through a summary analysis of your overall readiness for professional social work. Prepare your analysis in the form of a two-to-four page word-processed report (500–1000 words) entitled "Summary Assessment of Motivation, Readiness, and Suitability for the Profession of Social Work." In your report, be sure to address the following dimensions. When finished, include the report in your Social Work Skills Learning Portfolio.

   a. *Career Plans.* Look ahead to the professional social work career to which you aspire after graduation. Describe the setting, the nature of the issues, and the kinds of people with whom you would prefer to work. Identify and describe the personal qualities and attributes that you think will be required of you so you can practice social work effectively in such a context.

   b. *Client and Setting Preference.* Identify those settings, issues, and people with whom you would prefer *not* to work. Discuss the reasons for these preferences. What are the implications of those reasons for your personal and professional development?

   c. *Critical Events.* Identify three major factors or incidents in your personal, familial, or situational experience that contributed to your choice of social work as a career. How do these three affect your current readiness for professional social work practice?

   d. *Satisfying and Challenging Aspects.* What do you anticipate will be the single most rewarding or satisfying part of being a professional social worker? What will be the single most difficult?

   e. *Readiness for Social Work.* Consider your family genogram, eco-map, timeline, the results of the questionnaires, your responses to the exercises, and then ask yourself, "Do I possess or can I develop the personal capacities necessary to function effectively as a professional social worker?" If your answer is No, check out your conclusion by meeting with an adviser, a social work professor, or a guidance counselor. If your negative answer is confirmed through discussions with others, proceed to identify other careers for which you may be better suited. If your answer is Yes, identify the personal areas requiring further exploration and indicate those capacities you need to strengthen. Outline a specific plan to do so.

2. Finally, based on your current level of self-awareness and self-understanding, use the following space to outline the three issues most significant to you that you would want to explore with an outstanding experienced social worker? Identify three specific questions that you would ask.

◆ CHAPTER 2 WORLD WIDE WEB EXERCISES

Log on to the World Wide Web and electronically visit each of the Web sites identified in the following exercises. In the spaces provided, identify something from each Web site that might be of value to you as a student and later as a practicing social worker.

1. Go to the Thomson Learning InfoTrac® College Edition Web site at http://www.infotrac-college.com. Click on the InfoWrite item on the menu at the left side of the home page. That should take you to the InfoWrite page. Click on the Critical Thinking item on the menu to go to the page about critical thinking at http://infotrac.thomsonlearning.com/infowrite/critical.html. Read the contents of that page. Then write a two or three sentence reaction to each of the following sections: (a) Distinguishing Fact from Opinion and Bias from Reason, (b) Distinguishing Between Primary and Secondary

Sources, (c) Evaluating Information Sources, (d) Recognizing Deceptive Arguments, and (e) Recognizing Ethnocentrism and Stereotypes.

2. Return to the Thomson Learning InfoTrac College Edition homepage at http://www.infotrac-college.com. Use the passcode that accompanies this book to log in to the InfoTrac College Edition bibliographic resources. Safeguard the PassCode and keep it available so that you may access InfoTrac College Edition via any computer connected to the Internet. Once you have successfully logged in to InfoTrac College Edition, click on the EasySearch Help button toward the top of the page. Review the guidelines for conducting searches. After you have read that information, use the following space to compare the features of EasySearch and PowerSearch/PowerTrac. Also, in a sentence or two, describe a subject guide search and a keyword search.

3. Return to the InfoTrac College Edition search page. Using the EasySearch feature, enter the term "social work" (include the quotes), check the Subject Guide Search button, and then click on search. You should find two pages of various subdivision categories within the subject of social work. Scroll to "Social Work Education" and click on the "See also Subdivisions." Review the more than 30 subordinate listings. Scroll to and then click on the "social aspects" listing. You should find several articles on the topic, including one entitled "The Relationship Between Attitudes: Homophobia and Sexism Among Social Work Students" by Beverly Black and colleagues (1998). Click on the view text and retrieval options line just below the title of that article to review a full-text version. Read the article and use the following space to prepare a one-to-two paragraph summary of the implications of the findings for you personally and professionally.

4. Use the InfoTrac College Edition system to conduct a keyword search using the term "reputations cracked" (without the quotation marks) to locate an article entitled "Reputations Are Easily Cracked Never Well Mended" by Harvey MacKay (2000). Read the article. Use the following space to prepare a one-paragraph discussion of implications for the integrity of professional social workers.

Chapter 2 Self-Appraisal

As you finish this chapter, please reflect on your current level of professionalism by completing the following self-appraisal exercise.

SELF-APPRAISAL: PROFESSIONALISM

Please respond to the following items to help you reflect upon professionalism as presented in this chapter. Read each statement carefully. Then, use the following four-point rating scale to indicate the degree to which you agree or disagree with each statement. Record your numerical response in the space provided:

4 = Strongly Agree

3 = Agree

2 = Disagree

1 = Strongly Disagree

_____ 1. I can describe the dimensions of professionalism presented in this chapter.

_____ 2. I can discuss the significance of integrity for social work practice.

_____ 3. I can discuss the relevance of professional knowledge and self-efficacy for social work practice.

_____ 4. I can elaborate upon the significance of critical thinking and lifelong learning for social work practice.

_____ 5. I can discuss the relevance of self-understanding and self-control for social work practice.

_____ 6. I can discuss the relevance of cultural competence and acceptance of others for social work practice.

_____ 7. I can discuss the relevance of social support for social work practice.

_____ 8. I can assess my readiness for professional social work practice.

_____ Subtotal

Reflect on the dimensions of professionalism addressed in this chapter and the results of your self-appraisal. Based on your analysis, word-process a succinct one-page summary report entitled "Self-Assessment of Professionalism." Within the report, be sure to discuss those dimensions you rated highly (e.g., scores of 3 or 4) along with those that require further development (e.g., scores of 2 or less). Outline plans to enhance these aspects of your professionalism. When finished, save the report for inclusion within your Social Work Skills Learning Portfolio.

Chapter 3

Ethical Decision Making

Social workers consider the legal, ethical, and sometimes moral implications of professional situations and reach ethical decisions concerning their responsibilities. Social workers confront ethical dilemmas daily in many aspects of their service. To process these complex issues, you need a thorough understanding of social work values and ethics (Reamer, 1997, 1998a) as well as those legal obligations that affect and inform your work. Such understanding involves a great deal more than general familiarity with legal statutes, case law, and ethical codes. You require a thorough grasp of the underlying principles. You should know your social work code of ethics and be able to identify the legal and ethical principles that apply in specific situations. When principles conflict, you need the capacity to address and resolve the dilemma. Specifically, you should be able to determine which ethical principle or legal obligation takes precedence over others in situations where several competing responsibilities apply.[1]

The topic of laws, values, and ethics in social work practice is extraordinarily complex. Nonetheless, as a professional social worker, you must pay constant attention to legal and ethical obligations because they apply to virtually every aspect of your professional life.

---

[1] The National Association of Social Workers (NASW) Code of Ethics may also be found at www.socialworkers.org. Publications about social work ethics from an international perspective may be obtained through the International Federation of Social Workers (IFSW) at www.ifsw.org. Information about the Code of Ethics of the Canadian Association of Social Workers (CASW) may be found at www.casw-acts.ca. The Code of Ethics for Social Work of the British Association of Social Workers may be accessed at www.basw.co.uk and those of the Australian Association of Social Workers at www.aasw.asn.au.

In serving clients, social workers use information from a variety of sources: theoretical knowledge, knowledge from research studies, wisdom gained from life experience and service to clients, the expertise of colleagues and supervisors, and agency policies and procedures. One source of information, however, serves as a screen for all others. The values, ethics, and obligations of the profession are preeminent. Every aspect of practice, every decision, every assessment, every intervention, and virtually every action you undertake as a social worker must be considered from the perspective of your professional ethics and obligations. This dimension supersedes all others. Ethical responsibilities take precedence over theoretical knowledge, research findings, practice wisdom, agency policies, and, of course, your own personal values, preferences, and beliefs. Ethical decision making is a central component of professionalism and should be included along with the other dimensions addressed in Chapter 2. This chapter focuses exclusively on this topic by providing learners (see Box 3.1) opportunities to develop proficiency in ethical decision making for social work practice in contemporary society.

BOX 3.1

Chapter Purpose

The purpose of this chapter is to contribute to the exploration of professional integrity by helping learners understand the knowledge, appreciate the values, and implement the skills necessary for ethical decision making within the context of contemporary social work practice.

Goals

Following completion of this chapter, learners should be able to

◆ Identify and discuss the legal duties of professional helpers
◆ Access the laws that regulate the practice of social work in their locale
◆ Identify and discuss the fundamental values of the social work profession
◆ Understand the ethical principles and standards that guide social work practice
◆ Identify and analyze relevant legal duties and ethics that might apply within a professional context
◆ Analyze and determine the relative priority of competing legal and ethical obligations through application of a case-specific conceptual screen
◆ Use critical thinking skills to reach an ethical decision and plan appropriate action
◆ Assess proficiency in the ethical decision-making skills

Service as a professional social worker entails considerable personal sacrifice, enormous intellectual effort, and extraordinary self-discipline. Because you affect, for better or worse, the lives of the people you serve, you bear a substantial burden of personal and professional responsibility. Numerous obligations derive from your commitment to a professional code of ethics and the laws that regulate the practice of social work in your locale. In carrying out your responsibilities, you will confront complex ethical issues time and time again. To be effective and professionally responsible, you need means to identify, address, analyze, and resolve the ethical issues inherent in virtually every action you take as a social worker.

Ethical decision making involves consideration of several dimensions and, of course, a great deal of careful thought. First, you need to understand those legal duties that apply to all professional helpers. Second, you must be familiar with the state, local, and federal laws and regulations that affect the profession and practice of social work in your locale. Third, you should thoroughly comprehend the core social work values and be extremely familiar with the social work code of ethics. Fourth, you must be able to identify those ethical principles and legal duties that pertain to specific social work practice situations. Fifth, when several competing obligations apply, you need to be able to decide which take precedence. This represents the greatest challenge and involves the most advanced critical thinking skills. When there is no conflict among the ethical and legal responsibilities relevant to a particular situation, making a decision and taking appropriate action is fairly straightforward. You merely conform to the appropriate legal and ethical obligations. Sometimes, however, the applicable principles and duties conflict with one another so that adherence to one obligation effectively means violating another. Deciding which obligation takes precedence is the most complex and challenging aspect of ethical decision making. Sixth, you must keep professional quality records about your ethical decision-making process as well as other aspects of your service to clients. In your records, describe your decision and summarize your rationale. Seventh, implement your decision. On occasion, the decision may be to take action but sometimes the best decision may be to take no action. Eighth, keep professional records about the implementation. Ninth, monitor and record the outcomes and effects of the implementation.

Understanding Your Legal Obligations

Along with counselors, nurses, psychiatrists, and psychologists, social workers are members of the professional helping community. As a social worker, therefore, you are subject to certain legally determined obligations or duties. These derive from common law, legislation, regulations, and various court decisions. Some legal obligations coincide with the responsibilities suggested by social work values and the code of ethics; others do not. You are responsible for understanding both the legal duties applicable to all professional helpers and those ethical obligations that apply specifically to social workers. In particular, you need information about the laws and regulations that govern the profession and practice of social work in your locale. In the United States, all 50 states, the District of Columbia, Puerto Rico, and the U.S. Virgin Islands have enacted laws regulating social work. Obtain a copy of the licensing law and accompanying regulations that apply in your locale. Many are available through the World Wide Web. For example, Title 25 Article 23.6 of the Indiana State Code governs the licensure and practice of social work in the state. That section may be found at www.in.gov/legislative/ic/code/title25/ar23.6.

Despite the plethora of laws and regulations, the legal duties of professional helpers are not always clear. They are certainly not permanent. Various professional and governmental bodies regularly promulgate new, or change old, policies. Thousands of court cases are processed every year. Many are precedent setting and lead to regulatory changes. As new laws and policies emerge, they influence the legal duties of professional helpers, including social workers. As a professional social worker, you are subject to these evolving responsibilities.

Consider, for example, the topic of malpractice. *Malpractice* is "a form of negligence that occurs when a practitioner acts in a manner inconsistent with the profession's standard of care—the way an ordinary, reasonable, and prudent professional would act under the same or similar circumstances" (Reamer, 1994, p. 9). Malpractice is

> willful or negligent *behavior* by a professional person that violates the relevant *code of ethics* and professional standards of care that proves harmful to the client. Among a social worker's actions most likely to result in malpractice are inappropriately divulging confidential information; unnecessarily prolonged services; improper termination of needed services; misrepresentation of one's knowledge or skills; providing social work treatment as a replacement for needed medical treatment; providing information to others that is libelous or that results in improper *incarceration;* financial exploitation of the client; and physical injury to the client that may occur in the course of certain treatments (such as group encounters). (Barker, 1995)

Malpractice or *Mal Praxis* by professional social workers is, in legal terminology, a form of *tort.* A person or group may file a lawsuit in civil court because of injury or suffering resulting from the "wrongful actions or inactions" (Saltzman & Proch, 1990, p. 412) of the professional person. The plaintiff, often a client and sometimes a member of a client's family, typically seeks monetary damages to compensate for injuries or suffering. Occasionally, additional *punitive damages* are imposed to punish the professional person guilty of malpractice.

Malpractice involves poor or substandard professional service that results in harm. Failure to meet an accepted standard of care and damage to a client are the two usual criteria on which malpractice cases are determined. There are three common forms of malpractice: (1) malfeasance—where the professional intentionally engages in a practice known to be harmful; (2) misfeasance—where the professional makes a mistake in the application of an acceptable practice, and (3) nonfeasance—where the professional fails to apply a standard, acceptable practice when action is needed. The first form of malpractice involves intent to harm or malice and may constitute criminal behavior whereas the other two entail negligence or carelessness. The first two forms of malpractice consist of acts of commission, and the third refers to acts of omission (Kitchener, 2000; Reamer, 1995b).

Malpractice lawsuits may be filed against helping professionals for a wide range of behaviors. For example, in California, following treatment by a psychiatrist and a family therapist, a woman accused her father of childhood sexual abuse. Based on his daughter's allegations that he had molested her when she was a child, the man was fired from his high-paying job, and his wife divorced him. Both his daughter and his former spouse have, since the time of the allegations, refused to have contact with him.

The man filed suit against the helping professionals for malpractice. He won the suit and was awarded monetary damages. The court concluded that the helping professionals involved had acted improperly by suggesting that the client's emerging recollections of previously repressed memories were necessarily true and valid. The topic of recovered memories has become extraordinarily controversial in recent years—both in and out of courtrooms. Research studies indicate that inaccurate recollections may occur when professionals ask leading questions and make suggestive comments to clients. Interestingly, in this particular case, the court did not assert that the daughter's memories were false—only that the validity of the retrieved memories could not be determined because the helping professionals' words and actions were leading and suggestive. The court awarded the accused father several hundred thousand dollars as compensation for the damage caused him by the malpractice of the helping professionals.

The precise number of lawsuits filed against social workers is difficult to determine. Different authorities (Besharov & Besharov, 1987; Reamer, 1994) provide estimates that range from a few hundred to several thousand. Reamer reviewed the malpractice claims against social workers covered by the NASW Insurance Trust from 1969 through 1990. He found that "only 1 claim was filed in 1970; 40 claims, however, were filed in 1980, and 126 claims were filed in 1990" (Reamer, 1995b, p. 596). A total of 634 claims were filed during that 20-year period. This represents a relatively small number of the approximately 60,000 NASW members insured through the Trust. However, the rate and frequency of claims against social workers will undoubtedly increase substantially as the years pass. Of course, should a lawsuit ever be filed against you, it would not necessarily mean that you are, in fact, guilty of malpractice. Some lawsuits are unwarranted, harassing, and even frivolous. You could be the best social worker in the country and still be sued. Nothing you do can guarantee you freedom from legal action. If you are sued, however, the best defense is undoubtedly ethical, competent, and well-documented service that is grounded in current practice-related theory and research.

Although the increasing frequency of litigation against helping professionals is cause for concern, it should not unduly frighten you. The probability of being sued, especially for social workers, is still quite low. Social work remains a personally and professionally satisfying career. The possibility of lawsuits, however, underscores the importance of understanding the current legal milieu as well as those duties that apply to all social workers and other helping professionals.

Several categories emerge from a review of lawsuits filed against social workers and other helping professionals (Besharov & Besharov, 1987; Corey, Corey, & Callanan, 2003; Kitchener, 2000; Myers, 1992; Reamer, 1995b; Saltzman & Proch,

1990; VandeCreek & Knapp, 1993). Litigation may result from the following kinds of professional misbehavior:

- *Treatment without consent.* A client may allege that professional treatment procedures were undertaken without informed consent; the parents of a minor child may assert that their child was treated without their awareness or consent.
- *Professional incompetence, incorrect treatment, or failure to treat.* A client may assert that a social worker did not provide competent professional services, as indicated by the use of inappropriate, inadequate, or unconventional assessment procedures or interventions, or by the failure to provide service when needed.
- *Failure to diagnose or incorrect diagnosis or assessment.* A client may assert that a social worker failed to recognize signs of a problem or disorder, assigned an incorrect diagnosis, or formulated an erroneous assessment.
- *Failure to report suspected abuse or neglect.* A client, a client's family, or a state agency may assert that a social worker who had information of possible child endangerment failed to report suspicions that a child was being abused or neglected.
- *Reporting suspected abuse or neglect.* A client or a client's family may assert that a social worker who reported to state authorities suspicions that a child was being abused or neglected did so without adequate evidence and, as a result, caused severe and irreparable damage to the affected parties.
- *Failure to consult or refer to other professionals or specialists.* A client or client's family may allege that a social worker should have consulted with a medical doctor when it became apparent that the problems and symptoms revealed by the client suggested the real possibility of a medical condition.
- *Failure to prevent a client's suicide.* The family of a client who committed suicide may assert that a social worker knew or should have known that the client was suicidal, yet failed to take action necessary to protect the client from his or her own suicidal impulses.
- *Causing a client's suicide.* The family of a client who committed suicide may allege that a social worker's words or actions provoked the client to take his or her own life.
- *Failure to warn or protect third parties.* A person injured by a client may assert that a social worker knew or should have known that the client was potentially dangerous and intended to harm the person in question, yet failed to take action to notify the targeted individual and protect her or him from the client's violent actions.
- *Inappropriate release of a client.* A client or a client's family may allege that the social worker and other professionals were negligent in permitting a client to leave a facility while the client was in a state of acute distress or incapacity.
- *False imprisonment or arrest.* A client may claim that his or her commitment to a facility such as a psychiatric institution or drug treatment center, or police arrest constituted wrongful detention or incarceration.
- *Failure to provide adequate care or supervision for a client in residential settings.* A client or a client's family may assert that the client was injured because of the

neglectful and inadequate care provided by a social worker and other staff members in a hospital or other facility.

◆ *Assault or battery.* A client may allege that a social worker was threatening or engaged in improper or inappropriate physical contact.

◆ *Intentional infliction of emotional distress.* A client may assert that a social worker's actions, such as a counseling procedure or perhaps the removal of a child from the home of a biological parent, so traumatized the client as to cause significant mental or emotional distress.

◆ *Sexual impropriety.* A client may allege that a social worker used professional authority and expertise for the purposes of sexual seduction and exploitation.

◆ *Breach of confidentiality.* A client may allege that a social worker inappropriately communicated confidential information to an unauthorized party.

◆ *Breach of contract, poor results, failure to cure.* A client may believe that a social worker indicated that his or her marriage would be saved through the process of marriage counseling—in effect, providing a guarantee; when the marriage ends in divorce, the client may assert that the social worker did not fulfill the terms of the agreement.

◆ *Invasion of privacy.* A client may assert that a child abuse investigation was overreaching or harassing in nature.

◆ *Defamation of character, libel, or slander.* A client may believe that a social worker, orally or in writing, made an untrue and derogatory statement that harmed the client's reputation.

◆ *Violation of a client's civil rights.* A client in a residential facility may allege that his or her civil rights were violated when personal property was confiscated by a social worker.

◆ *Failure to be available when needed.* A client may assert that a social worker was inaccessible or unavailable when he or she was in urgent need of service.

◆ *Inappropriate termination of treatment or abandonment.* A client may allege that a social worker concluded treatment abruptly or unprofessionally.

◆ *Malicious prosecution or abuse of process.* A client may allege that a legal action initiated by a social worker, for instance in a child protection case, was undertaken with full knowledge that the case would be dismissed by the court and therefore was maliciously intended.

◆ *Inappropriate bill collection methods.* A client may assert that the social worker used invasive and improper means in an attempt to collect on bills that were outstanding.

◆ *Statutory violations.* A social worker might be sued for violating requirements of the state law under which social workers are legally certified or licensed.

◆ *Inadequately protecting a child.* A client, the client's family, or a state agency may assert that a child was injured because of the neglectful and inadequate care provided by a social worker.

◆ *Violating parental rights.* The parents of a child may assert that their rights were violated by a social worker who provided professional services to their child without their informed consent.

◆ *Inadequate foster care services.* A client, the biological parents of a child, or a state agency may assert that a social worker placed a child in a foster care setting that provided inadequate or injurious care.

In a review of the 634 malpractice claims filed against social workers covered for liability through the NASW Insurance Trust, Reamer (1995b) found examples of malfeasance and misfeasance that included

> flawed treatment of a client (incorrect treatment), sexual impropriety, breach of confidentiality or privacy, improper referral to another service provider, defamation of a client's character (as a result of slander or libel), breach of contract for services, violations of a client's civil rights, improper civil commitment of a client (false imprisonment or arrest), wrongful removal of a child from a home (loss of child custody), assault and battery, improper termination of service (abandonment), improper licensing of staff, and improper peer review. (p. 596)

Examples of nonfeasance included "failure to diagnose properly, failure to protect third parties from harm, failure to treat a client successfully (failure to cure or poor results) or at all, and failure to refer a client for consultation or treatment" (Reamer, 1995b, p. 596). The most common allegations involved incorrect treatment (18.6%), sexual impropriety (18.45%), breaches of confidentiality or privacy (8.68%), failure to assess or diagnose, or misdiagnosis (5.21%), and client suicide (4.42%). Not all of the claims were substantiated. However, the array and distribution of claims are revealing.

Certain forms of practice and certain settings constitute a greater risk for litigation against social workers. For example, because child welfare work often involves the provision of *involuntary* services, there is a greater likelihood of both civil and criminal legal action against social workers employed in such settings. In recent years, practice that involves the exploration of "repressed memories" has led to numerous malpractice lawsuits. Some of these resulted in multimillion-dollar judgments against the helping professionals involved. In June 1996, the NASW issued a Practice Update urging that "social workers who practice in the area of recovered memories should be mindful that this is a high-risk area of practice in an environment of intense controversy" (NASW National Council on the Practice of Clinical Social Work, 1996).

Although most malpractice litigation occurs in civil court, social workers may occasionally be subject to criminal action related to the nature and extent of their professional services.

> In Colorado, for example, a caseworker and her supervisor were criminally prosecuted when a child with whom the caseworker was working was killed by her parents. The parents had been reported to the worker as abusive but the worker had chosen to keep the child in the home. The worker and her supervisor were convicted. (Saltzman & Proch, 1990, p. 428)

The criminal convictions in the Colorado case were later overturned on technical grounds by an appellate court. Nonetheless, the case illustrates the enormous responsibilities associated with professional social work practice as well as the litigious nature of contemporary society.

You should carefully review the laws and regulations that affect the practice of social work in your locale. Also, examine laws that may relate to your service areas. Laws related to child abuse and neglect, elder abuse, domestic violence, civil rights, sexual harassment, psychological testing, psychotherapy and counseling, child custody, marriage and divorce, and adoption probably pertain in some way to most social workers. You should be familiar with the Americans with Disabilities Act (ADA), Public Law 101-336 (available online at www.usdoj.gov/crt/ada/publicat.htm), the Health Insurance Portability and Accountability Act of 1996 (HIPAA), and other federal laws that directly affect social workers and their service to others. Undoubtedly, as time passes, there will be changes in the nature and extent of the legal responsibilities that apply to social workers, but the general legal duties or obligations listed in Box 3.2 are likely to remain in effect for the next several years (Everstine & Everstine, 1983, pp. 227–251).

BOX 3.2

Legal Obligations of Helping Professionals

- Duty of care
- Duty to respect privacy
- Duty to maintain confidentiality
- Duty to inform
- Duty to report
- Duty to warn and protect

Legal duties tend to parallel those human rights that are highly valued by a society. In the United States, many fundamental rights are evident in the Constitution, the Bill of Rights, and in the decisions of the U.S. Supreme and federal courts.

Internationally, the Universal Declaration of Human Rights (General Assembly of the United Nations, 1948) describes the protections afforded all persons. Article 1 of the Universal Declaration begins with the phrase, "All human beings are born free and equal in dignity and rights." Most of the legal duties of helping professionals reflect some aspects of one or more fundamental human rights.

Duty of Care

As a professional social worker, you are legally obligated to provide a *reasonable standard of care* in delivering social work services. Clients have a right to expect that you will be competent in discharging your professional responsibilities. There is an implied contract to that effect. Services provided should meet at least an adequate standard of care—as determined in part by the social work profession and in part by common expectations of helping professionals. Social workers provide services to a diverse clientele in a wide range of settings. As a result, social workers must not only be competent in the fundamentals of social work practice but must also reflect competence in helping clients address specific problems and goals. For example, social workers who work with families addressing child abuse and neglect issues must be competent in both social work and child welfare practice. Those who serve diverse population groups must reflect cultural competence as well. Social workers attempting to help Buddhist immigrants from Laos must know a good deal about Laotian culture, Buddhist beliefs, and, of course, the problems and processes associated with transitions into a new society.

The NASW has published numerous booklets related to basic standards of practice in various contexts (e.g., *NASW Standards for School Social Work Services* [NASW, 2002a]; *NASW Standards for Social Work Practice in Child Protection* [NASW, 1981a]; *NASW Standards for Social Work Services in Long-Term Care Facilities* [NASW, 2003b]; *NASW Standards and Guidelines for Social Work Case Management for the Functionally Impaired* [NASW, 1984]; *NASW Standards for Social Work in Health Care Settings* [NASW, 1987]; *NASW Standards for the Practice of Clinical Social Work* [NASW, 1989], *NASW Standards for Social Work Case Management* [NASW, 2002b]; and *NASW Standards for the Practice of Social Work with Adolescents* [NASW, 2003a]). Beyond basic standards and guidelines, as a professional you are expected to be knowledgeable about information presented in scholarly books and professional journals related to effective social work practice generally. Spurred by demands for increased accountability and expectations that professionals adopt "best practices" in their service, social work authors and researchers have recently published books summarizing approaches that have research support (Thyer & Wodarski, 1998; Williams & Ell, 1998; Wodarski & Thyer, 1998). In addition, you should be familiar with the knowledge from scholarly works that pertain to specific populations you serve as well as those issues and problems you help clients to address. The assessments, diagnoses, treatments, and interventions that you choose should have at least theoretical and probably empirical support.

During the past decade, the American Psychiatric Association has begun to approve and publish "practice guidelines" for the treatment of certain mental health problems (APA, 1996, 1997a, 1997b). These guidelines are developed through comprehensive reviews and analyses of the relevant practice research literature. We expect the social work profession to follow suit by approving and publishing social work practice guidelines based on comprehensive analyses of "best practice" evidence.

If your social work activities are congruent with generally accepted theory and research, and current practice guidelines, you probably meet the basic standard of care expectation. Unusual interventions, activities, or procedures that do not have a sound professional rationale and evidence to support their safety and effectiveness could place you at increased risk of liability.

Several additional responsibilities may be included under the general duty of care. For example, as a professional social worker you must be available to the clients you serve. Clients should be educated about whom to contact and what to do in case of an emergency. Similarly, before going on vacation, you should inform clients well in advance and arrange for equivalent, substitute professional coverage. You must also take action to ensure the physical protection of clients you determine to be (1) imminently dangerous to other persons, (2) imminently dangerous to themselves, or (3) so gravely disabled as to be unable to provide minimal self-care (Everstine & Everstine, 1983, p. 232). You might have to arrange for the supervision or hospitalization of such clients.

Professional record keeping also relates to the "standard of care" obligation. Complete, accurate, timely documentation of the nature, scope, provision, cost, progress, and outcomes of your professional service is considered reasonable and usual professional behavior. At a minimum, you should include information concerning the identity of the persons you serve, relevant consent forms, dates and kinds of services, assessments and plans, progress reports, and closing summaries. Records, of course, are primarily *for* the client in that they help you, the social worker, remember relevant information and maintain your focus on agreed upon goals for work. If you were to become ill or injured, or in the event of your untimely death, your records could be used to maintain service continuity with your clients.

The keeping of records suggests at least a modicum of professionalism. Of course, records may also support the quality of your professional service. Accurate, complete, descriptive records are your single most important defense in the event of a malpractice lawsuit. Professional records that are absent, notations that are sparse, or notes that seem to have been altered after the fact may be viewed as evidence of inadequate care.

Duty to Respect Privacy

As a professional social worker, you have a duty to respect the privacy of people you serve. Under most circumstances, you are not entitled to intrude on the privacy of prospective or actual clients. Privacy includes an individual's physical space (home or residence, locker, automobile, wallet or purse, or clothing) as well as those aspects of personal life that constitute a *symbolic region* (Everstine et al., 1980), which is that person's alone to share or reveal as he or she sees fit. Consider, for example, the case of a penniless traveler who seeks your professional help in locating transportation to her home in a neighboring state. If you were to ask her for information about her sexual history—a topic clearly unrelated to her stated issue of concern—you would probably violate her right to privacy.

Similarly, suppose you hold strong religious beliefs. Your personal faith provides much needed spiritual support and comfort in your daily life. However, you serve as a social worker in a public child and family welfare agency. If you were to proselytize your religious beliefs with clients, you would violate their privacy. In a sense, this would be similar to a telemarketer who calls your home or a door-to-door salesperson who, uninvited, tries to sell you a product. You have not requested the information but you get it anyway. Social workers must have sound professional reason for entry into these private physical or symbolic regions.

Although a right to privacy is more implicit than explicit in the United States Constitution, it has grown in significance both inside and outside the helping professions

(Etzioni, 1999; McWhirter & Bible, 1992). Article 12 of the Universal Declaration of Human Rights indicates, "No one shall be subjected to arbitrary interference with his privacy, family, home or correspondence, nor to attacks upon his honour and reputation. Everyone has the right to the protection of the law against such interference or attacks" (General Assembly of the United Nations, 1948). As rights to privacy have evolved, so have the threats to them. Technological advances in the form of video and audio recording and other sensing devices; the explosion in computer software and hardware technology, cell phones, the Internet; and, of course, developments in DNA, urine, and blood testing increasingly endanger privacy.

However, the value of privacy rights is not universal—even among helping professionals and consumers. For example, cameras are sometimes placed in waiting areas, hallways, or parking areas of agencies and organizations; case records may be stored on a computer that is linked to the Internet; children or adolescents may be observed or videotaped without their knowledge; school lockers may be examined; individuals may be body-searched; and drug testing may be required as a condition for the receipt of service. Media reporters and television or movie producers may also be interested in the stories of clients and perhaps your services to them. Educators may seek to audio or videotape interviews or use the stories of clients in books or other publications. Even when clients sign releases, they may not fully understand or appreciate the implications of the widespread publicity that may follow publication. These actions and circumstances risk the privacy rights of clients and possibly their friends, neighbors, and family members as well.

Duty to Maintain Confidentiality

Professional social workers have a duty to maintain the confidentiality of what is said by clients. Derived from the right to privacy, this obligation applies, in general, to all helping professionals. The laws that certify or license social workers require that information shared by clients remain confidential. Indeed, some laws use the term *privileged communication* in describing this legal obligation. "*Confidentiality* refers to the professional norm that information shared by or pertaining to clients will not be shared with third parties. *Privilege* refers to the disclosure of confidential information in court proceedings" (Reamer, 1994, p. 47). When laws specify that your communications with clients are privileged, then you must meet an even higher standard of confidentiality. When information is privileged, it becomes much more formidable, even for a judge, to force social workers to reveal confidential information without their clients' consent.

In 1996, the U.S. Supreme Court (*Jaffee v. Redmond*) specifically upheld a U.S. Court of Appeals decision extending privilege for confidential client communications to licensed social workers during the course of psychotherapy. Redmond, a police officer, had been counseled by a licensed social worker whose case records were subpoenaed following an on-duty shooting death. In an earlier civil proceeding, the social worker and Redmond, the client, refused to provide the requested information. Based partly on that refusal, the plaintiffs were awarded damages. The Court of Appeals overturned that decision and the U.S. Supreme Court upheld that reversal. This decision is notable in reinforcing privilege for psychotherapy clients and specifically including licensed social workers with psychiatrists and psychologists as professionals who might provide such covered services.

The advent of computerized record keeping; organizational networks; management information systems; agency, governmental, and insurance company databases; the Internet; and managed care systems have seriously complicated the confidentiality issue. Advances in computer and communications technology may have contributed to increased productivity and efficiency, and perhaps even to improvements in the quality of social services. However, as information about clients becomes increasingly easy to access, use, and share, safeguarding client records becomes more difficult. Despite these complicated challenges, the basic duty remains intact. Indeed, in some areas the responsibilities of professionals to protect client privacy and confidentiality have increased.

The United States Health Insurance Privacy Protection Act (HIPPA) and the associated Standards for Privacy of Individually Identifiable Health Information (the "Privacy Rule") reflect the importance society increasingly places on the confidentiality of health information.

> A major goal of the Privacy Rule is to assure that individuals' health information is properly protected while allowing the flow of health information needed to provide and promote high quality health care and to protect the public's health and well being. The Rule strikes a balance that permits important uses of information, while protecting the privacy of people who seek care and healing. (Office for Civil Rights, 2003, May, p. 1)

All individually identifiable health information is protected under the Privacy Rule. Data such as name, address, telephone number, birth date, Social Security Number, date of birth or death, diagnosis, treatment, bank information, and any other information that could identify an individual person are included.

> *"Individually identifiable health information"* is information, including demographic data, that relates to:
> ◆ the individual's past, present or future physical or mental health or condition,
> ◆ the provision of health care to the individual, or
> ◆ the past, present, or future payment for the provision of health care to the individual, and that identifies the individual or for which there is a reasonable basis to believe can be used to identify the individual. (Office for Civil Rights, 2003, May, p. 4)

Generally speaking, material shared by clients is their property. It is not yours, even though you may remember it or record it in a case record. You are merely using the knowledge to serve them. It does not become your property simply because you have heard and recorded it. Under most circumstances, clients must give *informed consent* before you may legally and ethically share information with another person or organization. Even when informed consent is provided, you should carefully consider the nature, form, and extent of what is shared. Suppose, for example, a client is relocating across the country and requests that a copy of her or his records be forwarded to another social worker who will provide continuing services. If the case record contains information that is no longer accurate, comments about third parties, or other irrelevant information, you might inform the client that you would like to exclude such references from the records before they are sent. Although it might represent more work for you, a summary of services rather than a duplicate set of the case records may provide more protection for the client and could actually be more useful to the other social worker.

Duty to Inform

As a professional social worker, you have an obligation to educate clients and prospective clients concerning the nature and extent of the services you and your agency offer. Under HIPPA, you must also inform clients about privacy practices. In addition, helping professions address matters such as cost, length, risks, probability of success, and alternate services that may be appropriate. This is where knowledge of "best practices," "practice guidelines," and community resources are needed. You should also provide information concerning relevant policies and laws that could affect clients during the provision of social services. For example, early in the process, you should notify clients about your legal obligation to report indications of possible child abuse and neglect and other crimes as required by certain states (e.g., elder abuse). Also, you should inform clients that, should a person's life be at risk you will take action to protect that person even if it means violating confidentiality. Typically, you should also give clients information about your qualifications, fields of expertise, and, when relevant, areas in which you have limited knowledge or experience. Similarly, clients should be informed about any actions you might take that pertain to their care—such as consultation with a nationally renowned expert or the provision of information to an insurance company. Of course, you should inform clients well in advance before you discontinue services or transfer them to another helping professional.

The duty to inform is supported by several fundamental human rights including due process, equal protection, privacy, and dignity. Some information is needed to enter into all binding contractual agreements. In effect, the understanding between a social worker and a client is a special kind of contract where the client employs the social worker to provide professional services within the context of a fiduciary relationship (Kutchins, 1991). "Fiduciary relationships emanate from the trust that clients must place in professionals. . . . The professional's obligations are far greater than those of a commercial vendor" (p. 106). Indeed, within the context of these special relationships, clients have a right to provide informed consent (O'Neill, 1998).

Informed consent involves the following dimensions: (1) Relevant information provided by the helping professional, (2) competence of the client to understand, rationally evaluate, and anticipate implications and potential consequences of decisions and actions, and (3) voluntary choice by the client to accept or reject proposed activities. If one or more of these aspects are absent or diminished, then clients cannot be considered to have provided fully informed consent (Koocher & Keith-Spiegel, 1990).

When you purchase services from an automobile mechanic or a house painter, you have certain rights. For example, you have a right to honest answers to questions you ask. Generally speaking, however, it is your responsibility to learn as much as you can before you buy. Caveat emptor—let the buyer beware—is a major principle. The mechanic or painter is not required to provide additional information or consider what might be in your best interest. Helping professionals assume added responsibilities because of the vulnerability of clients and the potential for exploitation. Therefore, social workers have an "affirmative obligation to disclose more information than is requested" (Kutchins, 1991, p. 106) to ensure that clients are fully aware of aspects of the services that they might not have asked about or even considered.

Duty to Report

Professional social workers have a legal obligation to report to designated governmental authorities indications of certain "outrages against humanity" (Everstine & Everstine, 1983, p. 240). Although the specific procedures for reporting may vary somewhat from place to place, as a social worker you must report knowledge of certain criminal behavior, including "child abuse, child neglect, child molestation, and incest" (Everstine & Everstine, 1983, p. 240). Increasingly, laws are enacted to expand the kinds of behavior that must be reported. These include abuse, neglect, and exploitation of persons who are elderly, physically or mentally challenged, or developmentally disabled.

The duty to report is supported by several fundamental human rights. Article 1 of the Universal Declaration of Human Rights holds, in part, "All human beings are born free and equal in dignity and rights." Article 3 indicates, "Everyone has the right to life, liberty and security of person." Article 4 states, "No one shall be held in slavery or servitude." Article 5 holds, "No one shall be subjected to torture or to cruel, inhuman or degrading treatment or punishment" (General Assembly of the United Nations, 1948).

The duty to report is perhaps most obvious in the case of child abuse and neglect. Within the United States, all states require that helping professionals report instances of suspected child abuse or neglect to governmental authorities. Along with medical doctors, psychologists, nurses, and teachers, social workers are typically included among the group of "mandated reporters" specifically mentioned in the legislation. Mandated reporters who fail to notify authorities of suspected abuse may be subject to severe legal penalties.

Duty to Warn and Protect

Social workers also bear a responsibility to warn potential victims and take action to protect people who might be harmed by a client. Derived from the same human rights that warrant reporting crimes against humanity, helping professionals bear some responsibility to safeguard the lives of others who might be in danger. Of course, accurate prediction of future dangerousness is hardly a science. Despite the risk of false positives (concluding that someone is dangerous when he or she actually is not), public safety sometimes outweighs the rights of clients (VandeCreek & Knapp, 2001; Woody, 1997). The famous *Tarasoff v. California Board of Regents* decision established that helping professionals are obligated to take some action to protect the lives of third parties (Kagle & Kopels, 1994). Suppose, for example, that during an interview, a client with a history of violence toward others reveals a specific intent to kill his former spouse. You ask additional questions and you conclude that the client indeed poses a clear and present danger to his ex-wife. Under such circumstances, you would (1) try to arrange for protective supervision of the client (for example, through temporary hospitalization), (2) warn the intended victim of the threat, and (3) notify legal authorities of the danger. Of course, because such actions violate some aspects of the client's right to confidentiality and perhaps to privacy, you should clearly document the reasons you have taken this course of action. In such instances, you would be wise to quote the words, cite the gestures, and provide related evidence to support your conclusion that the client is potentially dangerous to another person. Also, document who, when, and how you contacted the relevant parties.

The duty to warn or the duty to protect others is similar but not equivalent to the duty to report. For example, legal statutes require social workers to report suspicions of child abuse. Indications of the presence of present or past child abuse are sufficient to warrant a report—which usually involves the identification of the alleged victim or alleged perpetrator if known. The social worker does not need to know that child abuse occurred to report. Suspicion alone is sufficient and social workers who report in good faith are typically immune from liability. In the case of potential violence toward others, however, suspicion alone is insufficient (*United States v. Hayes*, 6th Cir. 2000). The social worker must have reasonable evidence to conclude and does in fact conclude that the client poses a real and significant threat of violence toward another (Recent cases, 2001). Immunity from liability is not guaranteed, as it usually is in cases involving suspected child abuse. The social worker must exercise due professional care in reaching a decision about a client's dangerousness and in carrying out the obligation to warn and protect.

◆ EXERCISE 3-1: LEGAL OBLIGATIONS

1. Use your password to log on to the InfoTrac College Edition resources at www.infotrac-college.com. Enter the string "duty to warn" (include the quotation marks) to conduct a keyword search for an article entitled, "Health Care Providers' Duty to Warn" (Regan, Alderson, & Regan, 2002). Read and reflect on the article. Use the following space to summarize its meaning to you as a social worker in a paragraph or so.

2. Log on to the InfoTrac College Edition www.infotrac-college.com. Enter the string "privacy rule FAQS" (without the quotation marks) to conduct a keyword search for an article entitled, "HHS Releases FAQs about Medical Privacy Rule" (Peters, 2003). Read the article. Use the following space to record the World Wide Web address (URL) where the Office of Civil Rights (OCR) privacy rule guidance document may be located.

Understanding the Fundamental Values and Ethics of Social Work

In addition to the legal obligations that apply to all helping professionals, social workers also conform to the fundamental values and ethics of the social work profession. Social workers and social work educators have energetically discussed the topic of social work values since the emergence of the profession around the beginning of the 20th century. The discussion will undoubtedly continue throughout the 21st century, especially as the world becomes increasingly interconnected and interdependent through globalization and internationalization.

In discussing values, the IFSW states,

Social work grew out of humanitarian and democratic ideals, and its values are based on respect for the equality, worth, and dignity of all people. Since its beginnings over a century ago, social work practice has focused on meeting human needs and developing human potential. Human rights and social justice serve as the motivation and justification for social work action. In solidarity with those who are disadvantaged, the profession strives to alleviate poverty and to liberate vulnerable and oppressed people in order to promote social inclusion. Social work values are embodied in the profession's national and international codes of ethics. (2000, Values section, para. 1)

Although there is some divergence of opinion regarding the *application* of fundamental social work values, there is considerable consensus about the values themselves. For example, the NASW identifies the core values for social work in the Preamble to its Code of Ethics (1999):

The mission of the social work profession is rooted in a set of core values. These core values, embraced by social workers throughout the profession's history, are the foundation of social work's unique purpose and perspective:

- ◆ service
- ◆ social justice
- ◆ dignity and worth of the person
- ◆ importance of human relationships
- ◆ integrity
- ◆ competence

This constellation of core values reflects what is unique to the social work profession. Core values, and the principles that flow from them, must be balanced within the context and complexity of the human experience. (Preamble section, paras. 3–4)

The Council on Social Work Education (CSWE) endorses the NASW Code of Ethics by specifically requiring accredited academic programs to

integrate content about values and principles of ethical decision making as presented in the National Association of Social Workers Code of Ethics. The educational experience provides students with the opportunity to be aware of personal values; develop, demonstrate, and promote the values of the profession; and analyze ethical dilemmas and the ways in which these affect practice, services, and clients. (CSWE, 2001, p. 10)

These fundamental social work values serve as an extremely useful foundation for thinking critically about ethical and practice issues. They are invaluable in helping social workers define a professional identity and establish a social work frame of reference. Such abstract concepts, however, are not usually specific enough to guide ethical decision-making. That function is served by codes of ethics. Ethical principles and standards are derived from the fundamental social work values but presented in more concrete and prescriptive terms. Reference to a social work code of ethics should help you make practice decisions that are congruent with fundamental social work values.

To practice ethically, you need a thorough understanding of both the fundamental social work values and the principles and standards that guide ethical decision making. As suggested earlier, the *Code of Ethics of the National Association of Social Workers* (NASW, 1999) serves as the primary reference throughout the United States. The purposes of the NASW code are outlined in the preamble:

The primary mission of the social work profession is to enhance human well-being and help meet the basic human needs of all people, with particular attention to the needs and empowerment of people who are vulnerable, oppressed, and living in poverty. A historic and defining feature of social work is the profession's focus on individual well-being in a social context and the well-being of society. Fundamental to social work is attention to the environmental forces that create, contribute to, and address problems in living.

Social workers promote social justice and social change with and on behalf of clients. "Clients" is used inclusively to refer to individuals, families, groups, organizations, and communities. Social workers are sensitive to cultural and ethnic diversity and strive to end discrimination, oppression, poverty, and other forms of social injustice. These activities may be in the form of direct practice, community organizing, supervision, consultation, administration, advocacy, social and political action, policy development and implementation, education, and research and evaluation. Social workers seek to enhance the capacity of people to address their own needs. Social workers also seek to promote the responsiveness of organizations, communities, and other social institutions to individuals' needs and social problems. (NASW, 1999, Preamble section, paras. 1–2)

To practice ethically, you should be thoroughly familiar with the social work code of ethics. Carry a copy with you during your professional activities. You will frequently need to refer to it throughout the course of your service with and for clients.

Violations of the Code may serve as grounds for malpractice lawsuits or grievances filed with social work licensing boards or professional associations such as the NASW. The *NASW Procedures for Professional Review* (NASW, 2001) contains detailed descriptions concerning the processes by which complaints are submitted and adjudicated.

In studies of 894 of 901 claims of ethical misconduct by NASW members from 1986 to 1997, Strom-Gottfried identified some 66 categories of professional misbehavior and then organized them into 10 clusters (1999, 2000a). Among the cases where findings were adjudicated, *boundary violations* were the most common form of misconduct (about 55%). Most of those involved sexual misconduct and many involved dual-relationships. *Poor practice* such as failure to employ standard interventions or misapplication of professional standards and principles represented the second most common finding (about 38%), followed by *incompetence* caused by ignorance or inadequate supervision or impairment, inadequate record-keeping, dishonesty or fraud, failure to maintain confidentiality or protect privacy, failure to describe policies necessary for clients to provide informed consent, improper behavior with colleagues, problems related to billing and reimbursement, and conflicts of interest between the worker and one or more clients (Strom-Gottfried, 2000a).

Strom-Gottfried (1999, 2000a, 2000b, 2003) found that about 52% of the misconduct claims were filed by clients or family members of clients, about 19.5% by employees or supervisees, about 10.4% by co-workers or colleagues, and about 4.5% by supervisors or employers. Slightly less than half of the complaints reached the hearing stage although more than 60% of those that did resulted in findings of ethical violations against the respondents (Strom-Gottfried, 2003).

Strom-Gottfried (1999, 2003) found that the most common ethical violations included the following:

1. Sexual activity
2. Dual relationship
3. Other boundary violations
4. Failure to seek supervision or consultation
5. Failure to use accepted practice skills
6. Fraudulent behavior
7. Premature termination
8. Inadequate provisions for case transfer or referral
9. Failure to maintain adequate records or reports
10. Failure to discuss policies as part of informed consent

◆ EXERCISE 3-2: SOCIAL WORK VALUES AND ETHICS

1. Use your password to log on to the InfoTrac College Edition resources at www.infotrac-college.com. Enter the string "evolution social work ethics" (without the quotation marks) to conduct a keyword search for an article entitled, "The Evolution of Social Work Ethics" (Reamer, 1998b). Read and reflect on the article. Use the following space to summarize its meaning to you as a social worker in a paragraph or so.

2. If you do not yet have a copy of the current Code of Ethics of the National Association of Social Workers, you may secure one electronically through the NASW Web site at www.socialworkers.org. Carefully read the Preamble. In the following space, summarize the mission of the social work profession and list its six core values.

3. Carefully read the section of the Code of Ethics entitled "Purpose of the NASW Code of Ethics." In the following space, briefly describe the six purposes of the Code.

4. Carefully read the section of the Code of Ethics entitled "Ethical Principles." In the following space, briefly summarize each of the principles associated with the six core social work values.

Identifying Ethical and Legal Implications

In addition to understanding the legal duties of professional helpers and the social work code of ethics, you will need to identify those obligations, principles, and standards that might apply in a given practice situation. This requires critical thinking skills as you consider a specific situation and determine which ethical principles and legal obligations may be relevant.

For example, imagine that you are a social worker in an agency that provides crisis intervention services. One day, while catching up on paperwork, a former client whom you had served some eight months earlier telephones to say, "I have locked myself in my basement. I have a gun, and I am going to shoot myself today. I wanted to let you know that you did not help me at all! Goodbye."

In addition to managing the various emotions you would undoubtedly experience, you would also have to consider several values, ethical principles, and standards as well as various legal obligations. The values, ethical principles, and standards described in the NASW Code of Ethics (1999) shown in Box 3.3 probably apply.

BOX 3.3

NASW Code of Ethics

♦ **Value:** Service
Ethical Principle: Social workers' primary goal is to help people in need and to address social problems.
♦ **Value:** Dignity and Worth of the Person
Ethical Principle: Social workers respect the inherent dignity and worth of the person.
♦ **Value:** Integrity
Ethical Principle: Social workers behave in a trustworthy manner.
♦ **Value:** Competence
Ethical Principle: Social workers practice within their areas of competence and develop and enhance their professional expertise. (NASW, 1999)

Social workers' primary responsibility is to promote the well-being of clients. In general, clients' interests are primary. However, social workers' responsibility to the larger society or specific legal obligations may on limited occasions supersede the loyalty owed clients, and clients should be so advised. (Examples include when a social worker is required by law to report that a client has abused a child or has threatened to harm self or others.) (Section 1.01)

Social workers respect and promote the right of clients to self-determination and assist clients in their efforts to identify and clarify their goals. Social workers may limit clients' right to self-determination when, in the social workers' professional judgment, clients' actions or potential actions pose a serious, foreseeable, and imminent risk to themselves or others. (Section 1.02)

In instances when clients lack the capacity to provide informed consent, social workers should protect clients' interests by seeking permission from an appropriate third party, informing clients consistent with the clients' level of understanding. In such instances, social workers should seek to ensure that the third party acts in a manner consistent with clients' wishes and interests. Social workers should take reasonable steps to enhance such clients' ability to give informed consent. (Section 1.03.c)

In instances when clients are receiving services involuntarily, social workers should provide information about the nature and extent of services and about the extent of clients' right to refuse service. (Section 1.03.d)

Social workers may disclose confidential information when appropriate with valid consent from a client or a person legally authorized to consent on behalf of a client. (Section 10.7.b)

Social workers should protect the confidentiality of all information obtained in the course of professional service, except for compelling professional reasons. The general expectation that social workers will keep information confidential does not apply when disclosure is necessary to prevent serious, foreseeable, and imminent harm to a client or other identifiable person. In all instances, social workers should disclose the least amount of confidential information necessary to achieve the

(continued)

BOX 3.3 *(continued)*

desired purpose; only information that is directly relevant to the purpose for which the disclosure is made should be revealed. (Section 10.7.c)

Social workers should inform clients, to the extent possible, about the disclosure of confidential information and the potential consequences, when feasible before the disclosure is made. This applies whether social workers disclose confidential information on the basis of a legal requirement or client consent. (Section 10.7.d)

Social workers should discuss with clients and other interested parties the nature of confidentiality and limitations of clients' right to confidentiality. Social workers should review with clients circumstances where confidential information may be requested and where disclosure of confidential information may be legally required. This discussion should occur as soon as possible in the social worker-client relationship and as needed throughout the course of the relationship. (Section 10.7.e)

Social workers should not disclose confidential information to third-party payers unless clients have authorized such disclosure. (Section 10.7.h)

Social workers should protect the confidentiality of clients during legal proceedings to the extent permitted by law. When a court of law or other legally authorized body orders social workers to disclose confidential or privileged information without a client's consent and such disclosure could cause harm to the client, social workers should request that the court withdraw the order or limit the order as narrowly as possible or maintain the records under seal, unavailable for public inspection. (Section 10.7.j)

When social workers act on behalf of clients who lack the capacity to make informed decisions, social workers should take reasonable steps to safeguard the interests and rights of those clients. (Section 114)

Social workers should terminate services to clients and professional relationships with them when such services and relationships are no longer required or no longer serve the clients' needs or interests. (Section 116.a)

Social workers should take reasonable steps to avoid abandoning clients who are still in need of services. Social workers should withdraw services precipitously only under unusual circumstances, giving careful consideration to all factors in the situation and taking care to minimize possible adverse effects. Social workers should assist in making appropriate arrangements for continuation of services when necessary. (Section 116.b)

Social workers should seek the advice and counsel of colleagues whenever such consultation is in the best interests of clients. (Section 2.05.a)

Social workers should keep themselves informed about colleagues' areas of expertise and competencies. Social workers should seek consultation only from colleagues who have demonstrated knowledge, expertise, and competence related to the subject of the consultation. (Section 2.05.b)

(continued)

BOX 3.3 *(continued)*

When consulting with colleagues about clients, social workers should disclose the least amount of information necessary to achieve the purposes of the consultation. (Section 2.05.c)

Social workers should refer clients to other professionals when the other professionals' specialized knowledge or expertise is needed to serve clients fully or when social workers believe that they are not being effective or making reasonable progress with clients and that additional service is required. (Section 2.06.a)

Social workers who refer clients to other professionals should take appropriate steps to facilitate an orderly transfer of responsibility. Social workers who refer clients to other professionals should disclose, with clients' consent, all pertinent information to the new service providers. (Section 2.06.b)

Social workers should take reasonable steps to ensure that documentation in records is accurate and reflects the services provided. (Section 3.04.a)

Social workers should include sufficient and timely documentation in records to facilitate the delivery of services and to ensure continuity of services provided to clients in the future. (Section 3.04.b)

Social workers' documentation should protect clients' privacy to the extent that is possible and appropriate and should include only information that is directly relevant to the delivery of services. (Section 3.04.c)

Social workers should store records following the termination of services to ensure reasonable future access. Records should be maintained for the number of years required by state statutes or relevant contracts. (Section 3.04.d)

When an individual who is receiving services from another agency or colleague contacts a social worker for services, the social worker should carefully consider the client's needs before agreeing to provide services. To minimize possible confusion and conflict, social workers should discuss with potential clients the nature of the clients' current relationship with other service providers and the implications, including possible benefits or risks, of entering into a relationship with a new service provider. (Section 3.06.a)

If a new client has been served by another agency or colleague, social workers should discuss with the client whether consultation with the previous service provider is in the client's best interest. (Section 3.06.b)

Social workers should accept responsibility or employment only on the basis of existing competence or the intention to acquire the necessary competence. (Section 4.01.a)

Social workers should strive to become and remain proficient in professional practice and the performance of professional functions. Social workers should critically examine and keep current with emerging knowledge relevant to social work. Social workers should routinely review the professional literature and participate in continuing education relevant to social work practice and social work ethics. (Section 4.01.b)

(continued)

Social workers should base practice on recognized knowledge, including empirically based knowledge, relevant to social work and social work ethics. (Section 4.01.c)

Social workers should not participate in, condone, or be associated with dishonesty, fraud, or deception. (Section 4.04)

Social workers should critically examine and keep current with emerging knowledge relevant to social work and fully use evaluation and research evidence in their professional practice. (Section 5.02.c)

The legal obligations that deserve consideration in this situation are the:

(1) *duty of care*, including the responsibility to try to prevent suicidal action

(2) *duty to inform*

(3) *duty of confidentiality*

(4) *duty to respect privacy*

Used by permission of NASW.

Even though this is, nominally, a *former* client who expresses anger toward you, the codes suggest that you should maintain your professional role and continue to provide high-quality service. His best interest continues to be your primary obligation. Because the client expresses disappointment in you and may not respond to your attempts to contact him, you should probably seek advice and consultation from your supervisor, colleagues, or other professionals competent in crisis intervention and suicide prevention. You should also try to respect the client's civil and legal rights. You should maintain the confidentiality of information that he reveals or share such information with others only for compelling reasons, such as when he threatens to harm himself or someone else. These last three principles apply if or when you consider contacting the caller's family members, a medical doctor, an ambulance service, paramedics, or the police in your determined efforts to protect his life.

As a professional social worker, you should attempt to prevent the client from taking his own life. This is consistent with the legal duty of care under which you are obligated to be available, to try to prevent suicidal action, to avoid causing suicidal action, and to ensure the physical protection of clients who are dangerous to themselves. You also have a duty to inform the client concerning actions you intend to take. Finally, you have a legal, as well as ethical, duty to maintain confidentiality and respect the person's right to privacy.

When you consider the relevance of these various ethical principles, standards, and legal obligations, it becomes clear that you cannot possibly meet all of them. If you attempt to serve the client with devotion and meet your legal duty to try to prevent his suicide by telephoning family members, a physician, or the police, you violate his right to confidentiality and, potentially, his privacy. His right to privacy would obviously be lost at the point that police or emergency medical personnel entered his home. If you maintain his right to confidentiality and privacy, you neglect your legal duty to attempt to prevent his suicide. This is indeed an ethical dilemma. How do you decide what to do?

◆ EXERCISE 3-3: IDENTIFYING ETHICAL STANDARDS

1. Refer to the NASW Code of Ethics. Turn to the section entitled "Ethical Standards." Read the portion that describes social workers' ethical responsibilities to clients (1.01–1.16). Use the following space to summarize in a paragraph or two what these particular standards mean to you as a social worker.

2. Review the portion of the NASW Code of Ethics that describes social workers' ethical responsibilities to colleagues (2.01–2.11). Use the following space to summarize in a paragraph or two what these particular standards mean to you as a social worker.

3. Review the portion of the NASW Code of Ethics that describes social workers' ethical responsibilities in practice settings (3.01–3.11). Use the following space to summarize in a paragraph or two what these particular standards mean to you as a social worker.

4. Review the portion of the NASW Code of Ethics that describes social workers' ethical responsibilities as professionals (4.01–4.08). Use the following space to summarize in a paragraph or two what these particular standards mean to you as a social worker.

5. Review the portion of the NASW Code of Ethics that describes social workers' ethical responsibilities to the social work profession (5.01–5.02). Use the following space to summarize in a paragraph or two what these particular standards mean to you as a social worker.

6. Review the portion of the NASW Code of Ethics that describes social workers' ethical responsibilities to the broader society (6.01–6.04). Use the following space to summarize in a paragraph or two what these particular standards mean to you as a social worker.

Addressing Ethical Dilemmas

Several authors have suggested sequential steps for the process of ethical decision making (Congress, 2000; Loewenberg, Dolgoff, & Harrington, 2000; Mattison, 2000; Reamer, 1995a; Rhodes, 1986) or ethical problem solving (Reamer & Conrad, 1995). Congress, for example, suggests that social workers adopt the ETHIC Model of Decision Making and proceed through the following steps or processes:

E—Examine relevant personal, societal, agency, client, and professional values.

T—Think about what ethical standard of the NASW code of ethics applies, as well as relevant laws and case decisions.

H—Hypothesize about possible consequences of different decisions.

I— Identify who will benefit and who will be harmed in view of social work's commitment to the most vulnerable.

C—Consult with supervisor and colleagues about the most ethical choice. (Congress, 2000, p. 10)

Reamer suggests a seven-step process for ethical problem solving:

1. Identify the ethical issues, including the social work values and duties that conflict.
2. Identify the individuals, groups, and organizations that are likely to be affected by the ethical decision.
3. Tentatively identify all possible courses of action and the participants involved in each, along with possible benefits and risks for each.
4. Thoroughly examine the reasons in favor of and opposed to each possible course of action, considering relevant: ethical theories, principles, and guidelines; codes of ethics and legal principles; social work practice theory and principles; personal values (including religious, cultural, and ethnic values and political ideology), particularly those that conflict with one's own.
5. Consult with colleagues and appropriate experts (such as agency staff, supervisors, agency administrators, attorneys, ethics scholars).
6. Make the decision and document the decision-making process.
7. Monitor, evaluate, and document the decision. (Reamer, 2000, p. 361; NASW Office of Ethics and Professional Review, n.d.; Reamer & Conrad, 1995)

The sequential steps identified by social work scholars such as Congress (1999, 2000), Loewenberg, Dolgoff, and Harrington (2000), and Reamer (1995a, 2000; Reamer & Conrad, 1995) reflect well-reasoned, logical processes—especially when you can adhere to all of the applicable ethical principles. Unfortunately, this is sometimes impossible. When numerous principles and legal duties apply and some conflict with each other, you are faced with an ethical dilemma. In other words, conforming to one standard (e.g., duty to report) necessarily requires that you violate another (e.g., client confidentiality). When ethical and legal obligations conflict, which do you ignore? Which do you respect? How do you decide?

How to address and resolve moral and ethical dilemmas has been the subject of philosophical discussion for centuries (Holmes, 2003). In contemporary times, many social workers have questions about whether decisions should be based on certain fixed moral values and principles through a deductive, deontological, absolutist process or on individual cases via inductive, teleological, consequentialist, utilitarian, or relativistic reasoning. A social worker adopting a utilitarian perspective would consider the relative good versus harm of the probable consequences of the ethical decision and accompanying action in the particular case. A social worker adopting a deontological view would apply the chosen principle, rule, or law regardless of the potential consequences (Mattison, 2000).

Codes of ethics and laws reflect a strong deontological theme. Such rules are written and codified so that they might be precisely followed. Indeed, sanctions may be imposed when the "rules are violated." On the other hand, social work also emphasizes a person-and-situation or person-in-environment perspective—suggesting that individual circumstances play a part in all processes, including those involving ethical dilemmas. In fact, the NASW Code contains these passages:

> Specific applications of the *Code* must take into account the context in which it is being considered and the possibility of conflicts among the *Code*'s values, principles, and standards.
>
> Further, the *NASW Code of Ethics* does not specify which values, principles, and standards are most important and ought to outweigh others in instances when they conflict. Reasonable differences of opinion can and do exist among social workers with respect to the ways in which values, ethical principles, and ethical standards should be rank ordered when they conflict. (NASW, 1999, Purpose of the NASW Code of Ethics section)

The NASW Code of Ethics does not assign a particular value, weight, or rank to each ethic. Therefore, you may and indeed should consider the array of applicable ethical principles as well as the particulars of the situation, circumstances, and potential consequences of ethical decisions and actions. Of course, this complicates the decision-making process. The shear number of factors inherent in each unique case situation that might be considered is daunting. A clear ranking of the principles or an ethics hierarchy would certainly make it easier to apply the principles—from a deontological perspective. However, fixed application of ranked principles reduces the opportunity to consider unique situational aspects.

There are risks associated with both the deontological and the teleological approaches—especially when taken to the extreme. Case-by-case, inductive reasoning may lead social workers to, in effect, justify or rationalize any decision on the basis of the exigencies of the situation (Jonsen & Toulmin, 1988). Conversely, strict deductive application of prioritized ethical principles can contribute to petty, bureaucratic-like, thinking that fails to appreciate the need to sometimes make exceptions to the "rules" (Toulmin, 1981).

In considering the contextual or situational aspects of moral and ethical issues, you might wisely consider dimensions such as *motives, means, ends,* and likely *effects* (Fletcher, 1966). Explore your own motives, examine the means by which you plan to address the issues and implement the decision, assess the ends you envision, and identify the probable effects of your proposed actions. These considerations reflect the age-old, intellectually challenging questions such as, "Do the ends justify the means?" "Are your motives pure?" "Have you considered the potential impact of your actions upon others?" "Who should participate in the decision-making process?" "Who should make the final choice?"

These lead to social work specific issues: "Is a social worker ever justified in using "bad means" to pursue a "good end"? Should a social worker steadfastly adhere to "good means" even when the outcome is likely to be "bad"? "Should a social worker ever make a decision that affects another without that person's knowledge and participation?" "Should a social worker ever place an ethical obligation above a legal duty or, conversely, a legal duty above an ethical standard?"

One of the hallmarks of professional social work status is continuous and ongoing consideration of moral and ethical issues in service to others. Because you have the potential to harm as well as help, to exploit as well as empower, and to restrict as well as liberate, you must consciously, deliberately, and reflectively examine your thoughts, feelings, and actions in both moral and ethical terms (Goldstein, 1987; Schon, 1990).

Motives

In exploring motives, consider your primary and secondary purposes both as a person and as a social worker. In accord with your privileged professional status, you assume weighty moral, ethical, and legal responsibilities for others and for society. Ideally, your primary motives and those that influence your decisions and action are consistent with professional values and ethics (e.g., service, social justice, respect for people, integrity, or competence). However, you also reflect personal motives as well (e.g., fear of legal action, desire to assert your own agenda or will, sympathy, pity, spite). In carrying out your social work functions, you may and indeed should acknowledge your personal motives as you shift focus and emphasize your professional motives.

In addition, ask yourself, "If I was a client, and my social worker acted on these motives, what would I experience?" "If social workers everywhere manifested these motives, how would society respond?"

Means

In exploring "means," consider the "ways" you might act. Determine who should participate in the decision and how the action might be implemented. Means include both the processes of decision making as well as the nature of the plan for action. Ask, "Are the means consistent with my professional values and ethics?" "Are the means likely to produce the desired end or outcome?" "How will people and situations likely to be affected by my use of these means?" If the means are not consonant with social work principles or the associated effects appear potentially harmful, ask, "Have I genuinely considered all other means to these ends that would enable me to adhere to my professional values and ethics?" If acceptable means are indeed unavailable, ask, "Do the ends justify these undesirable means and the associated effects?"

Finally, you might ask, "If I was a client and my social worker adopted these means, what would be my reaction?" "If these means were applied routinely and universally by all social workers, what would be society's reaction?"

Ends

Consider the nature of the envisioned "ends" (goals) and determine if they are personal or professional. Ask yourself, "How were these goals determined?" "Who participated in their identification and definition?" "Toward whom or what are these goals targeted?" "Are the people affected by the pursuit and accomplishment of these goals aware of their existence?" "Would I be professionally proud to accomplish these goals?" "Are these goals consistent with our mutual understanding of the issues for work, the mission of the agency or program, and the functions of the social work profession?"

You could also ask yourself, "If I was a client in similar circumstances, how would I respond to these goals?" "If these goals were pursued and achieved by all social workers and their clients, what would be society's response?"

Effects

In exploring "effects," consider the additional consequences that could result from use of the identified means and accomplishment of the envisioned ends. Beyond the direct impact on the targeted persons-and-situations, you, your clients, other persons, and related social systems may also be affected by your decisions and actions. These "side effects" may be positive or negative, energy enhancing or energy depleting, depending on their nature, intensity, duration, and a host of other factors. Sometimes, the side effects are so potentially damaging that they outweigh even the most desirable ends. For example, a social worker might find an instrument that successfully identifies adult males that abuse children. However, the rate of "false positives" is extremely high. There is an inaccurate identification for every accurate one. The goals (ends) are certainly desirable: to protect children from abuse and to identify adult male offenders who need service. However, the side effects are so onerous (false identification of innocent persons) that the means could not reasonably be used without several additional safeguards.

Another example: Suppose an intervention (means) designed to reduce or prevent drug abuse among urban adolescents successfully enables 42% of participants who previously abused drugs to discontinue drug usage altogether. What great news! However, 48% of participants who had not previously used drugs begin to do so—evidently because of the information and connections established through the program. If these figures were accurate, the severity of the side effects or the "collateral damage" would warrant suspension or alteration of the service (e.g., limit the program to substance-abusing youth only).

You might finally ask yourself, "If I were subject to these side effects, how would I react?" "Would I personally willingly accept the side effects to achieve the intended goal?" "If these side effects were experienced widely throughout the world, how would society react?"

Of course, consideration of motive, means, ends, and effects occurs in an integrative fashion. They are explored in relation to each other and within the context of personal views, laws and policies, and, of course, professional values and ethics.

Consider a social worker in the following situation:

Hoping to protect a small child from physical harm (desirable motive), a social worker decides to lie to the allegedly abusive parent (undesirable means) in an effort to prevent injury to the child (desirable end). In reaching the decision and taking the action, the social worker, in effect, decides that the means are justified by the ends and willingly accepts responsibility for whatever happens.

This is contextual, teleological, or utilitarian thinking and is based on an estimation of the likely consequences of the action—in this case, the lie. A major danger in such analysis is that the means (the lie) may or may not yield the intended consequence of protecting the child from harm. You cannot predict or guarantee the future. The lie may achieve the anticipated ends, may have no effect whatsoever, or may exacerbate the problem. Whatever happens, the social worker may conclude, "My intentions were good. I wanted to protect the child from injury, so I lied."

Another social worker in a similar situation may adopt a deontological approach and conclude that lying is always wrong. The social worker may think, "I cannot lie (desirable means) to the allegedly abusive parent even if I anticipate an adverse response that increases the likelihood of physical injury to the child (undesirable end). I cannot predict the future with 100% certainty, therefore I should at least be truthful." Whatever happens, the social worker may conclude, "At least I was ethical—I did not lie." However, the act of not lying may have directly led to physical harm to the child. The means may have been good but the ends disastrous.

Relying exclusively on the ethical or legal standards or exclusively on the characteristics of the situation does not necessarily lead to a clear decision or plan of action. Both the teleological and the deontological approaches reflect strengths as well as weaknesses.

Despite the risks associated with efforts to rank moral or ethical values, some scholars have developed hierarchies to help social workers address ethical dilemmas where one ethic conflicts with another. Loewenberg, Dolgoff, and Harrington (2000) suggest that the protection of human life is the paramount moral and ethical obligation. Ranked first or highest, it takes precedence over all other moral values or ethical principles. Therefore, a social worker who learns that a client intends to kill a former lover would take action to protect the potential victim, even if other ethical principles are abridged in the process.

Loewenberg, Dolgoff, and Harrington place equality and inequality in the second position. A complex principle, it refers to fairness and justice. This principle "suggests that all persons in the same circumstances should be treated in the same way; that is, equal persons have the right to be treated equally and nonequal persons have the right to be treated differently if the inequality is relevant to the issue in question"

(Loewenberg et al., 2000, p. 70). For example, competent adults of equivalent status usually have the right to engage in consensual sex. However, because of unequal status and power, an adult does not have the right to engage in sexual activities with a child, even with the child's apparent consent. Similarly, because of the power associated with professional status and function, a social worker may not have sex with an adult client, even when the client takes the initiative, because of the social worker's special status as a helping professional.

Consistent with social work's traditional emphasis on respect for individual rights and self-determination, autonomy and freedom occupies the third position. This principle encourages social workers to "make practice decisions that foster a person's autonomy, independence, and freedom" (Loewenberg et al., 2000, p. 71). Of course, a client's right to independent action is not unlimited. A person does not have the autonomous right to kill him- or herself, or someone else, abuse or exploit a child, or scream "fire" in a crowded theater.

The principle of least harm is ranked fourth, indicating that a "social worker should always choose the option that will cause the least harm, the least permanent harm, and/or the most easily reversible harm. If harm has been done, the social worker should attempt where possible to repair the harm done" (Loewenberg et al., 2000, p. 71).

The fifth principle holds that a "social worker should choose the option that promotes a better quality of life for all people, for the individual as well as for the community" (Loewenberg et al., 2000, p. 71).

Privacy and confidentiality is placed in the sixth position, indicating that a "social worker should make practice decisions that strengthen every person's right to privacy. Keeping confidential information inviolate is a direct derivative of this obligation" (Loewenberg et al., 2000, p. 71).

Truthfulness and full-disclosure occupies the seventh most important position. This principle holds that social workers should be honest and truthful with clients and others. "Social and professional relationships require trust in order to function well, and trust—in turn—is based on honest dealing that minimizes surprises so that mutual expectations are generally fulfilled" (Loewenberg et al., 2000, p. 72).

Loewenberg, Dolgoff, and Harrington offer their Ethical Principles Screen to social workers as an aid in organizing and ranking aspects of ethical dilemmas when two or more ethical obligations conflict. Facets of the dilemma are organized into each of the fundamental ethical principles. Once categorized, the screen may be used as part of the ethical decision making process. In most cases, Ethical Principle 1 is superior to Principles 2 through 7; Principle 2 is of higher rank than Principles 3 through 7, and so on. If you can conform to all aspects of the ethical code, the Ethical Principles Screen is not needed. It is applicable when conflicts exist among various legal obligations and ethical standards so that decisions must be made about which should take precedence.

Loewenberg, Dolgoff, and Harrington's hierarchical screen is useful in stimulating thinking about specific dilemmas within the context of abstract principles. Indeed, philosophers have long argued that certain fundamental moral principles exist and they can and should guide decision-making in all aspects of life. Other helping professions have adopted these basic moral values, notably medicine, in the following manner (Beauchamp & Childress, 1983; Koocher & Keith-Spiegel, 1990):

Beneficence. The principle of beneficence suggests that helping, protecting, and promoting the well-being and welfare of clients and others is a primary moral value. In other words, professionals engage in "good deeds" through "good works" and must sometimes accept personal risk or sacrifice to carry out their responsibilities. Beneficence incorporates Loewenberg, Dolgoff, and Harrington's first principle by including the protection of human lives and is reflected in the legal duty of care and the duties to inform, report, and warn.

Nonmaleficence. The principle of nonmaleficence suggests that the professional should do everything possible to avoid harming clients or others through efforts to serve. The value is often captured through the admonition, "Do no harm!," and is reflected in ethical and legal codes concerning the quality of care so that clients and others do not suffer unnecessary harm because of services they received. This moral value incorporates Loewenberg, Dolgoff, and Harrington's fourth principle, that of least harm. The concept of *utility* is part of this value because the nature and extent of harm must be considered in attempts to implement "good acts." In essence, utility involves a combination of beneficence and nonmaleficence by suggesting that actions should be taken to promote the greatest good with the least harm. Nonmaleficence may be incorporated within the legal duty of care. For example, if efforts to help one person injure a dozen others, then the question of utility must be considered. Similarly, a client and worker might consider becoming more assertive a desirable goal. However, if assertiveness with an employer leads the client to lose a desperately needed job, then the harm done might well outweigh the good.

Justice. The principle of justice suggests that people have a right to be treated equally unless a disparity of power or capacity warrants differential treatment. Equal access and equal opportunity are components of justice as is consideration of extenuating or mitigating factors and environmental circumstances. Helping professionals are thus obligated to provide fair and equitable treatment to all. In social work, the value of justice applies to individuals, groups, communities, and societies. This moral value includes Loewenberg, Dolgoff, and Harrington's second principle, that of equality and inequality, and the fifth, quality of life. Justice may be implicitly considered part of the legal duty of care. Indeed, unjust practices may well fail to meet the minimal standard of professional care.

Autonomy. The principle of autonomy suggests that people generally have a fundamental right to liberty and self-determination. They have a right to govern their own affairs and make decisions about actions that may affect them or their well-being. This value reflects Loewenberg, Dolgoff, and Harrington's third principle, that of autonomy and freedom, and is implicit in the legal duty to respect privacy.

Privacy. The principle of privacy derives partly from the right to self-determination. In the context of privacy, people have a right to control the nature and extent of intrusion into or publicity about their personal lives and homes. Even the publication of clients' names threatens privacy. For example, when social workers call out the full name of the next client in a waiting area so that clients and visitors may overhear, they have abridged that person's right and violated the legal duty to respect privacy.

Confidentiality. The principle of confidentiality is associated with those of autonomy and privacy. In essence, clients retain ownership of information shared with helping professionals. Therefore, social workers may not share clients' information without their expressed permission. To do so would also violate the legal duty to maintain confidentiality. As illustrated in Loewenberg, Dolgoff, and Harrington's sixth principle, clients maintain fundamental rights to privacy and confidentiality. The role of client or the receipt of service does not diminish these rights.

Fidelity. The principle of fidelity or "good faith" suggests that clients and others may expect helping professionals to be honest and to keep their commitments. This moral value incorporates Loewenberg, Dolgoff, and Harrington's seventh principle, that of honesty and full-disclosure, and is inherent in the legal duty of care. Fidelity involves honesty, veracity, and integrity. Professionals are expected to tell the truth; to refrain from any forms of dishonesty, fraud, and deception; and to honor commitments made to clients and others.

Recognizing the limitations of any attempt to rank the core moral values in advance of specific information about a particular ethical dilemma, you may need to do so once you understand the applicable duties and obligations. Indeed, as part of your decision-making process, you may establish a case-specific moral values hierarchy that reflects your judgments about the relative importance of the relevant responsibilities. For example, in one instance, you—perhaps in conjunction with a client—may determine that autonomy is more important than beneficence. In another situation, the risk of harm (nonmaleficence) may outweigh the potential good (maleficence). Developing your own hierarchy requires more judgment and analysis than would applying a universal hierarchy such as proposed by Loewenberg, Dolgoff, and Harrington. However, ethical dilemmas tend to reflect idiosyncrasies that warrant modification of even well-conceptualized value hierarchies. Intellectual flexibility and integrity is consistent with a persons-and-situation perspective and professionalism. Critical thought and careful judgment are hallmarks of all aspects of professional social work practice. They are especially needed within the context of ethical decision making.

Return now to the case of the man who has locked himself in his basement and threatened suicide. You have already identified several ethical principles, standards, and legal duties that may apply in this situation. You have undoubtedly found that several of these conflict. To determine which of these conflicting responsibilities should take precedence in this particular instance, develop a case-specific moral values hierarchy.

If you examine the specifics of the situation in relation to the moral values, you would readily recognize the importance of beneficence. This is consonant with the principle of service, the ethical responsibility to "help people in need," and your obligation to safeguard human life. This moral value is consistent with the legal duty of care that includes the obligation to prevent suicidal action. Based on evidence that your former client intends to attempt suicide, you would take action to protect his life. In this situation, beneficence might well take precedence over other values. If so, you would intervene—even if such intervention involves a risk of harm or a loss of autonomy. Of course, if possible, you would first try to intervene in a manner that does not infringe on other values and human rights. For example, in this situation, you or perhaps your supervisor—because the client has targeted you as a source of dissatisfaction—might attempt to engage him in conversation and defuse the situation before initiating more invasive action.

An effort to intervene directly with the client by telephone is congruent with the moral value of autonomy. The man, however, may not answer the telephone—or it may become apparent that further contact by you or your supervisor would exacerbate the situation. If such is the case, you may have to infringe on the client's autonomy and his rights to privacy and confidentiality—should temporary police arrest or involuntary hospitalization become necessary.

In your attempt to save the man's life, you may have to call his relatives to inform them about the situation and request their cooperation. You may have to telephone the local police or paramedics and ask them to go to the house. At some point in the process, you may need to provide evidence to a judge or magistrate, or perhaps to a court-appointed physician, to facilitate hospitalization. Such actions obviously infringe on several of the client's fundamental human and civil rights. They represent violations of some of your own ethical principles and legal duties. Nonetheless, if a client in such a situation reports his intention to commit suicide, you are morally and ethically bound to temporarily forgo other principles as you try to save the person's life.

Summary

The values, ethics, and legal obligations that guide social workers pertain to every aspect of professional practice. Indeed, you should consider ethical principles more important than theoretical knowledge, research findings, agency policies, and, of course, your own personal views.

To make sound ethical decisions in social work practice, you should be familiar with the fundamental human rights of all people and the basic moral values involved in ethical decision making. You also need to know and understand the values of the profession, the code of ethics, and the legal obligations affecting social work practice. In addition, you need to identify the ethical principles, standards, and legal duties that may apply to particular situations. Finally, when several obligations conflict, you must determine which take precedence.

The skill of ethical decision making is fundamental to social work practice. Without such skill, you cannot legitimately claim professional status. Indeed, attempting to provide social work services without regard for the ethical principles would be, literally, unconscionable.

◆ CHAPTER 3 SUMMARY EXERCISES

In the space provided, identify the ethical principles, standards, and legal duties that you believe apply to each of the following case examples. Then, for each case, develop a moral values hierarchy through which to rank-order competing principles and duties. Finally, based on your case specific ranking, describe the actions you might take as a social worker in each situation. You will need to refer to information presented in this chapter and a copy of the NASW Code of Ethics to complete these exercises.

1. As a social worker in the oncology unit of the general hospital, you frequently work with clients who are dying. An intelligent, articulate 88-year-old woman, Ms. T., who has suffered from intense pain for several months, informs you that she has hoarded powerful analgesic medicines and intends to take her own life during the night. She says that she wants to say goodbye to you and to thank you for all your help during this time. However, she asks that you please do not interfere with her plans.

2. As a social worker in an elementary school system, you frequently work with young children in small groups. During a meeting with several girls in the 8-to-10-year-old age range, one girl says that almost every night, her father comes into her bedroom, puts his hands under her pajamas, and touches between her legs.

3. A 25-year-old man, father of two children (1 and 3 years old), comes to a first interview with you, a social worker in a family counseling agency. During the course of the interview, he reveals that he and his wife argue a lot. He says that she won't stop arguing once she starts and that when he tries to walk

away, she pursues him, yelling. He indicates that in those situations he becomes enraged. He reveals that on several occasions, he has pushed her and once he punched her in the face, breaking her nose.

4. You have recently been employed in an agency whose clientele is primarily African American and Latino. All the professional staff members are white. Several of the secretarial and support personnel are African American. No one employed by the agency is fluent in Spanish.

5. You have been working with a married couple that has indicated a desire to improve the quality of their relationship. You and the clients have agreed that direct, open, and honest communication is a relationship goal. Each has also expressed that sexual fidelity is an important dimension of their marriage. Between the fifth and sixth meetings, you receive a telephone call from one of the partners who says, "I think it would help you to know that I am involved romantically with another person. My spouse does not know and I know that you will not reveal this information because of your legal obligation to maintain confidentiality. I want you to know about this other

relationship because I think it will help you to help us. I have come to respect your expertise. You are doing a wonderful job. Thank you."

◆ CHAPTER 3 WORLD WIDE WEB EXERCISES

1. Go to the NASW Web site home page at www.socialworkers.org. Use the search feature to locate the NASW Standards for Cultural Competence in Social Work Practice. The search term "Cultural Competence" (quotation marks included) should reveal the titles of several documents, one of which contains the standards. Click on that title to go to www.socialworkers.org/sections/credentials/cultural_comp.asp. Review and reflect on the standards. Then, use the following space to write a two-to-three paragraph essay entitled, "What the Standards for Cultural Competence Mean to Me."

2. Go to the Thomson Learning InfoTrac College Edition site at www.infotrac-college.com and use your passcode to log in. Enter the search string "universal moral values" (without the quotation marks) to locate an article entitled "A Short List of Universal Moral Values" (Kinnier, Kernes, & Dautheribes, 2000). Carefully review the article and pay special attention to the Appendix. Reflect on the contents of the article and then use the following space to write a two-to-three paragraph reaction entitled, "The Implications of Universal Moral Values for My Social Work Practice."

3. Go to the Thomson Learning InfoTrac College Edition site at www.infotrac-college.com and use your passcode to log in. Enter the search string "Gandhian ethics" (without the quotation marks) to locate an article entitled "Gandhian Principles in Social Work Practice: Ethics Revisited" (Walz & Ritchie, 2000). Review and reflect on the article. Then use the following space to write a two-to-three paragraph reaction entitled, "The Implications of Mahatma Gandhi's Philosophical Principles for My Social Work Practice."

Chapter 3 Self-Appraisal

As you conclude this chapter, please assess your proficiency in the ethical decision making skills by completing the following self-appraisal exercise.

SELF-APPRAISAL: THE ETHICAL DECISION MAKING SKILLS

Please respond to the following items to help you undertake a self-assessment of your competency in the ethical decision making skills addressed in this chapter. Read each statement carefully. Then, use the following four-point rating scale to indicate the degree to which you agree or disagree with each statement. Record your numerical response in the space provided:

4 = Strongly Agree

3 = Agree

2 = Disagree

1 = Strongly Disagree

_____ 1. I can readily identify and describe the legal duties that apply to all helping professionals.

_____ 2. I can readily identify and describe the fundamental values of the social work profession.

_____ 3. I can readily summarize the principles of my social work Code of Ethics.

_____ 4. I can readily identify the ethical principles and legal duties that might apply in social work contexts.

_____ 5. In circumstances where two or more conflicting ethical principles or legal duties apply in social work contexts, I can determine their relative priority through the development and use of a case-specific conceptual screen.

_____ Subtotal

Note: These items are taken directly from the ethical decision-making skills section of the Social Work Skills Self-Appraisal Questionnaire contained in Appendix 3. Earlier, when you reviewed Chapter 2 and completed the exercises, you responded to these questions. You may now compare the responses you made on that occasion with those you made this time. Also, compare the two subtotals. If you believe that you have progressed in terms of your proficiency with the ethical decision making skills, the more recent subtotal should be higher than the earlier.

Reflect on the skills addressed in this chapter and the results of your self-appraisal. Based on your analysis, prepare a succinct one-page summary report entitled "Self-Assessment of Proficiency in the Ethical Decision Making Skills." Within the report, be sure to identify those skills that you know and do well (e.g., scores of 3 or 4). Also, specify those that need further practice (e.g., scores of 2 or less) and briefly outline plans by which to achieve proficiency in them. When finished, include the report in your Social Work Skills Learning Portfolio.

Chapter 4

Talking and Listening:
The Basic Interpersonal Skills

This chapter (see Box 4.1) is intended to help you develop proficiency in the basic interpersonal skills of talking and listening (i.e., the processes used to send and receive messages fully and accurately). In this context, the term *talking* is used to refer to the processes involved in sending and *listening* to refer to those involved in receiving messages—regardless of the means of transmission.[1]

Well-developed communication skills are needed in all phases and forms of social work practice. Indeed, they apply to all aspects of human social interaction. Inadequate skills in sending and receiving messages can impede the development of a productive professional relationship and prevent a successful outcome. The basic interpersonal skills of talking and listening facilitate social interaction. They enable you to understand accurately and express yourself clearly during exchanges with other people.

---

[1] People vary widely in their physical ability to speak, hear, and see. In this workbook, we use the terms talking and listening to refer to the transmission and reception of communication messages—regardless of the medium. Many superbly effective social workers communicate through alternate means (e.g., sign language, mime, and through interpreters, speech synthesizers, TDD, voice recognition systems, and other forms of augmented communication systems).

Chapter Purpose

The purpose of this chapter is to help learners develop proficiency in the basic interpersonal skills of talking and listening (i.e., sending and receiving messages).

Goals

Following completion of this chapter, learners should be able to demonstrate the following:

◆ Understanding of the talking, listening, and active-listening skills
◆ Appreciation for culturally competent communications
◆ Proficiency in nonverbal communications and body language
◆ Proficiency in the talking skills
◆ Proficiency in the listening skills
◆ Proficiency in active listening
◆ Ability to assess proficiency in the talking and listening skills

Culturally Competent Communications

Despite the fact that "everyone communicates," effective interpersonal communications are among the most difficult activities human beings undertake. The challenges for the worker-and-client in a professional encounter are even more challenging than those that occur in other kinds of relationships. The difficulties involve the various meanings that individuals have for the verbal and nonverbal conscious and unconscious messages they express. Cultural dimensions play a large part. Indeed, cultural competence is essential for effective communications.

Furthermore, the importance of culturally competent communications will increase with each passing decade. According to population projections of the U.S. Census Bureau, the 1999 U.S. population of approximately 280 million is expected to grow to about 480 million by the year 2075. The implications of a population that approaches one-half-billion—even in a country as resource-rich as the United States—are staggering. Growth in overall size, however, reflects only part of the picture. The racial and ethnic composition will change dramatically as well.

By 2075, the Hispanic population in the U.S. is predicted to grow from 11.5 to 29.5% of the population, and the non-Hispanic Asian and Pacific Islander population from 3.8 to 11.0%. The Native American Indian and the non-Hispanic black populations are expected to reflect modest changes, from 0.7 to 0.8 and from 12.1 to 13.2%, respectively. The largest percentage change is anticipated among the non-Hispanic, white population, which is expected to decrease from 71.9 to 45.6% of the population (U.S. Census Bureau Population Division Population Projections Branch, 2002). At some point during the 21st century, non-Hispanic whites are expected to represent less than half the total U.S. population.

When you addressed issues related to professionalism in Chapter 2 and ethical decision making in Chapter 3, you began to explore the importance of cultural competence for social work practice. Such competence emerges most profoundly during exchanges with others. Each person has culturally based expectations about all sorts of things, including roles related to help seeking and receiving as well as help giving, and beginning and ending social encounters. Among the most important aspects of culture are communications. Language, for example, is an obvious aspect of culture and affects the processes and outcomes of communications. Within a few years, most social workers will need to be proficient in at least one other language besides English. Schools and departments of social work would be wise to encourage students' bilingual proficiency. The increase in the number of Hispanic persons suggests that many social workers should know Spanish—but competency in American Sign and other languages is also needed to serve diverse populations, including the large numbers of first- and second-generation immigrants and refugees that come to North America.

The understanding of the meaning of words is, of course, only one aspect of the numerous challenges associated with intercultural communication. Pedersen (1981; Pedersen & Ivey, 1993) used the phrase "multicultural three-step" to describe the stages of developing competence among counselors: (1) *awareness*, (2) *knowledge*, and (3) *skill*.

Awareness refers to the recognition of your own cultural patterns, expectations, perceptions, and how they differ from and influence communication with people from different cultures. Awareness also involves realizing the limitations in your knowledge about other cultural traditions.

Knowledge involves appreciating and understanding clients' cultures. Such understanding is based on knowledge gained from the professional and scientific literature, resource persons from other cultures, and findings from research studies about communications between your culture and your clients'.

Skill includes those interpersonal abilities based on awareness and knowledge that enable you to communicate effectively and provide helpful services to people from other cultures. As professionals interested in service, social workers need interpersonal competencies as well as cultural awareness and knowledge. Without skill, you might be quite educated but unable to make a difference in others' lives. Among other competencies, social workers must be able to communicate verbally and nonverbally with persons from other cultures and, when necessary, use interpreters in appropriate and effective ways.

Several scholars have published valuable works in the area of intercultural communication competence for helping professionals (Arredondo, 1998; Arredondo & Arciniega, 2001; Arredondo et al., 1996; Blount, Thyer, & Frye, 1992; Braithwaite, 2000; Chung & Bemak, 2002; Fong, 2001; Fong & Furuto, 2001; Harrison & S. Dziegielewski, 1992a, 1992b; Hartley, 1999; Ivey & Ivey, 1996, 2003; Ivey, Simek-Morgan, D'Andrea, Ivey, & D'Andrea, 2001; Leigh, 1998; Liu & Clay, 2002; Mindess, 1999; Payne, 2001; Pedersen, 2000a, 2000b, 2002, 2003; Pedersen & Ivey, 1993; Ponterotto & Casas, 1991; Pope-Davis, Heesacker, Coleman, Liu, & Toporek, 2003;

Roysircar, 2003; Sue & Arredondo, 1992; Sue et al., 1998; Sue & Sue, 1999; Wamback & Harrison, 1992; Wodarski, 1992a, 1992b, 1992c). The sheer quantity of scholarly work related to intercultural communication in counseling and social work reflects the growing recognition that professional helpers must be culturally competent during the 21st century.

Numerous excellent resources are available for social workers seeking to enhance their awareness and improve their knowledge of and competence in serving persons from various cultures (Acevedo & Morales, 2001; Bird, 2001; Brammer, 2004; Daly, 2001; Davis, 2001; Devore, 2001; Fong, 2003; Fong & Furuto, 2001; Furuto, San Nicolas, Kim, & Fiaui, 2001; Galan, 2001; Gilbert & Franklin, 2001; Heart, 2001; Kanuha, 2001; Leung & Cheung, 2001; Lie & Lowery, 2003; McRoy, 2003; Negroni-Rodriguez & Morales, 2001; Villa, 2001; Walters, Longres, Han, & Icard, 2003; Weaver, 2003; Westbrooks & Starks, 2001; Zuniga, 2003). Indeed, whenever possible, begin to learn about specific population groups you will serve in your field practicum or in your professional roles following graduation before you start. Try to gain some personal experience as well. Visit neighborhoods, attend religious services, and talk with community leaders to gain understanding that cannot occur through scholarly materials alone.

Awareness and knowledge go hand-in-hand. Initial awareness of your thoughts, feelings, attitudes, and social behaviors toward and with another culture is very likely to change as you gain knowledge about the norms, values, history, religious beliefs and practices, dress, and social customs. Suppose, for example, that you experience negative judgmental thoughts about a culture that reflects a formally structured, patriarchic family structure where women and children assume lesser overt status and power. Your critical reaction might change if you learn that historically such a family structure served survival needs in a society where social deviance was commonly punished by death. You might also learn that within that culture's religious traditions, the father is viewed as the primary connecting linkage between women and children and God or heaven. Without such knowledge, you might adopt a negative view of men in the culture; with it, you might be more understanding and able to communicate with respect and empathy. Without cultural knowledge, you might, for example, begin an initial family meeting by talking first with a teenager rather than the father. As a result, you might unwittingly express disrespect for the father and the culture. Your ignorance could lead the family to withdraw from a service program and perhaps avoid additional professional help in the future. Cultural incompetence by social workers and other helping professionals might well lead members of certain cultural groups to avoid human service and mental health organizations altogether. Does it surprise you that certain population groups seek services at lower rates than do others or that the dropout rates of some groups are much higher than are those of others? Cultural incompetence may be part of the explanation.

As you proceed on the never-ending path toward competence, first learn about various facets of culture that directly relate to the nature of the services you expect to provide and the professional roles you hope to fulfill. For example, if you served as a social worker in public child welfare, you might well seek to develop the following:

(1) knowledge of the other groups religious/spiritual orientations and views of metaphysical harmony, (2) cultural views of children, (3) cultural style of

communication—whether information is transmitted primarily through spoken words or through the context of the situation, the relationship, and physical cues, (4) culturally prescribed and proscribed behaviors in formal and informal relationships, (5) family structures and roles; child-rearing practices including nurturing, meeting physical and psychosocial needs, methods of discipline (including use of corporal punishment), (6) norms of interdependency, mutuality, and obligation within families and kinship networks, (7) health and healing practices, and (8) views of change and intervention. (Samantrai, 2004, p. 34)

Of course, many other aspects of culture may pertain to communication with persons from other cultures. For example, the concept of time as measured by "the clock" may be highly valued in a culture. Being "on time" may be associated with responsibility, reliability, courtesy, commitment, and perhaps wealth. In such a culture, the phrase "time is money" may be used. In another culture, clock time may hold much less value. The natural rhythms of the movement of the sun and moon, the changing of the seasons, and the ebbs and flows in human relationships may assume greater importance. The concept "when the time is right" may be evident in social relations and interpersonal communications.

Other culturally relevant dimensions of communication include preferences about proximity or the degree of space between people, the expression of emotion, the nature and extent of eye-contact, the degree of hand or other physical movements, and the ease with which intimate or personal topics are discussed.

History is often a remarkably significant aspect of culture and could be overlooked in your efforts to deal with current issues. For instance, suppose one cultural group experienced severe oppression by another for several generations. Their ancestors may have been enslaved or perhaps subject to ethnic cleansing. What might happen if your name or appearance reminds a client of peoples who committed atrocities? In such circumstances, the cultural history may well become a powerful part of the immediate present.

Indeed, powerfulness and powerlessness tend to remain significant phenomena for individuals and groups that have experienced either or both. Being a "somebody" or a "nobody" (Fuller, 2002) profoundly affects people and the way they communicate with others. Fuller used the term *rankism* to refer to the uses and abuses of power by those of higher rank toward those of lower rank. The feelings of shame, humiliation, indignity, or inferiority felt by a "nobody" when abused, oppressed, enslaved, imprisoned, or exploited or even when addressed with superiority, arrogance, or condescendence by a "somebody" are pretty much the same whether it appears as racism, sexism, ageism, ableism, lookism, heterosexism, or other insidious "isms." When a professor demeans a student, a colonel ridicules a private, an employer humiliates an employee, a Senator ignores a citizen, a social worker belittles a client, or the people of one culture deny the humanity of another, the resulting dehumanization frequently has long-lasting effects.

Social workers' expression of cultural competence involves awareness and management of rankism in all its myriad manifestations. The role of social worker involves a position of status and rank relative to clients. The difference in rank is not, in itself, a negative. Indeed, as you in learned Chapter 2, the prestige and competence implicit in professional status are significant factors contributing to effective service outcomes. However, when helping professionals begin to view themselves as "somebodies" and others as "nobodies," the beneficial aspects of the differential status can easily turn into the deleterious effects of rankism.

In communications with and about others, a prominent sign of rankism is judgmental reference to "us" and "them" or sometimes to "you" and "them." In their efforts to understand and support clients, social workers may unwittingly adopt moral metaphors that actually hinder their professional efforts.

Perhaps the most well-known depiction of a common moral metaphor is the "dramatic triangle." Apparent in the Greek tragedies and many novels, plays, movies, TV soap operas, and in common gossip, the triangle reflects tension or conflict among three parties, forces, themes, or perspectives. A typical form includes a *hero* or *heroine* who confronts a *villain* or an *obstacle* to rescue a worthy or desirable *victim*.

Although the concept of dramatic triangles is commonly applied in literary criticism, they are also readily apparent in most cultural mythologies (Campbell, 1972; Campbell & Moyers, 1988), religions (Campbell, 1986), and political philosophies (Morone, 2003). Wartime tends to emphasize moral metaphors and dramatic triangles where one country, tribe, people, or coalition is viewed as "good," another as "bad," and a third as "victimized." The European theater of World War II provides a clear example of the morally based triangle: Great Britain, the United States, and their allies tend to represent the "good" coalition whereas Hitler and the Nazis represent the "bad" and the innocent victims included Poland, Belgium, France, and other countries invaded by Hitler's forces. Much later in the war, disturbingly so, Jews, Gypsies, gay and lesbian persons, and other cultural groups imprisoned and murdered during the Holocaust were finally formally identified and recognized as victims.

U.S. President George W. Bush's reference to an "axis of evil" represents another illustration of the use of triangular moral metaphors. The governments of certain countries are categorized as "evil," their oppressed citizens as "innocent," and the United States and its allies as "beneficent protectors." As is common in such triangles, however, the roles often shift—sometimes quite rapidly. A victim's view of a rescuer can quickly change from hero to persecutor or oppressor. Indeed, a victim can sometimes feel quite victimized by a rescuer soon after the purported rescue.

Communications within family systems often reflect triangular patterns, and they appear regularly within the context of social worker and client relationships as well. A typical form—at least from the point of view of the social worker—involves the assumption of the role of hero or heroine, the client as innocent victim, and selected other people or forces as villainous. A common variation occurs when the client is viewed as villainous or sinful (e.g., a substance abusing person or an offender of some sort), other persons as victims of the sinner, and the social worker as minister who hopes to help the sinner by changing his evil ways. Views derived from morally based triangles have enormous psychosocial, religious, political, and even advertising power. However, when unwittingly adopted by social workers, they can interfere with their professionalism and their helpfulness to clients.

Karpman referred to a common "drama triangle" in families, groups, and organizations that includes the roles or positions of Persecutor, Victim, and Rescuer (Karpman, 1968, 1971). Of course, these terms convey potentially negative connotations and simultaneously reflect rankism. The persecutor demeans and subordinates the victim; the rescuer—sometimes from a position of moral superiority—attempts to obtain the freedom and secure the safety of the vulnerable person or group. Occasionally, the rescue may occur without the implicit or explicit consent of the rescued and, of course, the rescuer may need to combat, defeat, control, or subordinate the persecutor in the process.

Learning about other peoples and their cultures, becoming aware of the many forms of rankism, and considering the nature and implications of various metaphors and conceptualizations are usually extraordinarily enriching endeavors—both personally and professionally. However, be aware of the dangers of stereotyping and overgeneralizing. The power of mass media, public education, and mainstream culture is such that other cultures tend to become quickly assimilated or acculturated. The often-dramatic differences between the first and third generations of immigrant families typify the speed with which cultures adapt to new social environments. Similarly, the amount of wealth, extent of formal education, age, degree of isolation from other groups, all influence the rate and extent to which adaptation occurs. Members of cultural groups vary greatly from one another. Indeed, individual differences within a culture may sometimes exceed group differences between cultures. Neither "we" nor "they" are "all the same."

Balance your growing knowledge of cultural groups with a consistent reminder that "diversity exists within diverse cultural groups." Consider this example: It is fairly common practice to assign a racial or ethnic category to people based on their physical characteristics. Some human service professionals may "check" a racial or ethnic category on an intake form because "he looks Hispanic." Such practices are extremely unwise. The person so labeled may think of himself as "Puerto Rican" rather than Hispanic. A woman classified as Asian might view herself as Thai, or that "white boy" might proudly consider himself part Cherokee.

Be aware of the strong psychosocial tendencies toward stereotyping, overgeneralization, rankism, and that extremely tempting process of "making assumptions." The most respectful approach is to ask the person about whom a categorization is to be made: "What is your racial or ethnic group?" If the answer does not fit the list of categories, add a new one!

To communicate productively with others, you require skills in *talking*—sending messages—as well as in *listening*—receiving messages. Skills in *active listening* are also needed. Active listening is that form of communication in which you expressively demonstrate that you have understood what the other has said.

Most people find it extremely challenging to communicate fully and accurately with one another. Social workers—and university professors—are no exception. Among the common errors social workers make in talking and listening are the following:

◆ Interacting in a patronizing or condescending manner
◆ Interrogating rather than interviewing by asking questions in rapid, staccato fashion

- Focusing on themselves (e.g., formulating questions before understanding the other's message, self-consciously monitoring their internal experiences, evaluating their own performance)
- Attending predominantly to a single dimension of a person's experience (e.g., just thoughts or just feelings; only the personal or only the situational; just the negative or just the positive)
- Interrupting frequently with a comment or question
- Failing to listen or remember, or selectively listening with an "agenda" so that messages are interpreted to match their own beliefs and opinions
- Neglecting to use a person's name, mispronouncing or changing it (e.g., referring to "Catherine" as "Cathy" or "Josef" as "Joe"), or assuming a degree of formality or informality that does not match that of the client's (e.g., "Mr. Jones" when he would prefer "Bill," or "Jane" when she prefers "Mrs. Smith")
- Neglecting to consider the cultural meaning of the interview for a particular person or family
- Failing to demonstrate understanding through active listening
- Using terms that stereotype people or groups
- Offering suggestions or proposing solutions too early in the process (on the basis of incomplete or inaccurate understanding of the person-issue-situation)
- Making statements in absolutist terms (e.g., *always*, *never*, *all*, or *none*)
- Disclosing one's own personal feelings and opinions or sharing life experiences prematurely
- Confronting or challenging a person before establishing a base of accurate understanding and a solid relationship
- Speculating about causes of issues before adequately exploring the person-issue-situation
- Pushing for action or progress from a person prematurely
- Using clichés and jargon
- Making critical or judgmental comments, including pejorative remarks about other persons or groups (e.g., other professionals, agencies, and organizations)
- Displaying inappropriate or disproportionate emotions (e.g., acting extraordinarily happy to meet a new client or sobbing uncontrollably when a person expresses painful feelings)

The words you choose, the sound and pitch of your voice, the rate and delivery of your speech, and your use of the language may suggest a great deal to clients and others with whom you interact.[2] During a typical first contact—whether face-to-face, via telephone, or by letter, fax or email—use easily understandable words and phrases. Keep it simple. Save arcane and esoteric language for professors! Avoid evaluative

---

[2] If you use augmented communication systems or other forms of "talking" (e.g., sign language) that do not involve voice and speech, please consider their potential effects on communication with others. Just as "tone of voice" may have meaning in a conversation between hearing persons, a signed message may convey "tone" as well.

terms. Even words such as *good*, *okay*, or *right*—through which you intend to convey support and encouragement—may suggest to a client that you regularly make judgments about people. A client may think, "If you judge me or my actions positively without knowing much about me, can you really be objective?" Or, perhaps, "At this point, you approve of me. I'd better not say anything that might lead you to disapprove. I guess I'll keep my real issues to myself."

Especially during the early stages of work, be careful about sharing opinions or hypotheses. Use of diagnostic medical or psychological terminology and legal jargon may suggest to clients that you are reaching conclusions about them or their situation before fully understanding all the intricacies of their circumstances. Labels of all kinds, even positive ones, can significantly affect the tenor of your relationships with clients and the course of your work together. Variations of the verb *to be* often result in a labeling effect. Suppose, for example, that you were to say the sentence, "He is a child abuser." Because the word *is* suggests an equivalence between *he* and *child abuser* (i.e., *he* equals *child abuser*), we would tend to view that human being through the conceptual screen of "child abuser." Rather than a human being who has abused a child, he becomes a child abuser who might possibly have some human qualities.

Of course, child abuse should not be tolerated. Perhaps especially among social workers, such offenses tend to elicit strong emotional reactions. However, even terms that are not so emotionally laden can have deleterious labeling effects. When you think or say, "She is young," "They were foolish," "He was manipulative," "She is seductive," "He is aggressive," "They are poor," "He is white," "He is disabled," or "She is unmarried," you reflect conclusions that are primarily derived from your own rather than from others' experience of themselves.

The human being convicted of the crime of child abuse may experience himself as a weak, impulsive person guilty of a terrible sin. The person who appears to you to be young may experience herself as old beyond her years. Indeed, she may even question her own sexual identity and wonder if she is truly female. The behavior that you consider foolish may have resulted from an excruciating examination of various possibilities. The manipulation that you infer may represent an attempt to maintain a sense of personal control or perhaps salvage some dignity by a person who feels humiliated. What you perceive as seductive may, in that person's family and culture, be a naturally warm and friendly interpersonal gesture. What you consider aggressive may constitute an effort to counter powerful feelings of fear and anxiety. What you see as poverty may be experienced by someone else as freedom from petty pursuit of money and material goods. The person you regard as a white male might view himself as Hispanic and may have adopted an androgynous philosophy in which the concepts of male and female or masculine and feminine have little relevance. The man you think is disabled may regularly play wheelchair basketball and tennis and possess computer skills beyond any you can imagine. And the person you consider unmarried may have long ago determined for herself that the institution of marriage was anathema to a liberated perspective.

Hypotheses, inferences, speculation, and labels about people are risky at all times, especially during the early phases of a relationship. As you interact with others, try to adopt the frame of reference of the person who is communicating. Be careful when you use forms of the verb *to be*. In general, try to use words that are descriptive rather than inferential, and simple rather than complex.

You may be tempted to make generalizations about people, perhaps because of their perceived membership in a certain class or group (e.g., male, female, poor, rich, black, white, Italian, disabled, diabetic, Catholic). As a social worker, you should, of course, be aware of sociological theory and research related to different groups, especially cultural groups common to your community, and populations generally at risk of oppression, exploitation, and discrimination. For example, in talking and listening with clients, you should be aware of research suggesting that men and women tend to adopt different conversational styles (Basow & Rubenfeld, 2003; Clark, 1993; Gray, 1992; Leaper, 1991; Mulac, 1998; Mulac, Bradac, & Gibbons, 2001; Nadler & Nadler, 2001; Tannen, 1990, 1994); that Native American clients may find a social worker's personal questions about their "individual identity" to be intrusive (Blount et al., 1992; Good Tracks, 1973; Heart, 2001; Lewis & Ho, 1975) or even foreign (Hobfoll, Jackson, Hobfoll, Pierce, & Young, 2002; LaFromboise, 1992; Mihesuah, 1996; Nelson, McCoy, Stetter, & Vanderwagen, 1992; Shutiva, 1994; Sutton & Nose, 1996); and that Latino clients may prefer a longer, more informal process of beginning (Aguilar, 1972; Bradford, Meyers, & Kane, 1999; Castex, 1996; Wodarski, 1992c; Zuniga, 2001). However, in using such knowledge, be alert to the danger of stereotyping. Many men use conversational styles quite different from many women, but *some* men adopt conversational styles that are quite similar to that of many women. *Some* Native Americans experience personal questions from a social worker as an expression of interest and concern, and *some* Latino clients prefer a direct, businesslike approach as they begin with a social worker. All women are not the same; nor are all men, all people of color, all children, all gay or lesbian persons, or even all professors! Therefore, be sensitive to and carefully consider the person's sex, class, ethnicity, able-ness, sexual orientation, religion, and cultural affiliation, but recognize that each individual client is unique. Each person will probably differ, at least to some extent, from common characteristics of the "average" member of his or her class or group.

As an interview proceeds, you may attempt to match the client's language mode. Some people favor words associated with *hearing;* others prefer those identified with *seeing;* still others like words that indicate *sensing* or *touching*. For example, if you use words such as *hear, sound, noise, loud,* or *soft* with people who favor an auditory language mode, you increase the probability of being understood and valued by them. A similarly favorable reaction is likely if you were to use *see, view,* and *perceive* with people who prefer a visual language mode, or *feel, sense,* and *touch* with those who favor tactile language (Bandler & Grinder, 1979, pp. 5–78).

In general, try to adopt a speaking style that is moderate in tone and speed of delivery. Through your speech, and language, convey that you are truly interested in what the client has to say (Ivey, 1988, p. 22). Sometimes, however, you may deliberately increase or decrease your rate of speech to match the pace of the client. On other occasions, you may purposely slow your pace to lead a fast-talking client into a slower speaking mode. In some circumstances (e.g., when working with a client with some loss of hearing), you may need to lower the pitch of your voice to be more audible. Generally, when you speak or write, active voice is preferable to passive voice, and each unit of speech should not be so long or complex as to impede understanding.

◆ EXERCISE 4-1: CULTURALLY COMPETENT COMMUNICATIONS

Complete the following exercises to become more aware of the nature of your speech and language patterns.[3]

1. Imagine that you work in an agency that provides a wide range of social services. You are about to meet for the first time with a prospective client who is dramatically different from you. If you are female, you might pretend the client is male. If you are Caucasian, you might imagine that the client is a person of color. If you are tall, you might assume that the client is of shorter stature. If you are well educated, you might consider the client to be poorly educated. If you are middle-class, your might pretend that the client is virtually penniless. If you have a residence, you might presume that the client is homeless. If you are hearing, you might imagine being hard-of-hearing. If you are sighted, you might assume you are blind. If you are able-bodied, you might imagine that you ambulate with a wheelchair. Now, use a recording device (e.g., audio or video) to capture yourself as you express the words you would say or sign as you begin work with this prospective client. Introduce yourself, describe something about the kinds of services your agency might be able to provide, and ask this imaginary person some of the questions you would like to ask. Continue this imaginary introduction for approximately three minutes.

   Now replay the recording and review your language usage. Examine the words you said and consider them from the point of view of the imaginary person you have created for this exercise. How would your prospective client be likely to experience the words and language you have chosen to use? If you have used spoken words, consider the implications for your vocal and speech patterns.

   In the space provided, indicate what you have learned through this exercise that may relate to your roles and functions as a professional social worker. In particular, consider how your use of speech and language is likely to be experienced by persons different from yourself in terms of age, sex, skin color, sexual orientation, educational background, socioeconomic status, ethnicity, physical appearance and ability, and other factors that distinguish human beings from one another.

---

[3] If you communicate primarily through sign language, computer-mediated speech, or some other means, please approximate this exercise in the message-sending mode you will use with clients. Be sure to consider the implications of your challenges in your analysis.

Nonverbal Communications and Body Language

A great deal of human communication is nonverbal. As a social worker, you should be keenly aware of the significance of body language. Factors such as posture, facial expression, eye contact, gait, and body positioning represent important forms of communication (Ivey, 1988; Kadushin & Kadushin, 1997).[4] In professional encounters with others, your body language should generally be congruent with your verbal language. Clients often notice discrepancies and incongruities between what you say verbally and what you express nonverbally. When you present yourself in an incongruent fashion, others may be confused about you and your message. When you express yourself congruently, people are more likely to understand your communications and to experience you as genuine and sincere.

In addition to verbal and nonverbal congruence, your body language should communicate attention and interest in the other person, as well as caring, concern, respect, and authenticity. On many occasions, you will need to express your message in an assertive manner that conveys authority. To emphasize one element or another, changes in body language may be necessary.

When beginning interviews with prospective clients, you should typically adopt an open or accessible body position (Egan, 1982a, pp. 60–62). If standing, you may hold your arms and hands loosely along your sides. If seated, you can place your hands on your lap. Arms held across the chest, behind the head, or draped over an adjoining chair may reflect inattention or nonreceptiveness. Tightly clasped hands, swinging legs or feet, pacing, looking at a watch or clock, or drumming fingers tend to communicate nervousness or impatience. Slouching in a chair may suggest fatigue or disinterest. Sometimes, however, you may need to assume an informal body position to increase the comfort and decrease the threat experienced by another person. For example, in working with children, you might sit on the floor and talk while playing a game. With teenage clients, significant encounters may occur while sharing a soft drink, shooting pool, or leaning against a fence or wall. Important exchanges may take place while you transport a client to a doctor's office or a food pantry, while you help a parent change a baby's diaper, or while you enjoy a snack together.

The frequency and intensity of eye contact varies according to the people involved, the purpose of the meeting, the topic under discussion, and a host of other factors. In general, you should adopt seating or standing arrangements that allow for but do not force eye contact between the participants. Although it is common for social workers to attempt rather frequent eye contact, especially when clients are talking, the degree and intensity should vary according to the individual and cultural characteristics of the person, the issues of concern, and the context of the meeting. In many cultures, regular eye contact is experienced as positive, but in several others, it is not. "Some cultural groups (for instance, certain Native American, Eskimo, or aboriginal

---

[4] If you are visually or hearing challenged, or move about with assistance (e.g., wheelchair, walking aids, guide dog), please reflect on the potential nonverbal communication effects on clients and colleagues. Also, consider how you might best address the nonverbal dimension of communication in your service to others.

Australian groups) generally avoid eye contact, especially when talking about serious subjects" (Ivey, 1988, p. 27). Dropping one's eyes to avoid direct eye contact, in certain cultures, conveys respect, whereas steady, direct eye contact signifies disapproval. For some groups, eye contact is more likely when talking than when listening, but the exact opposite is true in other cultures.

In all cases, however, you should not stare. Staring almost universally constitutes a violation of the other's territorial space and may be experienced as a challenge. It may also suggest a power differential. Many persons of majority status and those affiliated with favored groups feel entitled to look at, peruse, and even stare at people of minority or less favored status. For example, many men believe it quite acceptable to stare at women. In North America, many Caucasians find it quite permissible to watch and observe people of color. There are numerous other examples. However, as a social worker interested in relationships characterized by equality, mutual respect, and joint participation, your eye contact should never be so intense or continuous that it becomes an intrusion, a privacy violation, or a form of intimidation or superior rank.

Attending (Carkhuff & Anthony, 1979, pp. 31–60) is a term frequently used to describe the process of nonverbally communicating to others that you are open, nonjudgmental, accepting of them as people, and interested in what they say. A general purpose of attending is, in fact, to encourage others to express themselves as fully and as freely as possible. During the beginning phase especially, your nonverbal presentation is at least as important as any other factor in influencing clients' responses to you.

There is a substantial literature regarding the skill of attending. For example, Carkhuff and Anthony (1979, pp. 39–42) suggest that counselors face their clients squarely, at a distance of three to four feet, without tables or other potential obstacles between the participants. They further recommend regular eye contact, facial expressions showing interest and concern, and a slight lean or incline toward the other person.

Many of these guidelines are useful, but they tend to reflect nonverbal characteristics common among adult, majority-member, middle- and upper-class North Americans. Many children, members of ethnic minority groups, and people of lower socioeconomic status commonly demonstrate quite different nonverbal characteristics in their social interactions. Facing some people too directly, too squarely, and too closely may infringe on personal territory and privacy. For others, a distance of four feet would be much too far for an intimate conversation. Therefore, please be flexible in your attending and physical positioning. Closely observe the nonverbal expressions of the other person and respect them. Also, within these general guidelines, assume a comfortable body position. Trying to understand another person requires energy and concentration. If you are distracted by discomfort, you may become less attentive. Do not, however, assume such a comfortable position that you lose interest. Dozing off during an interview does not convey attention and concern!

When seated positions are desirable and available (e.g., when interviewing an adult in an office setting), place the chairs so that they create an angle of between 90 and 135 degrees. This allows other people to direct their eyes and bodies toward or away from you as desired, and it affords you the same opportunity. Matching, movable chairs are preferred for their flexibility and to avoid symbolic distinction between your chair and clients'. Physically leaning toward clients at points when they are sharing emotionally charged material usually demonstrates concern and compassion. However, carefully observe their reactions. Some clients may find the added closeness too intimate or even intrusive, especially during the early stages of the working relationship.

Of course, many times you have limited control over the placement of chairs or even the interview setting. Often an exchange occurs during a walk or an automobile drive, in a kitchen during mealtime, while someone cares for children, and sometimes even while a person watches television. As a relationship develops and you begin to understand the meaning of various gestures to the client, it may become possible to ask to move a chair closer or to lower the volume on the television. Such requests may be quite meaningful to clients as they realize that you actually do want to hear what they say!

◆ EXERCISE 4-2: NONVERBAL COMMUNICATIONS AND BODY LANGUAGE

Recruit a friend or colleague to join you in a few nonverbal experiments.[5]

1. Maintaining eye contact, slowly move toward your partner, who remains in position, until it becomes uncomfortable for you. Then stop. Observe the approximate distance between you. Describe your thoughts and feelings as you moved closer and closer to your partner. Ask your partner to express what he or she experienced as you approached. Make note of your experience as well as your partner's.

2. Position yourself face-to-face with your partner at a distance of approximately four feet. Look directly into his or her eyes until you become uncomfortable. When that occurs, simply avert your eyes. Now, move to three feet, then to two feet, each time looking directly into your partner's eyes until you experience discomfort. Then turn away. Share your reactions with each other.

---

[5] If you are visually or physically challenged in some way, please adapt these exercises accordingly. Be sure to incorporate the implications of your challenges in your discussions.

Now, experiment with different kinds and degrees of eye contact within a two-to-four-foot range. For example, try looking at your partner's cheekbone or mouth instead of directly into her or his eyes. Share your reactions. Experiment further by looking into your partner's eyes for several seconds and then slightly change your focus so that you look at a cheekbone for a few seconds, and then return your gaze to the eyes. Follow that by looking at your partner's mouth for a few seconds, and then return to the eyes. Share your responses to this manner of eye contact. Make note of the form of eye contact you and your partner seem to prefer as well as those that you dislike.

3. Place two chairs squarely facing one another (front to front) approximately two feet apart. Be seated. Share your thoughts and feelings as you sit face-to-face and knee-to-knee. Is it comfortable for both of you, for only one, for neither? If it is uncomfortable, alter the distance until it becomes comfortable. Ask your partner to do the same. Finally, compromising if necessary, move the chairs until they are placed at a mutually comfortable distance. Make note of your partner's remarks as well as your own experiences in this exercise.

4. Change the placement of the chairs so that instead of directly facing each other, they now are side by side in parallel position, approximately six inches apart. As you and your partner take your seats, share your respective thoughts and feelings. Now increase the angle so that the chairs form a 90-degree angle. Share with one another your reactions to this arrangement. Now increase the angle an additional 45 degrees. Describe your reactions to this position. Which arrangement does your partner prefer? Which do you?

5. Based on the results of your experimentation, place the chairs in the position and at the angle that is reasonably comfortable for both you and your partner. Some compromise may be necessary. Now, maintaining a more or less neutral facial expression and without saying a word, try to show through your body language, but without changing your facial expression, that you care about your partner and are interested in his or her thoughts and feelings. Continue to experiment with three or four different body positions, attempting to demonstrate concern and interest, for approximately one minute each. Following each position, seek verbal feedback from your partner concerning her or his reactions. Make note of your partner's comments as well as your own reactions.

6. Based on what you have learned through your experimentation with various body positions, assume a position that your partner indicates reflects caring and interest. Now begin to experiment with different facial expressions. First, let your face become relaxed in its more or less usual state. Retain this facial expression for about one minute while your partner experiences the effect. After a minute, seek feedback from your partner about his or her observations and reactions. Then experiment with other facial expressions through which you hope to express silently, in turn, affection, compassion, joy, sadness, disappointment, disapproval, fear, and anger. Hold each facial expression for a minute or so while your partner tries to determine the feeling you are trying to express. Note your respective thoughts and feelings about this exercise.

7. In the following space, summarize what you discovered from these nonverbal experiments that may help you to become a more effective social worker.

Listening

Listening involves the use of your sensory capacities to receive and register the messages expressed verbally and nonverbally by others.[6] The listening skills include *hearing* or *receiving* others' words, speech, and language; *observing* (Carkhuff & Anthony, 1979, pp. 42–47) their nonverbal gestures and positions; *encouraging* (Ivey, 1988, pp. 93–95) them to express themselves fully; and *remembering* what they communicate. Most people are rather poor listeners, tending to pay more attention to their own thoughts and feelings than to the messages others are trying to convey. Competent listening rarely comes naturally. Yet listening, perhaps more than any other skill, is essential for effective social work practice. It requires two actions. First, you minimize attention to your own experiences (e.g., thoughts, feelings, and sensations). Then, you energetically concentrate on the client with a determination to understand—not to evaluate—what the client is experiencing and expressing.

For most people, being truly understood by another person is one of the genuinely humanizing events in life. It conveys respect. It demonstrates that you value them and are interested in what they have to say. In a real sense, careful listening is a gesture of love. Because of this, listening is a dynamic factor in social work practice. It has several purposes. First, effective listening enables you to gather information essential for assessment and planning. Second, it helps clients feel better—often reducing tension or anxiety, heightening feelings of personal safety and well-being, and encouraging greater hope and optimism. Third, attentive listening encourages clients to express themselves freely and fully. Fourth, effective listening usually enhances your value to clients. Finally, attentive listening often contributes significantly to positive change in clients' self-understanding, self-efficacy, problem-solving, and goal-seeking capacities.

To listen effectively, you need to manage your own impulses, tendencies, and predispositions. Containing self (Shulman, 1984, p. 61; 1992, pp. 115–116) is essentially a matter of restraint, self-control, and self-discipline. You hold back from fully experiencing and freely expressing your own reactions, ideas, or opinions. Containing self involves temporarily suspending judgment and action so you can better hear and understand other people. As a social worker, you are probably highly motivated to help people who are troubled. In your desire to serve, you may sometimes be tempted to rush to conclusions and solutions. Although immediate intervention is certainly warranted in life-threatening situations, engaging in premature assessment, advice, or action interferes with effective listening. Frequently, it also has unintended adverse consequences. In most circumstances, you would be wise to listen carefully and fully before assessing or intervening. As Shulman (1984, p. 61) suggests, "Workers who attempt to find simple solutions often discover that if the solutions were indeed that simple, then the client could have found them alone without the help of the worker."

---

[6] If you have hearing loss, please reflect upon the potential implications for clients and colleagues. Also, consider how you might use other resources in your efforts to understand the meaning of others' messages.

Containing self is related to the use of silence. Social workers "frequently perceive silence as a hindrance and a hazard to the progress of the interview. . . . The professional assumption is that talking is better" (Kadushin, 1983, p. 286). This is certainly not always the case. Periods of silence, pauses in the exchange, are vital elements in effective communication. Of course, you should not let silence continue so long that it becomes a test to see "who will speak first" (Shulman, 1984, p. 63). However, do recognize that with some clients, at certain moments, silence can be a powerfully helpful experience. "Instead of a threat, silence should be seen and utilized as an opportunity" (Kadushin, 1983, p. 294).

Hearing refers to the process of listening (i.e., receiving messages) that involves attending to the speech and language of other people. Hearing can be prevented or impeded by numerous factors. A room might be noisy, or another person might speak in a soft or mumbled fashion, a foreign language, or an unfamiliar dialect. Another person might use words you do not understand or in ways that differ from your understanding of those words. Effective hearing involves diminishing the obstacles and focusing entirely on the words and sounds of the other person. It also involves reducing tendencies to hear selectively as a result of judging, comparing, criticizing, or evaluating the words and sounds of the other person. In attempting to hear clearly, you hope to take in and remember the messages sent by the speaker. In listening, *process* is as important as content. Therefore, try to hear more than the words themselves. Listen as well to the person's manner of speaking. Try to hear the meaning and feeling just beyond or beneath the words that are actually said.

Another vital element in the listening process is the skill of observation. *Observing* (Carkhuff & Anthony, 1979, pp. 42–47) occurs when you pay attention to the client's physical characteristics, gestures, and other nonverbal behavior. Nonverbal communications are at least as informative as verbal expression, and sometimes more. As a social worker, try to observe nonverbal manifestations of energy level, mood, and emotions. Quite often, clients do not directly express their feelings through verbal speech. Without staring, try to observe carefully so you notice nonverbal expression of feelings.

The purpose of observing is to gain a better and more complete understanding of the ways in which the client experiences the world. During interviews, attend to subtle or indirect communications. These may relate to themes of power or authority, ambivalence about seeking or receiving help, difficulties in discussing topics that involve a stigma or taboo, and inhibitions concerning the direct and full expression of powerful feelings (Shulman, 1984, pp. 20–22, 85–91). You are often more likely to pick up indirect communications from nonverbal rather than verbal expressions, so observe closely. Be careful, however, to avoid the tempting conceptual trap of reaching conclusions. The most you can do is formulate a tentative hypothesis about a theme based on the words and the nonverbal gestures a client used. Such tentative hypotheses are not, in any sense, true or valid. They represent, rather, preliminary hunches!

Among the specific aspects to observe are (1) facial expression, (2) eye contact, and (3) body language, position, and movement. When observing, look for predominant facial expressions, head and body positions, physical gestures, and patterns of eye contact during communication exchanges. Also look for the nature and timing of changes in these nonverbal indicators. These may suggest feeling states such as contentment, calmness, acceptance, joy, sadness, fear or anxiety, and anger. Based on these observations, ask yourself what these expressions, gestures, and behaviors might suggest about how this person experiences her- or himself and the issue of concern. Also, consider what the person might think and feel about you and this meeting.

Encouraging (Ivey, 1988, pp. 93–94) is form of listening that involves some talking. You can encourage other people to continue expressing themselves by making very brief responses in the form of single words, short phrases, or sounds and gestures that invite them to continue their expression. Some examples of brief verbal encouragers are *Please go on; and?; Uh huh; Mmmm; Yes; Please continue.* Nonverbally, you may further communication by nodding, making attentive eye contact or certain hand motions, and leaning or inclining slightly toward the client.

Repeating a portion of a phrase or a key word that a client uses may also constitute encouragement. Such brief responses enable you to demonstrate that you want to hear more, without interrupting with a lengthy statement of your own. However, be sure you avoid using the same encouragers repeatedly. After a while, their repeated use may suggest a lack of sincerity. Also be aware that encouraging is not sufficient in itself to demonstrate empathic understanding. More complete communications in the form of *active listening* are necessary for that.

The final dimension of listening involves *remembering* what the client communicates. Hearing and observing are skills without much inherent value unless you can retain the information received. Remembering is the process of temporarily storing information so that it may later be used, for example, to communicate understanding, make thematic connections between messages expressed at different times, prepare a written record, or develop an assessment.

◆ EXERCISE 4-3: LISTENING

Recruit a friend or colleague to join you in a listening exercise. Indicate that the purpose of this exercise is to determine how well you can understand and remember what is said. Tell your partner that you would like to record (e.g., audiotape or videotape) a conversation between the two of you and, following the conversation but before replaying the tape, you will attempt to write down what was said. Then you will compare what you remember with what was tape-recorded. Ask your partner to identify a topic of interest that the two of you might discuss for approximately ten minutes. As the listener, your tasks are to *encourage* your partner to discuss the subject; *hear, observe,* and *comprehend* what she or he communicated; and *remember* what was said and done. Keep in mind that your partner's perspective is paramount. Withhold your own opinions. This is your partner's time. Let the discussion proceed in whatever way and direction your partner wishes. Encourage him or her to communicate freely and fully, and try not to interfere with the flow of expression. As your partner talks, listen attentively and observe carefully. At the end of the ten-minute period, thank your partner and proceed with the following.

1. Ask your partner to rate on a scale of 0 to 10 (where 0 = did not listen at all and 10 = listened extremely well) how well she or he thinks you listened to what was said. Explore with your partner the reasons for the rating.

   Thank your partner again and say goodbye. Record your partner's rating and make note of his or her other comments, questions, and suggestions.

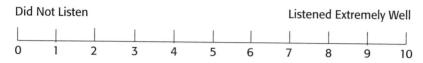

2. Now, before reviewing the tape recording, (a) try to reconstruct from memory (and word process or write on notepaper) the words your partner expressed during the discussion; (b) describe your partner's speech and language patterns; (c) prepare a physical description of your partner's clothing, hair and eye color, approximate height and weight, body build, and apparent physical condition; (d) describe your partner's predominant facial expression and body positions as well as any significant changes or gestures that occurred during the course of the conversation; and (e) based on these, tentatively hypothesize about your partner's overall mood and the primary emotions that she or he might have experienced during the exchange.

3. Now play the tape recording of the conversation. As you listen, compare it to the written account that you reconstructed from memory. Approximately what percentage of your partner's comments did you recall? Record your rating here.

Use the following space to identify factors that helped and those that impeded your ability to remember what was communicated. If your recall rating is less than 75%, develop a plan and a schedule for practicing the listening skills.

Active Listening

Active listening combines the talking and listening skills in such a way that others feel understood and encouraged toward further self-expression. It is a form of feedback. You listen carefully and communicate your understanding of a speaker's messages by reflecting or mirroring them back. In essence, you paraphrase the client's message. Ideally, your words should be essentially equivalent to or synonymous with those of the client. If factual information is expressed, your active listening response should convey that information. If feelings are communicated, your active listening response should reflect those feelings and should be of equivalent intensity. If ideas are expressed, you should paraphrase those ideas so that the other's meaning is accurately captured.

Active listening represents a clear and tangible demonstration that you have understood, or at least are trying to understand what a client has expressed. It indicates that you want to comprehend fully and accurately the messages communicated. Active listening shows that you are interested in the client's views, feelings, and experiences. Because it conveys empathy and furthers understanding, there is simply no substitute for active listening. It constitutes a major element of the vital feedback loop between you and your client. If you do not listen actively, you are more likely to miss part of a client's message and thereby misunderstand, distort, or misrepresent it. Furthermore, if you do not listen actively or if you do so in a consistently inaccurate fashion, you discourage the client from free and full expression. You also significantly diminish your own value in the relationship. Clients look forward to being understood. If you do not accurately communicate understanding, clients may feel unheard, disappointed, and alienated. Experiences of oppression, discrimination, abuse, or exploitation have left many clients feeling profoundly misunderstood throughout their lives. When you, as a professional social worker, communicate sincere and accurate understanding, the effect can be positive indeed. However, if the clients feel that you too, like so many before, also misunderstand, a powerfully adverse effect may result. Experiencing yet another repetition of alienation, such clients may wish they had never sought your services in the first place.

Active listening combines the talking and listening skills into three steps:

- ◆ *Step One: Inviting.* By your body position, facial expression, speech, and language you indicate that you are prepared to listen. Often, you can invite the other person to express himself or herself by asking a question such as "What happened?" or "How did this all come about?" It is not always necessary, however, to ask a specific question. Many clients begin to talk about themselves and their concerns as soon as you begin to attend to them with your eyes, face, and body.

- ◆ *Step Two: Listening.* When a client responds to your invitation to speak and begins to talk, you listen carefully by attempting to *hear, observe, encourage,* and *remember.* In this step, you essentially use your ears and brain to receive and retain the messages sent by the other person.

- ◆ *Step Three: Reflecting.* Periodically, as the client pauses at the conclusion of a message segment, paraphrase his or her statement. For example, a client might say, "I'm really frustrated with my boss. He says he wants production, production, production! But then he comes down to my shop and spends hours shooting the breeze." In active listening, you could say in response, "You're annoyed with him because he tells you he wants you to work harder and harder but then he interferes with you when you're trying to do so." Here is another example. Suppose a client says, "Ever since I was seven years old, I felt fat and ugly." You might say in active listening, "From the time of your childhood up through the present time you've thought of yourself as overweight and unattractive." By communicating an equivalent message, you demonstrate empathic understanding.

Active listening is, of course, most useful when you have accurately understood and paraphrased the client's message, but it can be helpful even when you have not. Sometimes a message is misunderstood or part of it is missed as your attention wanders; or the client may misspeak and send an incomplete or confusing message. In such cases, your sincere attempt to understand by active listening almost always elicits further expression from the client.

When your response accurately reflects the client's message, he or she may spontaneously confirm that fact by saying something such as, "Yeah, that's right." Then the client often simply continues to talk. On those occasions when your response is not entirely accurate but is close enough to demonstrate that you have heard some of the message and are genuinely trying to understand, the client may say, "Well, no. What I meant was . . ." He or she may then try to restate the message so that you can understand. However, when you are extremely inaccurate, perhaps due to your own lack of interest or attention, the client may very well respond with an emphatic "No!" and then become much less expressive. A similar phenomenon can occur when you do not actively listen frequently enough. If you only talk or only listen but do not actively listen, you may discourage clients from free and full expression.

Social workers tend to make several common errors when first developing skill in active listening:

- Using so many of the client's own words that your paraphrased reflections sound like mimicry
- Using the same lead-in phrases (e.g., "I hear you saying . . ." "It sounds like . . .") repeatedly
- Trying to be clever, profound, or interpretive—playing the role of "brilliant analyst" or "clever detective" tends to indicate that you are listening more to your own thoughts and speculations than to the client's message
- Responding only to facts, thoughts, and ideas, or just to feelings and emotions rather than active listening to all dimensions of the client's expression
- Interrupting frequently to reflect the client's message
- Using active listening following every short phrase or statement

◆ EXERCISE 4-4: ACTIVE LISTENING

In the spaces provided, write the words you might say in active listening to the following statements:

1. *CLIENT:* My life is in shambles. My wife is divorcing me and she's going to take me to the cleaners.

2. *SUPERVISOR:* I am disappointed that you did not follow up on the Sanchez case. You know that those children are at risk.

3. *PROFESSOR:* I wonder if the match between your personal values and those of the social work profession is a good one. It appears to me that your attitudes are quite different from those required of social workers.

4. *CLIENT:* My husband thinks I'm an alcoholic. I'm here because he made me come. Sure, I drink. I drink a lot. But he's the reason I drink.

5. *CLASSMATE:* I've missed the last three classes and don't know what's going on in here. Today is the day of the midterm exam and I know I'm going to flunk. I'm so uptight, I can't think straight.

6. *COLLEAGUE:* I am working with a family that is driving me up the wall. I know I have a problem here. I get so angry at this family for not trying to help themselves. I work so damn hard and they don't do a thing!

7. *CHILD:* Sometimes my mommy's boyfriend is mean to her. He hits her and she ends up crying a lot. I don't like him at all.

Summary

The basic interpersonal skills of talking and listening (i.e., sending and receiving messages) are fundamental to all aspects of human interaction, including the phases and processes of social work practice. To communicate effectively as a social worker, you use all the sensory faculties at your command in sending and receiving messages. In addition, you regularly combine the talking and listening skills in the form of active listening. Active listening conveys empathy by overtly demonstrating that you are making a genuine effort to understand.

◆ CHAPTER 4 SUMMARY EXERCISES

The following exercises are intended to aid you in refining the talking, listening, and active listening skills.

1. With the consent of a friend or colleague from another cultural tradition, make an audiotaped or videotaped recording of a 15-minute conversation. Indicate that you are trying to practice your interviewing skills and would like to conduct an interview about his or her choice of career. Inform your partner that she or he will not have to answer any questions about which there is discomfort. Also, be sure to tell your partner that your professor and perhaps some of your classmates may review the tape to provide feedback about the quality of your interviewing skills. During the interview, explore with your partner how she or he came to make the career choice. Explore influential and motivational factors. Ask about your partner's hopes and aspirations as well as issues and concerns regarding the chosen career.

   During the conversation, encourage your partner to share as much as possible about the career decision. Use the skills of talking, listening, and active listening. At the conclusion of the interview, ask your partner for feedback concerning the experience. Make note of his or her responses. Also, ask your partner to rate on a scale of 0 to 10 (where 0 = completely misunderstood and 10 = completely understood) how well you listened and understood what was said. Ask your partner to identify those factors that contributed to the rating. Thank your partner again and say goodbye. Use the following space to record your partner's rating and make note of other comments, questions, and suggestions.

Completely Misunderstood   Completely Understood

| 0 | 1 | 2 | 3 | 4 | 5 | 6 | 7 | 8 | 9 | 10 |

2. Consider your own reactions to the interview. How did you feel about the exchange? What did you like and what did you dislike about your part in the conversation? What would you do differently if you were to engage in the conversation again? Summarize your reactions in the following space.

3. Next, play the tape. Prepare a transcript that accurately reflects what was said and by whom. Identify the talking and the listening skills you used during the conversation. For example, identify as talking a statement you made or a question you asked that came from your frame of reference. Identify as active listening your attempts to communicate your understanding of your partner's expressions. Use the following format:

	Transcript	Skill Used
Interviewer	Record here the words you said.	Identify the talking and listening skill used, if any
Interviewee	Record here what the interviewee said.	

4. At the conclusion of the transcript, evaluate your use of the talking and active listening skills. How would you characterize this sample of your speech and language? Evaluate your choice of words and your language usage, particularly as it relates to the individual and cultural characteristics of the person you interviewed.

In this conversation, do you talk more or less than your partner? Do you tend to interrupt or to be interrupted? How many of your words are factual, descriptive, and informational in nature? What proportion suggests feelings or emotions? How much do you reveal your opinions or assumptions? Do you tend to use extraneous fillers such as *uhh* or *you know?* Are there indications of nervousness or tension? If so, what are they? Do your speech and language reflect interest in what your partner says? Does your colleague seem interested in what you have to say? What sources of evidence do you use to determine his or her degree of interest? If you could change anything about your speech and language, what would it be?

How often do you engage in active listening? Do you do so too often or not often enough? How accurate are you in your attempts to communicate understanding through active listening? Do your words equate to those of your partner? Does your partner appear to feel understood? Does your partner communicate fully, freely, and easily? Does she or he pause or hesitate at points during the interview? How do your partner's sex, age, class, ethnicity, and cultural affiliation influence the communication process? How does yours? In the space provided, summarize the major elements of your self-evaluation.

5. Consider your body position, body language, and facial expressions as revealed on the videotape or as you recall from memory. It may be particularly enlightening to view the videotape with the sound turned off. Evaluate the nonverbal dimensions of your communication during this interview. How well do you physically attend to your partner? What do you think your body position and body language communicate to your partner? What emotions do your facial expressions convey? What is the nature and extent of your eye contact? How comfortable and confident do you appear? How do factors such as your sex, age, class, ethnicity, and cultural affiliation affect your nonverbal style? Summarize your assessment in the space provided.

6. Consider your partner's nonverbal expressions as displayed on the videotape or as you recall from memory. Make note of facial expressions, eye contact, body position and body language, gestures and movements, and the rate and nature of speech. Indicate what you think are your partner's overall mood, predominant feelings, and energy level. What is your impression of your partner's general attitude about you, this meeting, and the topic of conversation? Would you say your partner is involved and interested in the exchange? Active? Cooperative? Responsive? How do your partner's sex, age, class, ethnicity, and cultural affiliation affect your impressions? Summarize your observations and conclusions in the following space.

7. Ask a colleague or instructor from the school of social work to evaluate your talking, listening, and active listening skills as reflected on the tape recording you made. Summarize his or her feedback in the space provided. With which points do you agree or disagree?

◆ CHAPTER 4 WORLD WIDE WEB EXERCISES

1. Go to the InfoTrac College Edition Web site at www.infotrac-college.com. Use your passcode to log in. Conduct a keyword search using the string "perspective taking" (include the quotation marks) to locate an article entitled "Perspective Taking: Imagining How Another Feels versus Imagining How You Would Feel" (Batson, Early, & Salvarani, 1997). Carefully read the research article, reflect on the findings, and use the following space to summarize its importance for you as an empathic listener.

2. Conduct a keyword search using the string "empathy another shoes" (without the quotation marks) to locate an article entitled "Empathy: Putting Yourself in Another Person's Shoes" (Donahue, 1997). Although the article is geared toward young people, it may help you to consider some aspects of empathic communication. Read the article and use the following space to summarize its importance for you as an empathic listener.

3. Conduct a keyword search using the string "Multicultural Counseling Competencies" (including the quotation marks) to locate an article entitled "Integrating Multicultural Counseling Competencies and Universal Helping Conditions in Culture-Specific Contexts" (Arredondo, 1998). Carefully review the article and use the following space to summarize its importance for your development as a culturally competent communicator.

4. Leave the InfoTrac College Edition Web site and go to the home page of the American Counseling Association at www.counseling.org. Click on "Resources" and then go to the section entitled "Multicultural & Diversity Issues" to locate an outline of "Cross-Cultural Competencies and Objectives" that informs curriculum development for counseling students in the United States. Review the outline and compare them with the NASW Standards for Cultural Competence in Social Work Practice that you considered in the first World Wide Web exercise in Chapter 3. The NASW Standards are available at www.socialworkers.org/sections/credentials/cultural_comp.asp. Use the following space to highlight the major distinctions in the two documents.

Chapter 4 Self-Appraisal

As you conclude this chapter, please assess your proficiency in the basic talking and listening skills by completing the following self-appraisal exercise.

SELF-APPRAISAL: THE TALKING AND LISTENING SKILLS

Please respond to the following items to help you undertake a self-assessment of your proficiency in the basic interpersonal skills addressed in this chapter. Read each statement carefully. Then, use the following four-point rating scale to indicate the degree to which you agree or disagree with each statement. Record your numerical response in the space provided:

4 = Strongly Agree

3 = Agree

2 = Disagree

1 = Strongly Disagree

_____ 1. I can effectively use nonverbal communications and body language skills.

_____ 2. I can effectively use the talking skills.

_____ 3. I can effectively use the listening skills.

_____ 4. I can effectively use active-listening skills.

_____   Subtotal

Note: These items are taken directly from the basic interpersonal skills section of the Social Work Skills Self-Appraisal Questionnaire contained in Appendix 3. Earlier, when you reviewed Chapter 2 and completed the exercises, you responded to these questions. You may now compare the responses you made on that occasion with those you made this time. Also compare the two subtotals. If you believe that you have progressed in your proficiency with the basic interpersonal skills, the more recent subtotal should be higher than the earlier.

Finally, reflect on the skills addressed in this chapter and the results of your self-appraisal. Based on your analysis, prepare a succinct one-page summary report entitled "Self-Assessment of Proficiency in the Basic Skills of Talking and Listening." Within the report, be sure to identify those skills that you know and do well (e.g., a score of 3 or 4). Also, specify those that need further practice (e.g., scores of 2 or less) and briefly outline plans by which to achieve proficiency in them. When finished, include the report in your Social Work Skills Learning Portfolio.

Chapter 5

Preparing

This chapter (see Box 5.1) is intended to help you learn the skills used in the preparing phase of social work practice. First meetings set the tone and influence the general direction of subsequent interactions. In fact, the nature of your initial contacts with prospective clients often determines whether they return and actually become clients. Preparation becomes essential for social workers who tend to encounter persons of diverse cultural traditions struggling with highly complex and extremely challenging issues (Gleeson & Philbin, 1996; Kovacs & Bronstein, 1999; Reeves, 1997; Sar, 2000).

In a meta-analysis of some 125 research studies, Wierzbicki and Pekarik (1993) found that the average early dropout rate for outpatient psychotherapy services was approximately 47%—a remarkably high incidence. Client factors associated with early dropout included limited formal education, lower socioeconomic status, and racial minority status. In a study of nearly 14,000 persons served in 17 mental health centers, Sue (1977) discovered that when compared with Caucasian clients, a significantly greater percentage of minority applicants did not return following an initial visit. Differences between the personal and perhaps cultural expectations of clients and professional helpers represent the clearest explanation for early dropout. Indeed, when professional helpers failed to express accurate understanding of clients' views of the problem (i.e., how clients conceptualized the issues), the rate of dropout tripled (Epperson, Bushway, & Warman, 1983; Pekarik, 1988; Wierzbicki & Pekarik, 1993). Similarly, the actual length of therapeutic service appears to be determined primarily by clients' expectations of anticipated duration (Pekarik,

1991; Wierzbicki & Pekarik, 1993). Although several factors are undoubtedly involved with premature discontinuation, insufficient and ineffective preparation for first meetings is certainly part of the problem. Effective preparation and careful planning can make the difference.

BOX 5.1

Chapter Purpose

The purpose of this chapter is to help learners develop proficiency in the preparing skills.

Goals

Following completion of this chapter, learners should be able to demonstrate proficiency the following:

◆ Preparatory reviewing
◆ Preparatory exploring
◆ Preparatory consulting
◆ Preparatory arranging
◆ Preparatory empathy
◆ Preparatory self-exploration
◆ Centering
◆ Preliminary planning and recording
◆ Ability to assess proficiency in the preparing skills

You need to be personally and professionally ready to perform competently from the first moment of contact. You should use the preparing skills before the first meetings with clients and other persons with whom you interact as part of your professional responsibilities. Then continue to use them in advance of each subsequent encounter. The preparing skills include (1) preparatory reviewing, (2) preparatory exploring, (3) preparatory consulting, (4) preparatory arranging, (5) preparatory empathy, (6) preparatory self-exploration, (7) centering, and (8) preliminary planning and recording.

Preparatory Reviewing

Preparatory reviewing involves examining and considering information available to you and your agency before an initial contact with another person (Kadushin, 1983, pp. 136–137). When a prospective client has received service at the agency before, review the relevant records the agency has on file. When a telephone contact or in-person intake admissions interview has preceded the first visit, examine notes concerning the nature and substance of that interaction. For first meetings with other persons, such as an agency director, a client's medical doctor, or a new supervisee, thoughtfully review relevant materials concerning the general purpose for the meeting and any topics likely to be addressed.

Preparatory reviewing helps you grasp significant factual information. This reduces the need for applicants, clients, or other persons to repeat information they have previously provided. It allows for more efficient use of time and helps people feel that what they say is valued and remembered. In some instances, failure to review available materials could constitute professional negligence. For example, suppose a teenage boy contacts the agency. He has a history of making serious suicide attempts following conflicts in romantic relationships. Your agency has served him off and on during the past several years, and the pattern of previous suicide attempts is clearly recorded in his case file. He requests an appointment for some time later that day, indicating that he needs help because his girlfriend recently "dumped" him, deciding that she wanted to date another boy. If you fail to review the case record, you may decide to give the teenager an appointment several days from now, not realizing the serious risk of suicide.

There are also numerous practical reasons for reviewing relevant information before a visit. You may learn, for example, that a prospective client is hard-of-hearing or does not speak any of the languages spoken in your agency, so an interpreter will be required. You might find out that a client uses a wheelchair or is accompanied by a canine companion, so that a chair must be removed from your office to allow enough open space.

Although there are many benefits associated with the review of materials, there are potential dangers as well. Some records contain hearsay information or opinions that are expressed as if they were undisputed facts. You may inadvertently accept at face value information that is essentially false, distorted, biased, or superficial. Some records contain personality profiles or psychiatric diagnoses that can lead you to form a stereotypical impression of a person before you actually meet. Such profiles and diagnoses may have been inaccurate when initially recorded, or they may have since become so. The person, the issue, or the situation may have changed, sometimes dramatically. In preparatory reviewing, recognize that information contained in case records or other forms of written material may be incomplete or mistaken. It is vital that you maintain an open mind during the preparatory reviewing phase.

◆ EXERCISE 5-1: PREPARATORY REVIEWING

CASE EXAMPLE: At 10:13 A.M. on January 12, an agency intake worker received a telephone call from a woman identifying herself as Mrs. Nancy Cannon. The intake worker jotted a few notes concerning the call on a form entitled Telephone Intake Report. The intake worker later gave the report to you, the social worker assigned to conduct the initial face-to-face interview and, if appropriate, provide needed professional services.

TELEPHONE INTAKE REPORT

January 12, 10:13 A.M. Mrs. Nancy Cannon telephoned from her place of work (the Capital Insurance Company—phone 234-6213). She sounded concerned. She said that on the previous Saturday night, her 14-year-old daughter Amy had come home after her 9:00 P.M. curfew, smelling of alcohol. She says that she "grounded" her daughter but now wants to talk with a social worker about the situation. Mrs. Cannon requested an appointment for herself alone, indicating that she wanted to sort things out with someone before she dealt further with her daughter.

Mrs. C. reported that this was the first such incident. She said, "I've never had any trouble whatsoever from Amy. She's been a wonderful child." She stated that she had not sought professional help before and that this was her first contact with any social service or mental health agency. She indicated that her husband, Amy's father, had recently filed for divorce and had left the home approximately six weeks ago. Mrs. C. wondered whether that might be connected with Amy's misbehavior over the weekend.

Disposition: An appointment was scheduled with an agency social worker for tomorrow at 12:00 noon. Mrs. C. requested a lunch-hour appointment, if at all possible, to reduce the amount of time away from her job.

Demonstrate your use of the preparatory reviewing skill by examining this telephone intake report. Using a pen or marker, highlight the information contained in the report that you, as the social worker, would want to remember for a first meeting with Mrs. Cannon.

Preparatory Exploring

The skill of *preparatory exploring* involves asking questions about a prospective client and the situation. This is an important but often neglected skill. Receptionists and intake workers from your own agency may talk with prospective clients before you first meet with them. They may have useful information that can improve the quality of the first contact. Similarly, referring persons from outside your agency may have knowledge that can help. As part of making a referral on behalf of another person, physicians, judges, teachers, ministers, and, of course, family members often contact social service agencies. They may possess important information concerning the prospective client, the presenting issue and situation, and sometimes even the nature of the service needs. As a natural part of the process of talking about the referral to your agency, you may appropriately inquire about the person, issue, and situation. Usually, you would not have permission to seek information from other sources. For that, you would need the informed consent of the client. However, when someone makes a referral for someone else, you may explore the circumstances with the referring person. Regardless of the source of information, realize that what you hear from others tends to reflect their own perspectives. The client may view things in quite a different way, and you may too.

Preparatory exploring is also applicable for people previously served by colleagues in your own agency. For example, by reviewing agency files, you may learn that another social worker in the agency, Ms. Castillo, had previously served the client you are about to see. You could ask Ms. Castillo for pertinent information about the case.

The use of the preparatory exploring skill can result in a more positive and productive first meeting. However, information gained through the preparatory exploring process should not lead you to stereotype people or form fixed impressions about the nature of an issue and situation. You can resist such temptations by consciously distinguishing fact from opinion and recognizing that the views of one person are likely to differ from those of others.

In preparatory exploring, you remain open to information that may help you be a more effective service provider. Names and approximate ages of the persons involved are often noted; so are phone numbers, addresses, and other demographic data. Details concerning the nature, severity, and urgency of the issue are extremely important, as are indications of the strengths and resources available to the client.

◆ **EXERCISE 5-2: PREPARATORY EXPLORING**

CASE SITUATION: At 3:15 P.M. on Wednesday, you receive a telephone call from Father Julio Sanchez, a Catholic priest in a largely Mexican parish. He indicates that a family of seven needs help. He says that the parents and older children are migrant workers. He reports that the family had been traveling to a new work site when their automobile broke down.

In the space provided, write the questions you would ask and identify the information you would seek as you use the skill of preparatory exploring with Father Sanchez.

Preparatory Consulting

The skill of *preparatory consulting* involves seeking advice from a social work supervisor or colleagues concerning an upcoming visit with a prospective client or other person. Commonly, you would seek such consultation to identify tentative objectives for an interview or to discuss other related practice considerations. The specific nature of the consultation, however, varies from situation to situation. On one occasion, you might discuss possible locations for the interview. In another, you might inquire about cultural customs of a particular religious or ethnic group about which you have limited knowledge. On occasion, you might seek advice concerning how best to ensure your own safety when you are about to interview a person who has previously been physically violent toward people in positions of authority. In still another, you might focus on the agency policies or legal obligations that could apply in a particular case. By engaging in preparatory consultation, you can enhance the quality of initial meetings. The usually modest investment of time it takes to consult with a colleague or supervisor can pay significant dividends in effectiveness.

Of course, as you gain actual social work practice experience, the felt need for preparatory consultation will probably decrease. Nonetheless, ongoing consultation with colleagues and supervisors after initial meetings and during the course of service is often useful and sometimes needed. Even after years of experience, there are unexpected, unusually complicated circumstances where preparatory consultation can make the difference between a helpful or unhelpful beginning.

◆ **EXERCISE 5-3: PREPARATORY CONSULTING**

CASE SITUATION: You work in an agency serving an elderly population in the community. On Tuesday morning, a woman telephoned the agency and talked with you about her neighbor, Mrs. Anderson. According to the caller, Mrs. Anderson is 82 years old and lives by herself in an apartment. The caller reported that Mrs. Anderson has not left her apartment in three days and would not answer her door or telephone. The neighbor did say, however, that she could hear movement in the apartment.

Immediately following the phone call, you examined agency files and discovered that Mrs. Anderson had not previously received agency services.

In the following space, please identify the information you would seek and the issues you would address as you consult with your supervisor before taking any action concerning Mrs. Anderson.

Preparatory Arranging

The skill of *preparatory arranging* involves logistical preparation for a first meeting. It includes scheduling an appointment, ensuring that there is adequate time and privacy, and organizing the physical environment. It may involve securing an interview room, locating an interpreter, or rearranging furniture. It includes considering the appropriateness of your apparel, appearance, and perhaps even hygiene. Some clients are offended by a social worker's noticeable body odors; other people are allergic to perfumes or colognes and react adversely to such scents. Some cultures reflect preferences that can easily be respected—if you know about them and make the necessary accommodations ahead of time. Rectifying cultural *faux pas* tends to be much more difficult than avoiding them.

Preparatory arranging could involve any number of considerations: locating transportation for a client, or perhaps organizing temporary child care so that you can meet separately with a parent. Also consider the significance of the environment for clients when making visits outside your agency (Kadushin, 1983, pp. 141–148). Many people assign special meaning to their homes and might feel ill at ease should you arrive before adequate preparations could be made. Food may also have significance to a client, or certain chairs in a home may be reserved for specific persons. Therefore, always pay close attention so you convey respect for these special familial and cultural meanings.

In agency settings, preparatory arranging includes considering the potential effects of the physical environment. Do clients have a comfortable place to sit when they arrive at the agency? Are interviewing rooms sufficiently soundproofed that privacy may be maintained? When you have office space assigned to you, arranging involves selecting and displaying pictures, posters, and other items such as college degrees, professional certificates, and your social work license. It may also include selecting paints or wallpapers and placing furniture.

The office environment can have a powerful impact on clients. Suppose, for example, that you provide social services in an area where firearms are widely prized. You would be unwise to decorate your office wall with a poster that reads, "Ban handguns." You could needlessly alienate many clients. Personal or political messages may interfere with clients' ability to experience you as an objective professional who genuinely respects them.

In sum, preparatory arranging should facilitate communication and diminish, to the extent possible, interference and distraction. Although it requires some time and reflection, the investment often pays substantial dividends.

◆ **EXERCISE 5-4: PREPARATORY ARRANGING**

CASE SITUATION: Assume that you are a social worker in a high-security men's prison. You have been assigned an office, which you share with another worker. The office contains two desks, chairs behind and next to each desk, two bookcases, two telephones, and two file cabinets. In addition, there is a small area containing a sofa, two comfortable chairs, and a coffee table. You have a 10:00 A.M. appointment scheduled with a prisoner, Mr. Somes. The topic for conversation is the serious illness of his wife of 23 years. According to a report you have just received from her physician, it appears that Mrs. Somes will die sometime within the next few days.

As the appointment time approaches, you notice that your social work colleague remains at his desk, actively engaged in paperwork. You had expected him to be out of the office, as he usually is at this time of day.

In the following space, discuss how you would use the skill of arranging in preparation for the meeting with Mr. Somes.

Preparatory Empathy

Preparatory empathy involves "putting oneself in the client's shoes and trying to view the world through the client's eyes" (Shulman, 1984, p. 22). You try to "get in touch with the feelings and concerns that the client may bring to the helping encounter" (Shulman, 1992, p. 56). Even before an initial face-to-face meeting, anticipatory empathy heightens your sensitivity to the prospective client's possible agenda, thoughts, feelings about himself or herself, the presenting issue, and the situation. Through preparatory empathy, you try to anticipate the client's subjective experience related to seeking or receiving social service. You put yourself in the other's shoes so you gain increased appreciation for the client's motivation for the contact, thoughts, and feelings about engaging an authority figure, and potential issues related to the client's sex, stage of life, culture, ethnic background, and socioeconomic status.

Preparatory empathy regarding cultural aspects is especially important. Members of some cultural groups may be ambivalent or conflicted about visiting a social worker. Certain people may prefer a slow and informal beginning. Others might find it difficult to share personal information about their families. Some may be concerned that their culturally appropriate, traditional sex and family roles might be challenged. For many people, visiting an agency is not a simple request for service. The meaning of this event can be extraordinarily complicated for members of many cultural groups. Therefore, as you engage in preparatory empathy with each new client, be sensitive to the potential cultural implications of the upcoming interview.

Preparatory empathy involves trying to experience, on the basis of whatever limited information is available to you, what the client may be thinking and feeling as this interview begins. Because preparatory empathy is done in advance of face-to-face contact, realize that much of the time you will be off target. Preparatory empathy is therefore always tentative, always preliminary, and always subject to immediate change based on the client's actual communications. Even when your preparatory empathy proves to be inaccurate, however, it is a productive activity because it enhances your readiness to listen carefully to the client when you finally do meet in person.

Returning to the upcoming visit with the new client, Mrs. Nancy Cannon, a social worker engaging in preparatory empathy might review the telephone intake report and then go through a mental process such as the following:

> If I were in Mrs. Cannon's shoes, I might feel anxious for, concerned about, and disappointed in my daughter. I would also love her a great deal. I might feel responsible and perhaps even guilty about my parenting behavior. I might feel uncertain about how to proceed. I could very well feel inadequate and maybe frightened. I would be concerned about what the future might hold for Amy and for me. I am aware that my husband's divorce petition and his recent departure from the home may have adversely affected my daughter, and I might feel angry at him—both on my own behalf as well as my daughter's. If I believed I could have been a better spouse or taken actions to prevent his departure, I might also feel guilty about the separation and upcoming divorce proceedings. I might perceive the divorce as the result of

some misbehavior of my own. Alternately, I may have initiated the divorce process and experience conflicted feelings about the decision to do so.

However the separation and divorce process began, I would feel a great deal of stress during this period. I would probably feel confused about the present and fearful about the future. I might be concerned about finances; about after-school supervision of Amy; about my ability to guide and discipline Amy; about whether there is another person in my husband's life; about whether there is now or ever will be someone else in my life; about my capacity to assume the roles of a single person and a single parent; about my ability to deal with my husband around parental issues concerning Amy; and about dozens of other issues provoked by my husband's departure and Amy's recent behavior. I would probably feel enormously burdened and perhaps overwhelmed by the events of recent weeks. If sadness and grieving have not yet occurred, I might begin to experience them soon. It is also possible that I may have begun to anticipate that not only has my husband left the household, but eventually Amy will also leave. After all, she is already 14.

Mrs. Cannon seems to be of a different ethnic background than my own and I am at least 10 years younger. I have never been married and do not have children of my own (Mrs. Cannon may ask about my marital and parental status.) As a result of these cultural and status differences, she may experience me as unable to understand and appreciate her situation. She may even see me as less able to help her, since I have not gone through some of these same difficulties.

Engaging in the skill of preparatory empathy helps to sensitize you to what others might experience as meetings get underway. By empathizing in advance, you increase the likelihood that you will approach the prospective client as a unique human being with all of the complexity that entails. A major challenge in this form of anticipatory empathy, however, is resisting the temptation to narrow your view of the person so that it becomes more of a fixed stereotype than an open set of possibilities.

◆ EXERCISE 5-5: PREPARATORY EMPATHY

CASE SITUATION: Assume that you are a social worker in a general hospital. This morning, a physician contacts you and asks that you accompany her while she informs the mother and father of a 23-year-old man that their son has AIDS. The physician wants you to provide support and social services to the family after she informs them of the diagnosis and prognosis.

Engage in the skill of preparatory empathy as if you were about to meet the parents of the AIDS patient in this situation. Record your thoughts and feelings in the following space.

Preparatory Self-Exploration

In addition to preparatory empathy, you should also engage briefly in *preparatory self-exploration* before meeting with clients or prospective clients. Preparatory self-exploration is a form of self-analysis or introspection through which you, a human being who happens to be a social worker, identify how you might be affected by your interaction with this particular person, this specific issue of concern, and this unique situation. In self-exploring, you would ask yourself questions such as "How am I likely to feel about this individual or family? How are the cultural and demographic similarities or differences between us likely to affect me? Given what I know about the issue and situation, what personal reactions might I expect to experience?"

The purpose of this skill is to identify the potential effects of your own personal history, characteristics, needs, biases, emotional tender spots, and behavioral patterns. Self-exploration helps you to bring into conscious focus those aspects of your personal self that might affect the nature and quality of your social work services to a particular client.

Preparatory self-exploration also involves identifying other personal factors that may affect your readiness to provide service. For example, there may be extraneous factors unrelated to the particular client that might influence you personally. If you have a splitting headache, are dealing with the breakup of a significant relationship, are in the process of repairing your furnace, have just lost out on an opportunity for promotion, did not sleep last night, or are worried about a family member of your own, the quality of your service might be affected. Identifying these factors and their effects on you constitutes the first step toward managing them so that they do not interfere with the high-quality professional service that all clients deserve.

◆ EXERCISE 5-6: PREPARATORY SELF-EXPLORATION

CASE SITUATION: Assume that you are a social worker in an agency that provides psychosocial counseling services to children who have been sexually abused. You have recently begun to work with Cathy, a 7-year-old who had been molested for a period of four years by her biological father. Approximately one month ago, Cathy's father forced her to perform fellatio. That incident led to his arrest and departure from the family home while awaiting further legal developments. You are about to interview Cathy's father for the first time. The general purpose for the interview is to gather information on which to base a tentative assessment of his potential to benefit from a counseling program.

In the following space, please write what you discover about yourself as you engage in self-exploration before meeting Cathy's father.

Centering

When, through preparatory self-exploration, you have identified personal factors that might affect your ability to provide high-quality service to a prospective client, you attempt to manage or contain them. As part of this centering process, you ask yourself, "What can I do to ready myself personally before the meeting begins?" *Centering* involves organizing your personal thoughts, feelings, and physical sensations so that they do not interfere with the performance of your professional obligations and delivery of social services. Depending on the personal factors involved, centering might include various kinds of activities. Among the more common are brief stress-management exercises intended to reduce emotional reactivity and promote self-control. Among the useful stress-reducing activities are positive self-talk, visualization, muscular relaxation, journal writing, and brief meditation.

Suppose, for example, you had once been the victim of date rape. At that time, you had somehow minimized the significance of the violation and have not addressed it since. Recently, you became aware that you still have strong feelings and some unresolved issues about the event. You have decided to seek out a social worker for help in this matter. As you look at the intake form of the new client you are scheduled to meet later today, you read that she was raped two weeks ago by a man she had dated once before.

Through preparatory self-exploration, you might recognize that you remain unsettled about the rape, even though it happened years before. You also realize that you would probably not serve this client well if you are caught up in the emotions of your own experience. Therefore, you might center yourself by taking a few deep breaths, engaging in a brief relaxation exercise, and compartmentalizing (temporarily putting into an enclosed area of yourself) your personal experience so you can provide full attention to the client. As part of the process, you say to yourself, "I'm still tender about being raped but I'm able to manage my feelings of rage and shame and fear so that they don't get in the way of my service to this client. Since it is obvious, however, that I still have some unresolved issues, I hereby commit myself to arrange for an appointment for myself with that social worker I've heard about. I promise that I will telephone her agency office at 11 o'clock when I have a free hour."

In centering, please do not deny or minimize your personal issues and strong feelings. Rather, manage them temporarily and develop a specific plan to address them at another time in a more appropriate context.

◆ EXERCISE 5-7: CENTERING

CASE SITUATION: Assume that you are scheduled to meet with a client in approximately ten minutes. While finishing a brief coffee break with a colleague, you learn that everyone else in the agency received a pay raise of 7%. Despite the fact that you have earned outstanding evaluations and were recently promoted, you know that you received only a 3% raise.

In the following space, please describe the activities you would undertake to center yourself before meeting with the client.

Preliminary Planning and Recording

As a social worker, you should engage in the skill of *preliminary planning* before meetings, contacts, and interviews with clients and other people with whom you interact as part of your professional duties. Begin the process of formulating a preliminary plan by asking and answering questions such as "Why is this meeting occurring? What is its overall purpose? What do I hope to accomplish through this meeting? What is my tentative agenda? What might be the other person's agenda? What would I consider to be a successful meeting? What are my functions or roles in this meeting? How do I wish to begin? What things should I say? What questions should I ask? What kind of interactional process would I like to see? How would I like the meeting to conclude?"

Kadushin suggested that the "general purposes of most social work interviews can be described as informational (to make a social study), diagnostic (to arrive at an appraisal), and therapeutic (to effect change)" (1983, p. 21). In *information-gathering interviews*, you encourage people to discuss their views and feelings about themselves, their preferences and strengths, issues and goals, and the situation. Basically, you gather data that may help you and your client reach a better understanding of the circumstances. In *information-giving interviews*, you share needed or useful knowledge. You might offer information about a program, policy, or resource in your attempt to respond to a request or address a perceived need. In *assessment-forming interviews*, your overall purpose is to arrive at an assessment, diagnosis, evaluation, or conclusion. Often, such an interview is followed by the preparation of a recommendation. In *change-making interviews*, you effect or help to effect movement or change somewhere within a targeted system. Change might occur within an individual person (e.g., thoughts, feelings, or actions), within a group of people (e.g., a family, organization, or community), or in the interactional processes that occur between persons and other social systems (e.g., communication practices or feedback mechanisms).

Most of the time, you should be able to identify, at least tentatively, a general purpose for a given interview. Sometimes, of course, a meeting serves more than one purpose. Once the purpose or purposes are identified, you may sketch out a preliminary plan for the meeting.

Many first meetings have as their primary purpose the gathering of information. In such cases, you might formulate a general but flexible plan concerning what data to seek and from whom. For example, in planning for a first meeting with a family, you may have to decide whether to see all family members together or to see some of them separately. If you plan to see members individually or in the form of smaller subsystems (e.g., mother-daughter dyad or parental dyad), you determine whom to interview first, second, and so forth.

Consider the case of a prospective client who telephoned expressing an interest in resolving a family problem. Your tentative plan might be as follows:

◆ Engage in introductions
◆ Identify a general purpose and direction for the meeting (information-gathering)
◆ Establish the ground rules for the process

- Address any questions or uncertainties concerning the agency, you as the social worker, the purpose, the process, or the ground rules
- Determine the identities and characteristics of the family or household members
- Explore the presenting issue that stimulated the phone contact
- Explore the history and development as well as the consequences of that issue
- Examine how the family has attempted to address this and other issues, and determine the effects of those efforts
- Explore strengths within the family systems and identify available resources that might contribute to a resolution
- Establish a preliminary goal for service
- Conclude the interview with some sense of what will happen next in the process.

Preliminary planning enables you to begin the interview in a coherent fashion and helps you formulate a tentative purpose to share with the client. The process yields a flexible structure, which can help you come across as organized and competent in your first meetings with other people.

The written recording that results from preparation in advance of meetings may take several forms and include various components. Many agencies use a telephone *intake form* to make relevant notations: the caller, the reason for the call, the substance of the conversation, and any plans that have been made. A more extensive *face sheet* provides space to record identifying characteristics of a person-issue-situation (e.g., name, sex, age, reason for contact, preliminary description of the issue of concern, occupation, family role, address, and phone numbers). The face sheet may be used instead of or in addition to the intake form. Although notes that result from telephone conversations should always be considered tentative in nature, they often provide valuable information to the worker who subsequently engages a person or family in a face-to-face meeting. Many workers also develop, often in outline form, a summary of their preliminary plan for the meeting.

For example, Rose Hernandez, the social worker assigned to interview Mrs. Cannon (see Exercise 5.1) might write the following notes in advance of her first meeting. Notice how useful these brief notes could be in helping her to be prepared from the very first moment of contact.

PRELIMINARY NOTES

January 13

Mrs. Nancy Cannon—seems to prefer "Mrs."—presenting concern: 14-year-old daughter Amy alleged to have drunk alcohol and come home after her 9:00 P.M. curfew. First such incident; may be related to separation and divorce petition by Mrs. Cannon's husband (Amy's father). He left the home about six weeks ago—uncertain who initiated the separation and divorce process. Mrs. Cannon wants a noontime appointment to avoid time away from work. Could there be financial constraints or concerns about keeping her job?

PRELIMINARY PLAN

◆ Introduce myself, my profession, and my affiliation with the agency. Use "Mrs. Cannon" as initial reference to her and ask how she would prefer to be addressed.

◆ General purpose for the meeting appears to be information gathering. Collect relevant information related to Mrs. Cannon, her daughter, estranged husband, the issue of concern, and the situation.

◆ Make sure that Mrs. Cannon understands limits of confidentiality including duty to report indications of child abuse or neglect. Indicate the mutual nature of this working relationship and invite her active participation.

◆ Explore the apparent presenting issue (Amy's drinking), as well as the related concern of the separation and divorce. Explore history, development, and current status of drinking and marital conflict.

◆ Clarify Mrs. Cannon and Amy's current household situation; inquire about Mr. Cannon's circumstances as well. Identify significant others who are involved with the three family members.

◆ Explore strengths of Mrs. Cannon, Amy, and perhaps Mr. Cannon. Identify available resources that might relate to a resolution.

◆ Explore in detail how Mrs. Cannon, Amy, and Mr. Cannon have attempted to deal with the separation and divorce processes, and with the issue of drinking or other "misbehavior" by Amy. Identify approaches that have been helpful and those that have been ineffective.

◆ Explore what Mrs. Cannon would consider an optimum resolution to the problems of concern.

◆ Conclude the interview with a specific next step. Consider the possibility of a second appointment, perhaps with Amy and Mrs. Cannon together, Amy alone, Mr. Cannon alone, or possibly Mr. and Mrs. Cannon together.

Rose Hernandez, B.S.W., L.S.W.
Licensed Social Worker

CASE SITUATION: Assume that you are a social worker who works in conjunction with a court that handles child custody disputes. You have been assigned the responsibility of collecting information and formulating a recommendation about the placement of a 12-year-old boy whose parents are divorcing. Each parent wants custody of the child.

1. Use the following space to develop and record a preliminary plan for the meeting or meetings you would have with the various parties involved in this situation.

CASE SITUATION: Assume that you are a social worker in a military veterans' center. You receive a telephone message from Ms. Francine Rivera concerning her brother Hector. Ms. Rivera indicates that Hector is 56 years of age and completed two tours of combat duty in Vietnam. She reports that he has had trouble keeping jobs, drinks alcohol (beer) every day, has nightmares at night, and occasionally has violent outbursts. She has become especially concerned lately because he has talked about ending "his own miserable life." She says that he won't go to an agency but he might be willing to talk with someone if a counselor came to the house. You agree to go for a first visit at 5:30 P.M. on the next afternoon.

2. In the following space, develop and record a preliminary plan for the meeting or meetings you would have with the various parties involved in this situation.

Summary

The preparing skills enable you to provide professional social work services efficiently and effectively from the first moment of person-to-person contact. The preparing skills are used extensively before initial interviews and in advance of later meetings as well.

The preparing skills include (1) preparatory reviewing, (2) preparatory exploring, (3) preparatory consulting, (4) preparatory arranging, (5) preparatory empathy, (6) preparatory self-exploration, (7) centering, and (8) preliminary planning and recording.

◆ CHAPTER 5 SUMMARY EXERCISES

Assume that you are a social worker with an agency that offers a broad range of social services. Using the skills requested, prepare for a first meeting with each of the following clients.

1. *CASE SITUATION:* A family of seven (two parents and five children, ranging in age from 1 to 7) has been sleeping in the family's dilapidated Chevy in a rest area on the highway. En route to another city where they hope to find work, they have run out of money and food and nearly out of gas. A highway patrolman has referred them to your agency.

a.   Engage in the process of preparatory empathy as you ready yourself to meet with this family. Describe the results here.

b.   Through preparatory self-exploration, identify those personal factors that might affect you as you provide social services to the family. Then use the following space to describe how you might center yourself to diminish any potentially adverse responses.

c.   In the following space, record a preliminary plan that reflects the results of your preparation activities before meeting with the family.

2. *CASE SITUATION:* A 33-year-old man is accused of molesting his girlfriend's 13-year-old-daughter. He is required to undergo counseling to stay out of jail while the judge considers whether to proceed with felony charges. The man was living with his girlfriend but has now been required to leave the house.

a.   Engage in the process of preparatory empathy as you ready yourself to meet with this prospective client. Use the following space to describe the results.

b. Through preparatory self-exploration, identify those personal factors that might get in the way of your helping the man. Then use the following space to describe how you could center yourself so you can manage your reactions.

c. In the following space, prepare a preliminary plan that reflects the results of your preparation in advance of meeting this man.

3. *CASE SITUATION:* You are a social worker with Child Protection Services (CPS), the agency that investigates allegations of child abuse or neglect. You receive a telephone report from a neighbor of the Smith family that the parents have neglected and abused their two children (ages 1 and 3). According to the neighbor, the mother sleeps while the children play in a filthy yard (which contains animal waste, junk, and potentially dangerous materials—glass and sharp metal objects). Also, the neighbor reports that the man in the house drinks heavily and beats both mother and children. Following the telephone call, you prepare to make a home visit to the family in question.

a.   Engage in the process of preparatory empathy as you ready yourself to meet with this prospective client family. Use the following space to describe the results.

b.   Through preparatory self-exploration, identify those personal factors that might affect the quality of your professional services. Then use the following space to describe how you might center yourself so you diminish any potentially adverse responses.

c. In the following space, prepare a preliminary plan for the meeting.

4. *CASE SITUATION:* You serve as a medical social worker on the cancer ward of a children's hospital. You receive a request from a physician that you join her as she informs the parents of an 8-year-old girl that their daughter has terminal leukemia.

a. Engage in the process of preparatory empathy as you ready yourself for this meeting with the physician and the parents. Describe the results here.

b. Through preparatory self-exploration, identify those personal factors that might inhibit your effectiveness in this situation. Then describe how you might center yourself so you diminish these potentially adverse responses.

c. In the following space, prepare a preliminary plan for the meeting.

◆ CHAPTER 5 WORLD WIDE WEB EXERCISES

1. Suppose in your role as social worker, you are scheduled to meet with a recently immigrated family that speaks a language that you neither speak nor understand. As you talk with your colleagues and supervisor, you realize that

although agency professionals have not regularly used interpreters, the need is growing because of the influx of immigrants from diverse parts of the world. Use the resources of the diversityRx Web site at www.diversityrx.org to locate and review information about the roles and standards of certified medical interpreters. Use the following space to summarize how you might adapt and apply that information about interpreters in preparing for initial meetings with clients that speak languages other than yours. Be sure to discuss the implications of differential degrees of enculturation for preparation.

2. Go to the InfoTrac College Edition Web site at www.infotrac-college.com. Use your passcode to log in. Conduct a keyword search using the string "counseling native adults" (include the quotation marks) to locate an article entitled "Honoring the Power of Relation: Counseling Native Adults" (Garrett & Herring, 2001). Carefully read the article and use the following space to reflect on the implications of the material in preparing for initial meetings with Native American clients.

3. Go to the InfoTrac College Edition Web site at www.infotrac-college.com. Use your passcode to log in. Conduct a keyword search using the string "counseling Arab Americans" (include the quotation marks) to locate an article entitled "Counseling Arab Americans: Counselors' Call for Advocacy and Social Justice" (Nassar-McMillan, 2003). Carefully read the article and use the following space to discuss the implications of the material in preparing for initial meetings with Arab American clients.

4. Go to the InfoTrac College Edition Web site at www.infotrac-college.com. Use your passcode to log in. Conduct a keyword search using the string "Multiculturally Responsive Counseling" (include the quotation marks) to locate an article entitled "Multiculturally Responsive Counseling: Effects on Asian Students' Ratings of Counselors" (Zhang & Dixon, 2001). Carefully read the article and use the following space to discuss the implications of the material in preparing for first meetings with Asian university students.

5. Go to the InfoTrac College Edition Web site at www.infotrac-college.com. Use your passcode to log in. Conduct a keyword search using the string "Deciding who to see" (include the quotation marks) to locate an article entitled "Deciding Who to See: Lesbians Discuss Their Preferences in Health and Mental Health Care Providers" (Saulnier, 2002). Carefully read the article and use the following space to discuss how you might use the information in preparing for initial meetings with lesbian clients.

Chapter 5 Self-Appraisal

As you conclude this chapter, please assess your proficiency in the preparing skills by completing the following self-appraisal exercise.

SELF-APPRAISAL: THE PREPARING SKILLS

Please use the following items to help you undertake a self-assessment of your proficiency in the preparing skills addressed in this chapter. Read each statement carefully. Then, use the following four-point rating scale to indicate the degree to which you agree or disagree with each statement. Record your numerical response in the space provided:

4 = Strongly Agree

3 = Agree

2 = Disagree

1 = Strongly Disagree

_____ 1. I can effectively use the preparatory reviewing skill.

_____ 2. I can effectively use the preparatory exploring skill.

_____ 3. I can effectively use the preparatory consulting skill.

_____ 4. I can effectively use the preparatory arranging skill.

_____ 5. I can effectively use the preparatory empathy skill.

_____ 6. I can effectively use the preparatory self-exploration skill.

_____ 7. I can effectively use the centering skill.

_____ 8. I can effectively use the preliminary planning and recording skills.

_____ Subtotal

Note: These items are taken directly from the preparing skills section of the Social Work Skills Self-Appraisal Questionnaire contained in Appendix 3. Earlier, when you reviewed Chapter 2 and completed the exercises, you responded to these questions. You may now compare the responses you made on that occasion with those you made this time. Also compare the two subtotals. If you believe that you have progressed in your proficiency with the preparing skills, the more recent subtotal should be higher than the earlier.

Finally, reflect on the skills addressed in this chapter and the results of your self-appraisal. Based on your analysis, prepare a succinct one-page summary report entitled "Self-Assessment of Proficiency in the Preparing Skills." Within the report, be sure to identify those skills that you know and do well (e.g., a score of 3 or 4). Also, specify those that need further practice (e.g., scores of 2 or less) and briefly outline plans by which to achieve proficiency in them. When finished, include the report in your Social Work Skills Learning Portfolio.

Chapter 6

Beginning

This chapter (see Box 6.1) is intended to help you learn the skills used during the beginning phase of social work practice. This phase formally begins when you, in your role as a social worker, and another person first encounter one another. Because first impressions are so important, the initial face-to-face contact often affects all future encounters. The beginning portion of each subsequent interview tends to influence the course of those meetings as well.

BOX 6.1

Chapter Purpose

The purpose of this chapter is to help learners develop proficiency in the beginning skills.

Goals

Following completion of this chapter, learners should be able to demonstrate proficiency in the following:

◆ Introducing yourself
◆ Seeking introductions
◆ Describing initial purpose

(continued)

BOX 6.1 (continued)

- ◆ Orienting clients
- ◆ Discussing policy and ethical factors
- ◆ Seeking feedback
- ◆ Ability to assess proficiency in the beginning skills

Competent use of the beginning skills helps ensure that meetings are positive and productive. An effective beginning results when you and the prospective client accomplish the purpose for which you first meet (e.g., information gathering, information giving, assessment forming, or change making) and reach some mutual conclusion concerning a next step in the process (e.g., conclude your relationship, continue to work together, or arrange for service from another professional or agency).

Typically, you make contact with prospective clients in one of two ways: "(1) The individual, family, or group may reach out for help with a problem they have identified as being beyond their means of solution; or (2) a community source may identify an individual, a family, or a group as having a serious problem threatening the welfare of themselves or others (a vulnerable person or group) and request that the social worker intervene to solve that problem" (Compton & Galaway, 1994, p. 346). During the early part of a first meeting, you generally hope to facilitate an exchange of introductions, establish a tentative direction or purpose for the meeting, outline the usual expectations of clients, describe the policies and ethical principles that might apply during this and future encounters, and ensure that the prospective client understands the parameters within which the interview takes place. This is a crucial part of the beginning process because it addresses your legal and ethical obligations with respect to informed consent. Commonly, at this point in the process, you give the prospective client an overview of relevant agency policies, as well as information about pertinent laws and ethical principles. The prospective client can thus understand the context within which helping endeavors take place. Throughout the beginning phase, you should frequently seek feedback concerning information discussed. Prospective clients sometimes need additional clarification about complex or confusing policies and principles.

The beginning skills are commonly used quite extensively during the first few meetings with clients. Use some of them in initial professional encounters with other people as well. Just as you are with clients, you should be clear about purposes and expectations when meeting with referral sources, colleagues from your own or other agencies, government officials, parents, and others with whom you interact as part of your professional responsibilities. Several beginning skills are also used during the early portions of later encounters. The beginning skills include (1) introducing yourself, (2) seeking introductions, (3) describing initial purpose, (4) orienting clients, (5) discussing policy and ethical factors, and (6) seeking feedback.

Introducing Yourself

At the beginning of any first interview, be sure to identify yourself by full name and profession, and by agency or departmental affiliation. For example, at the beginning of a meeting in the agency where he works, a social worker might say as he holds out his hand in greeting, "Hello Mr. and Mrs. Adabu. I'm Dan Majors. I'm a social worker here at the family service agency. I specialize in helping people who are dealing with family issues of one kind or another."

At the start of a visit to the home of a prospective client, another social worker might say, "Hello Ms. White [offers hand to shake]. I'm Joanna Samples. I'm a social worker with the local school system. I specialize in service to families of the students in our school district. Please call me Joanna." In meeting a bilingual Mexican-American family for the first time, an English-speaking social worker might nonetheless say a few words of greeting in Spanish along with a brief statement of regret that she is not fluent in that beautiful language. At first contact with some Asian clients, a respectful lowering of the head to approximate a modest bow may augment the introductory ritual.

In most circumstances, a friendly facial expression and a warm, firm handshake are helpful gestures. A few informal comments about such things as the weather may also help prospective clients feel more at ease with you, but do not overdo it. Spending too much time with chitchat may frustrate clients who are grappling with serious concerns and urgently wish to talk about them. Your introduction and informal remarks should always be considered in light of the context. Be especially sensitive to cultural factors. Prospective clients fully realize that you do not yet truly know them as individual people. Therefore, too much informality or effusiveness with some clients may be premature and, in some cultures, quite rude. Sometimes, clients experience exaggerated informality and effusive introductions as disingenuous and affected.

In addition to identifying yourself by name, profession, and agency affiliation, you might also want to provide formal identification. As part of her introduction to families, Joanna Samples routinely gives out her business card:

Joanna Samples, M.S.W., L.S.W.
Licensed Social Worker
Center Township School District
902 West New York Street
Indianapolis, IN 46202-5156
Telephone 317-274-6705

In office settings, display of your university degrees, social work license, and professional certificates can contribute to the introductory process. Clients may notice where you earned your college degree and that you are licensed to practice social work in your locale. Indeed, some licensing laws specifically require the public display of the license. Along with pertinent agency brochures, you might provide clients brief type-written summaries of your professional background, training, and expertise.

◆ EXERCISE 6-1: INTRODUCING YOURSELF

The following exercises give you an opportunity to practice the skill of introducing yourself. In the spaces provided, write the words you would say and describe the actions you would take in introducing yourself in the following circumstances.

1. Assume that you are a social worker in a residential nursing facility for eld-erly persons. You are scheduled to meet with family members concerning the possibility of placing their 85-year-old parent there. What would you say and do in introducing yourself?

2. Assume that you have recently been hired as a social worker in a training cen-ter for developmentally disabled children and young adults. Today, you are about to lead a group of six or eight teenage residents. The students are al-ready seated in the room when you arrive. Although a few of them may have seen you walking around campus, none of them actually knows you and you do not know any of them. What would you say and do in introducing yourself?

Seeking Introductions

People's names tend to hold special significance. Early in first meetings, encourage clients to say their names, and then try to pronounce them correctly. Thereafter, periodically throughout the interview, refer to your clients by name. For example, after introducing yourself, you might say, "And your name is . . . ?" If you already know the person's name, you might ask, "And you're Mr. Nesbit? Is that right? Am I pronouncing your name correctly?" Then ask how the person prefers to be addressed (Miss, Ms., Mrs., Mr., Reverend, first name, or nickname). Persons from cultural groups that experienced oppression may be especially sensitive to premature informality. In the United States, for example, slaves were often addressed by first name only or by the terms "boy" or "girl." Indeed, the original African surnames were often replaced by those of slave owners. Similarly, male Native Americans were frequently sarcastically referred to by some European Americans as "Chief" in a form of rankism and ridicule. Although most social workers would never intentionally insult other people, sometimes ignorance and insensitivity may lead to just such a result.

Frequently, clients may share additional forms of identification during the exchange of introductions. Suppose a new client introduces herself by saying, "I'm Mrs. Jones. I'm the mother of this mob of children." From her words, you might infer that she prefers to be addressed as "Mrs. Jones" and that a significant part of her personal and social identity is related to her role as parent.

In family and group contexts, you may find it useful to ask members to "go around" and introduce themselves. Because initial group meetings often provoke anxiety, you could incorporate a stress-reducing, ice-breaking dimension to the introduction process. For example, you might ask group members to introduce themselves and share a few of the thoughts they had as they anticipated coming to this first meeting.

◆ EXERCISE 6-2: SEEKING INTRODUCTIONS

For these exercises, assume that you are a social worker at a family social services agency. Respond in the spaces provided by writing the words you would say in each situation.

1. You are about to begin an interview with a recently divorced 55-year-old man. As you walk together to your office, you smell a strong odor of alcohol. How would you introduce yourself and seek an introduction from him? What else, if anything, would you say or do? Discuss your rationale for the words you choose and approach you propose.

2. You are about to begin an interview with a 77-year-old widow who has a hearing impairment. She can make out most words if they are spoken clearly, distinctly, and at a low pitch. How would you introduce yourself and seek an introduction from her? What else, if anything, would you say or do? Discuss your rationale for the words you choose and the action you propose.

3. You are about to begin a first interview with a family of seven members. You know that it is a blended family and that not all of the children have the same last name. You do not, however, know which children are from which relationships. How would you introduce yourself and seek introductions from the family members? What else would you say or do? Discuss your rationale for the words you choose and the action you propose.

4. You are about to begin an interview with a prospective client. As you introduce yourself and seek an introduction from her, you realize that she speaks neither English nor Spanish but another language, which you do not understand. What would you do? Discuss your rationale for the approach you would take.

Describing Initial Purpose

As part of the process of preparing for a meeting (see Chapter 5), you identify a tentative general purpose (Schwartz, 1976, pp. 188–190; Shulman, 1992, pp. 79–101) for the meeting. Especially in initial meetings, new clients tend to look to you, as the professional person in an authority role, for leadership. Therefore, you should clearly and succinctly describe your view of the purpose for the meeting. Without some beginning guidance from you, prospective clients are likely to feel even more uncertain about a process that is usually quite stress provoking. By tentatively sharing a general purpose, clients usually feel a sense of relief, as they conclude that you do, in fact, know what you are doing.

Building on the work of Vinter (1963) and Hansenfield (1985), Garvin (1997) identified the following overarching purposes for most social work agencies, programs, and services:

◆ *Socialization* "involves helping persons viewed as 'normal' and who are progressing from one status to another. Examples of this are assisting adolescents to assume adult responsibilities, middle-aged persons to plan for retirement, and school children to make better use of their learning environments" (Garvin, 1997, p. 40).

 ◆ *Identity Development* is an aspect of socialization service in which social workers help people to clarify their own goals and roles. Supporting adolescents as they explore social identity issues or consider career goals; facilitating a women's consciousness raising group; or helping gay, lesbian, or bisexual persons decide whether or not to "come out" are examples of identity development purposes.
 ◆ *Skill Development* involves helping persons develop the abilities needed to achieve the goals they've decided upon. Educational counseling, training or "coaching" activities (e.g., assertive training, social and communication skills, parenting skills, budgeting skills, time-management skills, study skills) and transition facilitation activities (e.g., retirement preparation, divorce adjustment—for adults and children, helping adults entering or returning to college) contribute to skill development. Such socialization activities help people to acquire the knowledge and skills associated with roles and goals to which they aspire.

◆ *Resocialization* involves "helping people viewed as not experiencing 'normal' phases of development or role transitions. Such people are often labeled 'deviant,' and therefore experience conflict with others" (Garvin, 1997, p. 40).

 ◆ *Social Control* efforts are often found in agencies that have a relationship with one or more aspects of the criminal and juvenile justice, child and adult protection, educational, and some medical systems. Typically, the "targets" of social control activities have not yet decided to accept a nondeviant, socially acceptable role. Although many social workers are reluctant to consider themselves as agents of social control, the purpose of such activities and the objectives of the agencies that sponsor them (and the constituencies that fund them) involve the control and management of the undesirable behavior of certain people. Activities offered within prisons, training schools, alcohol and drug treatment centers, many residential organizations, and some hospitals are often solely or primarily social control in nature. Persons reflecting classifications associated with crime and delinquency, sexual offenses, violence, substance abuse, and deviance often receive services intended to serve the purpose of social control. Indeed, in many educational, mental health and social service agencies, social control is frequently an unspoken but strong element of the (sometimes hidden) agenda.

◆ *Rehabilitation* services are often found in agencies and institutions such as psychiatric facilities, mental health centers, social service agencies, and the treatment programs of correctional settings. Typically, persons that voluntarily seek rehabilitation services identify certain behavior patterns as problematic (deviant, maladaptive, dysfunctional, or sick) and choose to pursue a more functional, healthful, or socially acceptable path. Rehabilitation services help the members develop the knowledge, skills, and attitudes necessary to fulfill functional, accepted, and socially desirable roles. Many social, psychiatric, educational, and substance abuse services fall into this category, as do many self-help programs where members openly acknowledge their faults, failures, or addictions (e.g., sex, relationship, drugs, alcohol, and so on) and undertake personal efforts to overcome them.

These overarching social work purposes may provide a context for the general reasons for initial meetings with clients. For example, when it is clear from a preliminary contact that a main issue requires rehabilitation services, you might identify that your purpose involves helping people develop new ways of thinking, feeling, and behavior so they can prevent past problems from recurring.

In some instances, the general purpose for the meeting is clear, and so is the professional social work role that matches that purpose. When such a strong degree of clarity exists, you may also appropriately describe one or more of the professional social work roles that you expect to assume during the course of your work together (Schwartz, 1976, pp. 188–190; Shulman, 1992, pp. 79–101).

Among the more common social work roles are *advocate, broker, case manager, counselor, educator, evaluator, facilitator, investigator, mediator,* or *therapist.* In serving as an advocate, you represent, defend, or champion the rights of clients and others who might be in need or at risk. As a broker, you help to locate community resources and link people with them. As a case manager, you coordinate delivery of several different services provided by personnel from one or more agencies or programs. As a counselor, you provide support and guidance to people in their efforts to address and resolve problems and accomplish goals. As an educator, you provide information, teach, train, coach, or socialize people in the development of knowledge, attitudes, or abilities to enhance their psychosocial functioning. As an evaluator, you make judgments and recommendations based on careful, fair, and systematic collection and analysis of pertinent information (e.g., recommending child custody arrangements, determining the effectiveness of a social service program, or assessing an applicant's eligibility for services). As a facilitator, you help bring people together, enhance their interaction and communication, and encourage them to cooperate in their efforts and actions. As an investigator (e.g., child or adult protective services worker), you carefully and systematically search to uncover hidden or secret information pertaining to the safety and well-being of potentially vulnerable people. As a mediator, you serve as a communication link or go-between in helping various parties address differences or conflicts, and to interact more productively. As a psychotherapist or social therapist, you use advanced knowledge, extensive training, and specialized strategies and techniques to help people cope with or resolve specific social, physical, or psychological problems, symptoms, illnesses, or disabilities.

In beginning with involuntary or nonvoluntary clients, both the purpose and your role warrant more complete and lengthy description. This is also the case in situations where clients seek a specific service offered through your agency. For example, your agency may sponsor an educationally oriented six-week group experience for teenagers considering marriage. Because it is a structured group that follows a predictable agenda, your social work roles are clear: educator and group facilitator. Therefore, you may appropriately describe to prospective members both an initial purpose and the professional roles that you expect to fulfill during the group experience.

Frequently, however, the exact nature of your professional role is unclear at the time of the first meeting. This often occurs with voluntary clients who seek service from organizations that have several programs and serve a variety of functions. When the professional roles you might assume remain uncertain, the tentative description of general purpose should suffice.

In the following examples, a social worker tentatively describes an initial purpose for a first meeting.

CASE SITUATION: The client is a woman (age 30) who called the agency a few days earlier to ask for help with a troubled marriage. The worker and client have already exchanged introductions. The worker begins to describe a tentative general purpose for this initial meeting.

WORKER: When you telephoned the agency the other day, you said that your marriage is on the brink of collapse and that you and your husband argue all the time. Is that correct? Yes? During our meeting today, I'd like to explore in detail with you the nature of your marriage, its history, and how it developed to this point. As we both gain a better understanding of the circumstances, we can decide together what to do next.

CASE SITUATION: The divorcing parents of a 9-year-old boy are involved in child custody proceedings. The social worker has been employed by the juvenile court to make recommendations to the judge about the placement of the child. The worker has just exchanged introductions with the father and describes a purpose and role as follows.

WORKER: Judge Bloom asked me to meet with you, your wife, and your son for the purpose of making a recommendation about the custody arrangements for Kevin. I'll be meeting with Mrs. Brown [spouse] this afternoon and with Kevin [son] tomorrow morning. After these three meetings, I should have a fairly good understanding of the situation. At that time, should further meetings be needed, I'll let you know.

I certainly recognize that this is a difficult time for you and for everybody involved. You may feel a bit like you're on trial here. It may seem that way. I'll try my best to make it as reasonable a process as possible. You should know, however, that your son Kevin will be fully considered in these processes. His well-being will be our primary focus. My efforts will be geared toward determining what is best for him and his development. I'm sure that you are also concerned about the consequences of the divorce and the upcoming court proceedings on Kevin too. I'd like to approach this interview with Kevin in mind as we try to determine the best custody arrangements.

CASE SITUATION: This is the first meeting of an educational group for persons arrested for driving under the influence (DUI). The participants range in age from 16 to 62 and cross gender, ethnic, and socioeconomic class lines. The group experience involves 12 weekly meetings of approximately two hours each. Members participate to decrease the chance of a jail sentence. The worker and group members have exchanged introductions and engaged in some small talk. The worker now proceeds to describe an initial purpose and role.

WORKER: The county prosecutor asked me to lead this educational group for the next 12 weeks. I understand that each of you was arrested for driving under the influence of alcohol and that you have chosen to participate in the group in order to reduce the chances of a term in the county jail. I imagine that you all have other places that you would rather be at this time. Some of you may be grateful for this opportunity to avoid a jail sentence. Others may be annoyed that you have to attend these meetings. If I were in your shoes, I'd probably have mixed feelings too. Whatever you feel, I hope the series of group meetings will help you learn a great deal about alcohol use and its consequences. Most importantly, however, I hope the experience will help you refrain from driving automobiles while under the influences of intoxicating substances.

CASE SITUATION: The interview setting is the front doorstep of the Frankel residence. It is a large home in an upper-middle-class neighborhood. The social worker knocked on the door and it was opened by a woman who appears to live there. Employed by the Child Protection Service (CPS) Division of the Department of Human Services, the worker is visiting the home unannounced because the agency received a complaint that Mrs. Frankel had severely beaten her 4-year-old son. Upon arriving at the home the worker exchanged introductions, learned that the woman is indeed Mrs. Frankel, and gave her a business card along with a brochure about CPS.

WORKER: Child Protection Services is responsible for investigating all allegations of abuse or neglect of minor children in this county. We have received a complaint concerning the treatment of your 4-year-old son. I'd like to discuss this situation with you and meet your son. May I come in?

◆ EXERCISE 6-3: DESCRIBING INITIAL PURPOSE

Use the following case situations to practice the skill of describing a tentative initial purpose for the meeting and, where you think appropriate, describing your social work role. Please respond to each situation in the spaces provided.

1. Assume that you are a social worker with a public housing agency. You are currently in the process of interviewing all residents of a building in an effort to determine their social service needs. You have just knocked on the door of Mrs. Strong's residence. Mrs. Strong is a single mother with five children who range in age from 9 years to 6 months. Write the words you would say to her as you describe an initial purpose for the meeting. If you think your social work role would be clear in this situation, describe that as well.

2. You are a social worker who works in the emergency room of a general hospital. Paramedics have just brought in an automobile accident victim. Doctors and nurses are providing lifesaving measures. Family members of the patient arrive. It is your function to provide them with a place to wait and to

inform them in general terms about what is happening to the patient. You go up to the family, introduce yourself, and guide them to a more private waiting area. Write the words you would say in describing an initial purpose for the meeting. In this case, your role is also likely to be fairly clear. Describe your role as well.

3. You are a social worker in a nursing residence for elderly persons. A new resident arrived over the weekend, and you go to her room for a first visit. You intend to introduce yourself and get acquainted. You realize that you will need to complete a social history and professional assessment before the week is out. You want to set the stage for that subsequent interview. Write the words you would say in describing an initial purpose for that upcoming meeting.

4. Along with other professional duties, you lead counseling groups for children who have been sexually abused. You are about to begin a new group, composed of five girls who range in age from 7 to 10. You have met individually

with each of the five before and talked with them at length. However, this is the first time they have been in a group, and they have not met each other before. You ask each girl to share her first name with the others. They all do so, although several introduce themselves in soft and tentative voices. You want to begin the group in a warm, safe, and secure manner. Write the words you would say in describing an initial purpose for the meeting. Then describe the professional role or roles that you might assume during the group experience.

Orienting Clients

During the beginning phase of the working relationship, many clients are quite uncertain about what is expected of them. Certain aspects of the anxiety and ambiguity may be the result of cultural factors, but others may be associated with potential vulnerability. Prospective clients are certainly concerned about the issues that led to the contact, but many are also worried that they may not be able to do what is needed to address them (Garvin & Seabury, 1997, pp. 80–82). In particular, prospective clients may be confused about how they may help you, the social worker, best help them. Ambiguity about what they are "supposed to do" is probably associated with the relatively high discontinuation or dropout rates of clients generally, and particularly members of minority groups (Sue, 1977).

Although mass media has contributed to popular familiarity with some facets of psychological and social services through television series such as *Bob Newhart, Judging Amy, Dr. Phil,* and of course, countless talk radio "psychotherapists," the actual history of formal "for hire" helping relationships with professionals external to the immediate community is quite short indeed. Throughout the centuries, most psychological and social problems were addressed with the help of family, friends, and shamans or religious leaders. Such problems were usually addressed internally within the family and local community.

Although social norms and mores have changed dramatically during the last several decades, receiving help from paid strangers about psychological and social issues remains an essentially anxiety-provoking experience for most people. It is sometimes associated with a sense of shame and perhaps stigma. You may help clarify the situation by describing how clients may join you as active participants in the helping process (Garvin, 1987, pp. 72–74; Garvin & Seabury, 1997, pp. 145–148). Indeed, orienting clients to the process and preparing them for likely activities may lower the early dropout rate and improve service outcomes (Atkins & Patenaude, 1987; Lambert & Lambert, 1984; Shuman & Shapiro, 2002; Yalom, Houts, Newell, & Rand, 1967).

For example, in the first meeting of a group for adolescents having school problems, you might orient group members in a manner such as the following:

ORIENTING CLIENTS (GROUP MEMBER)

We all have problems at some point in our lives. It's part of being human. We've found that talking with other people who are in similar situations often helps resolve those problems. We've planned this group so you can share with each other your issues and concerns as well as your hopes and dreams. Although you are not required to say anything that you wish to keep to yourself, we hope that you will talk openly with one another, listen carefully to what others say, and offer suggestions about how things could be better. We expect all group members to follow the rule of confidentiality. That means that whatever is said within the group setting stays here. Nothing discussed here should be repeated outside this room.

You might attempt to orient an individual client in the following way:

ORIENTING CLIENTS (INDIVIDUAL)

You can best help in this process by sharing your thoughts and feelings as freely and as fully as you possibly can. Please ask questions when you do not understand, offer suggestions about what might work better, and give feedback about what helps and what doesn't. Finally, you can be helpful in this process by trying as hard as you can to take the steps that we plan together. If we work together as a team, there's a good chance we'll be able to resolve the issues that prompted this visit.

In orienting clients, recognize that expectations necessarily vary according to the reasons clients seek or receive social work services. They also differ according to the agency setting, its mission and programs, and the composition of the client system—its size and the ages, capabilities, and motivations of its members. As you can imagine, the expectations for an adult male client about to begin an intensive, three-month therapeutic and educational group experience for men who batter women would be quite dissimilar from those for an 8-year-old child who witnessed her father shoot and kill her mother.

◆ EXERCISE 6-4: ORIENTING CLIENTS

Use the following case situations to practice the skill of orienting clients. Please respond to each situation in the spaces provided.

1. Assume that you are a social worker meeting for the first time with a couple that wants help to deal with relationship difficulties. Mr. and Mrs. Koslow have been married for ten years and have two children (8 and 10 years old). They have an adequate income. You have introduced yourself, secured introductions from Mr. and Mrs. Koslow, and have identified as a purpose for this first meeting to explore the problems and concerns that led the couple to come to the agency. You now want to orient them to this process. What would you say?

2. Assume that you are a social worker meeting for the first time with a family of four (a single parent and three children, ages 11, 13, and 16). The eldest child, a daughter, has reportedly begun to use marijuana and to drink beer and wine. The mother is very concerned and has brought the entire family to meet with you. You have introduced yourself, secured introductions from

each of the family members, and stated as a purpose for this first meeting to explore the problems and concerns that led the family to come to the agency. You now want to orient them to this process. What would you say?

Discussing Policy and Ethical Factors

An extremely important beginning skill involves discussing potentially relevant legal, policy, and ethical factors. Understanding the ground rules is a critical element in developing an authentic, honest, and trusting relationship. This constitutes part of the informed consent process and is an essential element of professional service. Failure to discuss relevant policy and ethical factors may be grounds for malpractice action.

As a professional social worker, you are bound by certain guidelines in the performance of your duties (see Chapter 3). Some of these originate with the agency with which you are affiliated (e.g., agency policies and procedures), others are promulgated by the social work profession (e.g., ethical codes and standards), and still others are formulated by governmental bodies (e.g., laws and regulations). Clients have a right to be informed of the policies and ethical principles that may apply to them. Many agencies wisely provide prospective clients with brochures and other publications describing relevant policies. Box 6.2 shows a sample document that social workers might provide to prospective clients and use in guiding the discussion of policy and ethical issues. However, some clients do not or cannot truly understand the full meaning of such written material. You should therefore discuss key policies with most, if not all, prospective clients.

BOX 6.2

Agency Policies

As a general guideline, whatever clients say during sessions remains confidential among agency personnel. There are, however, a few exceptions. If a client wants the agency to provide information to another person or agency (for example, to a medical doctor), he or she may sign a *Release of Information* form specifying which information to transfer and to whom. Also, as required by law, indications of possible child abuse or neglect will be reported to child protection authorities. Similarly, evidence that a person represents a danger to himself or herself or to others will not be considered confidential. Action will be taken to protect the lives of the persons involved. In potentially life-threatening circumstances, the value of human life takes precedence over that of confidentiality.

The agency operates on a *sliding fee* basis. This means that the cost of each individual or family session varies according to clients' ability to pay: the higher the family income, the higher the cost—to a maximum of $55.00 per session. Group sessions are lower. Reimbursement from insurance companies, where applicable, is the responsibility of the client, but agency staff will help clients complete the necessary claim forms.

If a scheduled meeting must be cancelled, the agency should be notified at least one day before the appointment

In this agency, we have a procedure for expressing concerns about the nature and quality of the services clients receive. If, for any reason whatsoever, you are uncertain about or dissatisfied with the services you receive, please discuss it with your social worker. If you do not receive an adequate explanation, if the service remains unsatisfactory, or if you feel uncomfortable talking directly with your social worker about the issue, please contact our agency's client representative, Ms. Sheila Cordula in Room 21 (telephone 789-5432). She will attempt to address your concerns.

Suppose, for example, an adult male client assumes that everything he says to you will remain confidential. During a counseling session, he tells you that he often uses a wire coat hanger to "discipline" his 2-year-old child. Operating on the assumption of "absolute confidentiality," he is likely to feel profoundly betrayed when you report to local child-protection authorities what he told you about the "spankings."

Social workers, of course, tend to be heavily invested in protecting children from abuse and may sometimes wonder if discussion of policy and ethical factors may unnecessarily inhibit people from revealing information. Although such discussion probably has little adverse effect on communications, some social workers believe that it does and consequently skim over policies that might provoke client anxiety. A few may even avoid them altogether. These are risky practices that not only clearly endanger the basic rights of clients, they also place social workers who use them at risk of malpractice action, and may in the long-run reduce the likelihood of learning about reportable activities such as child abuse. If consumers conclude that social workers cannot be trusted to tell the whole truth or keep promises, they may well avoid seeking professional help altogether.

In discussing relevant policy and ethical factors, however, you would consider several aspects of the person-issue-situation, including the relative urgency of a situation, timing, and context. Suppose, for example, you serve as a social worker in the emergency room of a hospital. An ambulance delivers a young child who has been severely injured in an automobile accident. When the visibly distraught parents arrive, you would obviously defer discussion of policy and ethical factors while you provide information about their child and try to comfort them. In such instances, their immediate needs take precedence over your obligation to discuss policies. Actually, all the social work skills need to be considered within the context of the person-issue-situation. Often, a skill applicable in one circumstance is completely inappropriate in another. Because social work practice is a professional rather than a technical endeavor, you continually make judgments about how to best use your self and your social work skills.

◆ EXERCISE 6-5: DISCUSSING POLICY AND ETHICAL FACTORS

Use the following case situations to practice the skill of discussing policy and ethical factors. Please respond to each situation in the spaces provided.

1. Assume that you are a social worker in a public housing agency. You are currently in the process of interviewing all residents of a building to determine their social service needs. You have just introduced yourself and described an initial purpose and role to Mrs. Strong, a single mother with five children who range in age from 6 months to 9 years. Write the words you would say in discussing policy and ethical factors.

2. You are a social worker in a nursing residence for elderly persons. A new resident had arrived during the previous weekend. Earlier in the week, you in-

troduced yourself, and now you are about to undertake a complete social history and psychosocial assessment. Following a reintroduction of yourself and a description of purpose and role, you want to outline the ground rules for the working relationship. Write the words you would say in discussing policy and ethical factors with this new resident.

3. You are a social worker for an agency that serves children who have been sexually abused. You are about to begin a new group for girls 7 to 10 years of age. You have introduced yourself, sought introductions from them, described an initial purpose for the group, and outlined your professional roles in the process. You have taken extra time to lessen their anxiety and encourage them to view the group experience as a "place of safety."

   Continue this beginning process by writing the words you would say in discussing policy and ethical factors as they might relate to this group of five girls.

Seeking Feedback

In using the skill of *seeking feedback* (Schwartz, 1976, pp. 188–190; Shulman, 1992, pp. 79–80), you encourage clients to comment about the initial purpose and your role, their roles, policy or ethical factors, or any other aspects of your introductory remarks. An important part of communicating effectively involves checking whether information has been accurately understood. Seeking feedback serves this function. As a social worker, you routinely seek feedback throughout the entire course of work with clients. By asking for feedback about your initial description of purpose and role and your discussion of policy and ethical factors during the beginning phase, you initiate the process of informed consent. You also invite clients to identify areas that are unclear, share thoughts that have occurred to them, introduce a new topic, or express any disagreement about your comments. By seeking feedback, you effectively send a message that this is a mutual and reciprocal process. You convey that you are genuinely interested in what clients have to say about what you have said and that you hope that they will actively participate in the process.

Among the more common ways to seek feedback about purpose, roles, and policy factors are questions such as "How does that sound to you? What do you think about what we've talked about so far? What questions or comments do you have?" Often, clients respond to your request for feedback by asking for clarification. This gives you an opportunity to elaborate about purpose, roles, or policy and ethical factors. In general, clients who clearly understand these ground rules and believe that you sincerely want their feedback are likely to feel both informed and respected.

◆ **EXERCISE 6-6: SEEKING FEEDBACK**

Use the following case situations to practice the skill of seeking feedback. Please respond to each situation in the spaces provided.

1. You, a social worker in an agency that serves children and their families, are meeting for the first time with a 32-year-old mother and her 8-year-old daughter. They have voluntarily sought help regarding some problems with the child's schoolwork. At this time, you do not know anything more about the school or family situation. You have introduced yourself and elicited introductions from them. You have learned that Ms. Pomerantz prefers to be called "Joan" and that her daughter prefers "Emily." You have asked them to call you by your first name. You have also outlined an initial purpose for this first meeting by saying, "In today's meeting I hope that we'll gain a beginning understanding of the concerns that led to this visit. Then, together, we'll try to find how best to address those concerns."

Write the words you would use in seeking feedback regarding purpose from Joan and Emily.

2. As you continue to interact with Joan and Emily, you state, "Everything that you and Emily say during our meetings will be treated as confidential. No one outside the agency will have access to information you share. The major exception to this policy of confidentiality is when you specifically and in writing request that we provide information to someone else. Of course, when someone's life is in danger or there are indications of possible child abuse or neglect, we'll take action to protect the safety of those involved—even if that means violating our basic rule of confidentiality."

   Write the words you would use in seeking feedback from Joan regarding policy and ethical factors.

3. You are a social worker in an agency that serves adults and children who have been involved in child abuse. You are meeting for the first time with a 22-year-old man who has been charged with severely beating his 4-year-old son. He has come to this first meeting involuntarily. He is required to receive counseling as part of an adjudicated court agreement that, depending on the results of the counseling, may enable him to avoid incarceration. Thus far, you have introduced yourself and elicited an introduction from him. You sense from the nature of his body position that you should address him in a formal manner. You refer to him as "Mr. Battle" and indicate that he may call you by your first name if he prefers. You have also outlined an initial purpose for this first meeting by saying, "In today's meeting I hope that we will be able to gain a beginning understanding of your current situation and identify

some preliminary goals for our work together. It is my understanding that you are required by Judge Koopman to participate in counseling sessions at least once per week for a minimum of six months."

Write the words you would use in seeking feedback from Mr. Battle concerning what you have said thus far.

4. As you continue to interact with Mr. Battle, you say, "I hope that we will be able to identify some of the reasons for the violence toward your son and that together we will work toward eliminating any future violent actions. You should know that in situations such as this, where the court is involved, I regularly provide reports to the judge. I will report to the judge the number of sessions you attend, the degree of your cooperation in the process, my evaluation of your progress, and my assessment concerning the risk of further violence toward your son."

Write the words you would use in seeking feedback from Mr. Battle concerning what you have said.

Summary

During the beginning phase, you introduce and identify yourself and seek an introduction from the prospective client. Following the exchange of introductions, you describe a tentative initial purpose for the meeting, possibly identify one or more professional roles that you might undertake, orient clients to the process, and identify relevant policy and ethical factors that might apply. Throughout this beginning process, you regularly seek feedback from clients concerning their understanding of and reactions to your introductory comments. By using the beginning skills, you help to clarify the nature and boundaries or ground rules of the helping process, lessen the initial ambivalence prospective clients often experience, and establish a tentative direction for work.

◆ CHAPTER 6 SUMMARY EXERCISES

Assume that you are a social worker with a human service agency that offers a broad range of social services. Prepare for a first meeting with each of the following prospective clients. In the spaces provided, write the words you would say and the actions you would take as you meet for the first time. Among the skills useful for this series of exercises are introducing yourself, seeking introductions, describing an initial purpose and (sometimes) your professional social work role, orienting clients, discussing policy and ethical factors, and seeking feedback. Please label each of the beginning skills you use in each case situation.

1. Earlier in the day, a woman telephoned the agency and said she wanted to talk with someone about an incident that had occurred about one week earlier. A man she had met in a bar drove her home and then raped her. She had thought that she would be able to manage her feelings about the crime by herself. However, she now realizes that she needs help to cope with the aftereffects of the violation. She said, "I'm falling apart." An appointment has been scheduled for the present time. What would you do and say in beginning?

2. The agency receptionist informs you that in the waiting room there is a 55-year-old man who is rapidly pacing back and forth in an agitated fashion,

saying, "I have to die. I have to die." You are the social worker responsible for interviewing all persons who come to the agency without appointments. You proceed to the reception area and ask him to accompany you back to your office. What would you do and say in beginning?

3. Recently, a 14-year-old African American girl told her schoolteacher that she is pregnant by her white boyfriend. She also told the teacher that she needs to get an abortion quickly, or "my parents will kill me if they find out I'm pregnant." The teacher urged her to talk with you, the school social worker, and secured the girl's permission to tell you about the situation. The teacher did so and arranged for a meeting at this time. What would you do and say in beginning?

4. An 8-year-old victim of sexual molestation seems to be in a state of emotional shock. She has not spoken a single word or expressed feelings since the incident was discovered several days ago. The child-protection caseworker tried

to encourage the child to talk about what happened, but her efforts were unsuccessful. The child has been referred to you, a social worker who specializes in work with victimized children.

A home visit has been scheduled for the present time. You drive to the girl's home, where she resides with her mother. The alleged perpetrator, a 15-year-old neighbor, has been detained in a juvenile center while awaiting a judicial hearing. The child's mother answers the door. What would you do and say in beginning, first with the mother and then with the 8-year-old girl herself?

5. A 42-year-old woman, beaten nearly to death by her husband several times during the past ten years, wants help in dealing with the situation. After the most recent episode, she sought refuge in a shelter for battered women, where you serve as a social worker. You are about to meet her for the first time. What would you do and say in beginning?

1. Go to the Peace Corps "Hello" Web page at www.peacecorps.gov /wws/views/hello/index.html, the "Say Hello" Web page at www.ipl.org/div /kidspace/hello, the New York Public Library's "Useful Expressions and Greetings in 26 Languages" Web page at www.nypl.org/branch/central _units/d/f/useful.htm, or to Jennifer's Language Page at www.elite.net /~runner/jennifers/index.htm. Use the following space to write how you would say, "Hello, my name is (insert your name)" in each of the following languages:

   a. Arabic

   b. Cherokee

   c. Spanish

   d. Korean

   e. American Sign Language

2. Suppose you were about to meet with a family that recently entered the United States from another country. Because of a preliminary telephone call, you know that they are interested in learning about immigration laws and procedures for obtaining a "Green Card." Go to the U.S. Immigration Bureau Web site at http://www.immigration-bureau.org to gain a preliminary appreciation of the requirements. Use the following space to summarize what is involved.

Chapter 6 Self-Appraisal

As you finish this chapter, please assess your proficiency in the beginning skills by completing the following self-appraisal instrument.

SELF-APPRAISAL: THE BEGINNING SKILLS

Please use the following items to help you undertake a self-assessment of your proficiency in the beginning skills addressed in this chapter. Read each statement carefully. Then, use the following four-point rating scale to indicate the degree to which you agree or disagree with each statement. Record your numerical response in the space provided:

4 = Strongly Agree

3 = Agree

2 = Disagree

1 = Strongly Disagree

_____   1. I can effectively use the skill of introducing myself.
_____   2. I can effectively use the skill of seeking introductions.
_____   3. I can effectively use the skill of describing initial purpose.
_____   4. I can effectively use the skill of orienting clients.
_____   5. I can effectively use the skill of discussing policy and ethical factors.
_____   6. I can effectively use the skill of seeking feedback.

_____   Subtotal

Note: These items are taken directly from the beginning skills section of the Social Work Skills Self-Appraisal Questionnaire contained in Appendix 3. Earlier, when you reviewed Chapter 2 and completed the exercises, you responded to these questions. You may now compare the responses you made on that occasion with those you made this time. Also compare the two subtotals. If you believe that you have progressed in terms of your proficiency with the beginning skills, the more recent subtotal should be higher than the earlier.

Finally, reflect on the skills addressed in this chapter and the results of your self-appraisal. Based on your analysis, prepare a succinct one-page summary report entitled "Self-Assessment of Proficiency in the Beginning Skills." Within the report, be sure to identify those skills that you know and do well (e.g., a score of 3 or 4). Also, specify those that need further practice (e.g., scores of 2 or less) and briefly outline plans by which to achieve proficiency in them. When finished, include the report in your Social Work Skills Learning Portfolio.

Chapter 7

Exploring

As the beginning phase ends, you engage the client in a mutual exploration of the person-issue-situation. This chapter (see Box 7.1) is intended to help you develop proficiency in the exploring skills that encourage clients to share information, thoughts, and feelings about themselves; the problems or concerns that led to the contact; and the social context and environment in which they function. Through this process of exploration, you and the client usually learn a great deal. You both derive a more complete and realistic understanding of the person-issue-situation. Clients often enhance their own self-understanding. Indeed, greater self-awareness is a common result because talking openly with another person also involves listening to oneself. As clients share their thoughts, ideas, and feelings, they not only perceive your reactions, they more fully experience their own. Through this process, you and the client together consider information regarding the person, the issue, and the situation. This helps both parties understand the factors associated with the origin, development, and maintenance of the issue of concern as well as those strengths, attributes, and resources that may later be useful in working toward resolution. Such information, in conjunction with your own professional knowledge, contributes to the development of an assessment and a plan for work.

The skills most applicable to the exploration phase are (1) asking questions, (2) seeking clarification, (3) reflecting content, (4) reflecting feelings, (5) reflecting feeling and meaning, (6) partializing, and (7) going beyond what is said. Consistent with a person-and-situation perspective, these skills are used for exploring the person, exploring the issue, exploring the situation, and looking for strengths.

The purpose of this chapter is to help learners develop proficiency in the exploring skills.

Goals

Following completion of this chapter, learners should be able to demonstrate proficiency in the following:

◆ Ability to explore relevant aspects of the person-issue-situation and look for strengths
◆ Asking questions
◆ Seeking clarification
◆ Reflecting content
◆ Reflecting feelings
◆ Reflecting feeling and meaning
◆ Partializing
◆ Going beyond what is said
◆ Ability to assess proficiency in the exploring skills

In undertaking the exploration process with clients, consider the matrix shown in Table 7.1. Following the introductions and other parts of the beginning phase, clients commonly feel a strong wish to discuss the problem or issue[1] of concern. As a result, you often proceed to an exploration of the issue as currently experienced (cell #1). You might then trace its emergence, history, and development (cell #2). As you do so, many clients naturally begin to describe aspects of themselves personally as well as dimensions of the situation. As needed, you may next explore clients' present view of themselves (cell #3), followed by a review of past experiences (cell #4). Then, to the degree that further information is needed, you encourage description of the present situation, including the social context and physical environment (cell #5) and then the situation as it has been in the past (cell #6). Finally, you encourage clients to envision what the future might be like if they, the issue of concern, and the situation were to continue as before (cells #7, #8, and #9). You also explore the possible effects if things should happen to change.

Of course, these nine dimensions overlap. As an issue is discussed, clients may share information about themselves and their situations. While exploring the present, clients may reveal material from the past or hopes and fears about the future. You do not need to interrupt to maintain a particular order or sequence. Generally, you may

---

[1] The term "issue" is used to refer to a topic of concern or interest to the client, the social worker, or other interested parties. In this context, an issue may be a problem, need, dilemma, symptom, goal, aspiration, or objective of relevance to participants in the professional relationship.

TABLE 7.1
Exploration Matrix

	Present	Past	Future
Issue	1	2	7
Person	3	4	8
Situation	5	6	9

encourage clients to share information in their own ways. Do not view the exploration matrix as a fixed interview schedule. Instead, consider it as a flexible guide to help you organize the exploration of relevant aspects of the person-issue-situation over time.

Exploring the issue involves examining the present status of the issue of concern—its intensity, frequency, and duration—and the context in which it tends to happen. As a social worker, you are interested in what happens before, during, and following its occurrence. In addition, you commonly explore the issue as it has been in the past. Trace or track its development from the time of its initial occurrence to the present. In your exploration, include a careful examination of clients' attempts to resolve, cope with, or avoid the issue (see *looking for strengths* later). Encourage exploration of efforts that have been successful, those that were partially successful, and those that were unsuccessful. Identify strengths and resources that were used in earlier attempts at resolution. As part of this exploration, encourage clients to share any thoughts, feelings, and actions associated with the issue of concern.

In exploring problems, clients often share their hypotheses about causes. They may offer an explanation about "why" something happened. Such hypotheses are often extremely useful. Sometimes, however, they appear unrelated to actual events or to potential solutions. Regardless of their relevance, make a mental note about clients' causal explanations because they may contribute to or hinder progress toward resolution. Indeed, some clients have fixed views about causes or solutions that represent genuine obstacles to change. For example, a teenage boy might view his mother's nagging as the cause of the problems for which he wants your help. He also sees the solution in terms of his mother's behavior: "If she would change, things would be better." If the youth retains that fixed view—or if you unquestioningly accept the validity of the hypothesis—the locus of responsibility and control shifts from the adolescent to his mother. From his perspective, the boy's mother becomes a "persecutor," the boy becomes a "victim," and you as the social worker are left to serve as "rescuer." Imagine the difficulties if the "real issue" involves the boy's severe substance abuse and the mother's "nagging" reflects her concerned attempts to help him recover. A social worker's uncritical confirmation of the boy's hypothesis might inadvertently contribute to his continued substance abuse.

Excessive attention to thoughts about and reasons for issues may limit the exploration process. Some clients and some social workers prefer analytic over descriptive expression of events or circumstances. Unfortunately, this preference for ideas may contribute to inadequate exploration of details or expression of feelings about the issues of concern. Through a process called intellectualization, people sometimes attempt to protect themselves from or defend against perceived powerful feelings and awareness by engaging in abstract, cognitive thought. Generally speaking, clients and social workers are wise to explore descriptive information before examining possible reasons for phenomena. The quality of cognitive analysis tends to improve when it is based on a solid understanding of the facts and circumstances. Questions such as, "Why do you think that happens?" or "What do you think causes that?" are postponed until both the client and the worker have explored the person-issue-situation in sufficient depth and breadth to warrant analysis. In general, descriptive exploration should precede and form the basis and context for analysis.

Exploring the person involves encouraging clients to explore aspects of themselves as individual human beings. In this dimension, you are especially interested in the *thinking, feeling,* and *doing* aspects of clients' experience. Seek information about personal strengths and assets as well as weaknesses and deficiencies. Within this dimension, explore both the substance of clients' thoughts—whether they occur as beliefs (the words people say to themselves) or as images (the mental pictures people visualize)—and the thought processes (the cognitive steps people take as they move from one thought or idea to another). Within the dimension of feeling, consider clients' emotions (e.g., anger, fear, or sadness) as well as physical sensations (e.g., energy, fatigue, muscular tension, nausea, or light-headedness). Within the dimension of doing, explore overt behavior (e.g., walking, speaking, hitting, looking) as well as the absence of behavior (e.g., behaviors, such as assertive requests, that clients might have used appropriately in a situation but, for whatever reasons, failed to do so).

Sometimes, the nature of the issue is such that exploration of personal style or personality characteristics may be needed. Clients may discuss traits or attributes that contribute to understanding. For instance, a middle-aged woman may describe an aspect of herself as "extraordinarily sensitive to criticism" or "my feelings are easily hurt." An older man might report that he is "emotionally shut down" or perhaps that he has "lost the ability to feel." Appreciating these characteristics may help in understanding the person-issue-situation and in developing plans to pursue goals.

The biological or medical history and condition of clients may be pertinent to the exploration process. For instance, diabetes, epilepsy, cardiac problems, and addictions are among the health-related factors that often contribute to an understanding of the person-issue-situation. Similarly, exploration of clients' spiritual or religious beliefs may be needed to further understanding. Indeed, certain religions prohibit the application of certain medical procedures. Others may consider certain misfortunes to be the result of sinful behavior. Core beliefs about life's meaning and how to live a good and proper life often influence clients' understanding of themselves and others, their circumstances, and the issues they confront.

Because most if not all issues have social aspects, social workers usually encourage clients to explore their significant relationships and their typical ways of relating to others. For example, clients may explore their preferred relational styles (e.g., aggressive, assertive, passive) and how they react socially during encounters involving conflict or intense emotion (e.g., confrontation, immobilization, withdrawal).

Clients' preferred coping processes and their problem solving strategies are also often relevant. Questions such as, "How do you cope with stress, disappointment, or frustration?" may lead to deeper understanding and reveal potential directions for work or perhaps avenues for resolution. Similarly, queries such as, "When you confront problems such as this one, how do you usually go about trying to solve them?" may contribute to understanding about problem-solving patterns and strategies.

Exploring the situation involves examining current and, when applicable, past circumstances. Collect pertinent information about social, cultural aspects, economic, environmental, and spiritual aspects of situations that may relate to the issue of concern or to those assets or resources that might be useful for resolution. Learn about significant other persons, family systems, communities, ethnic affiliations, religious involvement, housing, education, employment, and finances.

Exploring the future involves examining the issue, the person, and the situation as they may be in the future. In particular, explore three possible future scenarios. First, consider how the issue, person, and situation would probably be if everything continues along as before. Second, examine how they might be in a "worst possible case" scenario where things seriously deteriorate. Finally, explore a "best possible case" where the issue is completely resolved. The latter process is often extremely revealing, as it helps you and clients identify possible directions for work. Exploring the future has the additional value of helping identify potential indicators of a successful outcome.

As you and your client explore the person-issue-situation together, you may recognize an imbalance in the amount of attention to problems and troubles versus strengths and resources. Occasionally, clients deny or minimize problems and stridently assert that everything is "just fine." Some nonvoluntary clients reflect such a "rosy" view—at least at first. Other clients, however, seem to focus primarily on problems, dilemmas, and distressing events. This is quite understandable. Many clients are so distraught that they focus almost exclusively on things that cause the greatest pain. Helping professionals are frequently educated to do much the same; that is to attend primarily to symptoms, problems, illnesses, pain, or disorders. Several factors contribute to this "tilt toward troubles." As a social worker, however, ensure that strengths and resources—as well as problems and needs—are adequately explored. Otherwise, you and your client could conclude the exploration process with an incomplete understanding of both the factors associated with the development and maintenance of the issue as well as the potential resources that might be used to address them.

By *looking for strengths*, you gently—without denying or minimizing the client's reality—explore the strengths of the person-and-situation. You can look for strengths by asking questions, seeking responses to "incomplete" or "fill in the blank" sentences, or by active listening. Clients frequently reflect remarkable strength and resilience as they cope with and accommodate to challenging problems and circumstances. Indeed, the term "heroic" is not too extreme to apply to many clients.

Of course, there are risks and dangers associated with a strengths perspective—just as there with other conceptual models. A major danger occurs when social workers prematurely force clients to look for positive attributes before they have explored the problems and circumstances in their own way so that they may feel heard and understood. You may recall a brief reference in Chapter 5 to dramatically increased dropout rates when helping professionals did not communicate accurate understanding of clients' experience of the problem (i.e., how clients view the issues) (Epperson, Bushway, & Warman, 1983; Pekarik, 1988; Wierzbicki & Pekarik, 1993). Determined searches for strengths that prevent or impede clients' ability to describe and discuss the issues of concern in their own way can leave clients feeling unheard, misunderstood, and extremely frustrated. Many may not return following an initial visit. Prematurely seeking strengths may paradoxically leave clients feeling diminished rather than supported. The effects can be similar to those experienced by a child who has just scraped her knee. It hurts and she is just about to cry. Suppose an adult (e.g., a parent or teacher) were to say, "You're so grown-up! You've just skinned your knee and I'm sure it hurts at lot. Yet, you're such a big girl you're able to keep yourself from crying!"

The statement might motivate the girl to keep control of those tears and she might feel more grown-up. However, she would not feel understood. Indeed, the position "I know what you feel and experience better than you do" is anathema to empathic understanding. She would also almost certainly inhibit full and accurate expression of what she really thinks, senses, and feels to avoid the censure of the adult or perhaps to maintain the image of herself as a "big girl."

Imagine how this pattern might play out between a social worker and a client of any age. Minimizing or denying the other's feelings and experiences—even in an effort to identify strengths—can powerfully affect clients' willingness to share. The absence of complete exploration of experiences, events, and circumstances—including the feelings associated with them—may interfere with the development of a favorable working relationship.

As you do look for strengths, keep the client's perspective and the timing of the exploration in mind. Typically, looking for strengths should occur after the worker has accurately communicated understanding of the client's view of the problems and issues, and explored pertinent aspects of the person and situation.

Table 7.2 may help you organize the process of looking for strengths in the areas of competencies, social support, successes, and life lessons.

TABLE 7.2
Looking for Strengths

	Person	Situation	Issue
Competencies			
Social Support			
Successes			
Life Lessons			

All clients possess numerous abilities, capacities, and talents. They also hold various beliefs about them. Social workers seek to help clients identify and explore strengths in both dimensions—beliefs as well as realities. By *looking for competencies*, you and your clients may discover an incredible array of useful traits and attributes associated with their sense of efficiency and effectiveness. Unless you consciously seek them out, however, they may never become apparent.

You can look for competencies by asking questions such as, "When people praise or compliment you about your talents and abilities, what things do they mention?" "If people were to brag about your special qualities and characteristics, what would they say?" "Some people have special talents or abilities that they keep pretty much to themselves, what are some of yours?" You can also help clients explore competencies through the use of "incomplete" sentences. You could ask clients to complete sentences that begin with phrases such as, "I am very good at . . ." "I am especially talented when it comes to . . ." Try to extend the exploration by considering how clients' talents, abilities, and competencies manifest in social roles and situations (e.g., family, work, and other social systems). "Of all the things you do with your family, what gets you the most praise or credit?" "What qualities or abilities do you possess that you wish your boss knew about?" "When it comes to relationships, which of your personal qualities help you the most?" Competencies also relate to the issue of concern. "Over the course of time that you've been dealing with this issue, what talents or abilities of yours have been most helpful?"

Social workers tend to recognize the importance of social support in all aspects of human life.[2] By *looking for social supports*, you encourage clients to identify and reflect on those individuals and groups within the social environment that have been or could be resources. Ask questions such as, "Over the course of your life, who have been the people that provided the greatest support?" "Where do you feel the most support?" Of course, you would also consider how those social supports have or might favorably affect the person, and contribute to resolution of the issue of concern.

Experiences of accomplishment and achievement tend to contribute to feelings of competency and optimism. *Looking for success* involves specific recognition of those events and may lead to the creation of a "success timeline." Try asking questions such as, "When you reflect back upon your life, what do you consider your greatest successes or achievements?" "When you were a child, what were your biggest accomplishments? When you were a teenager? When you were a young adult?"

Over time, people tend to gain perspective and make their significant life experiences meaningful in some way. Successes and failures, good times and bad, pain and pleasure, all become part of a personal philosophy. By *looking for life lessons*, you encourage clients to consider what they have learned and realized. In effect, you help clients to acknowledge their own wisdom. Frequently, lessons learned before, perhaps in different circumstances, can be applied to current issues and concerns. You can look for life lessons by asking questions such as, "You've been through a great deal and

---

[2] Please refer to the discussion of social support and to the Social Support Appraisal Scale presented in Chapter 2.

somehow survived. What have you learned about life from these experiences? What have you learned about yourself? What have you learned about people?" As you proceed, you may find opportunities to look for life lessons that might apply to the current issue of concern. "Of all the things you've learned from these experiences, which lessons might help you address this issue?"

Usually, within one or two meetings, you and the client have discussed the more pressing issues, explored a good deal about the person and situation, and discovered various strengths, assets, and resources. At this point in the process, you can decide whether you and your agency have the authority, resources, and expertise necessary to provide the needed social work services to this particular client system. Because of a lack of familiarity with social service, health, and mental health networks, prospective clients sometimes contact providers and organizations that are not well prepared to help them address their particular issues. Through exploration of the person-issue-situation, you may be able to determine that another organization in the community would be better prepared to provide helpful service. Then, if the client concurs, you could contact the other agency to initiate a professional referral. Of course, the referral process should be done with great care, so that the client does not feel rejected by you or your agency. Also, the other agency's personnel should be treated with professionalism and courtesy. The nature of your relationships with other community professionals often determines whether prospective clients receive a warm or a cool reception. Therefore, relate to your colleagues in other agencies with the same high degree of professionalism you show to clients.

When the issue of concern is congruent with your agency's function and range of services, and falls within your areas of expertise, you and the client may appropriately continue the exploring process. Before long, both of you should gain a fairly clear sense of direction for the work that you will do together.

Asking Questions

Questions are used to elicit facts, ideas, and feelings concerning the person, the issue, the situation, and potential means or processes for resolution. Questions help identify strengths, competencies, assets, and resources. Questions often yield information necessary for mutual understanding, assessment, contract formulation, movement toward resolution and goal attainment, evaluation, and ending.

The first primary use of the questioning skill typically occurs as you and the client conclude the beginning phase. By this time, you have introduced yourselves, reached a tentative understanding of the purpose for meeting and your respective roles, discussed relevant policies and ethical principles, and sought feedback from the client. The initial exploratory question represents the first substantive consideration of the issue that led to the contact with you (Perlman, 1957, p. 88). Commonly, the question is phrased in such a way as to allow clients maximum opportunity to express themselves freely and fully. For example, you might ask, "When you telephoned the other day, you mentioned something about family problems. What's happening within the family that concerns you?" It may also be useful to ask about precipitating events related to the presenting concern. For instance, you might ask, "What led you to contact us about the family problems at this time?"

Questions may occasionally be phrased as directives. You could say, "Please share your concerns about the difficulties that trouble you at this time." In the case of an involuntary client, you might say, "I understand that the judge required you to come here for counseling. I know quite a bit about the situation, but I'd like to hear the full story from you. Please describe what happened." In general, questions are preferred over directives because of the suggested power imbalance. "Tell me . . ." or "Talk about . . ." is, in effect, a command that may subtly suggest that the social worker is the most important person in this encounter.

"Tell me . . ." requests also tend to imply that the primary reason for client sharing is for you, the social worker, to acquire information that you will then use to formulate an assessment and prescribe a treatment plan. In most circumstances, social workers hope to foster a collaborative working relationship where the client is a full participant in the process. Indications that the social worker is the expert authority who provides answers and solutions often lead clients to assume a passive, subordinate role akin to the "doctor-patient" relationship rather than the "client-and-social worker" partnership.

As you might expect, the questioning skill is applicable at many points throughout the exploration phase and, of course, all other phases as well. Questions are used to explore relevant aspects of the person-issue-situation, including the circumstances surrounding the origin, development, and status of the presenting concerns. Examples of common questions include: "How did these difficulties begin?" "Who was included in your family as you were growing up?" "What were your parents like?" "Who lives with you now?" "What did you feel when she left?" "What were you thinking about when that happened?" "What would you like to be different?" "What did you do then?"

The questions you ask derive from your active pursuit of information regarding the person-issue-situation over time. There are two general types of questions: closed-ended and open-ended. *Closed-ended questions* (Goodman & Esterly, 1988, pp. 123–127) are phrased to elicit short responses, sometimes simply yes or no. Closed-ended questions yield a great deal of information in a brief amount of time. They are especially useful in crises where vital information must be gathered quickly.

Here are a few examples of closed-ended questions that you might ask. "What is your phone number?" "What's your address?" "Do you have a car?" "Do you live at home?" "When were you born?" "How old are you?" "Where do you work?" "Who is your family doctor?" "When was your last physical exam?" "Does anyone live with you?" "Is somebody there in the house with you right now?" "Which do you prefer?" "Have you taken some medicine?" "How many pills did you take?"

Usually, answers to such questions are quite brief. This can be advantageous or not, depending on the purpose of meeting and the needs of the situation. Sometimes the rapid collection of specific information is so important that you postpone free and full exploration of other aspects of the person-issue-situation. However, too many closed-ended questions, asked one after another, may lead clients to feel like suspects in a criminal investigation. They may feel interrogated rather than interviewed, and the quality of your professional relationship may suffer. Therefore, unless the situation is immediately life threatening or otherwise urgent, you would usually be wise to mix closed-ended with open-ended questions and active listening responses.

Some closed-ended questions are, in legal terminology, *leading*. A leading question is phrased in a way that elicits (i.e., "leads to") a specific answer—one that the questioner wants to hear. For example, suppose a social worker asked a client, "Haven't you experienced lots of pain in your pelvic area? Yes? And, haven't you felt that pain since you were a young child? Yes? Aren't these painful symptoms common among people who were sexually abused as children? Yes? So, isn't it likely that you were sexually abused as a child?" Such a series of questions would clearly lead or suggest to a client that a certain conclusion held by the social worker is the right and valid one. During the exploration phase, such leading questions are generally counterproductive because they tend to narrow a process that should usually be quite open and expansive. In particular, whenever you serve an investigative function in your service as a social worker, choose your words and the phrasing of questions carefully. If you frequently ask leading questions in such interviews, your courtroom testimony could be easily challenged and perhaps disallowed. During the exploring phase especially, try to avoid leading or suggestive questions.

Open-ended questions (Goodman & Esterly, 1988, pp. 127–137) are phrased in a manner that encourages people to express themselves expansively and extensively. Open-ended questions are designed to further exploration on a deeper level or in a broader way. They are usually not leading questions because they enable the client to respond in any number of ways. Often they are phrased as "how" questions, which nearly always yield open responses from clients. For example, "How did that come to happen?" "How did he react?" "How do you feel right now?" "How did he act in that situation?"

"What" questions may also be used to elicit expansive expressions from clients. "What is the nature of your concern?" "What is she like?" "What happened then?" "In what way did you . . . ?" "What did you say then?" However, they may also be phrased in a closed-ended fashion as well. "What is your phone number?" "What is your date of birth?"

Unless you specifically request a feeling response, "what" questions usually elicit much needed descriptive information. In seeking feelings, you often have to ask for them. For example, "What feelings did you experience when he left?" encourages clients to identify and perhaps share emotions. Indeed, some evidence indicates that open questions about feelings may encourage clients to share more emotion than do active-listening responses (Hill & Gormally, 1977). When exploring emotions, it may help to combine active-listening responses with specific open questions about feelings.

Directives can serve the functions of open or closed-ended questions. For example, "Please say more about that," "Please elaborate," "Please continue," "Please share more about that part of your life," all encourage open responses. "Please spell your name," "Please tell me your street address," serve as closed-ended requests for brief responses. Remember, however, the earlier caution about the potential effects of directives on the working relationship. In most circumstances, you seek to develop a collaborative partnership rather than a hierarchical relationship in which you are the "expert-in-charge." Try to avoid indications that you are the superior party in this relationship.

"Why" questions can be used to encourage expression—especially when phrased in a tentative fashion. However, they may also generate defensiveness. Clients may conclude that you are judging them critically and feel compelled to defend or justify some aspect of their behavior or circumstances. Therefore, be cautious about the use of "why" questions. If you use a gentle tone of voice combined with a warm, open, and accepting facial expression, you may be able to use them occasionally. Also, the way you phrase the question can help. For example, the defensive-eliciting quality of a "why" question may sometimes be moderated by qualifying phrases such as "I wonder why (that is)?" or "Why do you think that happens?" When asking "why" questions, be certain to communicate nonverbally an attitude of interest and acceptance.

During the exploration process, intersperse your questions with active listening responses. Otherwise, an interview can quickly turn quite unpleasant. When clients must answer one question after another—even when they are open questions—they often begin to feel interrogated rather than interviewed. Realize that questions can suggest blame, judgment, evaluation, or advice. They are not always simply neutral requests for information. For example, "Have you talked with your mother yet?" might imply that you expected the client to talk with his or her mother. "Have you completed that form?" may convey a similar message. Although it is sometimes useful to express a statement of opinion or preference in the form of a question, be aware that you are doing so. Sharing your personal or professional views within the context of a question does not relieve you of responsibility for the substance of the message. Also, try to avoid asking either-or questions, multiple-choice questions, or a string of questions at the same time. For example, "Are you still going with Jackie or have you given up on her and are now dating only Jill? And what about Cathy?" would confuse most clients. They would not know whether to respond to your first, second, third, or fourth question. Try to ask one question at a time.

Questions can be extremely useful for providing a sense of coherence and continuity to the exploration process. As clients talk about themselves as people, the issue of concern, and the situational contexts in which they function, they sometimes (quite understandably) focus a great deal on one topic while entirely avoiding or only briefly touching on important related information. When that occurs, you can ask questions that guide clients toward an exploration of other pertinent aspects of the person-issue-situation. For example, you might ask, "As you were growing up, how was your relationship with your older sister?" in order to gather information about an aspect of a client's family and social situation that had been neglected. Be careful, however, to respect clients' psychological and interpersonal sensitivities. This is particularly important during the exploring phase. When a client is especially fragile concerning a particular topic or theme, you would usually postpone inquiry into that specific dimension until your working relationship becomes more established. Then, when the client feels more secure, you may return to delve into areas that require further exploration.

The exploring skill of asking questions is extremely useful for gathering and considering information about the person-issue-situation, and to look for strengths and resources. As you might imagine, however, questions are also needed throughout the entire helping process.

◆ EXERCISE 7-1: ASKING QUESTIONS

For these exercises, assume that you are a social worker at a social service agency for families and children. In the spaces provided, write the words you would say in each situation.

1. You are in the midst of the first interview with Mr. K., a recently divorced 55-year-old man. You have introduced yourself and have addressed the other aspects of the beginning phase of practice. You are now ready for an initial exploratory question. At this point, you know only that Mr. K.'s concern relates in some way to the divorce. Therefore, you want to encourage him to explore that topic in depth. Write the words you would say in asking this first question. Once recorded, indicate whether it is open- or closed-ended. Discuss your rationale for choosing this particular question. How do you think Mr. K. would respond?

2. You have just begun to interview Mrs. O., a 77-year-old widow who lives alone in a small apartment. You have already introduced yourselves, outlined some of the services that might be of interest to Mrs. O. (e.g., transportation, meals on wheels, or in-home medical services), and addressed other dimensions of the beginning phase. Now write the words you would say in asking an initial exploratory question. Once recorded, determine whether it is open- or closed-ended. Discuss your rationale for choosing this particular question and anticipate how you think Mrs. O. would respond.

3. You have begun the first interview with the S. family, a seven-member blended family who sought your help with problems of family tension and conflict. You have gone through the introductions and addressed other aspects of the beginning phase. Your initial question was, "What do you see as the major issues within the family?" The father responded to this question first, then the mother answered, followed by other family members. Although the specific nature of the responses varied somewhat, there appeared to be considerable agreement that the strained relationship between the two teenage boys (biological children of the father) and their father's wife (the boys' stepmother) is a major issue. Their relationship appears to involve a great deal of tension, conflict, and anger. As the social worker, you now want to explore the origin and development of the difficulties in this relationship. Write the words you would say in doing so. After you have written your question, determine whether it is open- or closed-ended. Is it directed to the boys, the other children, Mrs. S., Mr. S., or the entire group? Discuss your rationale for asking this question and selecting the person or persons you decided to address. What do you anticipate would be the boys' reaction? How might Mrs. S. respond?

Assume that you continue to explore the issue, the family, and the situation. Write the words you would say in formulating three additional questions. For each one, determine whether it is open- or closed-ended. Also, identify which aspect of the exploration process (person, family, issue, situation; present, past, future) each question addresses. Finally, anticipate how various family members might react to each question.

4. You have begun to interview a prospective client of Latino background who speaks both Spanish and English fluently. You have completed the introductions, addressed the policy and ethical factors, and established a tentative purpose for the meeting: to explore the concerns Mrs. F. has about her two children, 7 and 9 years old. According to Mrs. F., they are the only Latino children in their school and have been harassed by several teenage boys. Mrs. F. is worried that her children might be in physical danger. She is also concerned that their attitude toward school might be negatively affected by these experiences.

As the social worker, you are now ready to explore the issue further. Write the words you would say in an initial exploratory question. Follow that by writing the words you might say in asking three additional questions concerning the issue, the children, Mrs. F., the family system, or the school situation. Identify whether each question is closed- or open-ended. Then, briefly discuss your rationale for the questions you have selected. Finally, predict the reaction that Mrs. F. might have to each question.

Seeking Clarification

Sometimes during an interview, clients may make statements that seem unclear. They may communicate in an apparently contradictory fashion, skim over a relevant issue, or neglect some significant aspect of themselves, the issue, or the circumstances. Such indirect, unclear, or incomplete messages often involve important aspects of the person's experience, so the manner in which you respond may substantially affect the nature of the relationship, the direction for work, and the outcome of the helping endeavor. In such instances, you may use the skill of *seeking clarification*. That is, you attempt to elicit a more complete expression of the meaning of previous words or gestures. In effect, you ask the client to elaborate about something he or she has just said. During the early portion of an interview, you seek clarification to generate more complete and comprehensible information about particular aspects of the person-issue-situation. Seeking clarification also subtly suggests that a particular term or topic may be of some special relevance.

Of course, you will not always completely understand everything that clients say. Sometimes, this is because you are not listening well. At other times, clients do not express themselves clearly because they are uncertain about what they actually do think and feel. After all, one purpose of exploring is to help clients understand themselves better. Also, clients sometimes send subtle or indirect messages that, at some level, they may hope you will notice. Many people are reluctant to ask directly for help. Such hesitancy is quite common among members of some cultural groups. This reluctance may be intensified if the social worker happens to be a person of majority status and the clients are from a different culture. In addition, many issues are so embarrassing or emotional in nature that clients find it difficult to talk openly about them. Therefore, subtle communications are common. Be sensitive to indirect expressions in the form of hints, nonverbal gestures, or incomplete or mixed messages and recognize that considerable anxiety may be associated with such communications. Some clients may send extremely significant messages in an indirect manner because they are not yet fully aware of or comfortable with some aspects of their thinking or feeling, or because they fear that you might disapprove.

In responding to indirect expressions, move carefully toward a greater degree of specificity and clarity by asking for further information about the term, phrase, or topic. For example, during a first meeting a 50-year-old client says to a 25-year-old social worker, "I've never had much luck with young social workers. You're all so innocent— still wet behind the ears." The worker might respond to such a statement by asking, "When you talk about not having 'much luck' with other young social workers, it sounds like there have been some problems. What sorts of difficulties have you had with young social workers?"

The skill of seeking clarification tends to encourage clients to explain a term or elaborate about the specific aspects of a thought, feeling, action, or situation (Shulman, 1992, pp. 115–123). People often communicate in vague or general terms. Seeking clarification about detailed aspects of an experience or the specific meaning of a term may enable you and the client to gain a more complete and realistic understanding.

Seeking clarification may be especially helpful in circumstances where the social worker and client reflect cultural differences. Words, phrases, and gestures commonly used in one culture may be nonexistent in another, or their meaning may differ dramatically. Although the client may know exactly what she or he means by a particular term, you may not—at least when it is first used. Even when a client uses Standard English, a term may have a unique meaning to that person. Clients may use words that you have never heard before, or they may use a familiar term in a manner that is unusual to you. The skill of seeking clarification can help in these circumstances. In seeking clarification, you seek additional specific information about a particular word or phrase, or some other aspect of a client's verbal or nonverbal communication.

Seeking clarification is a discrete form of questioning. Rather than encouraging clients to provide more general information about a current or new topic, its purpose is to further understanding of specific aspects of a previous message. Seeking clarification may appear as an open or closed question or as a directive. To practice this skill, use the following formats.

PRACTICE FORMATS: SEEKING CLARIFICATION

What, specifically, do you mean when you say_____?

or

Could you be more specific about _____?

or

Would you please elaborate on_____?

or

Explain what you mean by _____?

Example: Seeking Clarification

CLIENT: My spouse and I just don't get along. We haven't for years. The relationship stinks.

WORKER: What do you mean, when you say "The relationship stinks"?

As is the case with most exploring skills, seeking clarification is useful throughout the entire helping process. It is especially relevant during the issue-definition and goal-setting phases, the working and evaluating phases, and the ending processes. Often, you can effectively precede your request for clarification with an active listening or reflective response.

◆ **EXERCISE 7-2: SEEKING CLARIFICATION**

For these exercises, assume that you are a social worker with an agency that serves families and children. Respond in the spaces provided by writing the words you would say to seek clarification in each situation.

1. You are in the midst of the first interview with Mr. K., a recently divorced 55-year-old man. You have introduced yourself and addressed other aspects of beginning. You are in the midst of exploring the person-issue-situation. Mr. K. says, "I feel so bad. It really hurts. I miss her terribly. I'm not sure I can go on." Write the words you would say in seeking clarification of what he has just said. After you have written your response, discuss your rationale for the words you have chosen. How do you think he might react to this ques-

tion? Now try preceding your attempt to seek clarification with an active listening response. What effect does that have?

2. As an outreach worker for elderly persons, you are in the midst of an interview with Mrs. O., a 77-year-old widow who lives alone. At one point in the conversation, Mrs. O. abruptly stops talking and looks blankly away. For perhaps 45 seconds, she does not respond to any of your questions. Then, suddenly, she shakes her head slightly and redirects her attention to you. Write the words you would use to seek clarification in this situation. After you have written your response, discuss your rationale for the words you have chosen. How do you think Mrs. O. might react to this question?

3. You have begun the first interview with the S. family, a seven-member blended family. You are in the midst of exploring the nature and development of the issue when one of the teenage boys (biological children of the father) angrily refers to their father's wife (their stepmother) as a "home wrecker." In reaction, Mrs. S. lowers her eyes and becomes very quiet. Write

the words you would say in seeking clarification from the teenager. Discuss your rationale for the words you have chosen. How do you think the teenager who made the remark might react? How might Mrs. S.? Mr. S.? Other members of the family? Now write the words you would say in seeking clarification from Mrs. S. concerning her nonverbal reaction to the term *home wrecker*. How do you think she and the other family members might react to your request for clarification from Mrs. S.?

4. Assume that you are exploring issues with Mrs. F., who is of Latino background and speaks both Spanish and English fluently. Mrs. F. is concerned about her children's safety at school. During the course of the exploration, Mrs. F. says angrily, "White men control this whole country and don't care about anybody but themselves!" Write the words you might say in seeking clarification. Discuss your rationale for the words you have selected. How do you think Mrs. F. might react to your question? Now write another way you might seek clarification in this situation.

Reflecting Content

Reflecting content (Carkhuff, 1987, pp. 95–97) is the empathic skill of communicating your understanding of the factual or informational part of a message. A form of active listening, you paraphrase or restate the client's words. By accurately reflecting content, you demonstrate that you have heard and understood what the client is trying to convey.

This skill is most applicable when a client has communicated factual or descriptive material, or ideas that lack an emotional dimension. Feelings have not been expressed so you, as the social worker, do not add them to the message. Indeed, accurately communicating understanding of what clients say is crucial for several reasons. For example, if clients do not believe that the social worker understands their view of the issues of concern, they may prematurely discontinue services. Accurate restatement of clients' expressions about the problems that led to the contact with you demonstrates that you understand their concerns. Accurate reflections of content also contribute to the development of a positive working relationship and can promote a sense of collaborative partnership between client-and-social worker. Without accurate reflections, clients are likely to assume a passive, subordinate role in the process and view the social worker as an expert who asks questions, collects information, diagnoses problems, and prescribes solutions for clients to complete.

To practice this skill, use the following format:

PRACTICE FORMAT: REFLECTING CONTENT

You're saying _____?

Example: Reflecting Content

CLIENT (MR. C): I'm a househusband. Every day, I cook the meals, clean the house, and do the laundry. That's my job now.

WORKER: You're saying that your current responsibilities include taking care of the family needs and doing the household chores.

In using the practice format for practice, recognize that repeated use of the same lead-in phrases might begin to sound artificial and mechanical. Imagine how it would seem to you if someone started six or seven sentences in a row with the words, "You're saying." Indeed, the phrase, "I hear you saying" has become a cliché. Therefore, vary the lead-in phrases or avoid them altogether. If you accurately reflect the content of the person's message, such lead-in phrases are usually unnecessary.

Try to use your own words to reflect, restate, or mirror the information the client has conveyed. If you repeat too many of the client's words, they may begin to feel that you are "parroting" or "mimicking" rather than truly listening. You can sound more like a tape recorder than a concerned human being.

Reflecting content is usually used when clients communicate information or ideas in an unemotional manner. On some occasions, however, you may purposefully choose to reflect only the content even when feelings are evident. Consider this example:

Example: Reflecting Content

CLIENT (MR. C): Several years ago, I lost my job. They closed the plant where I had worked for years and years. There was a huge layoff. Most of my buddies and I were let go. Since then, my wife has worked part-time and that keeps some food on the table. My unemployment compensation ran out long ago. We've not been able to pay the mortgage on the house for about the last 6 months. I think the bank is going to foreclose on us soon.

WORKER: You haven't had an adequate income for a long time and it's beginning to look like you may lose your home.

Mr. C. is probably experiencing a lot of emotion while he expresses himself. Although, he has not actually mentioned his feelings, he may do so nonverbally by shedding tears or dropping his head and shoulders. In using the skill of reflecting content, you stay with the factual content of the message. Even when a client does explicitly express feelings along with facts or opinions, you might occasionally choose to use the skill of reflecting content rather than a more complete form of active listening to highlight the informational portion of the message. You might do so when the urgency of a situation requires that *facts*, *ideas*, or *preferences* be elicited quickly; when you determine that the meaning of a client's message is more relevant at that particular point than feelings; or when you are trying to help a client maintain emotional self-control. In general, during the early stages of the exploration process, you should carefully respect clients' defensive and coping mechanisms. Follow their lead. If a client is expressing primarily facts and opinions in an unemotional or intellectualized fashion, use the skill of reflecting content. At this stage, there is usually no pressing need to reflect feelings that clients have not directly expressed. Mr. C., for example, may be trying to maintain control of his emotions by expressing himself in a matter-of-fact, businesslike fashion. He may not yet trust the worker enough to risk full and free expression of his true feelings. The worker could further develop the relationship by accurately reflecting the content of Mr. C.'s stated message and then, perhaps later during the interview, return to an exploration and reflection of his feelings.

◆ EXERCISE 7-3: REFLECTING CONTENT

For these exercises, assume that you are a social worker at an agency for families and children. Respond in the spaces provided by writing the words you would say in reflecting content in each situation.

1. You are in the midst of the exploration process with Mr. K., a recently divorced 55-year-old man. He says, "The divorce was final about three weeks ago. She said she'd had enough of my constant criticism and sarcastic comments, and that she was leaving me." Write the words you would say in reflecting the content of what he has said. After you have written your response, discuss your rationale for the words you have chosen. How do you think he might react to your reflection?

2. You are in the midst of an interview with Mrs. O., a 77-year-old widow who lives alone. Following an episode in which she appeared to lose awareness of her surroundings, Mrs. O. says, "I do occasionally have these spells. I don't pass out or fall down or anything like that. I just kind of wake up after a while." Write the words you would use in reflecting the content of Mrs. O.'s message. After you have written your response, discuss your rationale for the words you have chosen. How do you think Mrs. O. might react to your content reflection?

3. You are in the midst of an interview with the seven-member blended S. family. During the course of the exploration, Mrs. S. says, "I fell in love with Hank [Mr. S.], and when we married I hoped that his children and mine would come to love one another as brothers and sisters. I also wanted his kids to know that I would love and treat them as if I had given birth to them myself." Write the words you would say to reflect the content of Mrs. S' message. Discuss your rationale for the words you have chosen. How do you think Mrs. S. might react? Now write another way you might reflect the content of her message in this situation.

4. You are interviewing Mrs. F., a Latina mother of two children who have been harassed at school by several boys. During the course of exploration, Mrs. F. says, "I have talked to the teachers and the guidance counselor. They listen politely but they don't care about what this does to my children. They won't do a thing about it." Write the words you might say in reflecting content. Discuss your rationale for the words you have selected. How do you think Mrs. F. might react to your response? Now write another way you might reflect the content of Mrs. F.'s message in this situation.

Reflecting Feelings

Reflecting feelings (Carkhuff, 1987, pp. 99–110) is another of the empathic, active listening skills. It usually consists of a brief response that communicates your understanding of the feeling expressed by a client. Some of the more effective responses consist of a simple sentence containing a single feeling word. For example, phrases such as "You feel ashamed," "You're really hurting," or "You're terrified!" can be powerful empathic reflections of feeling. Despite their brevity and utility, some social workers are hesitant to reflect emotions. Reflecting feelings requires that you, at least to some extent, feel those same emotions yourself. Empathy can be uncomfortable, even painful. Partly because of such discomfort, you may be tempted to convert feeling reflections into content reflections by neglecting to use words that convey emotions. For instance, suppose a client says, "I am devastated." You might reflect the feeling by saying, "You feel crushed." If, however, you were to respond by saying, "It feels like you've been hit by a freight train," you imply the feeling; you do not actually say it. The message conveys an idea rather than a feeling. Although *hit by a freight train* is an apt phrase to amplify the feeling of devastation, it is much more effective when used in conjunction with one or more feeling words. For example, "You feel crushed. It's like you've been hit by a freight train" includes both a feeling word and a powerful idea that amplifies the emotion. Certain lead-in phrases, such as *You feel like . . .* , tend to be followed by ideas, analogies, or metaphors rather than words that connote actual feelings. Therefore, until you develop proficiency, practice by using a format such as the following:

PRACTICE FORMAT: REFLECTING FEELINGS

You feel (*insert appropriate feeling word*).

The single most important aspect in reflecting feelings is to capture accurately the primary emotion experienced by the client and mirror it back so that she or he *feels* your empathic understanding. When two feelings are in evidence, you may respond to both. For example: "You feel _____ and _____." Sometimes, you may be able to identify a single word that communicates both feelings. For example, *burdened* and *discouraged* might be reflected as *overwhelmed*.

Example: Reflecting Feelings

CLIENT: (*His former wife remarried about a year ago. Last month she and her current husband left the area with the client's 5-year-old son. They moved 2,000 miles away. The client tried to stop their relocation by filing a motion with the court, but his former spouse won the right to move with her son.*) I just can't stand it. I miss my son terribly, I know that he'll gradually lose interest in me and I can't do a thing about it.

WORKER: You feel sad and powerless.

Example: Reflecting Feelings

CLIENT: (*16-year-old girl who wanted desperately to be selected to the school's cheerleading team but was not chosen*) It's awful. I can't go back to school. I can't face them. I wanted to be on the team so bad. It hurts. It really hurts.

WORKER: You feel terribly rejected and you're awfully disappointed.

During the early portions of your work with clients, you might reflect only the feelings that are expressed verbally. After establishing a foundation of accurate reflections, or when the nonverbal, emotional message is very clear, try to reflect what you perceive as the unspoken feeling message. Nonverbal messages in the form of facial expressions, body positions and movements, tone of voice, and so on are important means for communicating emotions. They should not be ignored. When you reflect a feeling suggested by nonverbal behavior, however, recognize that you are taking a modest risk. Use the skill in an especially tentative fashion because the client has not actually used feeling words. Also, a client may not be ready to acknowledge certain feelings and, of course, members of certain cultural groups may feel especially vulnerable or uncomfortable when feelings are directly recognized. Therefore, please be cautious when reflecting unspoken emotions, particularly early in the working relationship. When you do so, use a gentle, tentative tone of voice. Be prepared to return to the skills of reflecting content, questioning, or seeking clarification if the client overtly or covertly indicates that your feeling reflection is premature or off target.

To use feeling reflections effectively, you need a large and sophisticated vocabulary of terms that connote emotions. Without such a vocabulary, it is extremely difficult to empathically capture the feelings, emotions, and sensations experienced and expressed by clients. To convey different kinds of emotions at various levels of intensity, you should be familiar with a wide range of feeling words commonly used by the cultural groups in your community. Otherwise, you will have difficulty accurately mirroring the feelings expressed. For example, anger is an emotion everyone experiences to one degree or another. A person who is mildly annoyed or irritated would probably not feel understood if you were to say, "You feel enraged." The words you use should match both the kind as well as the intensity of the feelings expressed by clients. As in other forms of active listening, your reflection should be essentially equivalent to the client's message.

◆ EXERCISE 7-4: REFLECTING FEELINGS

To begin to develop a feeling vocabulary of your own, consider the six categories of emotional experiences listed in Table 7.3.

TABLE 7.3
Standard English Feeling Vocabulary

Happiness	Hurt & Loss	Anxiety & Fear	Sadness	Anger	Guilt

Identify at least 10 feeling words that connote some degree of the emotion listed for each of the six categories of feelings. For example, under the *happiness* category, you might include the word *satisfied;* under the *anxiety & fear* category, you might list *stress* as an associated term. If you become stuck, review the alphabetized list of feeling words in Appendix 4. That should help you generate 10 Standard English feeling words for each category. Once you have listed them, rate each one in terms of relative intensity (1 = mild; 2 = moderate; 3 = strong). For example, under the *anger* category, you might assign a "3" (strong) rating to the words *enraged* and *furious.* Similarly, you might assign a "2" (moderate) to the term *irritated,* and a "1" (low) to *annoyed.*

Next, develop feeling vocabularies for different cultural groups. For example, you might develop separate lists of feeling words for contemporary North American teenagers, persons of African ancestry, Latinos, Asians, gays and lesbians, and so forth. Focus your efforts one or two of the cultural groups you would most like to serve as a social worker in your community.

Now that you have developed some familiarity with a range of feeling words, begin to practice some feeling reflections. Assume that you are a social worker with a family services agency. In the spaces provided, write the words you would say to reflect feelings in each situation.

1. During your first interview with Mr. K., a recently divorced 55-year-old man, he says, "I am absolutely lost. There is no reason to go on. I feel like someone reached into my gut and wrenched out my insides." Write the words you would say in reflecting the feelings Mr. K. has expressed. After you have written your response, discuss your rationale for the words you have chosen. How do you think he might react to your reflection? Identify two alternative feeling reflections that might also apply in this situation.

2. In the midst of an interview with Mrs. O., a 77-year-old widow, she says, "I feel just fine. Sure, I have my low points, but everybody does. I still cook my own meals and care for myself. I'm proud of that—but, with these spells, I'm afraid I won't be independent much longer." Write the words you would use

to reflect the feelings contained in Mrs. O.'s message. After you have written your response, discuss your rationale for the words you have chosen. How do you think Mrs. O. might react to your reflection? Identify two alternative feeling reflections that might also apply in this situation.

3. You are interviewing the seven-member, blended S. family. Mrs. S. has just said, "I fell in love with Hank [Mr. S.], and when we married I hoped that his children and mine would come to love one another as brothers and sisters. I also wanted his kids to know that I would love and treat them as if they were my own children." Following her statement, she hangs her head as tears fall down her cheeks. Mr. S.' eyes are also watery. Although specific feeling words were not used, write the words you would say in reflecting the feelings suggested by Mrs. S' nonverbal messages. Then do the same for Mr. S. Discuss your rationale for the words you have chosen for each feeling reflection. How do you think Mrs. S. might react to your response? Mr. S.? Identify another way you might reflect the feelings suggested by their communications in this situation.

4. You are interviewing Mrs. F., a Latina mother who is concerned about the safety at school of her two children. At one point, Mrs. F. says, "I'm so angry. Talking with the teachers and the guidance counselor does not help at all. It's so frustrating having to fight so hard for fair treatment. My kids deserve to be protected." Write the words you might say in reflecting her feelings. Discuss your rationale for the words you have selected. How do you think Mrs. F. might react to your response? Now write another way you might reflect the feelings indicated by Mrs. F.'s message in this situation.

Reflecting Feeling and Meaning

Reflecting feeling and meaning (Carkhuff & Anthony, 1979, pp. 78–82) is probably the most complete form of active listening. It is certainly the most complex. By reflecting both emotional and informational or ideational elements of a message, you convey a great deal of empathy.

For practice purposes, use the following formats:

PRACTICE FORMATS: REFLECTING FEELING AND MEANING

You feel _____ because _____.

or

You feel _____ and _____.

or

You feel _____ but/yet/however _____.

Reflecting feeling and meaning mirrors clients' emotions along with the facts or beliefs associated with them. As with other reflections, your response should represent an accurate and equivalent form of the message expressed by a client. Do not speculate or interpret. Rather, paraphrase or mirror the feeling and meaning as experienced by the other person. When clients convey their view of the cause of feelings they experience, reflect their perspective even though you might personally believe it to be incomplete or inaccurate. Often the meanings that clients convey suggest external or situational causes for their feelings (e.g., "My mother makes me feel guilty."). At other times, clients refer to aspects of themselves (e.g., attitudes, habits, traits, psychological patterns, fears, or physiological conditions) as the reason for their feelings. Whether the meaning associated with the feelings is externalized or internalized, try to remain congruent with the client's experience when reflecting feeling and meaning. Resist the temptation to modify the meaning of the message. As with other empathic reflections, accuracy is fundamental. Your response should be essentially equivalent to the message communicated by the client. Here are two examples:

Example: Reflecting Feeling and Meaning

CLIENT: (*60-year-old man who has just lost his job after 35 years of employment*) I have nowhere to turn—no job—no income—no nothing. They just let me go after 35 years of pain and sweat for them. I'm scared and angry.

WORKER: (*reflecting feeling and meaning*) You feel desperate because the company has turned you out after so many years of hard work, and it does not look like you'll be able to find something else.

Example: Reflecting Feeling and Meaning

CLIENT: I'm a wreck. I can't sleep or eat; I can't concentrate. I know my head is really messed up.

WORKER: (*reflecting feeling and meaning*) You feel awful. You're anxious and confused, and you know you're not thinking straight right now.

◆ EXERCISE 7-5: REFLECTING FEELING AND MEANING

For these exercises, assume that you are a social worker for a social service agency. In the spaces provided, write the words you would say in reflecting feeling and meaning in each situation.

1. In the midst of your first interview with Mr. K., a recently divorced 55-year-old man, you are exploring his feelings about his situation. He says, "I was so used to her being there. I needed her but I never told her so. Now that she's gone, I realize just how much she meant to me." Write the words you would

say in reflecting the feeling and meaning contained in what Mr. K. has said. After you have written your response, discuss your rationale for the words you have chosen. How do you think Mr. K. might respond? Identify two alternative feeling and meaning reflections that might also apply in this situation.

2. You are in the midst of an interview with Mrs. O., a 77-year-old widow who lives alone and occasionally has blackouts. During the conversation she says, "I'm afraid of being a burden to somebody. I'd rather be dead than be treated like a small child who cannot care for herself." Write the words you would use to reflect the feeling and meaning contained in Mrs. O.'s statement. After you have written your response, discuss your rationale for the words you have chosen. How do you think Mrs. O. might react to your response? Identify two alternative feeling and meaning reflections that might also apply in this situation.

3. You are interviewing the seven-member, blended S. family. Following a moment when both Mr. and Mrs. S. began to cry, one of the teenage boys

(Mr. S.' biological children) says, "Well, it just seems that she came into the house expecting to be Mom. She'll never be my mother, and I resent it when she tries to be." Write the words you would say in reflecting the feeling and meaning contained in his statement. Discuss your rationale for the words you have chosen. How do you think the teenager might react to your response? Mr. S.? Mrs. S.? Identify another way you might reflect the feeling and meaning suggested by the boy's words.

4. You are interviewing Mrs. F. While exploring the issue, Mrs. F. says, "I'm frustrated with the whole system! This society is racist to the core! Money and power are the only things they respect." Write the words you might say in reflecting feeling and meaning. Discuss your rationale for the words you have selected. How do you think Mrs. F. might react to your response? Now write another way you might reflect the feeling and meaning indicated by Mrs. F.'s words.

Partializing

The *partializing* skill (Perlman, 1957, pp. 144–149; Shulman, 1992, pp. 141–143) is used to help clients break down several aspects and dimensions of the person-issue-situation—complex phenomena—into more manageable units so you can address them more easily. Partializing is especially helpful during the exploration phase. If you and a client tried to deal with a multitude of facts, ideas, or feelings simultaneously, one or both of you would probably end up quite confused. Sometimes, there are simply too many phenomena to address effectively all at once. The partializing skill helps you and clients to maintain a sense of coherence by exploring smaller, more manageable units of information one at a time. For practice purposes, please use a format such as the following:

PRACTICE FORMAT: PARTIALIZING

You've addressed a number of topics here. You've talked about _____, _____, _____, and _____. There are so many aspects of what you've said that we could lose track if we try to consider them all at once. Could we explore them one at a time? (Yes) Which would you like to consider first? (or) Would it make sense to start with _____? That seems to be very important to you right now?

Example: Partializing

CLIENT: (*40-year-old mother and wife*) My whole life is a mess. My husband drinks two six-packs every night and even more on weekends. I think he's an alcoholic. He's out of work—again! My teenage son smokes dope. I've found marijuana in his room. And he's just been expelled from school for stealing money from another kid's locker. So, both of them are at home now. I'm the only one working and I'm falling apart. I'm a nervous wreck. And, I'm angry as hell!"

WORKER: You sure have a lot happening all at once. It sounds like everybody in the family has their own share of problems—and you're affected by all of them. I wonder, since there are so many issues to address—your husband's behavior, your son's, and your own feelings about it all—could we start by looking at them one at a time? Does that make sense to you? Okay? Which piece of all of this concerns you most right now? Let's start with that one."

◆ **EXERCISE 7-6: PARTIALIZING**

Assume that you are a social worker at a social service agency. In the spaces provided, write the words you would say in using the skill of partializing in each situation.

1. You are interviewing Mr. K., a recently divorced 55-year-old man. He says, "I think I'm on the brink of a nervous breakdown. I can't do my work. I can't sleep at night. I don't eat. All I do is think about her. I wonder what she's doing and whether she ever thinks of me. It's affecting my job. I think my boss is getting tired of my mistakes. I've also forgotten to pay some bills. Creditors are calling all the time. My whole life is a mess." First, separate and identify each of the elements in the client's message. List them in outline fashion. Which do you think is most important? Now write the words you would say in attempting to partialize what Mr. K. has said. After you have written your partializing response, discuss your rationale for the words you have chosen. How do you think Mr. K. might react?

2. You are in the midst of an interview with Mrs. O., a 77-year-old widow who lives alone. During the conversation, Mrs. O. says, "Sometimes I get so lonely. All my friends have moved away or died. And my children don't visit me any more. One of them lives in town, but he doesn't even telephone me. I don't get birthday cards from them. It's like I'm already dead. And I'm really worried about these spells. I don't know what's going to happen to me." First, separate and identify each of the elements in the client's message. List them in outline fashion. Which do you think is most important?

Now write the words you would use in attempting to partialize Mrs. O.'s statement. After you have written your response, discuss your rationale for the words you have chosen. How do you think Mrs. O. might react to your words?

3. You are interviewing the seven-member, blended S. family. During the course of the exploration, Mr. S. says, "Since we married, we've had troubles with both my kids and hers. Basically, they dislike each other, they seem to hate us, and lately my wife and I have begun to fight. Finances have become a problem, and there's no time for anything. I don't think I've had a single minute to myself in six months. My wife and I haven't been out of the house on a weekend evening since our wedding." First, separate and identify each of the elements in the client's message. List them in outline fashion. Which do you think is most important? Now write the words you would say to partialize the complex message communicated by Mr. S. Discuss your rationale for the words you have chosen. How do you think Mr. S. might react?

4. You are interviewing Mrs. F. During the conversation, she says, "I've had troubles ever since I moved into this community. The school system is totally insensitive to the Latino population. My kids have begun to disrespect me and berate their own heritage. All the neighbors are white and haven't even introduced themselves to us. My mother is seriously ill in Peru, but I don't dare leave the children here while I feel they're in danger." First, separate and identify each of the elements in the client's message. List them in outline fashion. Which do you think is most important? Now write the words you might say in partializing this message. Discuss your rationale for the words you have selected. How do you think Mrs. F. might respond?

Going Beyond

Going beyond what is said (Hammond, Hepworth, & Smith, 1977, pp. 137–169) occurs when you use your empathic understanding of the other person to extend slightly what was expressed. Instead of mirroring exactly what clients have said, you use your knowledge, experience, and intuition to add modestly to the feelings or meanings actually communicated. Through a process called *additive empathy*, you take a small leap beyond the spoken words to bring into greater awareness or clarity information that a client already knows. Your responses "go beyond what the client has explicitly expressed to feelings and meanings only implied in the client's statements and, thus, somewhat below the surface of the client's awareness" (Hammond et al., 1977, p. 137).

Going beyond sometimes involves combining what clients say verbally with what they express nonverbally. In doing so, however, continue to remain generally congruent with clients' overall direction and perspective. Although departing somewhat from their actual words, stay with their frame of reference. Rather than changing directions, build on the agenda your client has previously established.

For example, during the early part of a first meeting, a client who recently immigrated to the United States from Haiti might say to a white worker, "Do they have any black social workers at your agency?" This may be an indirect communication (Shulman, 1999, pp. 42–44) by a client who wonders whether a white worker has the capacity to understand him and to value his culture. He might prefer a black social worker. Perhaps he has had a negative experience with a white social worker at some point in the past. A white worker might respond to this question by saying something such as, "Yes, we have several black social workers [sharing information], although not as many as we should [sharing opinion]. Since you ask that question though, I wonder, are you saying that you'd prefer to work with a black social worker if that's possible [going beyond]?"

Example

CLIENT: (*41-year-old mother*) I've been depressed for months. I've been down in the dumps ever since my son died in that terrible motorcycle crash. I feel so ashamed. Just before he drove off that morning I yelled at him for not picking up the dirty clothes in his room. Why did I have to say anything? That's my last memory of him.

WORKER: (*reflecting feeling and meaning; going beyond what is said*) You feel guilty because of the last words you said to your son before he died. Do you sometimes feel that if you hadn't yelled at him about those dirty clothes, he might somehow still be alive?

Going beyond is not an interpretation, nor is it a wild speculation or guess. Rather, it involves putting into words those thoughts and feelings that a person probably thinks or feels but which have not yet been verbally expressed.

Example

CLIENT: (*12-year-old girl who was sexually molested by her mother's male friend*) My mother loved him very much and now he's gone.

WORKER: (*going beyond what is said*) You sometimes wonder whether you should have said anything. You think that maybe your mom might be happier and still have her boyfriend if you had just kept quiet about what he did to you?

◆ EXERCISE 7-7: GOING BEYOND

For these exercises, assume that you are a social worker with a social service agency. Respond in the spaces provided by writing the words you would say in using the skill of going beyond what is said.

1. You are interviewing Mr. K., a recently divorced 55-year-old man. You are in the process of exploration when he says, "I guess I'm a real wimp! I want so bad for her to come back home. All I do is think of ways to get her back. I make these plans about how to contact her; how to persuade her to change her mind. I constantly wonder what she's doing and whether she ever thinks of me." Write the words you would say in going beyond what Mr. K. has said. After you have written your response, discuss your rationale for the words you have chosen. How do you think he might react to your response? Identify another way you might go beyond what he said.

2. You are in the midst of an outreach interview with Mrs. O., a 77-year-old widow who lives alone. Mrs. O. says, "Oh, I guess all children forget about their parents when we get old. They have so much to do, what with their work and their own children and all. They're busy. I know that. I guess I should be grateful for what I do have." Write the words you would use in attempting to go beyond Mrs. O.'s verbal statement. After you have written your response, discuss your rationale for the words you have chosen. How do you think Mrs. O. might respond? Identify an alternative means for going beyond what she said.

Exploring

3. You are interviewing the seven-member, blended S. family. During the course of the exploration, Mrs. S. says, "Things are so bad between my kids and his kids that I've begun to wonder whether it's worth trying to continue like this. Maybe my children and I should just leave. We made it on our own before, and we can do it again." Write the words you would say in going beyond what Mrs. S. has said. Discuss your rationale for the words you have chosen. How do you think Mrs. S. might react to your response? Identify another way you might go beyond what she said.

4. You are interviewing Mrs. F. At one point, she says, "Maybe it's not worth fighting this racist system. Maybe I should just accept things as they are. I'm just one person—just one woman—what can I do?" Write the words you might say in going beyond her verbal message. Discuss your rationale for the words you have selected. How do you think Mrs. F. might respond? Now write another way in which you might go beyond Mrs. F.'s statement.

Summary

During the exploration phase of social work practice, you encourage clients to share thoughts, feelings, and experiences about the issue or concerns that led to the contact. Through the process of exploration, you and the client gather and review information regarding the person-issue-situation from the perspective of time: present-past-future. Both the social worker and the client participate in an attempt to understand the development, maintenance, and status of the issue. By looking for strengths, you and your client identify assets, talents, abilities, and resources that may be applied in resolution efforts. In particular, you look for strengths in the areas of competencies, social support, successes, and life lessons. When combined with your professional knowledge and the client's input, the information collected contributes to the development of an assessment and plan for work.

Although the exploring skills of (1) asking questions, (2) seeking clarification, (3) reflecting content, (4) reflecting feelings, (5) reflecting feeling and meaning, (6) partializing, and (7) going beyond are especially useful for encouraging mutual consideration of information regarding the person, issue, situation, and strengths, they are also functional throughout the entire helping process. Along with the beginning skill of seeking feedback, the exploring skills are used repeatedly as you and your clients work together toward resolution of the issues of concern.

◆ CHAPTER 7 SUMMARY EXERCISES

Assume that you are a social worker with an agency that offers a broad range of social services. You are actively exploring various aspects of the person-issue-situation. For each of the following cases, write the words you would use and describe the actions you might take in using the requested skills.

1. *CASE SITUATION:* You are in the midst of the first interview with a teenage couple (an African American male and white female) who have sought counseling in advance of their forthcoming marriage. She says, "I know there are going to be lots of difficulties, and that's why we're here. We don't want the problems to get in the way of our feelings for each other."

   a. Write the words you would say in reflecting the content of her statement.

   b. Formulate an open-ended question to follow her statement.

c. Write the words you would say in seeking clarification of her expression.

Following your response, she says, "One of the biggest problems has to do with my parents. My mom is fit to be tied and my dad is even worse. He's ready to kill Johnny, and he doesn't even know him. I'm afraid they won't even come to the wedding. That would really hurt."

d. Write the words you would say in reflecting the feeling and meaning contained in her message.

e. Demonstrate how you would use the skill of going beyond in response to her words.

2. *CASE SITUATION:* You are interviewing a family of seven (two parents and five children, ranging from 1 to 7 years of age) who had been sleeping in their dilapidated Chevy in a rest area on the highway. En route to another part of the country, where they hoped to find work, they ran out of money and food, and nearly out of gas. A policeman referred them to the agency. During the interview, Mrs. Z., says, "We don't want charity. We just need enough money and food to make it there."

a. Write the words you would say in seeking clarification following her statement.

b. Write three questions that might yield useful information in your effort to understand and help the family.

Following one of your questions, Mrs. Z. says, "The baby hasn't been eating well. She's sleeping all the time and has a fever. Yesterday she vomited three times."

c. Write how you would seek clarification following her statement.

d. Then write the words you would say in asking three additional questions concerning the baby's health.

3. *CASE SITUATION:* You are interviewing for the first time a man, Mr. T., who has been accused of molesting the 13-year-old daughter of his woman friend. Mr. T. is required to receive counseling to stay out of jail while the judge considers whether to proceed with felony charges. He had been living with the girl's mother but has been required to leave the house during this period. During the interview, Mr. T. says, "I don't know why she said that I did those things. It really hurts me. I've been good to her and her mother. She's just lying and I don't know why. Maybe she's jealous."

a.   First, write the words you would say in seeking clarification concerning his message.

b.   Write three open questions that might follow his statement.

c.   Reflect the content of his statement.

d.   Reflect the feeling and meaning contained in his message.

e.   Demonstrate how you might use the skill of reflecting feeling in response to his statement.

f.   Write how you might go beyond the words he has said.

4. *CASE SITUATION:* You serve as a social work investigator for Child Protection Services. Recently, your agency received a telephone call in which the caller alleged that Mr. and Mrs. D. have neglected and abused their children (ages 1 and 3). According to the caller, the mother sleeps while the children play in a filthy yard that contains animal waste, junk, and potentially dangerous materials—pieces of glass and sharp and rusty metal objects. The caller also reported that Mr. D. drinks heavily and beats both mother and children. Mrs. D. has permitted you to enter the house, and the two of you have begun to talk. Mrs. D. says, "I know who made the complaint. It's that nosy neighbor from down the street. She's always poking into things that are none of her business."

   a. Which of the exploring skills would you use in responding to Mrs. D.'s message? Discuss the rationale for your choice. Write the words you would say in using that skill.

   b. Write two questions you would want to ask at some point during this interview with Mrs. D.

◆ CHAPTER 7 WORLD WIDE WEB EXERCISES

1. Go to the InfoTrac College Edition Web site at www.infotrac-college.com. Use your passcode to log in. Conduct a keyword search using the string "learning from clients and Marsh" (without quotation marks) to locate an editorial by Jeanne C. Marsh (2002). Carefully read the piece and use the following space to summarize its significance for the exploring phase of practice.

2. Go to the InfoTrac College Edition Web site at www.infotrac-college.com. Use your passcode to log in. Conduct a keyword search using the string "Working with Men: A Prison Memoir" (quotation marks included) to locate an article by Jack Sternbach (2000). Carefully read the piece and use the space below to summarize the significance of "lessons learned" for the exploring phase of practice.

3. Go to the InfoTrac College Edition Web site at www.infotrac-college.com. Use your passcode to log in. Conduct a keyword search using the string "using windows opportunity interviews" (without quotation marks) to locate a brief research article about interviews by highly regarded medical doctors (Branch & Malik, 1993). Carefully read the piece and use the space below to summarize its significance for the exploring phase of social work practice.

4. Go to the InfoTrac College Edition Web site at www.infotrac-college.com. Use your passcode to log in. Conduct a keyword search using the string "mental health multiethnic society" (without quotation marks) to locate a

brief article about the influence of culture on mental health (Dein, 1997). Carefully read the piece and use the following space to summarize its significance for the exploring phase of social work practice. In your summary, refer to the contents in the section entitled "Making Mental Health Services Accessible for Ethnic Minorities." Also, briefly describe the phenomena of "obeah," "possession," "amok," "koro," "evil eye," "susto," and "latah."

◆ CHAPTER 7 SUPPLEMENTAL EXERCISES

Now that you have had some practice with the exploring skills, it is time to attempt an actual interview. Recruit a colleague. Inform your peer that you are practicing some social work skills and would like her or him to assume the role of client while you practice in the role of social worker. A fellow learner or someone who has already completed the workbook might be receptive to your request. Inform your colleague that you would need a few hours of time during the next several weeks. Indicate that he or she would be expected to serve in the role of client and would be asked to behave as if voluntarily seeking help from a social worker. Inform your colleague that she or he would be expected to identify at least one issue or concern for exploration. Be sure to indicate, however, that you will only meet together a few times. Your peer should understand that you may not be of any actual help with the identified concerns, except to the extent that talking about them might be beneficial.

You might mention that it is often professionally useful for social workers and social work students to take on a client role. By assuming the role of clients, social workers may become more sensitive to the experience of seeking help. It is not always easy to ask for and receive assistance. Being clients can also significantly heighten social workers' awareness of things to do or not do in their own social work practice. The experience often leads to greater understanding of how to be an effective social worker.

Inform your colleague that you would like to record (e.g., audiotape or videotape) the meetings, and that you will prepare a written recording based on the interviews.

Exploring

Indicate that you might discuss the interviews with others (e.g., a professor, fellow learner, or a social worker) but that you will not reveal your colleague's name or other identifying characteristics. Mention that, as the client, he or she may read your written records when they are completed. Assure your colleague that in your notes about the interview, her or his identity will be disguised to ensure privacy. State that you will not reveal his or her full name to anyone without his or her consent. Indicate that your colleague will not have to discuss any aspect of her or his personal life that would better be kept private. Tell your peer that if you happen to address a topic that he or she does not want to talk about, simply say, "I prefer not to talk about this." Notify your colleague that this is an entirely voluntary exercise. It is perfectly all right to decline this invitation. Finally, advise your colleague that you are still learning about social work and have not perfected the social work skills. You will probably make mistakes. The primary purpose of the exercise is for you to practice the social work skills. It is certainly not to provide actual social work services, nor to help your peer.

Request that your colleague identify an issue for which he or she might conceivably seek social work services. However, the issue should be modest and manageable. Avoid issues that have the potential to overwhelm your colleague's coping mechanisms. Try not to recruit colleagues who are dealing with major issues, significant life change, pressing concerns, or crises. After all, you are practicing skills here, not actually providing social work services. Your colleagues should realize that they are helping you to learn. The purpose is not to help them with serious concerns.

If your colleague understands what is requested and provides consent, arrange for a time and place during the next week to meet privately for approximately 30 minutes. Inform your peer that you will assume the role of social worker during that entire period. Remind your partner that you will ask about an issue or concern for which social work services might be sought. Indicate that your peer should assume the role of client from the moment you come together at the time of the scheduled meeting.

With your partner's consent, tape-record the interview. The overall purpose of the interview should be the exploration of your colleague's issue or concern as well as those aspects of the person and situation that may have relevance. Limit the interview to the preparing, beginning, and exploration phases only. Do not attempt to assess, contract, or in any way try to work toward resolution. Resist any temptation to speculate about underlying reasons or causes. Do not offer theoretical interpretations. Do not give any advice. At the conclusion of the meeting, arrange for a second 30-minute meeting in approximately one week.

1. When you have finished the 30-minute interview, leave your respective social worker and client roles. Then ask your partner for feedback concerning his or her thoughts and feelings about the experience. Request completely candid reactions to the following questions: (a) Did you feel comfortable and safe with me? (b) Did you feel that I was sincerely interested in you and in what you had to say? (c) Did you feel that I understood what you were trying to communicate? If so, what suggested to you that I did understand? If not, what indicated that I did not understand? (d) Were there aspects of yourself, the issue of concern, or your situation that we should have explored that we

did not? If so, what were they? (e) What information would you have liked to share that I did not ask you about? (f) In general, did you enjoy the experience? If so, what made it enjoyable? If not, what contributed to that? (g) What suggestions do you have for me concerning how the interview could have been better or more productive for you? Summarize your partner's feedback in the space below.

2. In the following space, discuss your own reaction to the interview. How did you feel about it? What did you like and what did you dislike about it? Discuss your performance of the social work skills. What would you do differently if you had a chance to conduct the interview again?

3. Play the audiotape or videotape. Use paper and pencil, typewriter, or word processor to prepare a transcript that reflects what was said by whom. *Be sure to disguise the identity of your colleague.* As part of the transcript, identify where you used specific skills. For example, if you responded to a statement of your partner by asking an open-ended question concerning his or her current situation, identify that response as an open-ended question. If you paraphrased the factual or informational aspect of a message, identify that as reflecting content. Please use the following format to organize your transcript. When finished, date the transcript and include in your Social Work Skills Learning Portfolio.

Format: Transcribed Record

	Content	Skill	Reaction	Reflection
Worker	Record the words you said.	Identify the social work skill you used, if any.	Describe the subjective reactions (thoughts, feelings, sensations) that you experienced when you expressed these words.	Analyze and evaluate the choice of words, the skill used, and the quality of your communication.
Client (or Interview Partner)	Record the words the client said.		Describe your subjective reactions to the client's verbal and nonverbal communications.	Briefly reflect on the client's words and gestures during the exchange.

Example: Segment of a Transcribed Record

	Content	Skill	Reaction	Reflection
Worker	How are you feeling during this difficult time?	Open-ended question	I have a hunch that the client wants to and probably needs to talk about her feelings, but I'm scared it might be too much for her—and perhaps for me—to handle.	I think this is an appropriate skill to use at this point. I also believe that I phrased it well. An open-ended question is more useful here than a closed one.

	Content	Skill	Gut Reaction	Reflection
Client (or Interview Partner)	I'm just so tired all the time.		I can believe it! I'd be exhausted too. If I were in her shoes. I don't know if I could even get out of bed to face the world.	Client's words appear to represent an accurate description of her feelings at this time. I wonder, might she be depressed enough that she should talk to her medical doctor?
Worker	You're simply exhausted.	Reflecting feeling	She looks and feels terribly fatigued. I feel depleted as I try to feel what she's feeling.	I believe that I'm on target with this feeling reflection. I also think that it's the right skill to use at this time.

4. Using the following exploration matrix, indicate the degree to which you have explored various dimensions of the person-issue-situation. Use approximate percentages to reflect the extent of exploration within each category. For example, if you believe you have discussed about half of the issue as it exists now, write 50% in that box. If you have not talked at all about the issue in the past, place 0% in that category. Identify those aspects of the person-issue-situation that you would like to explore in a subsequent interview.

Exploration Matrix			
	Present	Past	Future
Issue			
Person			
Situation			

In the following space, write three open-ended questions for each matrix category needing further exploration.

5. Now use the looking for strengths matrix to indicate the degree to which you looked for strength in the areas of competencies, social support, successes, and life lessons.

Looking for Strengths			
	Person	Situation	Issue
Competencies			
Social Support			
Successes			
Life Lessons			

In the following space, write three open-ended questions for each strengths dimension needing further exploration.

Chapter 7 Self-Appraisal

As you finish this chapter, please assess your proficiency in the exploring skills by completing the following self-appraisal exercise.

SELF-APPRAISAL: THE EXPLORING SKILLS

Please respond to the following items to help you undertake a self-assessment of your proficiency in the exploring skills. Read each statement carefully. Then, use the following four-point rating scale to indicate the degree to which you agree or disagree with each statement. Record your numerical response in the space provided:

4 = Strongly Agree

3 = Agree

2 = Disagree

1 = Strongly Disagree

_____ 1. I can effectively use the skill of asking questions.

_____ 2. I can effectively use the skill of seeking clarification.

_____ 3. I can effectively use the skill of reflecting content.

_____ 4. I can effectively use the skill of reflecting feelings.

_____ 5. I can effectively use the skill of reflecting feeling and meaning.

_____ 6. I can effectively use the skill of partializing.

_____ 7. I can effectively use the skill of going beyond what is said.

_____ Subtotal

Note: These items are taken directly from the exploring skills section of the Social Work Skills Self-Appraisal Questionnaire contained in Appendix 3. You have responded to these items before. You may now compare the responses you made on earlier occasions with those you made this time. Compare the subtotal scores. If you believe that you have progressed in your proficiency with the exploring skills, the more recent scores should be higher than earlier.

Finally, reflect on the skills addressed in this chapter and the results of your self-appraisal. Based on your analysis, prepare a succinct one-page summary report entitled "Self-Assessment of Proficiency in the Exploring Skills." Within the report, be sure to identify those skills that you know and do well (e.g., a score of 3 or 4). Also, specify those that need further practice (e.g., scores of 2 or less) and briefly outline plans by which to achieve proficiency in them. When finished, include the report in your Social Work Skills Learning Portfolio.

Chapter 8

Assessing

Assessment is a fundamental process in professional social work practice (Compton & Galaway, 1999, pp. 271–295; Cowger, 1994, 1996; Gilgun, 1999; Hudson & McMurtry, 1997; Meyer, 1993, 1995; Perlman, 1957, pp. 164–203; Richmond, 1944; Ripple, 1955; Zastrow, 1995, pp. 75–104). When the exploration process has progressed well, you and the client have gathered and begun to reflect on a substantial amount of relevant information about the person-issue-situation. You have traced the origin and development of the issue and identified factors that might be associated with its occurrence. You have learned about aspects of the person, issue, and situation in the present and the past, and even considered various scenarios in the future. You have identified strengths and resources of various kinds (e.g., competencies, social support, successes, and life lessons)—some of which might be useful in addressing issues and achieving goals. During the assessment phase, you—usually in collaboration with the client—try to make sense of this information so you can help the client address the issue or issues that have emerged. You analyze how the person and situation influence the issue of concern, and vice versa. Most importantly, you consider how the issue of concern might be addressed, often drawing on strengths and resources within the person or the environment.

Understanding gained from these reflective and analytic processes usually leads to an emerging focus or direction for you and your client. The assessment represents the basis on which to establish a clear and detailed contract for your work together. This chapter (see Box 8.1) helps learners develop proficiency in the primary social work skills commonly involved in the assessment process: (1) organizing descriptive information, and (2) formulating a tentative assessment.

Assessment involves both lifelong learning and critical thinking as you bring your professional knowledge and the client's experience together in a process of reflection, analysis, and synthesis. Using theoretical and empirical knowledge within the context of a person-and-situation perspective, you assess individuals, families, groups, organizations, or environments. You may use conceptual or assessment tools of various kinds. You might reflect on diagrammatic representations such as a family genogram, an ecomap, or a timeline (refer to Chapter 2). You might consider the results of scales or questionnaires such as the Social Support Appraisals Scale (see Chapter 2) or any of the hundreds of valid and reliable instruments that might pertain to an issue of concern (Corcoran & Fischer, 2000a, 2000b). You might examine a phenomenon in relation to a set of criteria or guidelines that have been derived from research studies or validated protocols. For example, in assessing the relative risk of child abuse, you might consider empirical factors such as those summarized by Herring (1996). Among others, certain conditions tend to be associated with a greater risk of child abuse: history of child abuse/neglect reports, parent abused as a child, youthful parent, single parent or extended family household, domestic violence in household, lengthy separation of parent and child, substance abuse by parent or caretaker, impairment (e.g., physical, intellectual, psychological) of the child, and impairment of the parent or caretaker (Brissett-Chapman, 1995, pp. 361–362). Using factors such as these as a guide, the worker thoughtfully considers the information learned during the exploring phase to determine the risk of child endangerment. The outcome of the assessment may powerfully affect, for better or worse, the well-being of a child and family. The consequences of both false positives (where the worker concludes there is high risk but the true danger is low) and false negatives (where the worker concludes there is low risk but the true danger is high) can be serious—in some cases, genuinely life-threatening.

Although social work assessments tend to have much in common, the specific form may vary considerably according to practice setting. For example, a gerontological social worker might refer to government guidelines in helping to determine whether a nursing home has adequate physical facilities and sufficient social stimulation to meet the basic needs of an elderly client. A psychiatric or clinical social worker might refer to criteria published in the *Diagnostic and Statistical Manual (DSM-IV-TR)* (American Psychiatric Association, 2000) to help determine if a client might be depressed and, if so, how seriously (Williams, 1995). A social worker serving in a crisis and suicide prevention program might use guidelines to estimate a distraught client's risk of suicidal action as low, moderate, or high.

Of course, certain kinds of issues commonly surface in almost all practice settings. Among others, violence toward self or others, child physical and sexual abuse, and substance abuse are likely to emerge as concerns wherever you serve. All social workers, therefore, need to be alert to their possible presence. Indeed, some agencies make it standard operating procedure to assess for substance abuse, child abuse and domestic violence, and risk of violence toward self or others. As a social worker doing so, you might consider various sources. The *DSM-IV-TR*, for example, contains these criteria for substance dependence and substance abuse (Reprinted with permission from the Diagnostic and Statistical Manual of Mental Disorders, Text Revision, Copyright 2000 American Psychiatric Association, pp. 197–199):

CRITERIA FOR SUBSTANCE DEPENDENCE

A maladaptive pattern of substance use, leading to clinically significant impairment or distress, as manifested by three (or more) of the following, occurring at any time in the same 12-month period:

(1) Tolerance, as defined by either of the following:

    (a) A need for markedly increased amounts of the substance to achieve intoxication or desired effect

    (b) Markedly diminished effect with continued use of the same amount of the substance

(2) Withdrawal, as manifested by either of the following:

    (a) The characteristic withdrawal syndrome for the substance (refer to Criteria A and B of the criteria sets for Withdrawal from the specific substances)

    (b) The same (or a closely related) substance is taken to relieve or avoid withdrawal symptoms

(3) The substance is often taken in larger amounts or over a longer period than was intended

(4) There is a persistent desire or unsuccessful efforts to cut down or control substance use

(5) A great deal of time is spent in activities necessary to obtain the substance (e.g., visiting multiple doctors or driving long distances), use the substance (e.g., chain-smoking), or recover from its effects

(6) Important social, occupational, or recreational activities are given up or reduced because of substance use

(7) The substance use is continued despite knowledge of having a persistent or recurrent physical or psychological problem that is likely to have been caused or exacerbated by the substance (e.g., current cocaine use despite recognition of cocaine-induced depression, or continued drinking despite recognition that an ulcer was made worse by alcohol consumption)

CRITERIA FOR SUBSTANCE ABUSE

A. A maladaptive pattern of substance use leading to clinically significant impairment or distress, as manifested by one (or more) of the following, occurring within a 12-month period:

(1) Recurrent substance use resulting in a failure to fulfill major role obligations at work, school, or home (e.g., repeated absences or poor work performance related to substance use; substance-related absences, suspensions, or expulsions from school; neglect of children or household)

(2) Recurrent substance use in situations in which it is physically hazardous (e.g., driving an automobile or operating a machine when impaired by substance use)

(3) Recurrent substance-related legal problems (e.g., arrests for substance-related disorderly conduct)

(4) Continued substance use despite having persistent or recurrent social or interpersonal problems caused or exacerbated by the effects of the substance (e.g., arguments with spouse about consequences of intoxication, physical fights)

B. The symptoms have never met the criteria for Substance Dependence for this class of substance. (American Psychiatric Association, 2000, pp. 197–199)

Although primarily a manual of psychiatric disorders, the *DSM-IV-TR* addresses several dimensions and contains materials that social workers and their clients may find pertinent. Axis III, for instance, includes "General Medical Conditions" that might relate to a psychiatric disorder. Such conditions, of course, might also affect various social problems as well. Furthermore, Axis IV refers to "Psychosocial and Environmental Problems" and includes the following subcategories:

◆ Problems with primary support group
◆ Problems related to the social environment
◆ Educational problems

- Occupational problems
- Housing problems
- Economic problems
- Problems with access to health care services
- Problems related to interaction with the legal system/crime
- Other psychosocial and environmental problems (American Psychiatric Association, 2000, p. 32)

Problem-focused assessment is often complemented with rapid assessment instruments of various kinds (Corcoran & Fischer, 1987, 2000a, 2000b; Fischer & Corcoran, 1994a; Hudson, 1982). In the case of substance abuse issues, instruments such as the CAGE Screening Test for Alcohol Dependence, the Michigan Alcoholism Screening Test, or the Drug Abuse Screening Test in conjunction with other information, can be used as aids for determining, for instance, whether a client might be physically addicted, perhaps indicating a need for detoxification in a hospital setting. Judgments of this nature and magnitude require perspective, objectivity, and extremely well-developed critical thinking skills. Your judgments also require a great deal of lifelong learning because of the changing nature of "knowledge" on which assessment criteria are based.

Axis V of the *DSM-IV-TR* (American Psychiatric Association, 2000) includes a Global Assessment of Functioning (GAF) scale through which a client's "psychological, social, and occupational functioning" may be rated "on a hypothetical continuum of mental health-illness" (p. 34) and several provisional tools including a Defensive Functioning Scale (pp. 807–813), a Global Assessment of Relational Functioning (GARF) Scale (pp. 814–816), a Social and Occupational Functioning Assessment Scale (SOFAS) (pp. 817–818), and an Outline for Cultural Formulation and Glossary of Culture-Bound Syndromes (pp. 897–903).

Although the *DSM-IV-TR* is extremely well known and widely used by practitioners from several professions, some social workers may find it useful to incorporate the person-in-environment (PIE) classification system (Karls & Wandrei, 1994a) in assessment processes. The PIE approach provides practitioners—presumably with the input and perhaps the participation of clients—an opportunity to classify or code problems within four dimensions or factors (Karls & Wandrei, 1994a, pp. 1–6):

- Factor I: Problems in Social Role Functioning
- Factor II: Environmental Problems
- Factor III: Mental Health Problems (classified with *DSM-IV-TR* codes)
- Factor IV: Physical or Medical Conditions (coded according to the *International Classification of Diseases*, 9th Revision, Clinical Modification [*ICD-9-CM*])

Problems in Factor I—Social Role Functioning (e.g., family roles, interpersonal roles, occupational roles, special life situation roles), may be identified and then classified and coded by *type* (e.g., power, ambivalence, responsibility, dependency, loss, isolation, victimization) as well as by the *severity* of the problem, its *duration*, and the client's *coping ability* (Karls & Wendrei, 1994a, pp. 4, 7–22).

Problem severity is rated on a six-point scale where 1 = *no problem* and 6 reflects a *catastrophic* level. Duration is evaluated via a six-level system where 1 = *more than five years* and 6 = *two weeks or less*. Problems of more recent origin and shorter duration receive a higher numerical number. Client coping ability is rated on a six-point index where 1 = *outstanding coping skills* and 6 = *no coping skills* (Karls & Wandrei, 1994a, pp. 35–37).

The practitioner may then use the classifications within Factor II—Environmental Problems, to identify those situational conditions that affect or perhaps are affected by the identified problems in social role functioning (Factor I). Environmental problems are categorized according to the following systems (Karls & Wandrei, 1994a):

1. Economic/basic needs
2. Education and training
3. Judicial and legal
4. Health, safety, and social services
5. Voluntary association
6. Affectional support

Each of these major categorical systems (e.g., Education and Training) contains subcategories (e.g., Discrimination), and each subcategory contains specific problems or conditions (e.g., Disability Discrimination). Once an environmental condition or problem has been identified, its *severity* and *duration* are determined and coded (Karls & Wandrei, 1994a, pp. 23–34).

A social worker and client using the *PIE Classification Manual* might, for example, identify the following problem classification (among others):

◆ Factor I: Parent Role Problem, ambivalence type, very high severity (5), six months to one-year duration (3), somewhat inadequate coping skills (4) [1120.534]
◆ Factor II: Absence of Affectional Support, high severity (4), six-months to one-year duration (3) [10101.43] (Karls & Wandrei, 1994a).

The PIE classification system (Karls & Wandrei, 1994a) has generated considerable interest among social work academicians and researchers (Karls & Lowery, 1997; Karls & Wandrei, 1992a, 1992b, 1994b, 1995; Williams, 1994; Williams, Karls, & Wandrei, 1989). Social work practitioners, however, appear to be less intrigued. Many may not be aware of the system, and others, especially those in health and mental health settings, may not see the value of additional classification beyond the *DSM-IV-TR* or the *ICD-10*. The potential utility of the PIE classification scheme may only become apparent in years to come when epidemiological and demographic studies establish the incidence and prevalence rates of various social role functioning and environmental problems. Like the *DSM-IV-TR*, the PIE classification system is primarily problem-focused in nature. To be truly useful to helping professionals and consumers, effective intervention strategies must be established for each problem classification or diagnosis. Indeed, such is the case for several psychiatric disorders included within the *DSM-IV-TR*. It has taken many years of clinical research for safe and effective medicines for conditions such as schizophrenia or psychosocial treatment protocols for disorders such as agoraphobia. You may expect much time to pass before effective prevention or intervention services can be established for many of the social role functioning problems and environmental conditions included within the *PIE Classification Manual* (Karls & Wandrei, 1994a).

During the last decade or two, many helping professionals have become concerned that exclusive or excessive focus on problems may interfere with clients' motivation and impede progress toward resolution. In addition, several scholars have questioned the assumption that detailed exploration of clients' personal and social histories and in-depth understanding of the contributing causes of psychosocial problems are necessary to effectively resolve those problems. Partly because of these concerns, professional helpers have become extremely interested in concepts and perspectives related to strengths, assets, resiliencies, and solutions.

Dozens of books, book chapters, and articles have been published on the topic of strengths-based practice or the strengths-model of social work practice (Clark, 1997; Fast & Chapin, 1997; Kisthardt, 1997; C. A. Rapp, 1998; R. Rapp, 1997; Saleebey, 1997, 1999, 2002). Indeed, Saleebey proposed the development of a diagnostic strengths manual (Saleebey, 2001) to counter-balance the problem-focused perspective reflected in the American Psychiatric Association's *Diagnostic and Statistical Manual (DSM)*.

Locating, enhancing, and promoting resilience (Greene, 2002; Masten, 1994; Norman, 2000; Walsh, 2003) and hardiness (Kamya, 2000; Lifton, Seay, & Bushko, 2000; Maddi, Wadhwa, & Haier, 1996) have generated similar interest, as has solution-focused or solution-oriented practice (Baker & Steiner, 1996; Berg, 1994; Berg & De Jong, 1996; Berg & Reuss, 1998; Birdsall & Miller, 2002; Corcoran & Stephenson, 2000; De Jong & Berg, 2002; de Shazer, 1988; LaFountain & Garner, 1996; Lee, 1997; Lipchik, 2002; MacKenzie, 1999; Metcalf, 1995; Miller, Hubble, & Duncan, 1996; O'Hanlon, 2003; O'Hanlon & Weiner-Davis, 1989; Zimmerman, Jacobsen, MacIntyre, & Watson, 1996).

Another theme or trend in psychosocial services involves the dimension of motivation enhancement—particularly as it relates to the "transtheoretical" or the "stages of change" model (Budd & Rollnick, 1996; Miller & Rollnick, 1991, 2002; J. M. Prochaska, 2000; J. O. Prochaska, 1999; Prochaska & DiClemente, 1982; Prochaska, Norcross, & DiClemente, 1994; Rollnick, 2002; Rollnick & Miller, 1995). According to the transtheoretical perspective, long-term change in the person-issue-situation generally tends to proceed sequentially in six stages (Prochaska et al., 1994, p. 39):

◆ Precontemplation
◆ Contemplation
◆ Preparation
◆ Action
◆ Maintenance
◆ Termination

Prochaska et al. (1994) assert that none of these stages may be skipped. Although the process may be spiral rather than linear in nature, each stage is eventually addressed.

Precontemplation is the first stage of change and is characterized by ambivalence, uncertainty, disinterest, or denial. For example, suppose you had agreed to help an unemployed, wheelchair-bound client find a job. When you first contact a prospective employer who has never employed someone who used a wheelchair, you might anticipate a precontemplative response. Despite the Americans with Disabilities Act, the employer could be quite reluctant to seriously consider the request. As a social worker, your first step toward change would be to help the employer to the next stage—contemplation.

Contemplation is the second stage of the change process. This stage is characterized by information-gathering, reflection, and analysis. The possibility of change is considered. There may even be a general sense of direction or a vague plan. Consider the situation of your wheelchair-bound client and the "reluctant employer." Suppose you provide written materials that outline the benefits of a diverse workforce and describe businesses that became successful after employing disabled workers. When the "precontemplative employer" reads and considers those materials, and thinks about the possibility of hiring a wheelchair-bound person, you would begin to see signs of contemplation and reflection. Unfortunately, thinking about change in general terms does not usually produce it. In trying to serve your client, you encourage the employer toward the preparation stage.

Preparation is the third stage of change. The transition from contemplation to preparation is associated with at least two notable shifts in thinking. First, there is a significant increase in thinking about solutions and resolutions. This is accompanied by a decrease in contemplation about the problem, issue, or need. Second, thoughts about the future increasingly replace those about the past and present. "The end of the contemplation stage is a time of anticipation, activity, anxiety, and excitement" (Prochaska et al., 1994, p. 43). Plan making characterizes the onset of the preparation stage. Specific steps are outlined and short-term dates are set. Importantly, public announcements of intent to change are made. You would notice signs of preparation when the "contemplative" employer tells colleagues, "We will hire at least one disabled worker this month and at least one more each month for the next six months." However, even extremely well-designed plans do not automatically lead to change. Change requires some kind of action.

Action is the fourth stage. Characterized by motivation, purposefulness, activity, and optimism, you notice actual differences in the person, the situation, or aspects of both. Indeed, the most long-lasting change tends to occur when several dimensions of the person-in-environment are addressed. All the activities of this stage, however, may not lead to durable change. The intensity may fade, sometimes remarkably quickly, and change-related activities may discontinue. The action stage can be short-lived and disappointing. Despite the public announcements, the plans, and the flurry of initial activity, your client may not be hired or, if he is, other disabled workers may not subsequently be employed. "Many people . . . erroneously equate action with change, overlooking not only the critical work that prepares people for successful action but the equally important (and often more challenging) efforts to maintain the changes following action" (Prochaska et al., 1994, p. 44).

Maintenance is the fifth stage in the change process. In some ways, it represents the greatest challenge of all. Requiring ongoing motivation, commitment, stamina, persistence, and follow-through, maintenance lacks the excitement of the preparation and the intensity of the action stages. Maintaining lasting change usually requires ongoing, detailed attention to small steps on a day-to-day and week-to-week basis. Human systems tend to reflect powerful forces of inertia that return them to traditional behaviors. Without continuous attention and consistent routines designed to maintain change, you may anticipate a return to previously established patterns. The recently "enlightened employer," who appears so motivated and "ready" to diversify the workforce, can easily become distracted by unrelated problems and challenges, and fail to monitor progress on a day-to-day basis. The person leading the effort to employ disabled workers may leave the company or be transferred to another area. There may be a downturn in the economy. When there is a surplus of applicants, workforce diversification may not seem as important or attractive as it does when a scarcity of dependable workers exists. Unless you persistently attend to maintenance, change is unlikely to last.

Termination represents the sixth and final stage of the change process. In this stage, the older forces of inertia lose their potency as the once-new changes become part of the established and traditional routine. At the point of termination, they reflect their own forces of inertia. Indeed, they would be quite difficult to change (Prochaska et al., 1994).

Although additional research is needed to provide further validation for the stages of change model, it represents a potentially extremely useful addition to the array of assessment models available to social workers and clients—regardless of the practice approach or intervention protocol. Clients who have progressed to the preparation stage would typically experience marginal benefit from additional exploration into historical events and relationships or examination of the problems of concern. They are ready to consider potential solutions and begin the process of formulating plans. At earlier stages (i.e., precontemplation and contemplation), clients would probably find the exploration of possible strategies for change premature and perhaps even frustrating.

Motivational enhancement or motivational interviewing (Baer, Kivlahan, & Donovan, 2000; Miller & Rollnick, 2002; Rollnick, 2002; Rollnick & Miller, 1995; Sellman, Sullivan, Dore, Adamson, & MacEwan, 2001) can lend encouragement and facilitate progression through the stages of change. Interestingly, some 50 years ago, leading social work scholars at the University of Chicago School of Social Service proposed a triadic model of assessment that included motivation, capacity, and opportunity (Ripple, 1955; Ripple & Alexander, 1956; Ripple, Alexander, & Polemis, 1964). Using the M-C-O framework, social workers and clients considered ways and means to solve problems and accomplish goals by intervening within these dimensions of the person-and-situation.

In contemporary social work, it probably makes sense to integrate several of these emerging perspectives for the purposes of assessment. Recognize, however, that knowledge is increasing at an exponential rate and the conceptual tools, classification manuals, and theoretical perspectives used today will probably change within a few years as researchers provide more valid, reliable, and relevant information.

Although social work assessment is an ongoing process rather than a finished product, a formal record is usually prepared. The record may be handwritten, audiotaped, typewritten, or word processed. Keep in mind, however, that assessments change, sometimes frequently and occasionally dramatically, during work with a client system. Also, remember to exercise caution with labeling terminology (see the section in Chapter 4 on the topic of Culturally Competent Communications).

Through assessment processes, you and the client reach an understanding of the factors and forces within the person-and-situation that affect and maintain as well as those that might be used to address and resolve the issue of concern. You also identify strengths, assets, competencies, and resources that could help in resolution and attempt to determine the transtheoretical stage that best reflects the status of the person-and-situation.

You and the client collaboratively determine the primary client-system and identify other persons or systems that should be involved in the helping process. You and the client determine potential targets for change—those aspects that, if altered, might resolve the issue. You identify potential obstacles or barriers to progress as well. You predict probable consequences if things remain the same and assess risk to determine how urgently intervention must be undertaken. In addition, you jointly explore potentially applicable intervention approaches or modalities, strategies, tasks, activities, and techniques and assess their probability of success. Finally, you determine a time frame for work and develop means for evaluating progress.

Social work assessments are multidimensional processes and serve many purposes. There are many ways to structure a social work assessment and record the results. The Description, Assessment, and Contract (DAC) outlined in Box 8.2 represents a comprehensive integrated format that might be useful in your practice context. You will probably find that some sections are irrelevant for use with some clients or certain agency settings. In addition, recognize that numerous other models are readily accessible in the professional literature. Some have been designed for use with specific population groups or for assessment of specific problems of concern and may be especially applicable to your particular social work role and function.

As you engage in assessment activities, please approach them as professional rather than technical endeavors, as collaborative rather than singular undertakings, and as dynamic rather than static processes. Avoid the temptation to adopt a checklist approach to assessment. Whenever possible, adopt a conversational style that reflects the core facilitative conditions of empathy, respect, and genuineness. Use available professional knowledge and judgment to determine the particular nature and style of assessment. It is highly unlikely that every client would have the same assessment experience. The unique nature of each person-issue-situation virtually requires certain adaptations or innovations. Be sure to consider the cultural implications and encourage clients to participate with you in formulating assessments. Seeking consensus about the assessment is likely to contribute to clients' sense of empowerment, encourage further collaboration, and enhance motivation for change.

BOX 8.2

Description, Assessment, and Contract (DAC)

I. Description
    A. Client identification

(continued)

BOX 8.2 *(continued)*

    B. Person, family and household, and community systems
       1. Person system
       2. Family and household system
       3. Community system
    C. Presenting issues of concern
    D. Assets and resources
    E. Referral source and process; collateral information
    F. Social history
       1. Developmental
       2. Personal, familial, cultural
       3. Critical events
       4. Sexual
       5. Alcohol and drug use
       6. Medical/physical/biological
       7. Legal
       8. Educational
       9. Employment
      10. Recreational
      11. Religious/Spiritual
      12. Prior psychological, social, medical, or educational service
      13. Other
II. Tentative assessment of the person-issue-situation
    A. Issues
       1. Nature and essential features
       2. Contributing factors and functions
       3. Exceptions
       4. Duration, severity, and urgency
    B. Person-and-situation
       1. Personal factors
       2. Situational and systemic factors
       3. Motivation and stage of change
       4. Personal beliefs and social norms
       5. Personal and situational strengths
       6. Challenges and obstacles
       7. Risk assessment
    C. Person-issue-situation
       1. Ideas and hypotheses
       2. Summary assessment
III. Contract
    A. Issues
       1. Client-identified issues
       2. Worker-identified issues
       3. Agreed upon issues for work
    B. Goals

(continued)

BOX 8.2 *(continued)*

C. Plans
1. Action plan
2. Client's tasks or action steps
3. Worker's tasks or action steps
4. In-Session tasks or action steps
5. Maintenance tasks
6. Plans to evaluate progress

As the title suggests, the DAC includes three major sections. First, the information gained through the exploration process is organized into a *description*. Second, ideas and hypotheses concerning the person-issue-situation that you and the client generate are formulated into a tentative *assessment*. Third, the *contract* for work that you and the client negotiate is summarized. The description and assessment parts of the DAC are addressed in this chapter. The contract portion is reviewed in Chapter 9.

Completing the description portion of the DAC helps organize a great deal of information about a client system, the situational context, and the issue of concern. The assessment section yields processed information that you and the client generate through analysis, synthesis, and the formulation of questions or hypotheses concerning the descriptive data. At first glance, the DAC may appear exhaustingly inclusive. Indeed, it includes many areas and dimensions. However, several of these would obviously be inapplicable for work with many clients, issues, and contexts. Please adapt the DAC format to fit the unique needs and functions of your specific social work setting and function. Realize that numerous alternate schemes are available to social workers. Ultimately, in consultation with your supervisors and agency colleagues, you determine the utility of any format for the particular circumstances of your social work practice.

Organizing Descriptive Information

Most social work interviews do not occur in such a logical fashion that a transcript of the interaction between worker and client would represent a coherent description of the available information. Therefore, your first step in the assessment process is to organize the information gained through exploration into a form that allows for efficient retrieval and examination. Typically, this involves arranging data according to certain categories that you and agency professionals consider significant.

Regardless of the organizational format you might adopt for record keeping, you should always distinguish clearly between reported and observed information. Also, ideas or conclusions that are the result of speculation or inference, deduction or induction should be stated as opinion or hypothesis and differentiated from factual data. Assertions or opinions are not facts and should never be presented as such.

Descriptive organization allows you to present information that you read, observe, or hear in a coherent fashion. The date and source of data should be noted. This information may be organized within the description part of the DAC in accordance with the following guidelines.

SUGGESTED FORMAT

DESCRIPTION SECTION OF THE DAC
(DESCRIPTION, ASSESSMENT, AND CONTRACT)

I. Description

    A. Client Identification

        In this section, place information that identifies the client and other relevant members of the person and situation systems. Such data as names and ages of household members, birth dates, Social Security numbers, home addresses, places of work, telephone numbers, email addresses, names and contact information of family doctors, and persons to notify in case of emergency may be included.

    B. Person, Family and Household, and Community Systems

        1. Person System

            In this section, include information that helps describe the client further. Whenever possible, use information that comes from clients themselves and your direct observations, rather than from your inferences. Also, identify the source of the information (e.g., "Client stated that he had 'just had his 32nd birthday.'" Or, "I observed that the client walked with a limp"). Whenever possible, quote significant words or phrases that the client uses in self-description. Be careful to use language that enhances the description rather than stereotypes the person. For example, the statement "Mary is a 45-year-old, white, divorced female" tends to emphasize age, race, and marital status in a manner that could unnecessarily narrow the focus. Contrast that with this description, "Mary describes herself as a person with a 'great deal of energy and zest for life.' She describes herself as 'single and happy to be so.' She says she 'just turned 45 years old but feels 30.'"

            Information based on your own observations of clients, such as their approximate height and weight, physical appearance, striking or characteristic features, speech patterns, and clothing may be included in this section. Ensure, however, that such information is actually relevant for the purpose of assessment, and note that it is based on your own observation.

2. **Family and Household System**

In this section, describe the client's family and household, or primary social system. If you have not included them elsewhere, include names, ages, and telephone numbers and addresses of significant persons. Family genograms and household eco-maps are useful tools for organizing this information. Cite the source of information and quote significant words and phrases.

3. **Community System**

In this section, describe the community system within which the identified client functions. Indicate the source of the information and include systems such as school, work, medical, recreational, religious, neighborhood, ethnic, cultural, and friendship affiliations whenever appropriate. The eco-map is an especially valuable tool for presenting this kind of information and can be included within this section.

C. **Presenting Issues of Concern**

In this section, describe the presenting issue or issues of concern as identified by the client or responsible party (e.g., parent, guardian, judge, teacher, or medical doctor). Clearly identify the source of the information and summarize the origin, development, and status of the issue. Quote significant words and phrases that help to describe needs, issues, concerns, or goals. In this section, outline how social services came to be sought or required at this time. Also, if identified, record the initial, desired outcome of the social service as envisioned by the client or responsible party. Unless the situation is of such an urgent or life-threatening nature that you are required to take action immediately, postpone your own view of issues and goals until you and the client have undertaken a more thorough exploration and assessment.

D. **Assets and Resources**

In this section, record information concerning the strengths, assets, and resources available within the client and situation systems. Competencies, social supports, successes, and life lessons may be noted here, as may specific resources such as the involvement of concerned relatives, sufficient financial assets, optimistic attitudes, or high energy levels. Identify the source of this information about strengths and resources (the client, a family member, or your own observations or inferences). Where possible, quote significant descriptive words and phrases.

As a social worker, you encourage identification of strengths and resources to provide a balanced picture—one not solely characterized by needs, problems, concerns, and deficiencies. Also, the assets identified here often become extremely relevant later, during the planning and intervention phases of work.

E. **Referral Source and Process; Collateral Information**

Summarize information concerning the source of the referral (who suggested or required that the identified client make contact with you) and the process by which the referral occurred. Information provided by sources other than the identified client or the client system (e.g., family member or a close friend) may be presented here. Cite the source by name, role, or position, and phone number. Try to quote specific words and phrases used in describing the person-issue-situation and the events that prompted the referral.

F. **Social History**

In this section, include summary information about the identified client's social history and current social circumstances. You may include one or more forms of "timelines" within this section. Include data that is relevant to the purpose of your involvement. Do not include information that is clearly irrelevant to the person-issue-situation. Cite the source of the information (e.g., the client, a family member, or your own observation or inference) and quote significant words and phrases wherever possible. In describing historical information, recognize that experiences may have effects that are energy enhancing, growth promoting, liberating, and empowering as well as energy depleting, growth limiting, oppressive, disenfranchising, or traumatic. As you describe historical information, be sure to reflect, where indicated, those aspects that represent strengths or successes. You may use a "Successes Timeline" in this context. Other kinds of timelines may be used to summarize relevant historical information (e.g., developmental, relationship, familial, critical events, sexual, alcohol or drug use, educational or employment).

Depending on the agency program, your social work function, and the specific circumstances of the person-issue-situation, this section could contain some or all of the following subsections.

1. **Developmental**

You might include a description of a client's developmental history. You might provide information such as the nature of the client's birth, infancy, childhood, adolescent, and adult developmental processes. Specific information regarding events or experiences might be included here.

2. **Personal, Familial, and Cultural**

You may summarize here information concerning the significant past and present personal, familial, and cultural relationships. Significant processes and events that influenced the client's biopsychosocial development and behavior may be recorded here.

3. **Critical Events**

   Summarize events or situations that might have been significant in some way. Identify critical liberating, empowering, or growth-enhancing processes and events such as successes, accomplishments, achievements, and experiences that may have enhanced psychosocial functioning. Also identify critical events such as violence, abuse, rape or molestation, suicides or suicide attempts, victimization, oppression, and discrimination that may have had traumatic effects. Describe how these experiences affected the client.

4. **Sexual**

   You may include here, if relevant to the social work purpose, information related to the person's sexual development and history.

5. **Alcohol and Drug Use**

   Because alcohol and drug abuse is so prevalent in our society, unless this topic is clearly irrelevant to the social work purpose, it is frequently useful to explore and summarize clients' history in these areas.

6. **Medical/Physical/Biological**

   Summarize here the person's medical and physical history. This might include identification of illnesses, injuries, disabilities, and current physical health and well-being. Be sure to include the date and results of the client's most recent physical examination. The client's family doctor or source of medical care should be identified.

7. **Legal**

   Include here, as relevant, history of involvement in the criminal justice and legal system as well as pertinent information such as citizen or residency status, custody, or guardianship.

8. **Educational**

   Summarize the client's educational history. Both formal and informal educational experiences may be noted.

9. **Employment**

   Include here the client's employment history, including military and volunteer experiences.

10. **Recreational**

    Where applicable, summarize recreational activities that the client has undertaken over the years. Often, these endeavors constitute strengths or resources.

11. **Religious/Spiritual**

Summarize current and past religious and spiritual affiliations and activities, and their meaning and significance for the client. Often, aspects of this dimension represent strengths or resources.

12. **Prior Psychological, Social, Medical, or Educational Service**

Summarize here previous involvement with psychological and social services. Where relevant, identify the names, addresses, and telephone numbers of agencies and service providers.

13. **Other**

Include here any additional, relevant historical and developmental information.

The following example illustrates how you might organize and record information about the case of Mrs. Lynn Chase into the description section of the DAC.

EXAMPLE

LYNN B. CHASE

I. Description

A. Client Identification

Date of Interview: January 13
Person Interviewed: Lynn B. Chase, Date of Birth: October 5, Age: 34
Residence: 1212 Clearview Drive, City
Home phone: 223-1234
Employment: Assembler at Fox Manufacturing Co., phone 567-5678
Household Composition:

Lynn Chase is married to Richard S. Chase, 35-year-old carpenter with Crass Construction Company—work phone 789-7890
Robert L. Chase, 12-year-old son, sixth-grade student at Hope Middle School
Referral Source: Sandra Fowles (former client of this agency and personal friend of Lynn B. Chase)

B. **Person, Family and Household, and Community Systems**

1. **Person System**

Lynn B. Chase prefers to be addressed as "Lynn." She described herself as "Irish-American" and said she was "raised as a Roman Catholic." She indicated that her maiden name was Shaughnessy. She looked to me to be approximately five feet six inches tall and of medium build. On the date of this interview, I noticed that she was attired in slacks and blouse. I noticed what appeared to be dark circles under her eyes and the small muscles in her forehead looked to be tense. She seemed to walk slowly and expressed an audible sigh as she sat in a chair. She spoke in an accent common to this area—although in a slow and apparently deliberate fashion. I noticed that she occasionally interrupted her speech to pause for several seconds, then sighed before resuming her speech.

2. **Family and Household System**

As reflected in the attached intergenerational family genogram [see Figure 2.1 in Chapter 2] that Mrs. Chase and I prepared during the initial interview, the household is composed of Lynn, Richard, Robert, and a mongrel dog, "Sly." They have lived on Clearview Drive for five years and "like it there." Their family life is "busy." During the week, Monday through Friday, both Lynn and Richard work from 8:00 A.M. to 5:00 P.M. One parent, usually Lynn, helps Robert ready himself for school and waits with him until the school bus stops at a nearby street corner at about 7:15 A.M. Then she drives herself to work. After school, Robert takes the bus home, arriving at about 3:45 P.M. He stays alone at home until his parents arrive at about 5:45 P.M.

Mrs. Chase indicated that Robert and his father have a very positive relationship. They go to sporting events together and both enjoy fishing. Robert was a member of a Little League baseball team this past summer. His dad went to every game. She described her own relationship with Robert as "currently strained." She also indicated that while she "loves her husband, there is not much joy and romance in the relationship at this time."

3. **Community System**

As reflected in the attached eco-map [see Figure 2.2 in Chapter 2], Mrs. Lynn Chase indicated that the Chase family is involved with several other social systems. Mrs. Chase reported that the family regularly attends the First Methodist Church, although "not every week." She said that she helps out occasionally with bake sales and other church activities. She indicated that Robert goes to Sunday school almost every week. Mrs. Chase said that her husband Richard is not really involved in many social activities. "He doesn't really have close friends. Robert and I are his friends." She said that Richard attends Robert's sporting events and goes fishing with him. Outside of work and those activities with Robert, Richard spends most of his time working on the house or in the yard. She said that Richard has a workshop in the basement and constructs furniture for the home.

Mrs. Chase reported that Robert has generally been a good student. She said that his teachers tell her that he is shy. When called upon in class, they said, he speaks in a quiet and hesitant voice but usually has thoughtful answers to questions. Mrs. Chase indicated that Robert had played very well on his Little League baseball team this past summer. She said that his coach thought highly of him and believed that he would make the high school team in a few years. Mrs. Chase said that her son has two or three close friends in the neighborhood.

Mrs. Chase reported that the family lives in a middle-class neighborhood. She indicates that, racially, it is minimally integrated and that the rate of crime is low and the neighbors friendly. She indicated that most of the home-owners tend to maintain their property carefully. Mrs. Chase said that their family is friendly with several families in the neighborhood and perhaps once every month or so, two or three of the families get together for dinner or a cookout.

Mrs. Chase reported that her job is "okay" and she likes the people there. She indicated that her husband truly loves his work: "Being a carpenter is what he's made for."

C. Presenting Issues of Concern

Mrs. Chase said that she has been concerned lately because she and her son have been getting into arguments "all the time." She said that she does not know what causes the trouble. She reported that she finds herself becoming critical and angry toward Robert at the slightest provocation. She said that Robert is "not misbehaving" and that "it's really my own problem." She indicated that about six months ago she began to become more irritable with Robert and, to some extent, with Richard as well. She reported that she hasn't slept well and has lost about ten pounds during that six-month period. She indicated that she took up smoking again after quitting some five years ago and has begun to have terrible headaches several times each week. Mrs. Chase reported that these issues began about the time that she took the job at Fox Manufacturing six months ago. "Before that I stayed at home to care for Robert and the household."

When asked what led her to take the job, she said, "We don't have any real savings and we'll need money for Robert's college education. I thought I'd better start saving while we have a few years before he leaves. Also, one of my friends said there was an opening at Fox and that she'd love me to work there with her."

Mrs. Chase indicated that she hoped these services would help her to feel less irritable, sleep better, have fewer headaches, discontinue smoking, and have fewer arguments with her son and husband.

D. **Assets and Resources**

Mrs. Chase acknowledged that she has an above-average intellect and a capacity to consider thoughtfully various aspects and dimensions of needs and issues. She reported that she is extremely responsible: "At times, too much so." She said that she is dependable in fulfilling her various roles. Mrs. Chase said that the family has sufficient financial resources and that her job has provided them with a "little bit more than we actually need." She indicated that the family lives in a "nice home in a safe and pleasant neighborhood." She said that her job is secure. She indicated that even though she has worked there only six months, her employer values her work highly, and her colleagues enjoy her company. Mrs. Chase reported that she has several close women friends who provide her with support and understanding. She mentioned, however, that "most of the time I am the one who provides support to them." She said that she feels loved by her husband and indicated that both her husband and son would be willing to do anything for her.

E. **Referral Source and Process; Collateral Information**

Mrs. Chase was referred to this agency by her friend and neighbor, Sandra Fowles. Ms. Fowles is a former client of this agency. In talking about Mrs. Chase, Ms. Fowles said that she is "an incredibly kind and thoughtful woman who would give you the shirt off her back. She may be too kind for her own good." Ms. Fowles made preliminary contact with the agency on behalf of Mrs. Chase and asked whether agency personnel had time to meet with her. A telephone contact with Mrs. Chase was subsequently made and an appointment scheduled for this date.

F. **Social History**

1. **Developmental**

Mrs. Chase reported that she believed that her mother's pregnancy and her own birth and infancy were "normal." She described her childhood as "unhappy" (see personal and familial section below).

2. Personal, Familial, and Cultural

As reflected in the attached intergenerational genogram [see Figure 2.1 in Chapter 2], Mrs. Chase reported the following about her personal and family history. She comes from a family of five. Her mother and father married while in their late teens. Her mother became pregnant with Lynn right away. Mrs. Chase is the eldest sibling. She has a brother one year younger and a sister five years her junior. Her parents are alive and, she says, "somehow still married." Mrs. Chase reported that during her childhood her father "was, and still is, a workaholic" who was rarely home. She described her mother as an "unstable, angry, and critical woman who never praised me for anything and always put me down." Mrs. Chase said that she "raised her younger sister" because, at that time, her mother was drinking all the time. Mrs. Chase indicated that her mother has refrained from drinking alcohol for the past three years and now goes to Alcoholics Anonymous meetings. She described the relationship between her mother and father as "awful—they have hated each other for years." She said, "They don't divorce because they're Catholic." Mrs. Chase said that her mother disapproved of her marriage to Richard because he had been married once before. She said that her mother would not attend her wedding. She said that her mother continues to berate Richard and "frequently criticizes the way I am raising Robert too."

Mrs. Chase reported that she rarely sees her mother, who lives 200 miles away, but does visit her sister about once a month. She said that her sister frequently needs emotional support, advice, and sometimes requires financial assistance. Mrs. Chase said that her sister had formerly abused alcohol and drugs, but the problem is "now under control."

Mrs. Chase said that her husband's family was "even more messed up than mine—if that's possible." She indicated that Richard also came from a family of five. She reported that his father abandoned the family when Richard was 9 and his sisters were 10 and 7. Mrs. Chase said that Richard's father had a serious drinking problem and that Richard remembered his father frequently beating both his mother and himself. Mrs. Chase indicated that Richard grew up in very destitute circumstances and learned to value money. She reported that even today he closely watches how the family's money is spent and worries that "we'll end up broke."

Mrs. Chase reported that her childhood was an unhappy one. She said that she remembers feeling "different" from other children. She indicated that as a child she was very shy, often afraid, and easily intimidated by other children. She reported that she often felt guilty and ashamed when parents or teachers criticized or corrected her. She indicated that she always tried to be "good" and, she continued, "for the most part—at least until my teenage years—I was." She said that she received excellent grades in school, although she remembered that she was sometimes taunted by other children, who called her a "teacher's pet." She said that she was slightly overweight during her childhood years and always thought of herself as "fat." She indicated that she had only a few friends during her younger years. She remembered one or two close childhood friends and described them as "shy and unattractive too." She recalled occasions when other children she had hoped would become friends "rejected" her. She remembered feeling sad and depressed on many occasions throughout her childhood.

3. **Critical Events**

As reflected in the attached critical incidents timeline [see Figure 2.3 in Chapter 2], Mrs. Chase described an incident that occurred when she was about 12 years old. She said that a boy she had liked said she was "fat" in front of a group of her peers. She said that she felt humiliated and "stayed at home and cried for days." She also recalled a time when she was about 14 or 15. She said she had begun to explore her body and to experiment with masturbation. She indicated that she found it pleasurable but believed that such activity was sinful. She said that she discussed it with a priest during a regular confession. Mrs. Chase said that the priest became "very angry" at her and told her in a forceful way to "stop abusing herself in that disgusting way." She said that she felt horribly guilty and ashamed. She reported that it was this experience in particular that led her to later leave the Catholic Church.

Mrs. Chase indicated that she has never been the victim of rape or any other violent crime. She did recall, however, several occasions when a male relative (maternal uncle) attempted to kiss her and fondle her breasts. She said that each time, she pushed him away but she remembered that she felt dirty and disgusted anyway. She said she was approximately 12 or 13 years old at the time and never told anyone about what had happened.

4. **Sexual**

Mrs. Chase reported that she did not date until her senior year in high school, when she went out with one boy a few times. She said that she "lost her virginity" in this relationship. She reported that had sex with "lots of boys" after that but that she "never really enjoyed it." She indicated that she met her future husband Richard about two years after graduation from high school and that, she was "pleased to say, has found it pleasurable and satisfying." She said that her marital sex life has been "great throughout our marriage" but she has not had much interest in sex during the last several months.

5. **Alcohol and Drug Use**

Mrs. Chase stated that she does not now have an alcohol or drug use problem but recalled drinking heavily as an 18-year-old. She said that after she graduated from high school, she ran around with a crowd that "partied all the time." She said that she drank a lot of alcohol at that time. She indicated that at that time she sometimes drank in order to "belong" and to feel comfortable in sexual relations with boys.

6. **Medical/Physical/Biological**

Mrs. Chase reported that she has not had any major medical or physical problems except for an enlarged cyst that was surgically removed from her uterus approximately eight years ago. She said that since that time she has been "unable to get pregnant again," although "both Richard and I wished we could have another child." She said that she has concluded that "it's not going to happen," and "I guess that's what's meant to be."

Mrs. Chase said that she "gained control of the weight problem" during the early years of her marriage by going to Weight Watchers. She reported that she has maintained her appropriate weight since that time. She indicated that she had recently spoken with her medical doctor about her occasional feelings of extreme fatigue, her change in sleep patterns, the loss of weight, and the periodic headaches. Her doctor could find nothing physically wrong and raised the question of "stress-related symptoms."

7. **Legal**

Mrs. Chase indicated that she and her family have not had any contact with the legal or criminal justice systems.

8. **Educational**

Mrs. Chase reported that she has a high school education and has taken approximately two years of college courses. She said that she had taken a course each semester until about six months ago, when she discontinued an evening course to "be at home more."

9. Employment

Mrs. Chase reported that she had worked in both secretarial and administrative positions following graduation from high school. She said that when Robert was born, she quit working outside the home to care for him. When he went to grammar school, she went back to work part-time. She said that about three years ago, she was laid off from that job and was unable to find another part-time job that would enable her to be home at the end of Robert's school day. She indicated that a little more than six months ago, she and Richard decided that Robert was old enough to be at home alone for a couple of hours each day. She therefore applied for and was appointed to the full-time position at Fox Manufacturing.

10. Recreational

Mrs. Chase reported that over the years she has found great pleasure in gardening. She also said, however, that during the last year or so she has discontinued that activity. She indicated that she thought she could rekindle that sense of satisfaction if she were to resume gardening again at some point in the future.

11. Religious/Spiritual

Mrs. Chase reported that she quit going to the Catholic Church at the age of 18 when she graduated from high school. She said she did not attend any church until the birth of her child. She indicated that she and her husband then decided that they wanted their children to be brought up with some religious involvement. She remembered joining the neighborhood Methodist Church because "it was nearby."

12. Prior Psychological, Social, Medical, or Educational Service

Mrs. Chase reported that she had not sought or received social or psychological services before. She reported that her mother has been in "therapy" for approximately four years.

◆ EXERCISE 8-1: ORGANIZING DESCRIPTIVE INFORMATION

For this exercise, assume that *you* are your own client. Use a word processor to draft the description section of a written record as if you had, as a social worker, learned what you know about yourself as a person and about your situation. Identify one or two issues or goals for which you might conceivably consult a social worker. As do all human beings, social workers also confront issues of various kinds throughout the course of life. Such challenges are inevitable. Therefore, build on the self-understanding exercises that you undertook in Chapter 2 by organizing information about yourself and your situation into a descriptive record. Use the DAC format to prepare the description portion of a "personal case record" for inclusion in a separate part of your Social Work Skills Learning Portfolio. Be sure to include your genogram, eco-map, and critical-events timeline. In creating your case record, it might be prudent to disguise your own identity to some extent. After all, these materials reflect a great deal about yourself and your own personal life. Instead of your full name, you might use one or two letters to identify yourself and the significant people in your life. Create a separate folder entitled "My Personal Case Record" to hold these materials within your portfolio.

Formulating a Tentative Assessment

After recording the available information in an organized fashion, you—with the active participation of the client—begin to formulate a tentative assessment through analysis and synthesis, the primary critical thinking skills involved in assessment. *Analysis* involves examining in fine detail various pieces of information about the person-issue-situation. For example, consider a 30-year-old woman who reports that she "feels anxious in the presence of men." Commonly, you and she would analyze how the different dimensions of anxiety interact. After collecting information about what the client thinks, feels, senses, imagines, and does when she experiences anxiety, you might piece together or track the precise sequence of events leading up to and following the feelings of anxiety. Such an analysis might reveal, for example, that the anxious feelings usually occur in the presence of men who are her own age or older, who are confident and appear successful, and who are eligible for romantic consideration. Further analysis might enable you to uncover that the client does not feel anxious when she interacts with men in business or professional contexts, men who are married or who are gay, or men who are much younger or less successful than she is. You and your client might also discover that when she first notices the early signs of anxiety, she immediately begins to say certain things to herself. For example, in such contexts, she might think, "I must not become anxious right now; if I become anxious, I will not say what I want to say and I will embarrass myself."

Analysis often leads you and the client to pinpoint critical elements or themes from among the various pieces of information. These become cornerstones in the formulation of a tentative assessment. *Synthesis* builds on what is gained from analysis. It involves assembling significant pieces of information into a coherent whole by relating them to one another and to elements of your theory, knowledge, and experience base. For example, you might consider the client's anxiety in the presence of certain men given her experience growing up as an only child, attending girls-only grammar and high schools, and later enrolling in a college for women only. These associations reflect the synthetic process of selecting various bits of data and configuring them into some form of relationship. Usually, social workers apply theoretical concepts to determine which pieces of information go with others, and to help grasp their relationship within the context of a unifying theme.

There are dozens of theoretical perspectives that you may find useful. For example, social learning theory may lead you to consider prior family and educational experiences in relation to certain concerns. Systems and ecological theories may lead you to consider how change or stress in one subsystem affects other subsystems. Ego-psychology might enable you to consider the defense mechanism of repression when attempting to understand certain behavior (e.g., a client's blocked memory in response to a question about combat experiences during a war). Fundamental concepts within role theory—role ambiguity, role change, and role conflict—may also be considered in relation to signs of frustration and stress. Crisis theory may help during emergencies, such as natural disasters, violent experiences, and other circumstances that involve sudden change. Family systems concepts may lead you to consider the effects of enmeshed boundaries or the absence of feedback processes within a family unit. Understanding individual, family, and organizational development theories may allow you to identify tasks necessary for further growth and to appreciate the possible communication value of a particular behavior pattern. Ecological and social network perspectives may help you to appreciate how a particular phenomenon might represent an understandable adaptation to social and environmental circumstances. A plethora of theories may prove useful as you and your client seek to understand and synthesize significant information about the person-issue-situation.

In the early stages of work with a client, the analysis and synthesis processes of assessment are tentative and speculative, because you and the client will usually not have conclusive support or confirmation for your ideas. In fact, analysis and synthesis typically yield a series of hypotheses or questions that guide the collection of additional information and the conduct of various intervention experiments. Throughout this assessment process, resist the temptation to conclude that you have the key or answer to understanding the person-issue-situation. There are very few situations for which there is only one key. Most of the time, there are many plausible hypotheses—your professional challenge is to identify those most likely to be useful for each unique set of circumstances. In addition to helping you formulate pertinent hypotheses and questions, analysis and synthesis usually lead you to highlight critical events and significant themes, patterns, and issues for further consideration.

As you do with descriptive data, organize the results of your analysis and synthesis into a coherent structure. The particular format varies from agency to agency, program to program, and indeed from worker to worker. Nonetheless, virtually all social work assessment schemes refer in one way or another to various theoretical dimensions and include consideration of the person, issue, and situation. The organizing structure may be derived from a single theoretical perspective or, eclectically, from several.

Guidelines for using the assessment part of the DAC to organize social work assessments are presented here. When prepared in written form, the assessment follows the description portion of the DAC.

SUGGESTED FORMAT

ASSESSMENT SECTION OF THE DESCRIPTION, ASSESSMENT, AND CONTRACT

II.   Tentative Assessment of the Person-Issue-Situation

    A.   Issues

        1.   **Nature and Essential Features**

        In this section, reflect on and analyze information gained during the exploration processes and reported in the description section to capture the nature and essence of the focal concerns. Go well beyond description to discuss "why" they are of concern and "how" they came to be so at this particular time. Include the client's as well as your own analyses about the issues. Incorporate professional and scientific knowledge to enhance understanding of the identified issues.

        2.   **Contributing Factors and Functions**

        In this section, discuss functions that the problematic issues might serve for the person-and-environment. Analyze factors or forces that contribute to the onset or maintenance of the issues. Analyze those personal and situational factors that may trigger, accompany, or follow occurrences of the issues of concern.

        3.   **Exceptions**

        Explore the circumstances and conditions that inhibit, impede, or prevent emergence of the issues of concern. Analyze the reasons the problematic issues do not occur during these exceptions—times when they are absent.

        4.   **Duration, Severity, and Urgency**

        Discuss the duration, severity, and urgency of the issues. Include your own assessment as well as that of the client and other significant persons.

    B.   Person-and-Situation

        1.   **Personal Factors**

        Analyze personal factors associated with the problematic issues. Discuss how they may affect the issues and, in turn, how the issues affect the person. Discuss their effects on the person's thinking, feeling, and doing. If relevant, include potential biochemical or physical factors and effects. Outline the strategies used to cope with or adapt to the issues and evaluate their effects and effectiveness. Consider the potential effects upon the person if the issues were resolved.

2. **Situational and Systemic Factors**

   Analyze situational and systemic factors for their relationship to the issues. Explore the effects of the issues upon family members and other significant persons and social systems. Analyze the systemic patterns, structures, and processes of primary social systems that promote or maintain the issues. Explore the strategies adopted by significant others in their attempts to cope or adapt. Include genograms, structural maps, and eco-maps as relevant. Assess the degree of energy, cohesion, and adaptability of primary social systems. Consider life cycle developmental issues and maturity of significant others' and of pertinent social systems. Explore how the needs and aspirations of significant others relate to the issues and the person-and-situation. Characterize the system by its dominant emotional climate; operating procedures; communication styles and process; affection and support patterns; distribution of power and availability of resources; assignment of roles; boundaries between members, subsystems, and other systems; and processes of decision making. Discuss the potential effects on the significant others if the issues were resolved.

3. **Motivation and Stage of Change**

   Assess the person's motivation to address and resolve the issues, and to work collaboratively toward change. Determine the transtheoretical stage that best reflects the person's current readiness for change. Consider factors associated with the person's motivation and consider how motivation might be enhanced. Assess significant others' motivation to contribute to resolution of the issues. Consider how others' motivation might be enhanced.

   Consider using a ten-point subjective rating scale (1 = low; 10 = high) to estimate various aspects of motivation (e.g., motivation to resolve the issues; motivation to take action; motivation to work with you).

4. **Personal Beliefs and Social Norms**

   Analyze the issues in relation to the client's personal, spiritual, religious, and cultural beliefs. Do the same for significant others' and for groups with which the client identifies or affiliates.

5. **Personal and Situational Strengths**

   Outline capacities, abilities, competencies, and resources within the context of the person-and-situation that may help to address and resolve the issues of concern.

6. **Challenges and Obstacles**

   Outline aspects of the person-and-situation that represent challenges, obstacles, or barriers to resolution. Be sure to consider deficiencies in basic needs for money, shelter, food, clothing, and social and intellectual stimulation. Assess social, political, and cultural obstacles such as oppression and discrimination. Also consider the impact of environmental conditions such as overcrowding, inadequate or excessive stimulation, and the presence of toxic materials.

7. **Risk Assessment**

   Analyze the risks to the person and to other people in the person's life if things remain the same. Also consider the potential personal-and-situational consequences of successful resolution. Certain negative effects usually accompany the positive. If relevant, also include an assessment of the risk of suicide, homicide, violence, abuse, neglect, and substance misuse within the context of the person-and-situation.

C. **Person-Issue-Situation**

1. **Ideas and Hypotheses**

   Outline ideas, questions, and hypotheses about the person-and-situation as they relate to the issues of concern. Incorporate concepts from theoretical and research-based knowledge. Include your own, as well as the client's, ideas, but identify the source. The nature of the professional knowledge that may apply varies according to the unique characteristics of the person-issue-situation. At times, assessments of the client's personality characteristics and style, self-concept, and self-esteem may be useful. At other times, hypotheses about interpersonal or relational styles may apply. Sometimes ideas about the person's primary personal, familial, cultural, and occupational role identities along with the extent of congruence or conflict among them may be noted. At times, the relative flexibility or rigidity of the client's personal boundaries, decision-making strategies, as well as the nature, strength, and functionality of the person's defensive and coping processes may be considered. Sometimes the ability to control desires and impulses and manage temptations may be explored. Often, hypotheses about the client's overall mood and emotional state are useful as are ideas about the phase of life-cycle development and degree of personal maturity. At times, assessments of the client' general competence to make significant life decisions, fulfill age- and situation-appropriate roles and tasks, care for self, and participate in the helping process are warranted. Sometimes, specific assessment processes such as mental status or substance abuse examinations are needed. Be sure to record when and why referral to an expert for specialized assessment is required (e.g., a neurological, medical, or psychiatric exam).

Ideas, questions, and hypotheses about the family and other social systems involved in the context of the person-issue-situation may also be recorded in this section. Hypotheses about systemic structures, patterns, and processes; developmental life cycle issues; external stressors; and other situational aspects may be noted. At times, ideas about family boundaries, roles, communication styles, and the nature and extent of affection and support may be relevant. Include clients' as well as your own questions and incorporate theoretical and research-based knowledge as appropriate.

2. **Summary Assessment**
   Provide a succinct summary synthesis of the person-issue-situation. Highlight the person-and-situation factors that influence the issues of concern and may contribute to their resolution. Also analyze the legal and ethical implications of the person-issue-situation. Finally, estimate the prognosis or probability that the issues might be successfully resolved.

The case of Mrs. Lynn B. Chase can be used to provide an example of a tentative assessment, organized as part of the DAC.

EXAMPLE

LYNN B. CHASE

DESCRIPTION, ASSESSMENT, AND CONTRACT

II. Tentative Assessment of the Person-Issue-Situation
   A. Issues
      1. Nature and Essential Features
         The issues of irritability and argumentativeness toward her son and husband; shame and guilt following expressions of anger or arguments; sleeplessness; weight loss; headaches; and resumption of cigarette smoking appeared to emerge at about the time Mrs. Chase accepted full-time employment outside the home. She indicated that she had not experienced these symptoms previously, although she did say that

her adolescent years were painful. At this point, it is not certain that her job is or will be as satisfying to her as child-rearing and homemaking have been and there may be role strain or conflict between the family and work roles. At first analysis, Mrs. Chase and I wondered if the symptoms might be indicative of increased stress associated with expanded demands on her time and energy and changes in roles and role identities. Although she now works at least 40 hours per week at her paid job, she also continues to perform all of the family and household duties she fulfilled before taking the outside job. Mrs. Chase appears to assume a protective, hard-working, caretaker role with her husband and son, siblings, and friends. Indeed, she seems to hold herself responsible for the thoughts, feelings, and behaviors of all members of her family.

Application of the *PIE Manual* criteria (Karls & Wandrei, 1994a) to Mrs. Chase and her situation might yield the following classification:

Factor I: Worker Role—Home, mixed type (ambivalence, responsibility, dependency), moderate severity, six months to one-year duration, adequate coping skills. also consider parental role or perhaps spousal role problems.

Factor II: Other Affectional Support System Problem, low severity, more than five-years duration.

Application of the *DSM-IV-TR* (American Psychiatric Association, 2000) criteria might suggest a "V-Code" classification. "V-Codes" are issues of concern but do not necessarily indicate or relate to a psychiatric disorder or mental illness. The "V-Codes" that seem most applicable to the person-issue-situation seem to be "Parent-Child Relational Problem," in recognition of the current strain between Mrs. Chase and her son, or perhaps "Phase of Life Problem" to reflect the stress associated with the change in role identity from primarily homemaker to homemaker plus full-time paid worker outside the home. The changing nature of the relationship with her teenage son may contribute as well.

The *DSM-IV-TR* diagnosis "Adjustment Disorder with Mixed Anxiety and Depressed Mood" might also be considered, although it is less applicable because the stressor—assumption of the full-time job outside the home—occurred six-months earlier. Most adjustment disorders are resolved—with or without professional aid—within six-months of onset.

2. **Contributing Factors and Functions**

In the general sense, assumption of the full-time job seems to have precipitated the onset of the issues of concern. It is conceivable that the symptoms may represent an indirect attempt—of which Mrs. Chase seems unaware—to secure greater appreciation and support from her husband and son or, if they worsen, to provide reasonable cause to quit the job and return to her previous family and household roles. The immediate precursors to the symptoms appear related to Mrs. Chase's beliefs and expectations about herself and perhaps others. She reports that she frequently worries about various things she "should" or "ought" to be doing and feels guilty that she is not fulfilling her parental, spousal, and household (home worker) roles as well as she previously did.

3. **Exceptions**

According to Mrs. Chase, there were two occasions during the past six-months when she felt a sense of contentment and happiness. The first occurred when Richard, Robert, and she went on a weekend trip to another city. They stayed in a hotel, ate in restaurants, went to a baseball game, and spent time talking and joking with each other. On the other occasion, Richard and she went on an overnight trip to attend a family friend's wedding.

4. **Duration, Severity, and Urgency**

The issues of concern have existed for about six months. Mrs. Chase and I estimated the severity of the problems and symptoms to be in the moderate range. She continues to fulfill all of her responsibilities in a competent manner. Mrs. Chase herself seems to experience the greatest discomfort from the issues—although Robert and to some extent, Richard, are affected by the irritability and argumentativeness. Mrs. Chase and I concur that the issues are not life-threatening and do not require immediate, emergency, or intensive intervention.

B. **Person-and-Situation**

1. **Personal Factors**

Mrs. Chase revealed a strong ethic of obligation and responsibility, especially toward her son and husband but to most other people as well. She holds herself to extremely high standards and often feels guilty or worried that she's not doing well enough, and ashamed when she makes mistakes or hurts someone else's feelings. She appeared less comfortable, however, when it comes to taking time for free and spontaneous play, relaxation, or recreation. She previously enjoyed gardening, but since she took the full-time job at Fox Manufacturing, she has become reluctant to allow herself time for "unproductive" leisure and relaxation. Shortly after we began to explore the nature and scope of her expectations and caretaking activities, she wondered aloud if she might do too much for others. If so, she might feel stressed and guilty at the possibility that she might be unable to fulfill her responsibilities in the superior manner that she expects. Indeed, she may feel guilty that she now spends less time with her son Robert and worried she may be unable to protect him from potential dangerous circumstances.

Mrs. Chase seems to view herself primarily as wife and mother and as hard-working, responsible member of the community. She appears to assume the role of a parent-like, big sister with her siblings. She seems open to input from others and from me, and has a well-established sense of personal identity in relation to family roles such as wife, mother, daughter, and eldest sibling. She and her husband had wanted more children, but a medical condition (the cyst or the surgery to remove it) prevented that. She seems less clear and secure, however, when it comes to other more playful or recreational roles. In these areas, she appears more uncertain and less inner-directed. She has yet to formulate personal life goals that are distinct from those of her family.

Mrs. Chase appears to have well-developed coping skills and defense mechanisms that have served her well over the years. Presently, however, the effectiveness of her usual coping capacities are diminishing somewhat. In addition to other worries, she may also be concerned that she might become more like her own mother, whom she described as "unstable, angry, and critical."

2. **Situational and Systemic Factors**

Based on information gained in the first interview, the Chase family system appears to be structured in such a way that Mrs. Chase is the primary executive or manager, or perhaps "parent-figure." She seems to have responsibility for the bulk of the home and family tasks, functions, and activities. Mr. Chase apparently assumes few household and parenting duties—although evidently takes care of yard work as well as home and auto repairs. She is the primary housekeeper and parent. She plans and prepares meals, does the shopping and cleaning, coordinates transportation for Robert, and pays the bills. Until Mrs. Chase began full-time work outside the home, the family rules and role boundaries were clear. Mrs. Chase sought ideas and input from Richard and Robert, but she made and implemented most family decisions. Now that she is home less often and there are increased demands on her, some of the rules and roles may be in flux. At this point, it seems that Mrs. Chase is trying to maintain her previous family and community duties while adding additional occupational responsibilities. She also appears concerned about certain "troubled teenage boys" in the neighborhood and worries that Robert might be negatively influenced by them.

It appears that communication and relational patterns within the Chase family are relatively open but inhibited and constrained. They are affectionate toward and seem to like each other. Based upon Mrs. Chase's description, however, the male family members sometimes appear to "hint" at rather than clearly state their preferences. Mrs. Chase seems to respond to such indirect expressions by guessing what they really want. She cited an example where, at a recent family dinner, Robert "made a face" when he was served his meal. Mrs. Chase then asked, "What's the matter?" Robert said, "Nothing." Mrs. Chase asked, "Don't you like the meal? I'll get you something else." Robert said, "Don't bother, this is okay." Mrs. Chase said, "No, I'll get you something else to eat." Robert said, "Oh, okay. Thanks." At this point, Mrs. Chase interrupted her own meal, got up, and prepared something Robert wanted to eat.

Members of the Chase family appear to have adopted many of the stereotypic rules and roles of men, women, and children projected by the dominant North American culture of the mid-20th century. Robert's adolescence and Mrs. Chase's full-time outside employment probably represent the most significant stressors the family system now faces.

As a system, the Chase family is moving into a phase when an adolescent child often stimulates a number of issues and decisions for the youth, the parents, and the family system as a whole. According to Mrs. Chase, Robert is beginning to experience bodily changes and has become more self-conscious and self-centered. These changes may be affecting the nature of the relationship between Robert and Mrs. Chase and perhaps that with his father as well. Mrs. Chase, directly or indirectly, may be uneasy and unclear concerning her parenting role during this time. Her own adolescent experiences and the shame she felt during the confession to a priest may continue to affect her today in relation to her son Robert. She may wonder about his unfolding sexuality and be concerned about how he will deal with adolescent changes.

3. Motivation and Stage of Change

Before the end of our first meeting together, Mrs. Chase concluded that throughout most of her life she has adopted a protective, parent-like, caretaking, and people-pleasing role toward people in general and the members of her family in particular. She also said that "not only has this pattern left me feeling guilty and stressed, it may have interfered to some extent with Richard and Robert's ability to care for themselves." She smiled as she said that "she might have to become more selfish—for the sake of her husband and son."

By the end of our first meeting, Mrs. Chase appeared highly motivated to make personal changes to allow her to lighten her burdens of responsibility and permit others to assume more control over their own lives. She looked forward to feeling more relaxed and playful, and more able to experience joy and pleasure. She indicated that this is very important to her as it could help her overcome her "family legacy" of anger, criticism, shame and guilt, and workaholism. Mrs. Chase seemed comfortable with and confident in my ability to help her address these issues and willing to work collaboratively with me in the process.

Relative to Prochaska's transtheoretical model (Prochaska et al., 1994), Mrs. Chase probably fits within the latter portions of the *contemplation* and the early parts of the *preparation* stages of change. She appeared motivated by the idea that she might change patterns of thinking, feeling, and behaving that had their origins during her childhood. She also seemed encouraged by the idea that making those changes could not only make her own life easier and more enjoyable but that it could also help her husband and son.

Mrs. Chase believed that Richard and Robert would be enthusiastic about any efforts to help her. She feels secure and confident in their love and affection for her. She thought they would place a high priority on addressing the issues of irritability, argumentativeness, shame and guilt, sleeplessness, smoking behavior, and excessive weight loss. She also believed that they would join in an attempt to alter the family structure so that she's less the "mommy" for both of them. She anticipated, however, that there might be times when all of them might be tempted to slip back into the old, familiar patterns.

She was less optimistic about her parents' and siblings' willingness to acknowledge or to help address the issues. She also seemed worried about the reactions of people at her job and friends within the church and community. She wondered if they might become confused and perhaps annoyed if she began to do less for them. However, she smiled when she said, "I'll talk with them about my issues, and we'll see what happens when I start to change."

4. **Personal Beliefs and Social Norms**

   Mrs. Chase and I observed that her beliefs about "thinking about and doing for others first," "don't make mistakes," "don't be a burden to others," "don't think about yourself," and "don't be selfish" may be related to the gender-related role expectations of her family of origin, her religious training and experiences, and her cultural background. She recognized the relationship of these beliefs to the current issues and was motivated to reconsider them.

5. **Personal and Situational Strengths**

   Based on information gained during the initial interview, Mrs. Chase reflects a high level of competence. She has coped well with life transitions and issues. In spite of the current concerns, she continues to function well in all important social roles. She appears to possess a coherent and integrated personality. She reflects superior thinking capacities, probably possesses above-average intelligence, and is insightful and articulate. Since the time of her marriage to Richard, her lifestyle has been stable and congruent. In addition, she seems highly motivated to function well in the role of client and agent of change in her own life.

   There are sufficient resources to meet basic and advanced needs of the Chase family. They have adequate assets and opportunities to pursue their aspirations. They have not been subject to overt oppression or discrimination. Mrs. Chase appears to have the affection and support of her husband and son. Although her mother, father, and siblings do not appear to provide much in the way of interest, understanding, or support, she has several friends who care a great deal about her. In these relationships as in most others, she seems to "give more than she receives" and "knows more about others than others know about her." She also believes strongly that both her husband and son would be willing to do anything they could to help her.

6. **Challenges and Obstacles**

   One aspect that may represent a personal challenge involves control. Mrs. Chase and I have not yet discussed the possible relationship between taking care of others and feelings of control. It's possible that as she worries less about others and reduces her caretaking behavior, she may experience increased anxiety associated with a decreased sense of control.

It's also likely that some elements of her primary and secondary social systems may resist changes she hopes to make. Despite their apparent love and support, Richard and Robert may well experience some resentment if expected to do more for themselves. Mrs. Chase's parents and siblings may also respond in a similar fashion, as might some of her work colleagues and church and community friends.

7. **Risk Assessment**

Despite the indications of stress and perhaps depression, Mrs. Chase and I concur that she does not represent any danger to herself or others. In response to a question concerning suicidal thoughts and actions, she indicated that she has never taken any self-destructive action and does not have suicidal thoughts. Similarly, she reported that she has never experienced thoughts nor taken actions intended to hurt another person. She also confirmed that she does not use drugs of any kind—only rarely takes an aspirin—and drinks at most one glass of wine per week.

C. **Person-Issue-Situation**

1. **Ideas and Hypotheses**

Might the fact that Robert is alone, unsupervised, and unprotected during two hours after school each weekday represent an important trigger to Mrs. Chase's feelings of stress, irritability, and guilt? Might she feel a conflict between working to save money for her son's college education and being unavailable to him when he returns from school? Might she be afraid that he could be in some danger? Might Mrs. Chase believe that she is less able to protect Robert from the influence of the neighborhood boys now that she works outside the home? Does she feel an obligation to keep Robert entirely away from negative influences? Does she suspect that Robert might be especially susceptible to such influences and that he might be unable to make responsible decisions? Might she be associating Robert's adolescence with her own teenage experience? Could she be worried that Robert might indeed be fully capable of making mature decisions and might not need her as much anymore? What would it take for Mrs. Chase to feel that Robert is safe during the two-hour "latch-key" period?

How much does she want to work outside the home? Does she enjoy the work? How does her husband feel about her working? How similar is Mrs. Chase to her father in terms of a workaholic, or compulsive, approach to life? Might her reactions to working outside the home be in some way related to her view of her father as "a workaholic who was never at home?" Might she feel guilty that "she's like her father?" Have the symptoms of irritability and argumentativeness led to a comparison with her mother—whom she views as angry, critical, and unstable. Might Mrs. Chase worry that if she does not do for others, they might not value, respect, or love her?

Are the communication patterns in the family such that the male family members tend to avoid full and direct expression? Does Mrs. Chase try to "read their minds" and subtly contribute to this process? Do Richard and Robert realize that they sometimes communicate indirectly through facial expressions and bodily gestures? What might be the consequence of more direct and full verbal expression within the family system? What would each family member stand to gain or lose?

Would Mrs. Chase be willing to let her husband and son assume greater responsibility for household and family tasks? Would they be willing to do so? How would the family members anticipate coping with the inevitable stress that accompanies change? What stress-reducing mechanisms do the family members have that might be applied during transitional periods such as this one?

What specific issues and dilemmas, if any, is Robert confronting? Is Mrs. Chase comfortable with her son's increasing autonomy and personal responsibility? How does Mr. Chase relate to his son during this time? What hopes and dreams do Mr. and Mrs. Chase have for Robert's future? What doubts and fears do they have about him?

2. **Summary Assessment**

Based on information gained during the initial interview, Mrs. Chase and her family have a lengthy history of competent functioning. The family members individually and as a system appear to be coherent and stable. However, Mr. Chase, Robert, and especially Mrs. Chase have begun to experience strain associated with changing demands on them. These demands were apparently initiated when Mrs. Chase began to work full-time outside the home. This has significantly increased the extent of her responsibilities and has caused her considerable stress. It appears that she has tried to continue to "do it all" and may feel worried and guilty that she is not as available to her son as he might need. She may be especially concerned about her son's well-being during the two hours that he's alone after school.

Several factors may have relevance to the identified issues. First, Mrs. Chase comes from a family of origin where she assumed adult responsibilities from an early age. She reported that her mother abused alcohol and her father was a workaholic. It is possible that Mrs. Chase tends to assume substantial responsibility for others—perhaps especially family members—because she was socialized to do so from an early age. Working full-time outside the home may represent a major psychosocial conflict for her. One part of her, perhaps like her father, may be strongly tempted to invest a great deal of time and energy in her employment. Another part may feel much anxiety and uncertainty when she is away from the home. She is so familiar with the role of caretaker for her husband and son that she may sometimes feel anxious when she is working and unable to meet their needs. Second, Mrs. Chase wanted to have more children, but a medical condition has prevented that. She may not, as yet, have fully explored and grieved for the loss of her hopes for additional children. She may also invest greater energy in her son Robert, since "he's my only child." Third, Robert, as an early adolescent, may be troubled by physical, psychological, and social changes he is undergoing. This, along with Mrs. Chase's employment, is probably causing considerable systemic stress within the family. As a person emotionally attuned to the family, Mrs. Chase is understandably affected during this transition period. She may be confronting the limitations of her family-centered role identification.

It's possible that the current issues of concern represent a kind of positive signal to Mrs. Chase to make some personal changes that could both liberate her from inhibitions that originate in childhood and prepare her for a more peaceful and enjoyable second half of life. Although assumption of the full-time paid job outside the home seems associated with the onset of the issues of concern, it is plausible that something was needed to help her and her family proceed to the next stage of individual and family development. Application of Erikson's psychosocial life-cycle stage theory (Erikson, 1963, 1968) might suggest that Mrs. Chase is proceeding through the "Generativity versus Stagnation" stage in preparation for greater meaning in life and a more coherent sense of personal identity and integrity. Some issues related to certain earlier life cycle stages may require exploration (e.g., autonomy versus shame and doubt, initiative versus guilt, identity versus role confusion). Indeed, Gilligan's theoretical approach to women's development might suggest that Mrs. Chase is indeed seeking enhanced intimacy and greater attachment to the most important people in her life (Gilligan, 1979, 1984). Although her commitment to and relationships with others have been strong, the degree of intimacy and closeness may have been inhibited by the dominance of the parent-like, caretaking role.

Mrs. Chase's intelligence, maturity, insight, and motivation along with the affection and support of her husband and son suggest a high likelihood that the issues can be effectively addressed. I estimate that the probability of full and successful resolution is greater than 85 percent. I also anticipate a satisfactory outcome in one to two months of weekly meetings with Mrs. Chase and her immediate family.

◆ EXERCISE 8-2: FORMULATING A TENTATIVE ASSESSMENT

For this exercise, please review the information that you organized into the description section of your own case record as part of Exercise 8-1. Based on what you know about yourself and what you included in the description, proceed to formulate a tentative assessment through analysis and synthesis of the available data. Record it in your own case record. In conducting your assessment, however, remember that much of what you determine remains tentative and speculative—even in this case, where you are assessing yourself. These ideas or hypotheses await later support and confirmation. Formulate your ideas in accord with the format provided in the assessment section of the DAC. Be sure that your identity is disguised, then place your description and assessment in the "My Personal Case Record" section of your Social Work Skills Learning Portfolio.

Summary

During the assessment phase of social work practice, you and the client attempt to make sense of the data gathered during the exploration phase. The assessment gives the parties involved a perspective from which to initiate the process of contracting. Two skills are especially pertinent to the assessment phase: organizing information and formulating a tentative assessment.

◆ CHAPTER 8 SUMMARY EXERCISES

Building on the first interview you had with your colleague (see the supplemental exercise in Chapter 7), conduct a second interview. Ensure that the interview setting is private, and again tape-record the meeting. Using the exploring and other relevant skills addressed thus far, interview your colleague with a view toward formulating an assessment. At the conclusion of the meeting, arrange for another meeting in about one week.

1. At the conclusion of the interview, ask your partner for feedback concerning his or her thoughts and feelings about the experience. Ask your colleague for a frank reaction to the following questions: (a) Did you feel comfortable and safe with me serving as a social worker? (b) Did you feel that I was sincerely interested in you and in what you had to say? (c) Did you feel that I understood what you were trying to communicate? If so, what contributed to this? If not, what led you to believe that I did not understand? (d) What information did we discuss that helped you to better understand or assess those factors that contribute to the issues of concern? (e) What material was neglected that might have contributed to a more complete and accurate assessment? (f) In general, was the experience satisfying? If so, what factors helped to make it so? If not, what contributed to that? (g) What would you suggest that I do in the future to improve the quality of my interviewing skills? Summarize your partner's feedback in the following space.

2. In the following space, record your own reaction to the conversation. How did you feel about the interview? What did you like and what did you dislike about it? Do you believe that you used all the relevant skills during the interaction? Which skills do you seem to perform well? Which skills need more

Assessing

practice? What information did you gain that will contribute to the formulation of an assessment? What additional information would be useful? What would you do differently if you were to redo the interview?

3. Organize the relevant information from both the first meeting (review your earlier transcript) and this second interview according to the format provided in the description section of the DAC. Type the description for inclusion in your Social Work Skills Learning Portfolio.

4. After completing the description, proceed to formulate a tentative assessment through analysis and synthesis of the available data. Type your assessment. Continue to completely disguise the identity of your colleague. Also, recall that much of what you determine remains tentative and speculative. These are ideas or hypotheses, not facts. They need further support and confirmation. Formulate your observations and ideas in accordance with the format provided above in the assessment section of the DAC.

5. After you have completed the description and assessment portions of the case record, play the audiotape or videotape. Study the tape and make note of significant information that you neglected to include in your description and assessment. Add it to the appropriate sections of your DAC. Make sure that the identity of your interview partner is fully disguised and then include your completed Description and Assessment in a separate section or folder within your Social Work Skills Learning Portfolio. You might label that section or folder "Practice Case Record."

◆ **CHAPTER 8 WORLD WIDE WEB EXERCISES**

1. Go to the InfoTrac College Edition Web site at www.infotrac-college.com. Use your passcode to log in. Conduct a keyword search using the string "social work assessment" (without the quotation marks) to locate several articles about the topic. Carefully read the article entitled "Social Work Assessment: Case Theory Construction" (Bisman, 1999), the one entitled "Strengths-

Based Social Work Assessment: Transforming the Dominant Paradigm" (Graybeal, 2001), and the one entitled "Incorporating Spirituality into Social Work Practice: A Review of What To Do" (Cascio, 1998). Reflect on the contents of the three articles and use the following space to summarize their import for assessment processes in social work.

2. Go to the InfoTrac College Edition Web site at www.infotrac-college.com. Use your passcode to log in. Conduct a keyword search using the string "mental status examination Dilsaver" (without the quotation marks) to locate the article entitled "The Mental Status Examination" (Dilsaver, 1990). Carefully read the article and use the following space to summarize the common dimensions of mental status examinations. Also outline the questions and scoring procedure for the "Short Portable Mental Status Questionnaire," which is included in the article. Finally, describe one or two circumstances where social workers might find it useful to incorporate a mental status examination as part of an assessment process.

3. Go to the InfoTrac College Edition Web site at www.infotrac-college.com. Use your passcode to log in. Conduct a keyword search using the string "alcohol problem Kitchens" (without the quotation marks) to locate the article

entitled "Does This Patient Have an Alcohol Problem?" (Kitchens, 1994). Carefully read the article and use the following space to summarize the questions contained in the CAGE, MAST, and AUDIT instruments for assessing alcohol problems? Finally, describe one or two circumstances where social workers might find it useful to incorporate evaluation of substance abuse as part of an assessment process.

4. Go to the InfoTrac College Edition Web site at www.infotrac-college.com. Use your passcode to log in. Conduct a keyword search using the string "child abuse assessment Patterson" (without the quotation marks) to locate the article entitled "Child Abuse: Assessment and Intervention" (Patterson, 1998). Carefully read the article and use the following space to summarize the factors to consider when conducting an assessment of child abuse in an orthopedic setting. Finally, describe one or two circumstances where social workers might find it useful to incorporate a sophisticated child abuse assessment procedure.

5. Go to the InfoTrac College Edition Web site at www.infotrac-college.com. Use your passcode to log in. Conduct a keyword search using the string "Suicide Assessment Checklist" (without the quotation marks) to locate the article entitled "Validity of the Suicide Assessment Checklist in an Emergency

Crisis Center" (Rogers, Lewis, & Subich, 2002). Carefully read the article and use the following space to summarize the factors to consider in conducting an assessment of suicide risk. Finally, describe one or two circumstances where social workers might find it useful to incorporate a sophisticated suicide risk assessment procedure.

Chapter 8 Self-Appraisal

As you finish this chapter, please assess your proficiency in the assessing skills by completing the following self-appraisal exercise.

SELF-APPRAISAL: THE ASSESSING SKILLS

Please respond to the following items. Your answers should help you to assess your proficiency in the assessing skills. Read each statement carefully. Then, use the following four-point rating scale to indicate the degree to which you agree or disagree with each statement. Record your numerical response in the space provided.

4 = Strongly Agree

3 = Agree

2 = Disagree

1 = Strongly Disagree

_____ 1. I am proficient in organizing descriptive information for social work purposes.

_____ 2. I am proficient in formulating a professional quality social work assessment.

_____ Subtotal

Note: These items are taken directly from the Social Work Skills Self-Appraisal Questionnaire contained in Appendix 3. You have responded to these items before. You may now compare your item responses to those you made on earlier occasions. You may also compare the subtotal scores. If you think you are developing greater proficiency in these skills, more recent scores should be higher than earlier.

Finally, reflect on the skills addressed in this chapter and the results of your self-appraisal. Based on your analysis, prepare a succinct one-page summary report entitled "Self-Assessment of Proficiency in the Assessing Skills." Within the report, be sure to identify those skills that you know and do well (e.g., a score of 3 or 4). Also, specify those that need further practice (e.g., scores of 2 or less) and briefly outline plans by which to achieve proficiency in them. When finished, include the report in your Social Work Skills Learning Portfolio.

Chapter 9

Contracting

Contracting follows integrally from the assessment process. This chapter (see Box 9.1) is intended to help you develop proficiency in the contracting skills that yield clearly identified goals for work and plans to pursue and evaluate progress toward those goals.

BOX 9.1

Chapter Purpose

The purpose of this chapter is to help learners develop proficiency in the contracting skills.

Goals

Following completion of this chapter, learners should be able to demonstrate proficiency in the following:

◆ Reflecting an issue
◆ Identifying an issue
◆ Clarifying issues for work
◆ Establishing goals

(continued)

BOX 9.1 *(continued)*

◆ Developing an action plan
◆ Identifying action steps
◆ Planning for evaluation
◆ Summarizing the contract
◆ Ability to assess proficiency in the contracting skills

The contracting process typically begins during or shortly after assessment. Skills especially applicable to this phase of practice include the following: (1) reflecting an issue, (2) identifying an issue, (3) clarifying issues for work, (4) establishing goals, (5) developing an action plan, (6) identifying action steps, (7) planning for evaluation, and (8) summarizing the contract.

Reflecting an Issue

By using the skill of *reflecting an issue,* you demonstrate to clients that you understand their view of an identified topic of concern. Reflecting an issue is an important form of active, empathic listening; it constitutes the beginning of the contracting process. When you empathically communicate your understanding of clients' experience of and perspective about the issue, the working relationship and clients' motivation to work with you tend to improve. It is very important to communicate your understanding of the nature of the issues of concern as the clients themselves see them. In effect, you show clients that you intend to help them address the issues *they* wish to address. By confirming that their view of the issues is legitimate, you communicate respect for them as persons and for their right to self-determination.

Of course, your reflection of an issue does not suggest moral *approval* or professional *agreement* to work toward its resolution. Occasionally, clients identify issues in such a way that a social worker could not morally, ethically, or legally help to address it. For instance, suppose you served as a school social worker in a high school. One of the students—a 16-year-old girl—says she has a problem and wants your advice. She states, "Everybody drinks at the school dances. It helps people feel better and have more fun. But the new regulations prevent us from going out to our cars during dances. It's a good policy. Everybody had to go out to the parking lot to drink and then come back into the gym to dance. It was, like, back and forth all night long. It would be so much better if we could just spike one bowl of punch with whisky. It would be safer and we wouldn't have to leave the building."

As a social worker, you obviously could neither condone nor help her put whisky in the punch. However, you could easily communicate your understanding of the student's view of the issue so that she feels heard and understood. That understanding can form the basis for further exploration and perhaps reconsideration of the issue.

Clients, especially adults who voluntarily seek social services, are usually quite ready to share their issues and concerns, but some clients may need support, guidance, and encouragement to do so. In certain involuntary circumstances or when clients' lack competency to participate in the process, you may have to assume major responsibility for both issue identification and goal determination.

Regardless of the context, do not assume that the issues clients first identify will necessarily remain the focus for work. They may do so, but during exploration with an attentive social worker, clients often identify different concerns that are more pressing or more fundamental than those they initially mention. Some clients test workers by trying out a relatively modest issue first. Based on the nature of your response, they may then move on to identify an issue of much greater significance.

As you begin to practice the skill of reflecting an issue, please use the format outlined here. Later, when you gain greater proficiency, experiment with alternate formats.

PRACTICE FORMAT: REFLECTING AN ISSUE

As you see it, one of the issues you'd like to address in our work together is _____.

Example

CLIENT: My wife left me—sure, for very good reasons—but I'm really down about it. She has left me before but always came back. This time I know she won't. She's gone for good, and I don't know what to do. I can't go on the way things are. I'm so sad and lost without her.

WORKER: (*reflecting issues*) As you see it, there are two major issues you'd like to address in our work together. First, you feel terrible. You're lonely and depressed, and you find it hard to function well when you feel that way. Second, you're unsure of how to get on with your life without your wife.

Reflecting an issue is, of course, a form of active listening. If you accurately paraphrase the issue as experienced by clients, they are likely to respond, "Yeah, that's right," or something similar, to verify your reflection. Nonetheless, it is often useful to precede issue reflections with reflections of feeling, content, or feeling and meaning, to show you understand clients' experience. Also, it may help to seek feedback following your reflection of the issue. For instance, following the worker's response in the example just shown, the client might be asked, "Are these the major issues you'd like to work on?"

◆ EXERCISE 9-1: REFLECTING AN ISSUE

For these exercises, assume that you are a social worker with a family-oriented social services agency. In the spaces provided, write the words you would say to reflect an issue as the client sees it.

1. You are interviewing Mrs. O., a 77-year-old widow who lives alone in a small apartment. She says, "Most of the time, I feel all right. But I'm really beginning to worry that these spells might be a sign of a serious illness." Write the words you would use in reflecting an issue as Mrs. O. sees it.

2. You are in the midst of an interview with the blended S. family. Mr. S. says, "I guess I can say this in front of the children—they know so much already. Anyway, today at work, I learned that there will soon be massive layoffs. It's likely that I will lose my job within the next three or four weeks. It's just what we need, to top off the rest of our problems!" Write the words you would say in reflecting an issue as Mr. S. sees it.

3. You are conducting an interview with Mrs. F., the Latina woman who is concerned that her children are mistreated. She says, "I guess I've never felt we really belong here in this town. Nobody really seems to like us or want us

here. I guess we just don't fit in." Write the words you might say in reflecting an issue as Mrs. F. sees it.

Identifying an Issue

Based on your exploration and assessment of the person-issue-situation, you may decide to identify an issue that the client did not mention. Or you may take a somewhat different perspective on one the client introduced. For example, a client may say that his wife's nagging is a major problem. After gaining some insight into what the client views as nagging, you might ask, "I wonder, might what you call *nagging* be a sign of a more basic communication issue? Could it be that the two of you have trouble really talking and listening to one another?"

Sometimes, you need to assume primary responsibility for issue identification and goal definition. For example, when the situation is immediately life-threatening (e.g., a client is suicidal, psychotic, or heavily intoxicated) or the client is involuntary (e.g., required to seek counseling or face felony charges for child abuse), you may need to define the issue for the client. Then the client decides whether or not to participate in the process.

Even when the situation is neither life-threatening nor involuntary, you may legitimately share your view of possible issues. Based on the tentative assessment, you may suggest that additional issues be considered, or that an identified issue be defined differently. You may have professional knowledge or previous experience that leads you to point out an issue not previously discussed. For example, suppose a client describes feelings of constant fatigue, difficulty sleeping, loss of appetite, decreased interest in pleasurable activities, and diminished social involvement. You would probably wonder whether the client might be mourning the loss of someone or something of value, be physically ill, or perhaps be significantly depressed.

You will naturally form opinions about what factors may be relevant to the clients' present situation. Often, you will share these ideas with clients—but this is done in the same way you share all your professional opinions. That is, you communicate them as opinions or ideas to consider, not as indisputable facts, and you allow clients the freedom to agree or disagree. As a part of this process, you routinely seek feedback from the client concerning these newly identified or redefined issues.

In practicing this skill, follow the format outlined here. Notice how the skill of seeking feedback is incorporated at the end.

PRACTICE FORMAT: IDENTIFYING AN ISSUE

As we have talked about you and your situation, I have been wondering about _____.

What do you think—is that an issue we should consider too? (*seeking feedback*)

Example

CLIENT: (*Lisa, partner in a lesbian relationship*) We fight all the time. Virtually every single day we have a knock-down-drag-out fight. Ever since we moved in together, two months ago, we have fought like cats and dogs. We were so great together before we decided to share the apartment. We don't hit each other, but there sure is a lot of yelling and screaming.

WORKER: (*identifying an issue; seeking feedback*) As we've talked about your relationship and how moving in together has affected it, I've been wondering about the question of roles and expectations. It seems to me that moving from a dating relationship to a live-in relationship represents a very significant change—one that might leave each of you uncertain about what the other wants and needs in this new form of relationship. What do you think—could this issue of unclear role expectations now that you live together be something we should address too?

◆ EXERCISE 9-2: IDENTIFYING AN ISSUE

For these exercises, assume that you are a social worker with a family social services agency. In the spaces provided, write the words you would say in identifying an issue.

1. You have spent nearly a full hour talking with Mrs. O., the 77-year-old widow who lives alone in a small apartment. She has expressed disappointment that her grown children no longer visit her. She worries about her spells and the possibility that she might be seriously ill; she is concerned that she might soon lose her independence and autonomy. Based on this summary of concerns and a review of exchanges that occurred earlier (Exercises 7-1.2, 7-2.2, 7-3.2, 7-4.2, 7-5.2, 7-6.2, 7-7.2, 9-1.1), write the words you would use in iden-

tifying an issue. Experiment with one or two other forms of identifying an issue as it might apply to Mrs. O.

2. You have spent approximately 75 minutes talking with the seven-member, blended S. family. Several issues have emerged: strain and conflict between Mr. S's children and Mrs. S., financial difficulties, marital distress, and most recently the threat to Mr. S.'s job. Based on this summary of concerns and a review of exchanges that occurred earlier (Exercises 7-1.3, 7-2.3, 7-3.3, 7-4.3, 7-5.3, 7-6.3, 7-7.3, 9-1.2), write the words you would use in identifying an issue. Experiment with one or two other forms of identifying an issue as it might apply to the S. family.

3. You have now talked with Mrs. F. for about 45 minutes. You've explored several issues, including her feelings that she and her family do not fit in this community, her children's apparently increasing disrespect for her and their Latino heritage, and most importantly, the concern for her children's safety at school. Based on this summary of concerns and a review of exchanges that

occurred earlier (Exercises 7-1.4, 7-2.4, 7-3.4, 7-4.4, 7-5.4, 7-6.4, 7-7.4, 9-1.3), write the words you would use in identifying an issue. Experiment with one or two other forms of identifying an issue as it might apply to Mrs. F. and her family.

Clarifying Issues for Work

Clarifying issues for work constitutes the first definitive indication that you and the client have agreed to work together toward resolving certain issues. It is a fundamental component of the social work contract. Usually, the issues for work are derived from those the client has identified, those you have contributed, or some negotiated combination or compromise of the two. Whatever their source, the issues for work provide a context for all your subsequent professional activities. Whenever possible, the issues for work should be stated in clear and descriptive terms. They may be recorded within the contract portion of the Description, Assessment, and Contract (DAC).

Specifying issues for work follows naturally from the processes of exploring and assessing the person-issue-situation. Typically, you use the skills of reflecting an issue and identifying an issue before you and the client jointly agree on the specific issues or focus for work. When you clarify issues, you suggest that there is an agreement—a contract—that these areas will be the primary focus of the work that you and the client will undertake together. In practicing this skill, consider the format outlined below.

PRACTICE FORMAT: CLARIFYING ISSUES FOR WORK

I think we agree about the primary issues that we will address in our work together. Let's review them, and I'll write them down so that we can refer to them as we go along. First, there is the issue of _____. Second, the issue of _____. Third,

_____. What do you think? Is this an accurate list of the issues that we'll address together?

Example

CLIENT: (*who has identified and explored two major issues for which she sought help from your agency; with the client's agreement you have contributed a third issue*) Well, that's my story. I hope you can help with the mess I'm in.

WORKER: (*clarifying issues for work*) I hope so too. It seems to me that we have identified three major issues to address during our work together. Let's review them once more, and I'll jot them down so that we can refer to them as we go along. First, there is the issue of housing. You have been living on the street now for three weeks and the weather is beginning to turn cold. Second, there is the diabetes. You have been without medicine for a week now and you have no insurance or money to pay for it. Third, you lost your job two months ago and need to find work so you can make some money. What do you think? Is this an accurate list of the issues that we'll address together?

◆ EXERCISE 9-3: CLARIFYING ISSUES FOR WORK

For these exercises, assume that you are a social worker with a family social services agency. Review your responses to Exercises 9-1 and 9-2 and then, in the spaces provided, write the words you would say in clarifying issues for work with each of the clients identified here. Use the format suggested earlier but feel free to be somewhat creative in preparing your response. You cannot actually interact with these clients, so you need a certain amount of flexibility.

1. Refer to Exercises 9-1.1 and 9-2.1 and then write the words you would use to clarify issues for work as they might apply to 77-year-old Mrs. O.

2. Refer to Exercises 9-1.2 and 9-2.2 and then write the words you would use to clarify issues for work as they might apply to the seven-member S. family.

3. Refer to Exercises 9-1.3 and 9-2.3 and then write the words you would use to clarify issues for work as they might apply to Mrs. F.

Establishing Goals

Following the clarification of issues, you encourage clients to participate in establishing goals. Setting effective goals is the second critical element of the contracting process. It is a vital step toward change. Goals are the aims toward which the social worker and client direct their cognitive, emotional, behavioral, and situational actions. Goals are essential. Consider the title of a book by David Campbell: *If You Don't Know Where You're Going, You'll Probably End Up Somewhere Else* (1974). Without clear goals, you and your clients are indeed likely to end up somewhere other than where you intend.

In constructing goals with clients, use a SMART format. SMART stands for

♦ Specific
♦ Measurable
♦ Action-oriented
♦ Realistic
♦ Timely

Objectives that are defined in a SMART manner are usually easier to understand, undertake, accomplish, and assess. As Egan (1982b, pp. 212–218) suggests, effective goals are

♦ Stated as accomplishments
♦ Stated in clear and specific terms
♦ Stated in measurable or verifiable terms
♦ Realistic (e.g., have a reasonable chance of success)
♦ Adequate, if achieved, to improve the situation
♦ Congruent with clients' value and cultural systems
♦ Time-specific (i.e., include a time frame for achievement)

According to Egan, effective goals meet the criteria just outlined. First, well-formed goals are described as accomplishments rather than processes. "To lose weight" is a process. "To achieve a weight of 125 pounds and maintain that weight for six months" is an accomplishment. Second, effective goals are clear and specific. They are not vague resolutions or general mission statements. "Securing employment" is un-specific. "Within six weeks, to secure employment as a waiter in a restaurant" is much more clear and specific. Third, well-stated goals are described in easily understood, measurable or verifiable terms. Both client and worker can clearly recognize when goals have been achieved. "To feel better" is hard to recognize and not sufficiently measurable. "To feel better as indicated by sleeping the night through (at least seven hours per night on at least five nights per week), completely eating three meals daily, and by scoring at least 15% higher on the Beck Depression Inventory" is much more measurable. Fourth, goals should be realistic. Given the motivations, opportunities, strengths, resources, and capacities of the person-issue-situation systems, the estab-lished goals should have a reasonably high probability of attainment. A goal "to get all straight A's" would not be realistic for a student who has never before received a sin-gle "A." Fifth, effective goals are adequate. A goal is adequate to the degree that its ac-complishment would significantly improve the situation. Goals that would not contribute to a resolution of the issues are therefore inadequate. Sixth, effective goals are congruent with the client's value and cultural systems. Unless a life-threatening sit-uation exists, you should generally neither ask nor expect clients to forsake their fun-damental personal or cultural values. Seventh, effective goals are described with a time frame. Both you and your clients need to know *when* the goals are to be achieved.

Although specifying smart goals in a manner consistent with Egan's criteria rep-resents an ideal, it is not always desirable or feasible to do so. Do not become so fa-natical in your attempt to define goals in a precise manner that you lose touch with the client's reality. Some clients are in such a state of uncertainty and confusion that pushing them too hard toward specificity would exacerbate their state of distress. Therefore, on occasion, you should postpone goal specification and instead establish a general direction for work. Indeed, sometimes the general direction involves "working toward clarifying goals for our work together." Later, when the confusion and ambiguity subside, you may appropriately return to encourage identification of clear and precise goals that conform more closely to Egan's ideal.

Whether stated in specific or general terms, goals should follow logically from and relate directly to the agreed-on issues for work. Usually, you and your client identify at least one goal for each identified issue. However, accomplishing one goal sometimes resolves more than one issue, so it may not always be necessary to have a separate goal for every issue. Nonetheless, be sure that accomplishing the array of goals would resolve all the identified issues.

Consistent with the values of the profession, goals are jointly determined with clients and have their consent. In effect, when you and a client establish goals, you implicitly agree to a contract in which both parties commit to work toward accomplishing them. Most of the time, clients are quite capable of active participation in goal identification. As part of that process, you request that they indicate a goal for one or more issues for work. However, you should ask them to do so in a special way. Clients often respond to direct questions such as "What is your goal for resolving this issue?" in vague and general terms. You can often encourage clearer goal descriptions by asking questions that require clients to describe specifically *how they will know* when a particular issue is resolved. In addition to furthering the purposes of goal establishment identified earlier, these questions serve another extremely important function. They encourage clients to envision, in considerable detail, a future in which the issue has indeed been resolved. In so doing, clients often begin to feel better, more energized, and more motivated to work toward goal attainment. To yield such results, however, these questions are phrased in a certain way.

For this purpose, the exploring skill of *seeking clarification* is adapted to encourage clients both to establish a goal and to imagine a future in which the issue has been resolved. Clarification-seeking questions, phrased in the following format, tend to yield these dual results.

PRACTICE FORMATS: ENCOURAGING GOAL IDENTIFICATION

In specific terms, how will you know when the issue of _____ is truly resolved?

or

What would indicate to you that this issue is truly a thing of the past?

Example

WORKER: Now that we have a pretty clear list of the issues, let's try to establish specific goals for each one. The first issue we've identified is that your 14-year-old son skips school two or three days each week. Let's imagine that it is now some point in the future and the issue has been completely resolved. What would indicate to you that your son's truancy is truly a thing of the past?

CLIENT: Well, I guess I'll know when Johnny goes to school every day and his grades are better.

WORKER: *(reflecting goal; seeking feedback)* When Johnny goes to school daily and improves his grades, you will feel that it's no longer an issue. Is that right?

CLIENT: Yes.

WORKER: *(seeking clarification)* Okay, now let's try to be even more specific. When you say, "Johnny will go to school every day" do you also mean that he will attend all his classes when he's there?

CLIENT: Yes.

WORKER: *(seeking clarification)* What do you think would be a reasonable period for accomplishing this goal?

CLIENT: Well, I don't know. I'd like him to start now.

WORKER: *(sharing opinion; seeking feedback)* That would be great progress! But I wonder if that might be expecting too much. Let's see, it's now one month into the school year. As I understand it, Johnny skipped school some last year too and this year he is skipping even more. What do you think about a two-month period for accomplishing the goal?

CLIENT: That sounds really good.

WORKER: *(establishing goal)* Okay, How does this sound as our first goal: "Within two months from today's date, Johnny will go to school every day and attend all his classes, except when he's sick enough to go to a doctor"? Let me take a moment to write that down for us. . . . Now about the grades. As I understand, he is currently failing most of his courses. How will you know when that is no longer an issue?

As should be apparent from this example, you often need to be quite active in encouraging goal identification. Notice that the questions reflect an implicit optimism. They require clients to envision a future in which the issue is indeed resolved. Therefore, in seeking goal identification, try to avoid phrases such as, "*If the issues were resolved . . .*" This could suggest to a client that you are pessimistic about the chances for success. In expressing optimism, however, be careful to avoid making promises that you cannot keep. Most of the time social workers cannot guarantee that their services will result in successful outcomes.

Sometimes, in response to your questions, clients formulate clear goals with which you can readily concur. When this happens, you may simply reflect the goal by paraphrasing the client's words. You may use a format such as the following.

PRACTICE FORMAT: REFLECTING A GOAL

As you see it, one goal for our work together is _____.

Example

CLIENT: *(responding to worker's request to state a goal)* Well, I guess I'd like to improve the quality of the communication between us.

WORKER: *(reflecting goal; seeking feedback)* As you see it then, one goal for our work together is for the two of you to become better at talking pleasantly and respectfully with one another. Is that right?

CLIENT: Yes.

Reflecting a goal involves communicating your empathic understanding of a client's view of a goal that he or she would like to pursue in your work together. As are all reflecting skills, it is a specific form of active listening. Reflecting a goal demonstrates that you have heard and understood a goal as the client expressed it. When reflecting goals, you may paraphrase or mirror the client's words even if the goal is stated in a general way. Alternately, you can go somewhat beyond what the client has said, phrasing your response so that the goal is stated in more clear and specific terms.

Sometimes, despite your active encouragement, a client cannot or will not identify a goal. In such instances, you may simply postpone the goal-setting process and engage in additional exploration of the person-issue-situation. Alternatively, you may propose a tentative goal, which the client may accept, reject, or modify. In *proposing a goal,* you may adopt a format such as the following.

PRACTICE FORMAT: PROPOSING A GOAL

I wonder, would it make sense to establish as one goal for our work together _____?

Example

WORKER: Now that we have a pretty clear understanding of the issues and a sense of the direction we'd like to go, let's establish goals for our work together. We've agreed that your pattern of alcohol consumption is a significant issue that we'll address. I wonder, would it make sense to establish as a goal for our work together to limit the amount of daily alcohol intake to one 12-ounce can of beer each day?

Example

CLIENT: Yes. It does feel like I've lost everything I had hoped for. I guess it's normal to feel sad when a marriage fails.

WORKER: (*reflecting feeling and meaning*) Your dreams for the future of your marriage have been shattered, and you feel a powerful sense of loss and sadness.

CLIENT: Yes, my marriage meant a lot to me.

WORKER: (*encouraging goal identification*) I wonder if it might be possible for us to identify a goal in relation to these feelings of sadness and loss. Let's imagine that it's now some time in the future when these feelings are long since past. What will you be thinking, feeling, and doing when these depressed feelings are no longer a problem for you?

CLIENT: Gee, I don't know exactly. I guess when I'm finally over her I'll feel a lot better.

WORKER: (*reflecting content; encouraging goal specificity*) So it will be a positive sign when you begin to feel better. And what will indicate to you that you're feeling better?

CLIENT: I guess once I'm over this, I'll be able to sleep and eat again and not think about her so much, and I might even be dating someone else.

WORKER: (*reflecting content; proposing a goal; seeking feedback*) So when you begin to eat and sleep better, and you think about her less, we'll know that things have taken a positive turn. Let's make the goals even more specific so that we will know when you have completely achieved them. How does this sound to you? "Within six months, to (1) sleep six or more hours per night at least five nights per week, (2) regain the weight that you lost, (3) at least 75% of the time, think about things other than your wife, and (4) go out on at least one date." What do you think?

CLIENT: Real good. Right now, I probably think about her 95% of the time, and the idea of going on a date sounds just awful. If I were thinking about other things, doing other things, and dating someone else, I'd know that I'd finally be over her.

WORKER: (*establishing goal*) Okay. Let me jot that down so we can remember it.

◆ **EXERCISE 9-4: ESTABLISHING GOALS**

For these exercises, assume that you are continuing in your role as a social worker with a family social services agency. In the spaces provided for each case situation, complete three tasks. First, write the words you would say in *encouraging the client to identify a goal*. Second, prepare a *general goal statement* that reasonably follows from one or more of the issues that you specified in Exercise 9-3. Third, prepare a *specific goal statement* that reasonably follows from one or more of the issues that you specified in Exercise 9-3. Try to write it so that it meets Egan's ideal criteria for effective goal statements.

Of course, the nature of this exercise does not allow you to interact with clients in negotiating goals. Therefore, simply formulate appropriate questions and then share your view of goals that might match the identified issues. The primary purpose here is to practice asking questions that encourage goal identification and to practice preparing two forms of goal statements.

1. a. Write the words you would say in asking a question that encourages Mrs. O., the 77-year-old widow, to identify a goal that relates to one or more of the issues specified in Exercise 9-3.1.

   b. On behalf of Mrs. O., write a general goal statement that relates to one or more of the issues specified in Exercise 9-3.1.

c. Now write a SMART goal statement that relates to one or more of the issues specified in Exercise 9-3.1.

2. a. Write the words you would say in asking a question to encourage members of the S. family to identify a goal that relates to one or more of the issues specified in Exercise 9-3.2.

b. On behalf of the S. family, write a general goal statement that relates to one or more of the issues specified in Exercise 9-3.2.

c. Now write a SMART goal statement that relates to one or more of the issues specified in Exercise 9-3.2.

3. a. Write the words you would say in asking a question that encourages Mrs. F., the Latina mother who is concerned about her children, to identify a goal that relates to one or more of the issues specified in Exercise 9-3.3.

   b. On behalf of Mrs. F., write a general goal statement that relates to one or more of the issues specified in Exercise 9-3.3.

c.   Now write a SMART goal statement that relates to one or more of the issues specified in Exercise 9-3.3.

4.   When you have completed these exercises, review the SMART goal statements that you wrote and then ask yourself the following questions. Are the goals described as accomplishments rather than processes? Are the goals clear and specific? Are they measurable or verifiable in some way? Are they realistic, given the circumstances? Are they adequate? Do they appear to be consistent with the fundamental values and cultural preferences that you might expect of these clients? Finally, are the goals congruent with the issues identified in Exercise 9-3? If your answer to any of these questions is No, revise your SMART goal statements so that they do meet Egan's ideal form.

Developing an Action Plan

Once goals have been established, you engage the client in the process of developing an action plan to pursue them. In doing so, you and the client identify pertinent others who will meet with you and who or what will be the target for change. Together, you and the client also determine who will be involved in the change efforts and how those efforts might affect others. For example, consider a case in which the mother of an 8-year-old boy expresses concern about his disobedience and aggression. You and the client would determine who should and could be involved and in what context. Will it be the mother and boy together; the mother separately; the boy separately; sometimes one, sometimes the other, sometimes both; the boy in a group with other boys; or the mother in a group with other mothers? There are numerous possibilities, and many decisions are required.

You also determine what social work role or roles you will play (e.g., *advocate, broker, case manager, counselor, educator, evaluator, facilitator, investigator, mediator,* or *therapist*) and what theoretical approach or intervention protocol to adopt in pursuing established goals. Clients participate in the process and, of course, must provide informed consent before any intervention or action may be undertaken. If, for example, you and the client decide that you will serve in the role of counselor, you also need to determine a theory, model, or protocol that will guide your actions (e.g., task-centered, family systems, ecological, behavior modification, problem-solving, or some combination thereof). You also select one or more counseling methods or formats (e.g., individual, dyadic, family, small group). You and the client also determine how to implement the change efforts. How active should you be? How direct should you be? Should you encourage the client to take the initiative, or should you assume primary leadership responsibility? You and the client decide how fast to proceed with change efforts and how to approach other persons who could or should be involved.

You and the client decide where to hold your meetings and where the change efforts will occur. Sometimes it is easier for clients, or more likely to yield positive results, to meet in their homes rather than in your agency office. On other occasions, an entirely neutral location may be the best choice. You and the client also determine when you will meet (e.g., morning, afternoon, evening on which days), how often (e.g., once per week, three times weekly, once per month), and how long (e.g., 15 minutes, 30 minutes, one hour, two hours). Typically, you and the client will establish a time frame for your work together. Will you plan to work together toward these goals for six weeks, three months, six months, or longer? In addition, you and the client should identify possible obstacles as well as potential resources that might affect the outcome of your plan. Importantly, you also generate and reflect on the likely beneficial results of a successful outcome.

Most social work action plans involve change of some kind—change that would help resolve an issue and achieve a goal. Sometimes a single decision or action is all that is needed. More commonly, however, the focus is on long-lasting change. Long-lasting change efforts may be directed toward some aspect of a person, some part of the situation, or, as is usually the case, toward elements of both the person-and-the-situation. For example, change in a person's thinking might be the focus (e.g., to think more favorably about oneself, to develop a more optimistic attitude, or even to accept that certain things will probably continue as before). Or, change in a client's feelings (e.g., to reduce the frequency and intensity of angry feelings or to become more relaxed) might be a target. Or, behavior change might be warranted (e.g., speak more often in a group context or become more proficient in certain parenting skills). As a social worker, you and your clients will also undoubtedly focus a great deal on situational change of various kinds. For instance, you might attempt to secure housing for a homeless person or improve the quality of care for someone living in foster care. You might try to find employment for someone out of work or obtain an exception for someone deemed ineligible for food stamps, health insurance, or social security benefits. Regardless of the focus of change, recognize that individuals, dyads, families, groups, organizations, communities, or societies that are not ready for planned change or motivated to take action, rarely do so. If you expect that change will always naturally and easily follow from a cooperative process of goal setting and action planning, you will be quite disappointed. Social systems vary in their readiness depending on their stage in the change process (Prochaska et al., 1994).

In developing an action plan, you and the client consider a number of factors, including the stages of change, and develop an approach to guide your work together. The following is an example of how an action plan might be succinctly recorded as part of the contract portion of the DAC. (See Summarizing the Contract later in this chapter for additional discussion of this part of the DAC.)

EXAMPLE

1. Action Plan

   Florence Dupre (client) and Susan Holder (social worker), agree to meet together for weekly one-hour sessions over the course of the next eight weeks. Our purpose is to accomplish the goals identified above. In particular, we will work to secure a full-time job that pays $15.00 or more per hour, and includes medical and retirement benefits. We will approach this work as a cooperative effort with each of us contributing ideas and suggestions, and each of us taking steps toward goal achievement. Susan Holder will serve in the roles of counselor, educator, and advocate in attempting to help Florence Dupre reach the identified goals for work. Sometimes we will meet in the agency, sometimes in Ms. Dupre's apartment, and sometimes at other locations within the community. In approaching this work, Susan Holder will adopt a "task-centered" approach. Throughout the eight-week period, we will keep track of tasks or action steps undertaken and their effects, and generally monitor the progress toward goal achievement. At the end of that time, we will determine whether to conclude our work, consult with or refer to someone else, or contract with each other for further work together.

EXERCISE 9-5: DEVELOPING AN ACTION PLAN

For these exercises, assume that you are continuing your work with the clients described in the previous exercises (Mrs. O., the S. family, and Mrs. F.). Review your responses to Exercises 9-3 (clarifying issues for work) and 9-4 (establishing goals). Then, in the spaces provided following each vignette, develop an action plan for your work with each client. Of course, it should be congruent with the identified issues and goals, and consistent with the dimensions discussed earlier.

1. Develop an action plan for your work with Mrs. O. Write it so it could be included as part of the Contract portion of a DAC.

2. Develop an action plan for your work with the S. family. Write it so it could be included as part of the Contract portion of a DAC.

3. Develop an action plan for your work with Mrs. F. Write it so it could be included as part of the Contract portion of a DAC.

4. When you have completed these exercises, review the action plans you have formulated. Ask yourself whether each plan adequately describes who is to be involved; who or what are the targets of change; where, when, and how long the meetings are to occur; how active you are to be; what role or roles you are going to assume; what strategy or approach is to be used; and what the time frame is to be. In addition, ask whether the action plan in any way infringes on the personal values and the cultural preferences you might expect of these particular clients. Finally, determine whether the action plan is logically congruent with the issues identified in Exercise 9-3 and the final goals established in Exercise 9-4. In the following space, summarize the results of your review and specify those aspects of the action planning process that you need to strengthen.

Identifying Action Steps

Sometimes, the goals that you and the client formulate are simply too large to accomplish in a single action, and it would be unrealistic and impractical to try to accomplish all of them at once. When this is the case, you engage the client in identifying small action steps or tasks (Reid, 1992) that are consistent with the action plan and likely to contribute to goal accomplishment. In a sense, these tasks or action steps are subordinate goals. They may be recorded within the Plans section of the Contract portion of the DAC.

In identifying action steps, you and the client use the information gained and the hypotheses generated during the description and assessment phases. You attempt to foster a flexible, creative, brainstorming atmosphere where all sorts of ideas are identified and examined. The skills of questioning, seeking clarification, reflecting, going beyond, and seeking feedback are commonly used during this process.

There are many ways to resolve issues and achieve goals. Some approaches require changes in the person, others involve changes in the situation, and many entail changes in both dimensions. Changes such as increasing one's knowledge about parenting or increasing one's skill in communicating assertively are examples of *person-focused* change. Securing adequate food and shelter or organizing a tenants union to lobby for improved building conditions exemplifies *situation-focused* or environmental change. In social work practice, changes are rarely limited to the individual person. Changes in the situation are usually needed as well. Whenever you serve as an advocate, broker, or mediator, you are working toward situational change. For example, an unemployed client's situation is likely to be dramatically improved when you intercede with a prospective employer to help the client secure a new job. Or consider the example of a female client living with a man who periodically beats her. With your help, several situational changes might be possible. Her male companion could be encouraged to join in a process of relationship counseling designed to enhance direct verbal communication and decrease the risk of future violence. Or he might be asked to participate in a program for abusive men. The client might file a criminal complaint with the police and courts, or she might leave the household for a safe shelter. All these involve changes in the situation, and all would affect the person as well. Although an action step in any given case may be primarily person-focused or primarily situation-focused, you should be aware of the following systemic principle: *Changes in one aspect of the person-issue-situation nearly always result in changes in other aspects as well.*

Completion of tasks or action steps contributes to the achievement of larger goals. Because they usually involve relatively small steps, they have a higher probability of success than would be the case if the final goal were attempted in a single action. For example, suppose you were 50 pounds overweight and wanted to lose that much to improve your health. Except by surgery, it is physically impossible to lose 50 pounds at one time. Reducing by one pound, then another, and then another, however, is conceivable. It is similar to the "one day at a time" principle of Alcoholics Anonymous. Abstaining from alcohol for the rest of one's life is indeed a large order for anyone who has drunk large quantities of alcohol every day for many years. Abstaining for one day, one hour, or even for one minute is more manageable and certainly more probable. By putting together and accomplishing several tasks or action steps (subordinate goals), a large goal that otherwise would seem insurmountable may be successfully achieved.

Identifying action steps of all kinds involves determining *what will be done.* These actions constitute steps, tasks, or activities that you or the client will take in your efforts toward goal accomplishment. Various action steps may be referred to as client tasks, worker tasks, in-session tasks (Tolson, Reid, & Garvin, 1994), or maintenance tasks. *Client tasks* are action steps that clients take during the intervals between your meetings. *Worker tasks* are those that you, the social worker, complete before you meet again with a client. *In-session tasks* are procedures, activities, or intervention techniques that you or clients undertake during your meetings together. *Maintenance tasks* are those regularly occurring personal or situational policies, practices, or activities that become routine or institutionalized to promote long-term change.

In attempting to specify these tasks or action steps, you and the client first engage one another in generating a first, small step toward the goal. You may initiate this process by asking questions such as "What would represent a first step toward achieving this goal?" or "What needs to change for you to be able to make a small step toward achieving this goal?"

Questions such as the following may also help to generate action steps. "What will be the first sign that you are beginning to make progress toward this goal?" "What will be the very first indication that there is progress in this matter?" "What will be the very first sign that you are taking steps to reach your goal?" Such questions tend to increase clients' optimism and motivation, as do those used in establishing goals. They do so by bringing the near future into their present thinking. You ask clients to imagine or visualize the situation being somewhat improved and to identify signs of that improvement. These signs often indicate the kinds of specific action steps that might be taken to progress toward goal attainment.

Notice the emphasis on identifying an action that might be taken. Your focus is on doing something that represents movement toward goal achievement. Depending on the nature of the agreed-upon goals, you may encourage clients to identify steps leading to changes in themselves (e.g., their thoughts, feelings, or behaviors) or in their situations that might help to resolve the identified issues.

When the agreed-upon goals require long-term change (e.g., maintain a 50-pound weight loss for one year, or abstain from all alcohol use for six months), you engage the client in identifying action steps that directly relate to the maintenance of durable change. Such *maintenance tasks* are not needed in circumstances where a single decision or short-term action is the goal. Lasting change, however, requires ongoing attention. Therefore, you and the client identify ways and means to maintain change over the long term. Maintenance is most likely when personal or situational policies, practices, or activities become routine or institutionalized. The most effective maintenance tasks occur regularly (e.g., hourly, daily, weekly, or biweekly), they function as reminders, incentives, or rewards for the individuals, families, groups, organizations, or societies involved.

In identifying maintenance tasks, you and the client anticipate that the action steps are underway. Together you address the question, "How do we maintain these changes over the long term?" You ask yourselves, "How can these changes become a natural and routine part of everyday life?" Building on the mutual understanding gained earlier, you jointly generate possible maintenance tasks within each relevant sphere of the person-and-situation.

During this part of the contracting processes, you ask questions that will yield small and manageable tasks or actions. As you and the client come to consensus concerning initial action steps, reflect them in clear terms.

In practicing the skill of identifying action steps, use a format such as the following:

PRACTICE FORMAT: IDENTIFYING AN ACTION STEP

So, the (first or next) step that (you, I, or we) will take is _____. (You, I, or we) will complete this task by (*insert date*) and talk about it at our next meeting.

Example

CLIENT: *(identifying an action step)* I'll go ahead and talk with her to see if she'd be interested in the idea of joint counseling.

WORKER: *(identifying an action step)* Okay, the next step that you will take is to talk with your partner and ask her if she might be interested in joining us for a few meetings. You'll talk with her within the next few days in order to give her a chance to think about it and give you her response before our next meeting. How does that sound? Fine, let me jot that down so we can keep it in mind.

By identifying an action step, you firmly cement the contract for your work with the client. The following are some examples of typical processes by which a worker might engage a client in establishing action steps.

Example

WORKER: *(reflecting a goal; seeking an action step)* You want to improve your sleeping patterns. Right now, you sleep the night through only about one out of every seven days. You want to be able to do so at least five days per week. Going from one to five nights is a pretty large jump. It might be helpful to start with something a bit smaller. What would represent a good first step toward achieving the goal?

Example

WORKER: *(reflecting a goal; seeking an action step)* You want to improve your sleeping patterns. Right now, you sleep the night through about one day per week and you want to be able to do so at least five times per week. What will be the first signs that you are beginning to sleep better?

Contracting

If the client cannot or will not respond to your encouragement by identifying a small action step, you may tentatively propose one for consideration. Of course, as always, be sure to seek the client's reactions to the idea. In proposing a task, you might use a format such as the following.

PRACTICE FORMAT: PROPOSING AN ACTION STEP

As a first step toward the goal of _____, what do you think about (*insert client task, worker task, or in-session task as needed*)?

Example

WORKER: *(proposing a client task)* We have identified the goal of graduating from high school by completing your General Education Diploma within the next 12 months. As a first step toward that goal, what do you think about contacting the school that you attended through the ninth grade to ask for your academic records?

Example

WORKER: *(proposing a worker task)* We have identified the goal of graduating from high school by completing your General Education Diploma (GED) within the next 12 months. As a first step toward that goal, I'd like to contact the department of education and ask for information about local GED programs. How does that sound to you?

Example

WORKER: *(proposing an in-session task)* Here's a copy of the application form for the GED program. I thought we might try to complete it together during our meeting today. What do you think?

◆ EXERCISE 9-6: IDENTIFYING ACTION STEPS

Continuing with the cases previously described, review your responses to Exercises 9-4 (establishing goals) and 9-5 (developing an action plan). Then, in the spaces provided, use the suggested format to write the words you might use to encourage each client to identify an initial, small task or action step. Then, write three action steps (client tasks, worker tasks, and in-session tasks) that you might propose to each client. Of course, they should be congruent with the identified issues and goals and, if completed, clearly represent a contribution to goal achievement.

1. a. Write the words you might say in encouraging Mrs. O. to identify an action step.

   b. Write the words you might say in proposing a client task to Mrs. O.

   c. Write the words you might say in proposing a worker task to Mrs. O.

   d. Write the words you might say in proposing an in-session task to Mrs. O.

2. a. Write the words you might say to help members of the S. family identify an action step.

    b. Write the words you might say in proposing a client task to the S. family.

    c. Write the words you might say in proposing a worker task to the S. family.

    d. Write the words you might say in proposing an in-session task to the S. family.

3. a. Write the words you might say in encouraging Mrs. F. to identify an action step.

    b. Write the words you might say in proposing a client task to Mrs. F.

    c. Write the words you might say in proposing a worker task to Mrs. F.

    d. Write the words you might say in proposing an in-session task to Mrs. F.

4. When you have completed these exercises, review the tasks or action steps identified and ask yourself the following questions. Are the steps described so that they involve actually doing something? Are the steps clear and specific? Would they in any way infringe on the personal values and the cultural

preferences that you might expect of these clients? Finally, are the action steps congruent with the specified issues, the goals, and the action plans identified in Exercises 9-3, 9-4, and 9-5? In particular, what is the probability that, if completed, the action steps would indeed contribute to and maintain the achievement of the identified goals? In the following space, summarize the results of your review and specify aspects of action step identification you need to develop further.

Planning for Evaluation

As a professional social worker, you are responsible for evaluating progress toward issue resolution and goal achievement. Regardless of the nature of the agency setting, the presenting issue, or the client's circumstances, it is possible to create some method for measuring progress toward goal attainment. Be sure to consider with clients the "goodness-of-fit" between the evaluation "tool" and their capacities and resources. Some clients are unable, for example, to create frequency charts or complete paper and pencil instruments. Nonetheless, some form of evaluation can almost always be found. In many practice contexts, failure to evaluate progress could constitute negligence.

You can measure progress toward goal attainment in several ways. One of the more applicable methods is called *goal attainment scaling* (Kiresuk & Sherman, 1968). Goal attainment scaling (GAS) is particularly well suited to social work practice because the dimensions for measurement are not predetermined (as is the case with standardized tests). In goal attainment scaling, the dimensions for assessment evolve from the goals negotiated by you and the client, so they are specific to each person-issue-situation. Compton and Galaway (1989, pp. 671–674) and Kagle (1984, pp. 74–76) provide useful summaries of goal attainment scaling procedures. To develop a goal attainment scale, you generate a series of five predictions concerning the possible outcomes of work toward achievement of each goal. The predictions provide you and your client with markers on which to base your evaluation of progress. The possible outcomes range from worst to best and are classified (Compton & Galaway, 1994, p. 551) as shown in Table 9.1.

TABLE 9.1
Goal-Attainment Scale

	Goal 1	Goal 2	Goal 3	Goal 4	Goal 5
1. Most unfavorable results thought likely					
2. Less than expcted success					
3. Expected level of success					
4. More than expected success					
5. Most favorable results thought likely					

Other means for evaluating progress toward goal achievement include counting and subjective rating. In *counting,* you, the client, or another person in the client's environment keeps track of the frequency of a particular phenomenon that is integrally related to the final goal. For example, consider self-esteem; people with low self-esteem often think disparaging and critical thoughts about themselves. You and such a client might identify as a final goal to increase the frequency of self-approving thoughts. You might provide the client with a small notepad in which to keep track of the number of self-approving thoughts during a given period (e.g., each day for one week). The frequency counts are then transferred to graph paper, with the expectation that the change program will lead the client to increase the frequency of self-approving thoughts per day. Counting is often used to establish a *baseline* for the targeted phenomenon, before implementing intervention plans. The baseline then is used as a measure to gauge the effectiveness of your approach. Counting can be applied to many different phenomena in the dimensions of person and situation.

Subjective rating requires that you, the client, or another person make a relative judgment concerning the extent, duration, frequency, or intensity of a targeted phenomenon. For example, you might ask a client to form an imaginary 10-point scale that runs from "worst" or "least" (number 1) to "best" or "most" (number 10). Then the client is asked to rate the phenomenon on the scale. For example, suppose a client is concerned about the quality of the relationship with her partner. You could make a request in this fashion: "Would you please imagine a scale that runs from 1 to 10, with 1 being the lowest possible and 10 being the highest possible? Now, on the basis of your best judgment, please rate the quality of the relationship as it has been today." Suppose that the client rates the day's quality of the relationship as 4. You could then ask the client (her partner might be invited to participate as well) to conduct such a subjective rating once each evening. The request might be phrased in this manner: "Each evening just before going to bed, please record in a notebook your subjective rating of the quality of the relationship during that day. Please do not share your ratings with your partner until we meet together again. We'll transfer your ratings onto a graph so we can determine how your views change as we work toward improving the quality of the relationship. How does that sound?"

Subjective ratings can be used in relation to almost all forms of human psychological and social phenomena. Of course, since they are subjective by definition, they are quite susceptible to individual bias and other forms of human error. Nonetheless, where more objective means are inappropriate or impractical, subjective ratings may be extremely useful.

As a social worker, you may also select from a vast array of paper-and-pencil instruments that are widely available. For example, Hudson produced *The Clinical Measurement Package: A Field Manual* (Hudson, 1982). The Clinical Measurement Package (CMP) contains nine scales that are useful to social workers. These scales assess phenomena that often apply to the issues and goals clients identify when they meet with social workers. The CMP scales address dimensions such as self-esteem, generalized contentment, marital satisfaction, sexual satisfaction, parental attitudes, child attitudes toward mother, child attitudes toward father, family relations, and peer relations. Each of the scales may be completed and scored quickly.

Two other social workers, Corcoran and Fischer, have published *Measures for Clinical Practice: A Sourcebook* (Corcoran & Fischer, 1987, 2000a, 2000b; Fischer & Corcoran, 1994a, 1994b). Their most recent edition includes two volumes of Rapid Assessment Instruments (RAIs) relevant for many aspects of social work practice. Volume 1 contains more than 100 measures relevant for assessing various dimensions of couples, families, and children. Volume 2 reviews more than 200 instruments relevant for adults. Included among the measures are instruments to aid assessment of various kinds of abuse, acculturation, addiction, anxiety and fear, assertiveness, beliefs, children's behavior, client motivation, coping, couple and martial relationships, death concerns, depression and grief, ethnic identity, family functioning, geriatric issues, guilt, health issues, identity, impulsivity, interpersonal behavior, locus of control, loneliness, love, mood, narcissism, pain, parent-child relationship, perfectionism, phobias, posttraumatic stress, problem-solving, procrastination, psychopathology and psychiatric symptoms, rape, satisfaction with life, schizotypal symptoms, self-concept and esteem, self-control, self-efficacy, sexuality, smoking, social functioning, social support, stress, suicide, treatment satisfaction, and substance abuse (Corcoran & Fischer, 2000a, pp. xxx–xlviii). The two volumes of *Measures for Clinical Practice* represent a rich resource of easily administered and rapidly scored instruments.

◆ EXERCISE 9-7: PLANNING FOR EVALUATION

Review your responses to Exercises 9-3, 9-4, 9-5, and 9-6 as they relate to the previously described case situations. Then, in the spaces provided, write the words you would say to identify two means for evaluating progress toward goal achievement in each of those case situations. First, plan an evaluation process that is more objective in nature. Then plan a subjective method to measure progress. The primary purpose is to encourage you to consider various means for measuring progress in your work with clients. Whatever evaluation plans you generate should, of course, relate directly to the identified issues and goals, so that progress can be determined.

    1.   a.   Prepare a brief subjective plan by which you might evaluate progress toward goal achievement in your work with Mrs. O.

          b.   Prepare an objective plan by which you might evaluate progress toward goal achievement in your work with Mrs. O.

2. a. Prepare a brief subjective plan by which you might evaluate progress toward goal achievement in your work with the S. family.

b. Prepare an objective plan by which you might evaluate progress toward goal achievement in your work with the S. family.

3. a. Prepare a brief subjective plan by which you might evaluate progress toward goal achievement in your work with Mrs. F.

    b. Prepare an objective plan by which you might evaluate progress toward goal achievement in your work with Mrs. F.

4. When you have completed these exercises, please consider the means of evaluation you have identified and ask yourself the following questions: How subject to evaluator bias and error are the means you have selected? What are the ethical implications of these forms of evaluation? Do the means appear to be respectful of the personal values and the cultural preferences you might expect of these clients? Finally, are the means likely to be accurate in determining progress toward the goals specified in Exercise 9-4? In the following space, summarize the results of your review and specify those aspects of evaluation planning you need to develop further.

Summarizing the Contract

Summarizing the contract involves a concise review of the essential elements of the understanding that you and the client have reached. It covers issues for work, goals, an action plan, tasks or action steps, and means by which progress will be evaluated.

Written contracts are generally preferred so that all parties to the process may have copies and can refer to them as needed (Hanvey & Philpot, 1994). The contract may be organized in accordance with the framework shown here and incorporated into the DAC. Alternately, it may be prepared separately as a formal contract, using letterhead paper, with spaces for you and the client to sign. In both written forms, the contract provides for descriptions of issues, goals, and plans. The contract represents your basic agreement with the client to work together toward the resolution of issues and the achievement of goals. You will probably find such contracts extremely applicable in your social work practice. Of course, the specific dimensions of the format shown here may not be relevant for practice in all social work settings or with all clients, all issues, or all situations. As a professional social worker, you assume responsibility for adopting contract guidelines that best match the needs and functions of your agency and your own practice.

SUGGESTED FORMAT

CONTRACT SECTION OF THE DAC
(DESCRIPTION, ASSESSMENT, AND CONTRACT)

III. Contract

A. Issues

1. Client-Identified Issues

In this section, you clearly outline the issues that the client identified.

2. Worker-Identified Issues

In this section, you outline the issues that you identify.

3. Agreed Upon Issues for Work

In this section, you outline the issues that both parties agree to address. These are the issues that remain the focus for work unless or until they are renegotiated by you and the client. Of course, either party may request that the issues for work be reconsidered or revised.

B. Goals

In this section, outline the final or outcome goals that you and the client have identified. They should, of course, relate to the issues for work. Ideally, final goals are defined in SMART format so that progress toward their attainment can be measured. Sometimes, of course, only general goal statements are possible or advisable. Whether specific or general, record the goal statements in this section.

C. Plans

1. Action Plan

In this section, summarize the action plan that you and your client have planned. You usually make note of factors such as who will be involved; where, when, and how often the work will occur, and for how long; and how the process will unfold. You should also identify, where applicable, the social work role or roles you will assume, and the theoretical perspective or model that has been selected for use in work with this particular client.

2. **Client's Tasks or Action Steps**
   In this section, outline the initial tasks or action steps that the client agrees to undertake in his or her attempt to achieve the agreed-upon goals.

3. **Worker's Tasks or Action Steps**
   In this section, outline the initial tasks or activities that you agree to undertake in your effort to help achieve the agreed-upon goals.

4. **In-Session Tasks or Action Steps**
   In this section, outline the initial tasks or activities that you and the client agree to undertake during your meetings together.

5. **Maintenance Tasks**
   If the goals involve long-term change, use this section to outline the tasks or activities that you agree will occur on a regular, ongoing basis to promote lasting change.

6. **Plans to Evaluate Progress**
   In this section, outline the means and processes by which progress toward goal accomplishment is to be evaluated.

The following is an example of the contract portion of a social worker's Description, Assessment, and Contract. Notice that it is a continuation of the Lynn B. Chase case presented earlier.

EXAMPLE

LYNN B. CHASE

III. Contract

  A. Issues

    1. **Client-Identified Issues**
      Mrs. Chase identified the following issues:
      a. Frequent arguments with her son Robert and, less often, with her husband Richard
      b. Increased irritability, criticism, and anger toward Robert and, to a lesser degree, toward Richard
      c. Shame and guilt following arguments with her son
      d. Unplanned weight loss (ten pounds) over the past six months

e. Sleep disturbance

f. Resumption of cigarette smoking after five years' abstinence

g. Fatigue

h. Headaches

2. **Worker-Identified Issues**

On the basis of our first interview, I tentatively identified the following as potential issues (tentative hypotheses only; they may be inaccurate).

a. Ambivalence about job at Fox Manufacturing

b. Feelings of depression

c. Ambivalence about Robert's adolescence

d. Feelings of loss, disappointment, and grief because client probably cannot have another child

e. Stress and tension; anxiety

f. Thoughts and feelings of excessive responsibility and possibly of control

g. Role strain and possibly role conflict among roles of mother, wife, homemaker, and employee

h. Issues related to childhood experiences (i.e., growing up in a family system with a parent who reportedly abused alcohol; largely absent and possibly workaholic father; unhappy incidents with childhood peers; feeling overweight and unattractive; church-related issues; reported episodes of attempted molestation by maternal uncle)

i. Interactional styles that may be classified as predominantly nonassertive with occasional periods of aggressive verbal expression

3. **Agreed Upon Issues for Work**

Mrs. Chase and I agreed on the following issues for work. These will provide us with a focus for our work together:

a. Frequent arguments with her son Robert and, less often, with her husband Richard

b. Irritability, criticism, and anger toward Robert and, to a lesser degree, toward Richard

c. Disproportionate feelings of shame and guilt

d. Sleep disturbance

e. Ambivalence regarding job at Fox Manufacturing

f. Stress and tension; anxiety

g. Thoughts and feelings of excessive responsibility and possibly of control

h. Role strain and possibly role conflict among roles of mother, wife, homemaker, and employee

B. Goals

Mrs. Chase and I agreed on the following goals for work:

1. Within six weeks, decrease by 50% the frequency of unwarranted arguments with Robert and Richard and increase the frequency of satisfying interactions with them by 50%.
2. Within six weeks, decrease by 50% the frequency and intensity of inappropriate feelings of irritability, criticism, and anger toward Robert and Richard and increase appropriate feelings of comfort and acceptance of them by 50%.
3. Within six weeks, decrease by 50% the frequency and intensity of disproportionate feelings of shame and guilt, and increase feelings of self-acceptance and self-forgiveness by 50%.
4. Within six weeks, sleep eight full hours per night and awaken feeling refreshed at least four of seven mornings a week.
5. Within six weeks, decrease the ambivalence about the job at Fox Manufacturing by deciding whether Lynn Chase really wants to keep the job.
6. Within six weeks, decrease the stress, tension, and anxiety and increase feelings of personal comfort and calmness by 50%.
7. Within two weeks, explore in greater depth the issue of excessive responsibility and control; by the end of that time, decide whether maintaining or lessening the current level of responsibility and control is desirable.

C. Plans

1. Action plan

To achieve the final goals, Mrs. Chase and I agreed on the following action plan:

Mrs. Lynn Chase and I (Susan Holder, social worker) will meet for eight one-hour sessions during the next two months. Our purpose is to work together toward achievement of the final goals identified above. We will approach this work as a cooperative effort, with each party contributing ideas and suggestions. I will serve as counselor and facilitator, and approach our work together from a combination of cognitive-behavioral and task-centered approaches, and a family systems perspective. On at least some occasions, we will ask Mrs. Chase's husband and son to join us. Throughout the two-month period, we will monitor the rate and degree of progress. At the end of that time, we will determine whether to conclude our work, consult with or refer to someone else, or contract with each other for further work together.

2. **Client's Tasks or Action Steps**

   Mrs. Chase and I agreed that she would undertake the following steps during the first week of our work together. Other tasks will be identified and implemented later in the program.

   a. As a first step toward decreasing the stress, tension, and anxiety and increasing feelings of personal comfort and calmness, Mrs. Chase agreed to spend 15 minutes each day during the next week planning for or working in her garden.

   b. As a first step toward decreasing the frequency of inappropriate feelings of irritability, criticism, and anger toward Robert and Richard and increasing appropriate feelings of comfort, understanding, and acceptance of them by 50%, Mrs. Chase agreed to do two things during the course of the next week. First, she agreed to resist "stuffing" her feelings. Whether by writing them down on paper, verbally expressing them in a place where no one can hear, or expressing them directly to the relevant person or persons, she agreed to express whatever feelings she experiences within a few minutes of the time that she first becomes aware of them. Second, she agreed to take five minutes every day to engage Robert and Richard pleasantly by inquiring about their thoughts, feelings, and activities.

   c. As a first step toward addressing the goal of determining whether a lessening of responsibility and control in some areas might be helpful, Mrs. Chase agreed to identify and write down as many reasons as she can why she should continue to maintain her current level of responsibility and control. Following that, Mrs. Chase agreed to identify as many reasons as she can why a lessening of her responsibility and control might be beneficial to her, her husband, and her son at this time. We agreed to review the two lists of reasons in our next meeting.

3. **Worker's Tasks or Action Steps**

   a. I, Susan Holder, agreed to prepare this contract or agreement in written form and provide a copy to Mrs. Chase.

   b. I agreed to assume responsibility for planning tentative agendas for our meetings together and to consult with Mrs. Chase concerning the implementation of the action steps and their effects.

   c. I agreed to provide Mrs. Chase with a notebook and related materials for completing written tasks and monitoring progress.

4. **In-Session Tasks or Action Steps**

   Mrs. Chase and I agreed that during our meetings together, we would undertake some or all the following activities (additional in-session tasks will be identified and implemented later in the program):

   a. Value-clarification exercises intended to aid Mrs. Chase in addressing various issues about which she experiences ambivalence.

   b. Self-talk analysis to help Mrs. Chase identify the "things she says to herself" that seem associated with the feelings of irritability, criticism, anger, depression, stress, and tension.

   c. Strength-oriented, "bragging" exercises to help Mrs. Chase heighten her feelings of calmness.

5. **Maintenance Tasks**

   Mrs. Chase and I agreed that the goals involve long-term change, and required ongoing attention. Mrs. Chase indicated that she would recite the serenity prayer at least once per day for the next 365 days.

6. **Plans to Evaluate Progress**

   Progress toward goal achievement will be evaluated in several ways. First, Mrs. Chase agreed to keep a daily log in her notebook, where she intends to record the time and date of all "arguments" and all "satisfying interactions." Second, Mrs. Chase also agreed to log the time and date of all inappropriate feelings of "irritability, anger, and criticism" toward Richard or Robert, as well as all feelings of "comfort, understanding, and acceptance" of them. Third, Mrs. Chase agreed to use the logbook to record the number of hours slept each night and to rate, on a subjective scale of 1–10, how refreshed she feels upon awakening. Fourth, Mrs. Chase agreed to register completion of her daily 15 minutes of "gardening." Evaluation of progress toward other goals will occur by asking Mrs. Chase for self-reports. In regard to the issues of excessive responsibility and ambivalence about her job at Fox Manufacturing, progress will be indicated when Mrs. Chase reports that she has decided whether to lessen responsibility and control and whether she wants to keep her job. A decision in either direction will be considered progress.

◆ EXERCISE 9-8: SUMMARIZING THE CONTRACT

For this exercise, please review the information you organized into the description and assessment sections of your own DAC in Exercises 8-1 and 8-2. Based on what you know about yourself and what you included in the description and assessment sections, proceed to type a written contract as if you were your own social worker. In creating your contract, be aware that you too, despite your considerable self-understanding, are still likely to miss some of the issues or issues that a professional social worker might help you to identify. Therefore, even though it concerns you, the contract you develop should be viewed as tentative. Prepare the contract in accordance with the format provided in the contract section of the Description, Assessment, and Contract. When complete, place the contract in your Social Work Skills Learning Portfolio within the section or folder that contains your personal case record. At this point, you have completed all three sections of a DAC—the Description, the Assessment, and the Contract.

Summary

During the contracting phase of social work practice, you, based on the assessment and in conjunction with the client, attempt to define clearly the issues and goals for work and to develop plans likely to resolve the identified issues and achieve the final goals. Skills that are especially applicable to this phase of practice include (1) reflecting an issue, (2) identifying an issue, (3) clarifying issues for work, (4) establishing goals, (5) developing an action plan, (6) identifying action steps, (7) planning for evaluation, and (8) summarizing the contract.

◆ CHAPTER 9 SUMMARY EXERCISES

Building on the earlier two interviews that you had with your colleague, conduct a third interview for the purpose of developing a contract for work. Ensure that the interview setting is private and again tape-record the meeting. Using the skills of exploring and contracting and other relevant social work skills, interview your colleague with a view toward negotiating a contract. At the conclusion of the meeting, arrange for another meeting in about one week.

1. Following the interview, ask your partner for candid feedback concerning his or her thoughts and feelings about the experience. Ask for a completely honest reaction to the following questions: (a) Did you feel comfortable and safe with me? Did you feel that I seemed like a person you could trust? (b) Did you feel that I was sincerely interested in you and in what you had to say? (c) Did you feel that I understood what you were trying to communicate? If so, what contributed to that? If not, what indicated to you that I did not

understand? (d) Does the contract as I summarized it really match your views of the issues that concern you? (e) Do the goals we've established fit your needs and preferences? (f) What is your reaction to the first action steps we've planned? (g) What do you think about our plans for evaluating progress? (h) Did you find the experience productive? (i) What could I do better or differently in order to improve the quality of this interview? (j) How could the interview have been better or more satisfying for you? Summarize your colleague's feedback in the space provided.

2. Review your own reaction to the conversation. How did you feel about the interview? What did you like and what did you dislike about it? Do you believe that you used relevant skills during the interaction? Were you able to develop the essential elements of a contract? If so, what helped you to do that? If not, what hindered you in that effort? What additional information would be useful? What would you do differently if you were to redo the interview? Summarize the results of your review in the space provided.

3. Based on your experience, type a contract according to the format provided in the DAC. After you have written the contract, play the audiotape or video-

tape. Identify the specific social work skills that you used. Make notes of significant exchanges that affect the way in which you drafted the contract, and revise the contract accordingly. Place the contract in the Practice Case Record section of your Social Work Skills Learning Portfolio.

◆ CHAPTER 9 WORLD WIDE WEB EXERCISES

1. Go to the InfoTrac College Edition Web site at www.infotrac-college.com. Use your passcode to log in. Conduct a keyword search using the string "Reflections on Empowerment-Based Practice" (include the quotation marks) to locate an article by that title (Rose, 2000). Carefully read the article and reflect upon its contents for establishing contracts with clients. Use the space below to write a one-two paragraph response to the article.

2. Go to the InfoTrac College Edition Web site at www.infotrac-college.com. Use your passcode to log in. Conduct a keyword search using the string "Co-Constructing Cooperation with Mandated Clients" (De Jong & Berg, 2001) to locate an article with that title. Carefully read the article and reflect upon its contents for establishing contracts with clients. Use the space below to write a one-two paragraph response to the article.

3. Go to the InfoTrac College Edition Web site at www.infotrac-college.com. Use your passcode to log in. Conduct a keyword search using the string "Participation in Treatment Planning" (include the quotation marks) to locate an article entitled "Opportunities and Barriers to Empowering People with Severe Mental Illness through Participation in Treatment Planning" (Linhorst, Hamilton, Young, & Eckert, 2002). Carefully read the article and reflect upon its contents for planning action steps with clients. Use the space below to write a one-two paragraph response to the article.

4. Go to the InfoTrac College Edition Web site at www.infotrac-college.com. Use your passcode to log in. Conduct a keyword search using the string "empowerment battered women" (without the quotation marks) to locate an article entitled "Choice and Empowerment for Battered Women Who Stay: Toward a Constructivist Model" (Peled, Eisikovits, Enosh, & Winstok, 2000). Carefully read the article and reflect upon its contents for planning action steps with clients. Use the space below to write a one-two paragraph response to the article.

5. Go to the InfoTrac College Edition Web site at www.infotrac-college.com. Use your passcode to log in. Conduct a keyword search using the string "knowledge direct social work practice trends" (without the quotation marks) to locate an article entitled "Knowledge for Direct Social Work Practice: An Analysis of Trends" (Reid, 2002). Carefully read the article and reflect upon its contents for engaging clients in planning action steps with clients. Use the space below to write a one-two paragraph response to the article.

Chapter 9 Self-Appraisal

Now that you have finished this chapter and completed the exercises, please assess your proficiency in the contracting skills by completing the following self-appraisal exercise.

SELF-APPRAISAL: THE CONTRACTING SKILLS

Please respond to the following items. Your answers should help you to assess your proficiency in the contracting skills. Read each statement carefully. Then, use the following four-point rating scale to indicate the degree to which you agree or disagree with each statement. Record your numerical response in the space provided.

4 = Strongly Agree

3 = Agree

2 = Disagree

1 = Strongly Disagree

_____ 1. I can effectively use the skill of reflecting an issue.
_____ 2. I can effectively use the skill of identifying an issue.
_____ 3. I can effectively use the skill of clarifying issues for work.
_____ 4. I can effectively use the skill of establishing goals.
_____ 5. I can effectively use the skill of developing an action plan.
_____ 6. I can effectively use the skill of identifying action steps.
_____ 7. I can effectively use the skill of planning for evaluation.
_____ 8. I can effectively use the skill of summarizing the social work contract.

_____ **Subtotal**

Note: These items are taken directly from the Social Work Skills Self-Appraisal Questionnaire contained in Appendix 3. You have responded to these items before. You may now compare your item responses to those you made earlier. You may also compare the subtotal scores. If you think you are developing greater proficiency in these skills, more recent scores should be higher than earlier.

Finally, reflect on the skills addressed in this chapter and the results of your self-appraisal. Based on your analysis, prepare a succinct one-page summary report entitled "Self-Assessment of Proficiency in the Contracting Skills." Within the report, be sure to identify those skills that you know and do well (e.g., a score of 3 or 4). Also, specify those that need further practice (e.g., scores of 2 or less) and briefly outline plans by which to achieve proficiency in them. When finished, include the report in your Social Work Skills Learning Portfolio.

Chapter 10

Working and Evaluating

As you engage clients in the process of working toward the goals you have jointly agreed on, you make a transition. Until this point in the helping process, you have used social work skills primarily for collecting information, developing a relationship, formulating an assessment, and negotiating the contract. Once you have agreed on a contract, however, you may now legitimately use skills to promote change within various aspects of the person-issue-situation. This chapter (see Box 10.1) is intended to help you develop proficiency in the *working and evaluating skills*. These skills build on clients' experience and frame of reference by introducing, in a much more active and expressive fashion, your own professional knowledge and expertise.

BOX 10.1

Chapter Purpose

The purpose of this chapter is to help learners develop proficiency in the working and evaluating skills.

Goals

Following completion of this chapter, learners should be able to demonstrate proficiency in the following:

(continued)

- ◆ Rehearsing action steps
- ◆ Reviewing action steps
- ◆ Evaluating
- ◆ Focusing
- ◆ Educating
- ◆ Advising
- ◆ Representing
- ◆ Responding with immediacy
- ◆ Reframing
- ◆ Confronting
- ◆ Pointing out endings
- ◆ Progress recording
- ◆ Assessing proficiency in the working and evaluating skills

The skills covered in earlier chapters are primarily empathic, exploratory, and contractual in nature. You use them to clarify policies under which you will operate; explore factors associated with the origin, development, and maintenance of the issues of concern; learn about and understand clients' experience of the person-issue-situation from their own perspective; develop an assessment; and agree on plans to pursue and evaluate progress toward the jointly determined goals for work. Throughout these processes, you listen actively, ask questions, and seek feedback. In empathic fashion, you regularly reflect understanding. This encourages further self-expression and self-exploration by clients, while strengthening your relationship. You may go slightly beyond client's literal statements, but your primary focus is on the client's experience and frame of reference.

The working and evaluating skills are significantly different. Here, you may appropriately proceed from your social work frame of reference—your own professional knowledge, experience, and expertise. These tend to be more active and expressive than empathic in nature. Through the working and evaluating skills, you express your professional agenda—your thoughts, feelings, beliefs, opinions, hypotheses, deductions, and conclusions. You first use such an active and expressive skill during the beginning phase of practice, when you suggest a tentative purpose for meeting and outline relevant policy and ethical factors. You also express your knowledge and experience when you identify an issue, suggest a goal, or propose an intervention during the assessing and contracting processes.

Occasionally, the expressive skills bear little obvious relationship to the words or actions of the clients. Most of the time, however, they reflect your attempt to expand or extend the client's experience. You use what you have learned from the client to process it from your own professional perspective. Then you express yourself in a fashion you believe will be useful to the client in progressing toward the agreed-upon goals.

Because the working and evaluating skills tend to be expressive rather than empathic, try to clarify your rationale for using them at a particular time. Your motivations should be professional, not personal. Resist temptations to share your knowledge, feelings, or opinions simply because they occur to you at the moment. Rather, the working skills you use should consistently relate to the contract for work. To help you determine whether an expressive working skill is indeed appropriate and applicable, ask yourself and critically think about the following questions. "Have we adequately explored the person, issue, and situation? Have I sufficiently communicated empathic understanding of the client's experience so that I may now reasonably consider using a work-phase expressive skill? Do we have a clear contract for work? What is my objective in choosing this skill at this time? Will my use of this skill now help the client with our agreed-upon work toward issue resolution and goal attainment? Does the use of this skill convey respect for the client's personal values and cultural preferences? How will the client react to my expression? What is the risk that using this skill now might endanger the client's individual or social well-being? Is there any risk to other people? How do I personally think and feel about this client at this time? Am I tempted to use a working skill now to express a personal view or satisfy my own impulse?"

Thinking critically about these questions and their implications should help you to determine the appropriateness and applicability of a work-phase expressive skill. If there is doubt, choose a more appropriate skill or return to an empathic, exploring skill until you and the client are ready.

During the work and evaluation phase, of course, you continue to use many of the empathic skills previously discussed. Reflective communications, seeking feedback, asking questions, and seeking clarification are needed throughout the entire helping process. During this phase, however, working skills such as rehearsing, reviewing, focusing, reframing, and advising are increasingly used. In using expressive working skills, you maintain your focus on the assessment and contract for work. In particular, your efforts are shaped by the agreed-upon goals for work and the service approach you and the client have established. Each application of a working skill should, in some way, relate to one or more of the goals.

The skills especially applicable to this phase include (1) rehearsing action steps, (2) reviewing action steps, (3) evaluating, (4) focusing, (5) educating, (6) advising, (7) representing, (8) responding with immediacy, (9) reframing, (10) confronting, (11) pointing out endings, and (12) progress recording.

Rehearsing Action Steps

As part of the contracting process, clients often agree to attempt a task or action step. In the work phase, the worker prepares and motivates them to carry out the task. Unfortunately, commitments made by clients during an interview frequently do not translate into action outside the context of your meeting together. This is one of the major challenges you and clients confront if your work together is to be effective. You need to incorporate means that facilitate transfer of learning into the real world of the client. Several things may be done within the context of the interview itself. Various in-session activities such as role-play, guided practice, and visualization bridge the gap between the special circumstances of the social work interview and the more common environment of everyday life. Rehearsal activities incorporate aspects of doing with thinking and feeling. Involving more than talk alone, these activities constitute action-step practice. Engaging several dimensions of experience (thinking, feeling, doing) in the rehearsal activity, the client moves closer to what is necessary in the real-world context.

Rehearsing an action step decreases anxiety associated with the idea of taking action, enhances motivation, and increases the probability that the step will be taken. It also improves the chance that the action step will be successful. In using this skill, you review the action step with the client and then consider probable scenarios. Although most clients are quite capable of generating alternate courses of action, some are not. When a client needs such help, you may appropriately assume a more active role in identifying options. You might propose a few different ways to undertake the step or present examples of how other people do so. As part of the rehearsal process, you could *model* an action step for the client by saying or doing what is needed. Or, in a *role-play*, you may assume the role of a person who will be involved in the client's enactment of the action step. During or following the role-play, you give the client guidance, feedback, support, and encouragement.

Another form of rehearsal involves clients *visualizing* themselves undertaking an agreed-upon action step (Lazarus, 1984). Before using visualization, you first determine whether a particular client has the capacity to create mental pictures. You might explore this by asking, "If I were to ask you to imagine in your mind's eye the kitchen in the place where you live, could you do so?" If the client says, "Yes," you could then say, "Good, some people aren't able to imagine as well as you do. Your mental capacity in this area will help us a great deal in our work together." You might then say, "Please assume a relaxed position and take a few slow, deep breaths. You may close your eyes if you wish but closing your eyes is not essential—many people can visualize just as well with their eyes open." Then you might go on to ask, "Please imagine a movie screen on which you can see the context where the step you'll take will occur. Now see yourself actually taking the action we have discussed." You might pause briefly and then ask the client to study the visualized scene in detail, noticing all aspects of the action step.

Visualization can be used for the purpose of identifying client fears and anticipating potential obstacles to successful action, as well as for the purpose of rehearsal. When you and a client clearly understand what needs to be done, you may ask him or her to imagine successfully completing the action step. Following that, you may also ask the client to identify the positive thoughts and feelings that accompany imaginary completion of the action step.

Returning to the Chase case, the following is an excerpt from an interview in which Susan Holder helps the client rehearse an action step through role-play.

EXAMPLE

WORKER: *(identifying an action step; seeking feedback)* One of the steps we identified is to express your affection for both Robert and Richard at least once each day. If I understand the usual patterns correctly, this would represent a change from the way you have recently related. Is that right?

CLIENT (MRS. CHASE): Yes, it would be a big change.

WORKER: It's been my experience that accomplishing changes such as this takes quite a bit of planning and preparation. By practicing an activity ahead of time, we increase the likelihood that we will actually do it. With that in mind, I wonder if you would be willing to practice with me what you are going to say and do each day?

CLIENT: Okay.

WORKER: Thanks. When you think of where and when you might make your first caring statement to Robert, what comes to mind?

CLIENT: Well, I think that I'd like to start off the day with something positive.

WORKER: Good idea! Where do you think you will be when you make your first affectionate statement?

CLIENT: Well, I think it will probably be in the kitchen.

WORKER: In the kitchen. . . . Let me assume the role of Robert. And, if you would, please let's imagine that it's tomorrow morning and we are now in the kitchen. What will you say to him tomorrow?

CLIENT: Well, I think I'll say something like, "Robert, I know that we have been on each other's nerves lately. I know that a lot of it has been my fault. I guess I've been more stressed out than I realized. Anyway, I want to say I'm sorry and I want you to know that I have never loved you more than I do now."

WORKER (AS ROBERT): Geez. Thanks, Mom. I love you too.

WORKER (AS HERSELF): Thanks Lynn. When you say those words to Robert, I can really feel your love for him. How does it feel to you?

CLIENT: It feels really good. I feel warm inside. Loving toward him and also better about myself.

WORKER: How do you think Robert will respond to your words?

CLIENT: I'm not sure. But I do think he'll like it, and it should bring us closer.

WORKER: That's exactly what you want to happen, isn't it?

CLIENT: Yes, it sure is.

WORKER: How do you feel when you realize that Robert will probably appreciate your comments and feel very loved?

CLIENT: Really good. I can't wait until tomorrow morning!

The following excerpt illustrates how Ms. Holder, the social worker, helps Mrs. Chase rehearse an action step using visualization.

EXAMPLE

WORKER: *(identifying the step; exploring probability of action; seeking feedback)* One of the steps we identified as a means to decrease stress and increase feelings of personal comfort is to spend 15 minutes each day planning for or working in your garden. I must admit to wondering about your ability to actually do that. You are very busy. You do so many things that I wonder whether you will really take the time to do the 15 minutes of gardening each day. What do you think?

CLIENT *(MRS. CHASE)*: Well, to be honest, I have known for some time that I need to get back to gardening and I just haven't done it. I keep on making promises to myself and I keep on breaking them.

WORKER: Thanks for being frank with me. If we're going to get anywhere with these issues, honesty and openness is the best policy. If you don't think you will actually take a step that we identify, please tell me.

CLIENT: Okay, I will.

WORKER: Thanks, Lynn. Making changes such as this takes a good deal of planning and preparation. Unless we practice ahead of time, things tend to stay the same. With that in mind, I wonder if you would be willing to try a little experiment that may make it a little easier to actually do the gardening that you'd like to do?

CLIENT: Well, I guess so. What kind of experiment?

WORKER: I'm sure that you've heard the old saying, "Practice makes perfect." Well, for many people, practicing in one's imagination is nearly as effective as practicing for real. If you happen to be one of the people who can form mental pictures, then we can use that capacity to increase the likelihood that you will actually begin to garden for real. Is that description clear?

CLIENT: Yes, I think so. How do I do it?

WORKER: First, let's find out about your picture-making ability. Please try now to imagine your garden as it used to be when it was in full bloom. Can you picture it?

CLIENT: Yes. I can see it now.

WORKER: Can you see it in color or is it black and white?

CLIENT: It's in color.

WORKER: Now please imagine yourself in the garden tilling the soil around the growing plants. Is that the sort of thing you might be doing?

CLIENT: Yes. I'd be down on my knees, working the soil.

WORKER: Can you visualize that in your mind's eye?

CLIENT: Yes.

WORKER: Now, please describe what you are feeling, what you are experiencing, as you work the garden.

CLIENT: Well, I feel warm and relaxed. I feel content. I feel happy. Working the soil is, well, it's pleasurable.

WORKER: Now please picture yourself in the garden this very evening. Can you do that?

CLIENT: Yes.

WORKER: And does that feel as good as the other picture did?

CLIENT: Yes.

WORKER: Now, let's shift to a different picture. Suppose it rains. Can you imagine planning or preparing for the garden in a way that would also be relaxing or pleasurable?

CLIENT: Yes. I can work on my drawings of the garden. I kind of draft out what plants, what fruits, what vegetables go where in the garden. I also work out what to plant when, and the approximate date they should be harvested.

WORKER: And what do you feel in this picture?

CLIENT: I feel just as relaxed and content as when I'm in the garden itself.

WORKER: Let's create a picture of you actually doing that on rainy days when you cannot go out into the garden.

CLIENT: Okay.

As a result of rehearsing, whether through role-play, guided practice, visualization, or some combination, clients are more likely to carry out the activity in their own worlds.

◆ **EXERCISE 10-1: REHEARSING ACTION STEPS**

For these exercises, assume that you are a social worker with a family services agency. Respond in the spaces provided by describing what you would do and say in using the skill of rehearsing the action steps you identified as part of Exercise 9-6.

1. You are in the midst of an interview with Mrs. O., the 77-year-old widow who lives alone. You have agreed on the issues and goals for work and have identified an action step. In the following space, describe what you would do and say in using the skill of rehearsing the action step with this client. In

formulating your description, anticipate what the client might say or do in response to your statements and actions.

2. You are in the midst of an interview with the seven-member, blended S. family. You have agreed on the issues and goals for work and have identified an action step. In the following space, describe what you would do and say in using the skill of rehearsing the action step with this client system. In formulating your description, anticipate what the clients might say or do in response to your statements and actions.

3. You are interviewing Mrs. F. You have agreed on the issues and goals for work and have identified an action step. In the following space, describe what you would do and say in using the skill of rehearsing the action step with this

client. In formulating your description, anticipate what the client might say or do in response to your statements and actions.

Reviewing Action Steps

There are three possible outcomes when a client agrees to undertake an action step: (1) the client may complete it; (2) the client may partially complete it; or (3) the client may not attempt any portion of the action step. The first two outcomes almost always represent progress; the third does not. Even the third outcome, however, may be useful if the process is carefully reviewed to improve the chance of success in the future. In working with clients, try to increase the probability that they will attempt and complete agreed-upon action steps. If clients rehearse an action step before attempting it for real, they are more likely to try it. Motivation is also enhanced when clients understand that they will have a chance to *review the action step* after attempting it. For most clients, when you demonstrate your interest in the process and outcome of their action steps by asking about them, you help to increase the probability that further action steps will be attempted. By reviewing what happened following the attempt, you also gather information that can be used in the evaluation of progress toward goal achievement and in identifying subsequent action steps.

In reviewing action steps, adopt an attitude of supportive curiosity. If the client has partly or completely undertaken the activity, express your pleasure. If a client has not attempted the action step, on the other hand, it is usually unwise to express disapproval or criticism. Rather, convey your interest by questions such as "What do you think got in the way of your attempt?" In such circumstances, explore with the client the thinking and feeling experiences that led him or her to defer taking the action step. Also inquire about situational factors that may have contributed to a change in plans. Often, it will become clear that unanticipated obstacles interfered with completion of the action step. Alternate plans can then be devised, and you and the client can proceed to rehearse the revised action step. When a client has completed an action step, you may appropriately express both pleasure and curiosity as you inquire about the factors contributing to the accomplishment. "What was different this time that enabled you to take this step?" For clients who have partly completed the activity, inquire with pleasure and interest about those differences that made it possible to take this "step in the right direction." Later, you may explore what factors blocked a more complete attempt and then, with the client, formulate a slightly revised plan. If clients have partially or completely undertaken the action step, encourage them to identify and express the satisfying thoughts and feelings that accompany action toward goal achievement. In many circumstances, you may also appropriately share your positive impressions about the client's efforts. Following such encouragement, you and the client may then proceed to identify and rehearse additional action steps.

EXAMPLE

Reviewing a Completed Action Step

WORKER (MS. HOLDER): Last time we talked, you agreed to spend 15 minutes each day in gardening activities. If you recall, we went through the process of visualizing those activities in your mind's eye. How did that work out?

CLIENT (MRS. CHASE): It was great! I gardened every day, sometimes more than 15 minutes, and I enjoyed it enormously. It spread out into other parts of my life too. I felt more calm and content throughout the day.

WORKER: Wonderful! So, it was truly effective in increasing your feelings of contentment?

CLIENT: Yes. It really worked. I had only one headache all week, and I felt much better.

WORKER: Terrific! Now is there anything about the gardening activity that we should change to make it better?

CLIENT: No. It's working just fine. Let's not change anything about it.

WORKER: Agreed. Let's keep the gardening activity just the same. That is, each day you will spend 15 minutes in a gardening activity. Is that right?

CLIENT: Yes.

EXAMPLE

Reviewing a Partially Completed Action Step

WORKER (MS. HOLDER): Last time we talked, you agreed to spend 15 minutes each day in gardening activities. If you recall, we went through the process of visualizing those activities in your mind's eye. How did that work out?

CLIENT (MRS. CHASE): Well, I gardened on two days this week but I couldn't find the time to do any more than that. I was just too busy.

WORKER: You were able to find time to do the gardening on two of the seven days. That's a very good beginning. On the two days that you gardened, what was it like?

CLIENT: Well, I guess at the beginning of the week I was just determined to do the gardening. I did it and I liked it. It's a lot to do, to start up a garden when you haven't worked on it for a long time. But I enjoyed it a lot and I felt good on those two days. On the third day, I just couldn't find the time.

WORKER: It sounds like the two days that you did the gardening were very good days for you. You enjoyed those days at lot. On the third day when you did not garden you didn't feel as well. Would I be correct in saying that the gardening is definitely a helpful activity?

CLIENT: Oh, yes! If only I would do it!

WORKER: Let's see if we can figure out some way to make it easier for you to do the gardening and gain the benefits from it. What was different about the days that you did garden from the days that you didn't?

CLIENT: Well, I was really motivated on the first two days. On the third day, I had a tough time at work, and I was exhausted when I got home. I just slumped onto the sofa and went to sleep. I guess I was tired every night after that.

WORKER: Let's assume then that when you come home from work really tired, it's much harder for you to do the gardening, even though it leads to relaxing and contented feelings. I wonder, when you fall asleep on the sofa after work, do you awaken feeling as rested and relaxed as you do when you garden?

CLIENT: Actually, I feel much worse after dozing on the sofa. I'm kind of grouchy for the rest of the evening. And, I don't sleep very well at night. It's better when I garden.

WORKER: Now that we know that, let's see what we can do to help you garden even when you're tired and exhausted from work. Imagine that you have just come home from a stressful day at work. You're exhausted. Your usual pattern has been to crash on the sofa. This time, however, imagine yourself taking a drink of ice water and walking out to the garden. You sit in a chair and look at your garden while drinking the ice water. You don't do anything. You just sit there. After ten minutes or so, you can feel the stress and exhaustion begin to lessen. You decide to do just a little bit of gardening. After 15 minutes, you pause, and notice that you feel calm and relaxed. You're no longer tired. Instead, you're ready to go on with the rest of your evening . . . How about it, Mrs. Chase, could you imagine that pretty clearly?

CLIENT: Yes. And I can see myself really relaxing during the gardening. I don't relax as well when I sleep on the sofa.

WORKER: In that case, what do you think about trying the 15 minutes of gardening again during this next week—only, let's go for four days instead of all seven?

CLIENT: That sounds good. I think I'll do it this week.

EXAMPLE

Reviewing an Unattempted Action Step

WORKER (MS. HOLDER): Last time we talked, you agreed to spend 15 minutes each day in gardening activities. If you recall, we went through the process of visualizing those activities in your mind's eye. How did that work out?

CLIENT (MRS. CHASE): Well, I thought about it but I couldn't find the time to do any gardening at all. I was just too busy.

WORKER: You were unable to find time to do the gardening at all during this past week. Tell me, during this week's time, have there been any signs that things are getting better?

CLIENT: Well, no. Things are about the same. I did feel a lot better after talking with you last time, but that lasted only a day or so.

WORKER: It sounds like there was some temporary relief from talking about the problems with me, but there hasn't been any real progress, is that right?

CLIENT: Yes, I'm afraid so.

WORKER: Let's talk some about the gardening activity itself. In our discussion last time, you were quite sure that if you began to garden again, even for a little bit, you would soon feel better. Do you think that still holds true, or have you reconsidered whether gardening would actually be helpful to you?

CLIENT: Well, I know it would help me, but I just can't find the time.

WORKER: If you still think the gardening would be helpful, let's see if we can identify what gets in the way of taking time to do it. During this past week, what did you end up doing instead of the gardening?

CLIENT: Well, on the first evening I planned to garden, Robert injured his knee playing basketball and I had to take him to the emergency room. He has been in bed all this week. I've been nursing him each evening after I get home from work.

WORKER: Your son's injury got in the way. How is his knee now?

CLIENT: Well, it's much better. He should be able to get out of bed about the middle of next week. Then he'll start walking around the house. By the first part of the following week, he should be able to return to school.

WORKER: It sounds as if your son is well on the way to recovery, and you will soon have more time once he can get around on his own. Do you think that when he does start to walk again, you will be more likely to do the gardening?

CLIENT: I think so. It depends upon how much help he needs.

WORKER: It sounds like you'll be nursing him at least for another several days. What is involved when you care for him in the evening?

CLIENT: Well, first I make him supper and then I take it to his room. Then we talk for a while. Then I clean up the kitchen and do the dishes. Then I check on Robert again. We usually talk some more. By that time, it's time for bed.

WORKER: Lynn, it seems to me that we have a choice to make here. First, if you really believe that once Robert is better you will begin the gardening, we can simply delay the starting date of the gardening activities. If you believe, however, that if it were not Robert's injury it would be something else that would prevent you from gardening, then perhaps we should take this opportunity to challenge the pattern of excessive caretaking. We have explored this before. If your decision not to garden is a matter of neglecting yourself rather than simply a matter of unusual circumstances, perhaps we might begin to change that right now while Robert is still injured. What do you think?

CLIENT: Well, honestly, I think it's some of both. Robert's injury gives me an opportunity to care for him—I guess it's really "caretaking"—and it provides me with a reason not to take good care of myself by gardening.

WORKER: Then, what do you think? Should we delay the startup date for the gardening activities, or should we start now in order to challenge the tendency to avoid caring for yourself?

CLIENT: Well, I guess I'd like to start right now. Even with Robert's injury, I should be able to find 15 minutes at some point during the evening.

WORKER: All right. I wonder, though, because of the extra responsibilities caused by Robert's injury, should we change the plan from 15 minutes every single day to 15 minutes three times during the next week? That might be more reasonable, given the current circumstances.

CLIENT: Yes, yes. I think that would be just about right. I know I can garden three times during the next seven days.

WORKER: Okay. We've changed the plan for gardening from once every day to three times during the next week. Now, what do you think about rehearsing this a little bit?

As a result of reviewing action steps, clients are more likely to believe that you are genuinely interested in them and progress toward the agreed-upon goals. Reviewing increases the probability that additional action steps will be attempted and successfully completed.

◆ EXERCISE 10-2: REVIEWING ACTION STEPS

For these exercises, assume that you are a social worker with a family services agency. In the spaces provided, create simulated dialogues between yourself and the client that reflect how you might use the skill of reviewing action steps. Follow up on the case situations for which you identified action steps in Exercise 9-6.

1. You are in the midst of reviewing action steps with Mrs. O., a 77-year-old widow who lives alone. She reports that she has fully completed the agreed-upon action step. In the following space, write the words you might say in reviewing the action step with this client.

2. You are in the midst of reviewing action steps with the seven-member, blended S. family. The family indicates that they partly carried out the agreed-upon action step. In the following space, write the words you might say in reviewing the action step with them.

3. You are in the midst of reviewing action steps with Mrs. F. She reports that she did not attempt the agreed-upon action step. In the following space, write the words you might say in reviewing the action step with this client.

Evaluating

Evaluation of progress is crucial during the work and evaluation phase. It often occurs while reviewing action steps. Through the skill of *evaluating*, you engage the client in reviewing progress toward goal attainment. Progress may be indicated by changes in such indicators as goal attainment scales, frequency counts, subjective ratings, or paper-and-pencil instruments. The presence or absence of progress, as well as the rate of change, if any, can be recorded in case notes or presented graphically. When reviewed with clients, evidence of progress may improve self-esteem and increase motivation to undertake further action. Over time, if evaluation reveals no progress, or change in a negative direction, you and the client should reconsider the assessment, the contract, and the action steps that you have planned. Obviously, when progress toward goal achievement is not forthcoming, you need to reexamine the approach to change.

Through the skill of evaluating, you engage the client in examining data that have been collected in accordance with your plan for evaluating progress. You and the client consider the information and determine whether it reflects progress toward goal attainment, no change, or a change in the wrong direction. As you do when reviewing action steps, you may appropriately express your pleasure when there is clear evidence of progress and encourage clients to identify those factors that contributed to make the positive changes. When there is no evidence of progress, you may ask the client to help analyze why. You and the client then consider whether a major revision in the plan is needed or whether relatively minor adjustments might suffice. Frequently, the evaluation instruments provide useful information to supplement the client's experience and your own observations. When issues worsen, you and the client engage in an intensive reanalysis. Together, you need to determine if the planned action steps, rather than helping, have contributed to the deteriorating situation. Often, initial negative effects are an expected but temporary phenomenon, subsequently followed by positive results. Because of the systemic nature of many issues, at first "things may become worse before they get better." Also, negative effects are not always the result of your approach or the action steps undertaken. They may be effects of ongoing changes in the person-issue-situation. Of course, sometimes they are indeed caused by the change program itself. When this occurs, a major revision to the contract is imperative.

As an example, consider Mrs. Chase's daily sleep log, in which she records the number of hours she sleeps each night. The social worker, Susan Holder, has reviewed these daily logs and converted the sleep data into the graph displayed in Figure 10.1.

As the graph shows, Mrs. Chase slept approximately four hours nightly during the period between January 13 and January 19. According to her, four hours has been the approximate amount she has slept each night over the last few months. On the evening of January 20, following the second interview with Susan Holder, Mrs. Chase implemented the change program they had jointly devised. Beginning on that night and continuing for the next 12 days, Mrs. Chase's daily log reflects general progress toward achieving the goal of sleeping eight hours nightly. There was only one night when she did not sleep at least seven hours.

In evaluating progress, Mrs. Chase and Susan can reasonably infer that, with regard to the goal of sleeping more, the plan is working successfully. They should also review Mrs. Chase's subjective ratings concerning how refreshed she feels on awakening in the morning. Those ratings may also be converted into graph form for ready review.

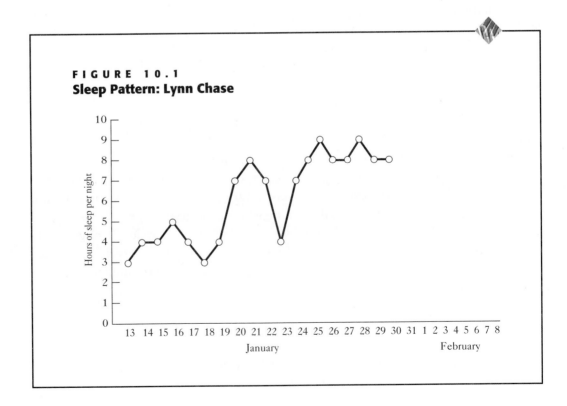

FIGURE 10.1
Sleep Pattern: Lynn Chase

Chapter 10

◆ EXERCISE 10-3: EVALUATING

For these exercises, assume that you are a social worker with a family services agency. In the spaces provided, create simulated dialogues between yourself and the client, showing how you might use the skill of evaluating progress toward goal attainment.

1. You are in the midst of evaluating progress toward goal attainment with Mrs. O. The measurement data clearly indicate that progress toward goal achievement has not occurred; in fact, the issues have worsened. In the following space, write the words you would use to initiate a review of the data and discuss the implications with Ms. O.

2. You are in the midst of evaluating progress toward goal attainment with the S. family. The measurement data indicate that progress toward goal achievement has not occurred. There has been no change in either a positive or a negative direction. In the following space, write the words you would use to initiate a review of the data and discuss the implications with the S. family.

3. You are in the midst of evaluating progress toward goal attainment with Mrs. F. The measurement data clearly indicate that progress toward goal achievement has occurred. There is a definitive change in a positive direction. In the following space, write the words you would use to initiate a review of the data and discuss the implications with Mrs. F.

Focusing

Focusing (Perlman, 1957, pp. 145–149) is a skill used to direct or maintain attention to the work at hand. Occasionally, both workers and clients wander away from the issues that are relevant to the agreed-upon purposes for work. These diversions are often productive, leading to greater understanding and improving the chances for effective change. Sometimes, however, these departures may be clearly unproductive. Through the skill of focusing, you redirect energy to relevant topics. Also, something of significance may occur that goes unnoticed by the client. By directing attention to it, you may heighten awareness and understanding. For example, in working with a family, you may observe that just as plans for an action step are about to be finalized, one sibling interrupts with a complaint about another family member's past misbehavior. As a social worker, you might hypothesize that the interruption represents a defensive or self-protective act, ambivalence about change, or perhaps an attempt to maintain family-system equilibrium. However you regard it theoretically, you may use the skill of focusing to respond to the interruption. You could say to the family member who interrupts, "Would you please hold on to that thought so that we can come back to it later? Let's complete our plans first. Thanks." Through such a form of focusing, you guide the family back to the work at hand. To accomplish a different purpose, that of enhancing process awareness, you might focus in a different way: "I noticed that just about the time we were reaching consensus on a step to address one of the issues, Johnny brought up his concern about Sheila's past behavior. I wonder, Johnny, what do you think led you to raise the topic at this particular time?"

◆ EXERCISE 10-4: FOCUSING

For these exercises, assume that you are a social worker with a family services agency. In the spaces provided, write the words you would say in using the skill of focusing.

1. You are reviewing action steps with Mrs. O. In the midst of this process, Mrs. O. begins to reminisce about a childhood girlfriend. It is your judgment that Mrs. O. would be better served at this time if you were to complete the process of reviewing action steps. You intend to return later in the interview to her childhood memory. In the space provided, write the words you would say in using the skill of focusing with Mrs. O.

2. You are in the midst of exploring a new topic of importance to the S. family. Only the parents and the teenage children are present for this meeting. The subject involves the emerging sexuality of one of the adolescents. As the discussion begins, you observe that Mrs. S. changes the subject to a less anxiety-provoking issue. This pattern seems to occur whenever the adolescent family members begin to express sexual concerns. Based on your professional judgment, you conclude that continuing with the topic of adolescent sexuality would be congruent with the values and cultural background of the family, helpful to the family, and would represent a step toward goal achievement. You therefore decide to use the skill of focusing. In the space provided, write the words you would say in demonstrating two forms of focusing with the

S. family. First, show how you would focus to redirect the discussion back to the topic of adolescent sexuality. Second, indicate how you might refocus to enhance the family's awareness of the pattern of shifting away from difficult topics.

3. You are in the midst of role-playing an action step with Mrs. F. She has assumed the role of her own daughter. A few moments after taking the part of her own daughter, Mrs. F.'s eyes begin to water, and then tears start to fall onto her cheeks. Mrs. F. shrugs and continues in the role of her daughter. You make a professional judgment that Mrs. F would benefit from a more complete expression of her feelings and an exploration of the meaning of the tears. You also realize that such steps would be entirely consistent with the contract for work. In the space provided, write the words you would say in using the skill of focusing to call attention to the tears as well as to the thoughts and feelings behind them.

Educating

During the work phase, it may become apparent that a client lacks useful or valid information or competencies that might aid in the achievement of the agreed-upon goals for work. In such circumstances, you may appropriately assume the role of teacher or educator. The skill of *educating* involves several dimensions. Often, you share knowledge and educated opinions. For example, you might inform parents about major developmental milestones that are to be expected in an infant's first year of life. You could share your ideas about how parents might facilitate childhood development through, for instance, mutual play activities. In educating, the information should be conveyed in such a way that clients may freely consider its relevance for their particular situation and decide whether to accept it. This is particularly true when the information you express is opinion rather than fact. Even when factually correct information is presented, you continue to respect the right of clients to disagree and choose their own course of action.

In educating clients, realize that all people do not learn in the same way. There are several different learning styles; some of your clients are likely to have learning styles that differ from your own preferred manner of teaching or learning. Therefore, try to individualize your educational approach so you can reach each client. For example, some clients have an affinity for deductive thinking. They enjoy theoretical concepts and principles. Once an abstract principle is understood, they can apply it through deductive reasoning to everyday life. Other clients possess strength in inductive thinking. They can take a specific incident or situation and reach a clear understanding of it. Sometimes, this understanding can then be applied to similar circumstances in the future, but at other times, these clients may have to go through the learning process all over again. Such clients frequently benefit more from examples, illustrations, and specific guidelines than from abstract presentations. Many clients also learn better when you tell a story, use a metaphor, or share an analogy. For example, in working with an adult male client who feels trapped by circumstances, you might—having thoroughly explored the situation with the client—realize that he is, in many ways, trapping himself. There are options, but the client has not really seen or seriously considered them. At such a time, you might tell a story in the following fashion.

EXAMPLE

I remember a comic strip I once saw. In the first frame, there is a desperate-looking man, staring out between the iron bars of a jail. His eyes and head are absolutely still. He looks only through the bars and nowhere else. He seems to be highly anxious, afraid, and depressed all at the same time. In the second frame, we see the scene from a more distant perspective. Again we notice the desperate man looking out between the bars. But then we notice that there are iron bars on one side of the room only. The other three sides don't have bars at all; there aren't even any walls. It's completely open. The prisoner, if he would only move his head out from between the bars and look in another direction, could easily see that he could walk away any time he wanted.

In addition, some clients learn best by hearing, others by seeing, and others through a multisensory learning approach (a combination of hearing, seeing, and physically experiencing). Some people learn best by working independently; others by working cooperatively with others, receiving guidance and feedback throughout the process. Certain individuals are more receptive to learning during the morning, others during the afternoon, and still others during the evening hours. Some people enjoy moving around while learning, whereas others prefer stillness. Some prefer to have stimulation in the form of music or background noise, while others learn best when it is absolutely quiet. As you try to educate clients, discover their preferred learning styles and adapt your teaching approach accordingly.

Sometimes, you can serve important educational functions by sharing personal feelings and experiences. It is very much like telling a story, but it is a story about yourself. In self-disclosing, you almost always become a more genuine human being to the client. In addition, the personal experience may carry special meaning to the client, who might attribute considerable significance to the message or moral of your personal story. In sharing your personal feelings and experiences, however, be careful not to become the client's client. There should be a clear relationship between your own self-disclosures and the established goals for work. Also, you should not take so much time in sharing your experiences and feelings that it detracts significantly from the client's opportunity for self-expression. If you share too much of yourself, especially personal difficulties or tragedies, the client may begin to view you as troubled or needy rather than as competent. If your client does begin to see you in this light, it could seriously diminish your effectiveness. The client might abruptly end the relationship with you and look for a healthier professional. Alternately, your client may start to take care of you, assuming the role of caretaker or surrogate parent. In addition, your client might begin to protect you from the full impact of the truth about the situation. Therefore, be cautious about speaking of yourself too often or to too great an extent. Remember, social work services are primarily for the client, not for you.

◆ EXERCISE 10-5: EDUCATING

For these exercises, assume that you are a social worker with a family services agency. In the spaces provided, write the words you would say in using the skill of educating.

1. You are in the midst of discussing Mrs. O.'s eating patterns with her. You discover that she almost never has a hot meal and rarely eats vegetables. Her most typical meal is a bologna sandwich. You and Mrs. O. agree that more balanced meals are desirable. You then begin to educate Mrs. O. about the meals-on-wheels program available in your community. Through this program, Mrs. O. could have delivered to her apartment one or two hot, nutritionally balanced

meals per day. In the space provided, outline the major elements of the information you would like to communicate to her. Then write the words you would say as you begin to educate Mrs. O. about the meals-on-wheels program.

2. You are in the midst of an individual meeting with a teenage member of the S. family. She reports to you in confidence that she is sexually active and "will continue to have sex with my boyfriend no matter what my mother says!" She reports that she and her boyfriend do not practice birth control but that she would like to have some protection. She also mentions that she has recently begun to feel some unusual itching and discomfort "down there" (in her vaginal area). In the space provided, outline the major elements of the information you would like to communicate to her. Then write the words you would say in beginning to educate the teenager about birth control possibilities and about medical care.

3. You are role-playing an action step with Mrs. F. She plays the role of her daughter while you play the part of Mrs. F. Through this experience, Mrs. F. becomes aware of her feelings of extreme guilt about the way she has reared her children. She sobs and says, "I tried not to repeat the bad things my parents did to me, but it looks like I did so anyway." In the space provided, outline the major elements of the information you might communicate to Mrs. F. in educating her about the human tendency to repeat intergenerational family patterns even when trying not to. Then, write the words you would say in telling a story or disclosing a personal experience of your own, to begin to educate Mrs. F. about this human tendency.

Advising

In working with clients, it is sometimes proper for you to provide advice. Making a suggestion or recommendation can be a perfectly appropriate action by a social worker. In using the skill of *advising*, you should almost always convey that the client may freely accept or reject your advice. As Maluccio (1979) observes, many clients very much value and appreciate professional advice. Nonetheless, particularly during the early stages of your professional development, you may experience conflict about advising. You may be tempted to give too much advice or perhaps too little. As a social worker, you are probably keenly aware of the values of self-determination and respect for the uniqueness of each person. In interpreting these values, you might conclude that you should never offer any advice at all. Or you might decide that clients are entitled to all the knowledge you possess; you might therefore provide a great deal of advice, whether or not it is requested or needed. These two positions represent the extremes of a continuum. Most likely, you will take a more moderate stance, giving advice in certain circumstances but not in all. Some advising is usually appropriate and helpful; the key is knowing when to, when not to, and especially how to give advice.

In general, resist the temptation to offer advice based on your own personal feelings, attitudes, and preferences. This can be difficult in situations when a client asks, "What should I do?" or "What would you do if you were in my place?" For example, suppose you have worked for several weeks with a 19-year-old man who is gay. As a result of your exploration together, the young man has become much more self-accepting and comfortable with his sexual orientation. Recently, he raised the issue of whether to tell his tradition-bound parents the truth about his sexual orientation. He asks you, "Should I tell them?"

You could, of course, deftly avoid answering his question by responding with a question of your own: "What do you think?" Or you might respond directly and share your personal opinion: "Of course. Tell them. You have nothing to be ashamed about." Or, not knowing what to do or say, you might become confused and uncertain. On the one hand, you might expect that the client would probably feel less distressed and more personally integrated if he were to tell his parents about his sexual orientation. On the other hand, you might also anticipate that such an encounter between the young man and his parents could be extremely stressful. It could conceivably lead to the loss of his parents' approval and support; he might even lose all contact with them. You might conclude that this decision is ultimately his and his alone to make. Following that line of thinking, you might respond directly to his question, but without advising him what to do: "I'd be more than glad to explore this issue with you and help you make a decision. But I cannot simply give you an easy, direct answer to that question. I cannot advise you what to do. The final decision is yours and yours alone to make."

Of course, there are also many occasions when you clearly should offer direct and specific advice. For example, suppose that you have been helping an adult female client become more assertive with her lover. You and the client have rehearsed assertive communication during your meetings together. The client is about to take a step toward greater assertion in her intimate relationship. You believe that soft or caring expressions tend to strengthen relationships and provide a basis for moving toward hard or confrontational assertions. You therefore advise the client to begin with affectionate, caring assertions and later, after some experience, to initiate assertive expressions that involve requests that her partner make changes.

Usually, it is preferable to provide advice in such a way that the client may freely accept or reject it. On some occasions, however, you may actually need to direct the actions of clients or other persons. For example, in an emergency where an injured child is in life-threatening danger, you might direct another by saying, "We must get this child to the hospital now!"

Advising is involved in many aspects of practice. You might, for example, advise an adult male client who grew up in a family where his father was regularly intoxicated and abusive to read selected books on the topic of children of alcoholic families. You might suggest that the client consider attending Adult Children of Alcoholics (ACOA) or Al-Anon meetings as an adjunct to your work together. You might advise another client concerning how best to complete a job application or how to request a raise. You might advise a client to seek medical care. You might appropriately give advice concerning a variety of life circumstances. In so doing, you would phrase the advice in slightly different ways to accomplish different objectives. Unless life-threatening circumstances exist, however, you should nearly always express advice in the form of a suggestion or perhaps a strong recommendation. Avoid communicating advice as commands or directives, such as an authoritarian boss might deliver to a subordinate employee or an angry parent might say to a disobedient child.

As you begin to practice the skill of advising, please use the format outlined here. As you become more proficient in using the skill, experiment with alternate formats.

PRACTICE FORMAT: ADVISING

I have a suggestion that I'd like you to consider. I suggest (or recommend) that you _____.

◆ **EXERCISE 10-6: ADVISING**

For these exercises, assume that you are a social worker with a family services agency. In the spaces provided, write the words you would say in using the skill of advising.

1. You have now provided Mrs. O. with information about the meals-on-wheels program available in your community. However, Mrs. O. seems uncertain and ambivalent about the service. In the space provided, write the words you would say in advising Mrs. O. to participate in the meals-on-wheels program.

2. During an individual meeting with a teenage member of the S. family, she describes clear symptoms that suggest she has contracted a sexually trans-

mitted disease (STD). In the space provided, write the words you would say in advising the teenager to seek medical care.

3. As you and Mrs. F. have explored more about the relationship between her parenting patterns and the childhood experiences in her own family of origin, you conclude that she might benefit from the construction of a family genogram. In the space provided, write the words you would say in advising Mrs. F. to help you complete her family genogram.

Representing

The skill of *representing* includes those actions you take on behalf of clients in pursuit of agreed-upon goals. Representational activities are usually intended to facilitate clients' interaction with members of various social systems. Representing incorporates the interventive roles of *brokering, advocating,* and *mediating* (Compton & Galaway, 1994, pp. 427–438). Therefore, representing is a complex process indeed. It builds on many of the skills of the preparing, beginning, and exploring phases, as well as those of assessing, contracting, and working. Instead of working for and with the client, however, you work for the client but with others. For example, suppose an unemployed adult woman is currently homeless and desperately needs immediate shelter, food, clean clothes, and financial support. Based on your joint assessment, you and the client concur that if she were to apply directly to a certain resource agency for help, she would probably be denied. Therefore, the client asks you to represent her in this matter. You agree to make an initial contact with the appropriate agency. Then, with the support of the client, you sketch out several action steps. As in the process of preparing for a first meeting with a client, you carefully prepare for the contact with the agency to improve your chances of effectively representing the client.

During the course of your social work career, collect the names and phone numbers of other social workers and representatives of various community resources. Get to know people at churches, community centers, hospitals, neighborhood associations, government welfare organizations, and other systems that might serve as resources for clients. Make notes about such people and keep them in a card file or computerized database for easy access. Periodically send them friendly thank-you notes and mail letters of praise to their supervisors and agency administrators. Such actions tend to enhance your value within the helping community and improve the chances that your clients will receive the high-quality service they deserve.

In the instance of the woman in need of food and shelter, you might decide that a good first step would be to contact a social work colleague at the agency in question. Once you make telephone contact, proceed in much the same manner as if you were beginning with a client. Introduce yourself and secure an introduction in return. Depending on the circumstances, you might make a few informal, friendly remarks to put your colleague at ease. Then outline the purpose for the contact: "I have a client here with me who is in need of assistance. She is unemployed, without money. She hasn't eaten for two days and has no place to stay tonight. I'm calling to determine whether she might be eligible to receive some help from your agency." Following this description of purpose, you may seek feedback to confirm that your message has been understood. At this point in the process, you could invite your colleague to provide information about eligibility requirements or to inquire further about your client's circumstances.

Representing clients in such cases is often extremely satisfying. Interactions with resource persons may be both pleasant and productive. Clients may receive what they need and be treated well. If you cultivate positive relationships with resource persons and know something about the mission and programs of various service organizations, you are more likely to be effective in representing your clients.

However, representing clients is not always enjoyable or satisfying. Sometimes, you must be an assertive advocate on behalf of clients who are not being treated fairly. It can be frustrating. For example, consider the situation of a client who seeks your help in dealing with a landlord. In the middle of a cold winter, heat, which is supposed to be provided to all tenants as part of their rent, is not reaching into the client's apartment.

Despite several complaints, the landlord has taken no action to correct the situation. The client then asks you to represent her by contacting the landlord on her behalf.

First, you would use the preparing skills to formulate a preliminary plan. You explore the situation more fully with the client, securing detailed facts about the heating problem and learning about her experience as a tenant there. You might then consult city officials who are knowledgeable about housing regulations and landlord-tenant laws, expanding your own knowledge base. You also prepare for the initial contact with the landlord. In this instance, suppose you decide to telephone first. You might call, give your name, and say, "I am a social worker with the tenants' advocacy program of the city social services agency. One of your tenants, Mrs. Wicker, has contacted us about a problem with the heating system. It seems that the family has been without heat for five days. Could you tell me what's being done to repair the problem and how much longer it will be before their apartment is warm enough for them to live there?"

If the landlord does not acknowledge the problem and, for example, begins to denigrate the client, you might respond, "Regardless of the complaints you have about Mrs. Wicker and her family, they still need heat. As you know, it's dangerously cold, and the lives of the family members could be in serious jeopardy if heat is not restored soon." If the landlord remains unresponsive, you might outline the steps you could take should the heating system remain unrepaired and the family continues to be in danger. In several respects, your comments are similar to those you might share in beginning with a client. You state your purpose, describe your role as client advocate, and discuss the actions you could take should your client continue to be in need or at risk (i.e., your policies and procedures). You also make a specific request for action from the landlord (i.e., you outline the landlord's role).

If the landlord acknowledges the problem, outlines a plan and a timetable for repair, and makes a commitment to provide the family with sufficient heat, you may appropriately express your thanks and credit him for being responsive to your request. You would then apprise the client of the landlord's plan and request that she notify you about the outcome. If the landlord follows through with the plan, you might again communicate appreciation for the positive action. If the landlord does not follow through, however, you would probably contact him again, report that the apartment is still dangerously cold, and inform him specifically about the steps you will now take to ensure the safety and well-being of your client.

You will probably represent clients quite frequently as a regular part of social work practice, to link clients with needed community resources and to secure fair and equitable treatment, as part of the processes of mediation and conflict resolution. In representing, ensure that you have clients' informed consent to act on their behalf, and always keep their best interests in mind.

◆ **EXERCISE 10-7: REPRESENTING**

For these exercises, assume that you are a social worker with a family services agency. In the spaces provided, outline the action steps you might take in representing the clients in the following situations. Describe how you would prepare to represent the client, and then write the words you would say in beginning with the person contacted on behalf of the client.

1. With her consent, you are representing Mrs. O., an elderly person who almost never has hot or nutritionally balanced meals. You are about to contact the community meals-on-wheels program to seek their help in providing Mrs. O. with at least one sound meal daily. In the space provided, outline the steps you would take before making contact, and then write the words you would say as you begin to represent Mrs. O. with the resource agency.

2. With her consent and that of her parents, you are representing Gloria, a teenage member of the S. family, in relation to some sexual issues. You have jointly decided that you will contact the office of her family physician to arrange for a prompt appointment to deal with a sexually transmitted disease. (When Gloria called for an appointment, she was too embarrassed to say why she needed one right away. An appointment was scheduled for a month later.) In the space provided, outline the steps you would take before making contact with the physician's office, and then write the words you would say in beginning to represent Gloria in this matter.

3. With the informed consent of Mrs. F., you are representing her during interactions with the principal of the school, where her daughters report that they
   have often been harassed by several teenage boys. According to the girls, the
   boys spit on them and used ethnic epithets in referring to their Latino heritage. In the space provided, outline the steps you would take in preparing
   for contact with the principal, and then write the words you would say as you
   begin to represent Mrs. F.

Responding with Immediacy

The skill of *responding with immediacy* (Carkhuff & Anthony, 1979, pp. 114–116) involves exploring the client's experiences and feelings about you, your relationship, or
your work together, *as they occur*. In responding with immediacy, you focus on the
client's experience of what is occurring here and now between the two of you. These
thoughts and feelings become the subject for immediate exploration. Responding with
immediacy makes things real. It intensifies the relationship and encourages the client
to explore relational concerns as they emerge. When you respond in an immediate
manner, you also demonstrate or model an open communication style. Such openness
may promote greater honesty and authenticity by clients, increase their understanding
of interpersonal patterns, and reduce any hesitation to address issues and goals. One
format for responding with immediacy is as follows.

PRACTICE FORMAT: RESPONDING WITH IMMEDIACY

Right here and now with me you seem to be (thinking/feeling/doing/
experiencing) _____.

Usually, the skill is applied directly to the client's immediate experience about you, your relationship, or the nature and utility of your work together. Your response becomes less immediate and less powerful as you move away from the context of "right here and right now with me." Responding with immediacy occurs in the present tense. Whenever the discussion shifts into the past or future tense, the interaction becomes less immediate. For example, if you comment about something that happened between you and the client a week or two ago, he or she may recall it differently or not at all, or the client may intellectually process the information without feeling its full impact. Although it may still be a useful comment to make, exploring a previous exchange rarely has the powerful effect of responding immediately to something that is occurring right now.

In many cases, the manner in which clients relate to you is representative of their general pattern of relating with people. Clients sometime recreate in the working relationship the same problematic conditions that emerge in other relationships. By responding immediately to such relational patterns as they come up, you can help clients learn to recognize them and to develop new, more useful styles of interaction.

Responding with immediacy is not appropriate for use with all clients. It depends on the nature of your contract, including the goals for work, and your plans for change. In general, you would not respond with immediacy unless the client's reactions are clearly relevant to the issues and goals for work. Also, social workers differ in the degree to which they emphasize and attend to immediate interactions in their relationships with clients. Some social work practice approaches regard worker-client relational factors as extremely important, whereas others consider them less so. Nonetheless, most social workers recognize that client reactions within the working relationship are often relevant to the helping process. Responding with immediacy is a skill for addressing client experiences as they occur.

For example, suppose that you have begun to work with an adult female client who identifies as an issue the fact that her spouse does not like her company. Indeed, her spouse has confirmed this: "It's true. I'm sorry to say that I don't much like her company. Every time we start to talk, she drifts off into the ozone—into some daydream world." During your meetings with this client, you notice that her attention frequently does seem to wander, in a fashion similar to her spouse's description. She seems to focus on her own thoughts and listens just enough to your comments to stay distantly aware of the conversation. You begin to observe, and to feel, that when you talk, she essentially tunes you out. Because this pattern relates to the agreed-upon contract, you might appropriately respond with immediacy: "Right here and now as I'm talking, I notice that your eyes are turned away from me. You seem to be looking off into the distance and thinking about something else. What are you experiencing right now?"

The use of responding with immediacy often results in a significant increase in energy between you and your client. Both of you are likely to become much more oriented to the present moment and more engaged with one another. Because immediate responses often heighten intensity and interpersonal intimacy within the professional relationship, use the skill only after rapport is well established and, of course, a contract agreed on. Your clients should know that you genuinely have their interest at heart before you move into the intimate realm of immediacy.

◆ EXERCISE 10-8: RESPONDING WITH IMMEDIACY

For these exercises, assume that you are a social worker with a family services agency. In the spaces provided, write the words you would say in using the skill of responding with immediacy.

1. During a discussion with Mrs. O. about her eating patterns, you advise her to enroll in a meals-on-wheels program so she can get at least one hot meal per day. As you share your recommendation, you notice Mrs. O. turn her body away from you and subtly shake her head. You conclude that her nonverbal behavior may be saying No to your advice. In the space provided, write the words you would say in responding with immediacy to Mrs. O.'s nonverbal reaction.

2. You are in the midst of an individual meeting with Gloria, a teenage member of the S. family. She confides to you that although she is sexually active with her boyfriend, she often fantasizes about another person. As she says that, she looks deeply into your eyes, blushes, and then looks away in what appears to be an embarrassed reaction. You suspect that she has had sexual fantasies about you. You know that it would be quite consistent with your

contract to discuss this directly. In the space provided, write the words you would say in responding with immediacy to the teenager's expression.

3. As Mrs. F. talks with you about her own parenting practices and those that she experienced as a child in her own family of origin, you observe that she sits back in her chair, crosses her arms in front of her, and appears to frown. You're not entirely certain what this reaction means, but you suspect that she may be feeling ashamed and vulnerable. You think she is afraid that you might be critical of her. In the space provided, write the words you would say in responding with immediacy to Mrs. F.

Reframing

The term *reframing* (Bandler & Grinder, 1982; Hartman & Laird, 1983; Tingley, 2001) refers to the words you say and the actions you take when introducing clients to a new way of looking at some aspect of themselves, the issue, or the situation. Usually, it involves sharing a different perspective from that which clients have previously adopted. Clients sometimes embrace a point of view in such a determined fashion that the perspective itself constitutes an obstacle to goal achievement. Of course, fixed views are not necessarily problematic. You should not indiscriminately attempt to challenge or reframe all of them. Reframing is applicable when the fixed attitude constitutes a fundamental part of the issue for work. It is similar to the skill of educating, but it differs in that the overall purpose of reframing is to liberate the client from a dogmatic perspective. As a result of reframing, clients may reconsider strongly held beliefs. This may, in turn, affect their feelings and behavior as well.

There are several forms of reframing. One of the more common is *reframing a negative into a positive.*

EXAMPLE

Reframing a Negative into a Positive

When you say that you're "stupid" and "indecisive" because you have difficulty choosing from among various courses of action, I feel confused. I mean, what you refer to as indecisive appears to me to be the ability to see different points of view. It sounds like you're open-minded and willing to consider many perspectives and options. To me, this sounds like flexibility—not indecisiveness. And what you call stupidity sounds a great deal to me like carefulness, thoroughness, and patience. These are attributes that I find extremely appealing and functional. Are you sure they are so bad?

Another form of reframing is *personalizing meaning* (Carkhuff & Anthony, 1979, pp. 95–131), through which you encourage clients to shift the attribution of responsibility away from other people, organizations, or external forces (i.e., the situation) and toward themselves. Personalizing meaning can help people assume greater responsibility for effecting change. It can be liberating, even empowering. Personalizing meaning can help clients see a relationship between their own beliefs, values, attitudes, and expectations, on the one hand, and the feelings they experience or the behavior they enact on the other. This form of reframing involves going beyond the communication directly expressed by the client. You slightly alter the client's expression to shift an externalized meaning toward a more internalized or personalized meaning, for which the client is likely to feel greater responsibility, personal power, and control. In personalizing meaning, you may use a format such as the following.

PRACTICE FORMAT: PERSONALIZING MEANING

You feel (do or experience) _____ because you think (believe/
value/perceive/expect) _____.

Because the skill of personalizing meaning is derived from your frame of reference rather than the client's, it constitutes an expressive rather than an empathic skill. Therefore, you should phrase your comments in a tentative manner. Personalizing meaning suggests that the client's thoughts, feelings, or actions are more associated with conscious individual processes than with external or situational factors. Occasionally, it may leave clients feeling more guilty or more burdened with responsibility. It also may convey a sense of considerable optimism, because such feelings are a result of one's own values, beliefs, or thoughts. These are aspects of a person that are not necessarily permanent—one's beliefs and attitudes can and do change. Notice how much more positive such an explanation is than the view that one feels a certain way because one is jinxed, has a deficient superego structure, had a lousy childhood, suffers from a personality disorder, or because "That's just the way I am."

Here is an example of a social worker talking with a client who happens to be a social work student.

EXAMPLE

Personalizing Meaning

CLIENT: I'm devastated! I got a C+ in my social work field placement. I'll never make it through the program. I'm a total failure.

WORKER: You're disappointed in yourself because you believe you should do better than C+ work, and you think that getting a C+ means that you won't be able to graduate?

Situationalizing meaning is another form of reframing through which you change the meaning suggested by clients' expressions. Although there is certainly an empathic element, in this form of reframing you also begin to alter slightly the meaning as presented by the client. In the case of situationalizing meaning, you reflect understanding of the client's feelings or behavior but then suggest that they may also be viewed as a result of external, societal, systemic, situational, or other factors beyond the client's individual control or responsibility.

Frequently, situationalizing meaning results in an expansion of clients' perspectives and a lessening of their sense of guilt, self-blame, or personal responsibility.

EXAMPLE

Situationalizing Meaning

CLIENT: I'm a wreck. I can't sleep or eat; I can't concentrate. I know my head is really messed up. I've always been kind of crazy.

WORKER: You feel awful; you're anxious and depressed and you have lots of issues. I wonder, though, might these feelings be an understandable re-action to the recent changes in your life? Wouldn't even the most well-adjusted person feel out of sorts and have some difficulty sleeping after being laid off from a good job and not having any immediate prospects for another?

◆ EXERCISE 10-9: REFRAMING

For these exercises, assume that you are a social worker with a family services agency. In the spaces provided, write the words you would say in using the skill of reframing.

1. You are in the midst of discussing Mrs. O.'s eating patterns. She says that she has not been eating balanced meals because "I cannot get anyone to drive me to the grocery, it's too far to walk, and when I telephone to have it deliv-ered they always get it wrong." In the space provided, write the words you would say in reframing Mrs. O.'s statement so that it reflects a personalized meaning.

2. You are in the midst of an individual meeting with Gloria, a teenage member of the S. family. She says, "My mother is always on my case. She's a wild

woman. She's so controlling. I can't do anything I want to do. She thinks that I'm five years old." In the space provided, write the words you would say in reframing her statement from a negative to a positive. Also, experiment by reframing her statement so that it has a personalized meaning.

3. During a meeting with Mrs. F., she confirms that she is indeed feeling guilty and ashamed that she may have harmed her children. She says, "I feel so ashamed. I've done just what I've always criticized my parents for." In the space provided, write the words you would say in reframing Mrs. F.'s statement so that it reflects a situationalized meaning. Also, record how you might reframe her statement so that it has a personalized meaning. Finally, respond to her words with the skill of reframing a negative into a positive.

Confronting

In *confronting* (Carkhuff & Anthony, 1979, pp. 116–119), you point out to clients—directly and without disapproval—discrepancies, inconsistencies, or contradictions in their words, feelings, and actions. In confronting, you challenge clients to examine themselves for congruence. For example, suppose an adult male client has requested help from you regarding a troubled marriage. The client says, "I am willing to do whatever is necessary to improve this relationship." Following a joint meeting with you and his spouse, during which he promised "to go out for a date with my spouse this week," he voluntarily worked overtime at his job and arrived home three hours late—too late for the date. After the client subsequently missed another planned date night, you might confront him by saying, "You said you want to improve the relationship and you agreed to two dates with your spouse. However, you worked late on the nights you had planned to go out with your wife. What do you think this might mean?"

In confronting, you may use the following format (Carkhuff & Anthony, 1979, p. 117).

PRACTICE FORMAT: CONFRONTING

On the one hand you say (feel, think, or do) _____ but (and or yet) on the other hand you say (feel, think, or do) _____.

Confrontation can have a powerful effect on clients. It has the potential to cause severe disequilibrium in people who are highly stressed or have fragile coping skills. Therefore, before confronting a particular client, be certain that person has the psychological and social resources to endure the impact. Certainly, the relationship between you and the client should be well established before any confrontation. In confronting, try to be descriptive about the incongruities or discrepancies that you observe. Avoid judgmental or evaluative speculations and conclusions. Finally, it is usually wise to "precede and follow confrontations with empathic responsiveness" (Hammond, Hepworth, & Smith, 1977, p. 280).

◆ EXERCISE 10-10: CONFRONTING

For these exercises, assume that you are a social worker with a family services agency. In the spaces provided, write the words you would say in using the skill of confronting.

1. You are in the midst of an interview with Mrs. O., approximately two weeks after she has begun to receive daily hot meals through the meals-on-wheels program. Before that, she had agreed that more balanced meals would be desirable and said that she would eat the food when it was delivered. During the course of this meeting, you notice that the day's meal remains untouched.

There is also evidence that Mrs. O. has not eaten the delivered meals for the past two days. In the space provided, write the words you would say in confronting Mrs. O. about the uneaten meals.

2. You are in the midst of an individual meeting with Gloria, a teenage member of the S. family. She reports that her physician had prescribed medication for treating the sexually transmitted disease. The doctor told her to abstain from sexual intercourse during the two-week period she is to take the medication. She was also told to inform her boyfriend that he should see his doctor and be treated before he resumed any sexual relations. Otherwise, they would continue to infect each other. The girl says that her boyfriend will not go to the doctor and continues to want to have sex with her. She says, "I'll probably just let him have what he wants because if I don't, he'll go somewhere else." In the space provided, write the words you would say in confronting the girl about this situation.

3. During the course of your interaction with the principal of the school where Mrs. F.'s daughters have apparently been harassed by several teenage boys, the principal says, "There is no racism at this school. The F. girls are simply too sensitive. They are the only Latino students we have in the school, and they will just have to learn to deal with the boys. We never had any trouble before they enrolled here." In the space provided, write the words you would say in confronting the principal.

Pointing Out Endings

In *pointing out endings* (Shulman, 1992, p. 206), you remind the client "some time before the last sessions that the working relationship is coming to a close." In most cases where a contract has been established, a time frame for working together has also been determined. This occurs as a significant part of planning an approach to your work together (see Chapter 9). Periodically during the work phase, you refer to this time frame for work. Of course, the timetable may be renegotiated when the situation warrants. Ideally, however, any such revision should be considered carefully and discussed openly with your client. Extending a time frame does not necessarily increase the probability of goal achievement. Additional time could imply that the goals are just too difficult to accomplish. Also, time extensions may leave an impression that your working relationship can go on indefinitely.

Social work in several practice settings (e.g., hospitals, residential facilities, prisons) has natural ending points that are partially or fully beyond either client or social worker control. There are numerous legal as well as practice implications related to the process ("Lawsuit seeks discharge treatment-planning at NYC jails," 1999). Consider, for example, the process of discharge following a stay in a medical or psychiatric hospital. Indeed, the process of "discharge planning" is widely discussed in the professional literature (Christ, Clarkin, & Hull, 1994; Clemens, 1995; Cox, 1996; Morrow-Howell, Chadiha, Proctor, Hourd-Bryant, & Dore, 1996; Oktay, Steinwachs, Mamon,

Bone, & Fahey, 1992; Proctor, Morrow-Howell, & Kaplan, 1996; Spath, 2002; Tuzman & Cohen, 1992), reflecting the complexity of an ending process that often involves additional assessment, contracting, and working activities.

By pointing out endings, you may help motivate clients to work hard on the action steps to complete them within the established period. As Perlman suggested (1979, pp. 48–77), the social work relationship is limited in time. After all, as a social worker you are not marrying or adopting your clients. You are a professional helper, not a member of their family. By establishing time limits and pointing out endings, you help clients to prepare psychologically for the process of concluding the working relationship. If the topic of the forthcoming conclusion to the relationship is avoided, you and your clients can deny the immediacy of the feelings. Such denial may allow temporary emotional respite from strong feelings, but it also prevents the parties from psychologically anticipating and preparing themselves for ending. Therefore, despite feelings of discomfort, you should occasionally refer to the upcoming conclusion to the relationship.

The skill of pointing out endings may be undertaken in several ways. Regardless of the specific form it takes, the skill leads the client to consider consciously and emotionally the fact that the relationship will end. Whether it involves a transfer, a referral, or a termination, you gently remind the client that there will soon be an ending and that there may very well be some thoughts and feelings triggered by the change.

For example, suppose you and family members have agreed to meet for eight sessions, with a goal of improving communication. The work has proceeded quite well. By the fourth meeting, the family members have progressed to such an extent that they are able to express differences of opinion without feeling devalued or rejected. There has also been a noticeable decrease in tension and an increase in humor. Toward the end of the session, you say, "We're now finishing up our fourth session. There are four meetings left. We're halfway there."

Following such a reminder, you might explore thoughts and feelings associated with the idea of ending. You might ask, "As we think about concluding our relationship, some thoughts or feelings may come up. I wonder, what comes to mind when you think about finishing our work together?" Or you might ask, "How will things be different once we have concluded our work together?" Although a specific format is not universally applicable, the primary element in pointing out endings is the reminder. Statements such as "We have ___ meetings left" or "We will be meeting for another ___ weeks" serve this function. In the case of transfers or referrals, clarify what will happen following your ending with the client. You might say, "We have ___ meetings left before you begin to work with _____," or "We will be meeting for another ___ weeks before you begin the program at _____."

◆ EXERCISE 10-11: POINTING OUT ENDINGS

For these exercises, assume that you are a social worker with a family services agency. In the spaces provided, write the words you would say in using the skill of pointing out endings.

1. You have been working with Mrs. O. for approximately two months. Her eating patterns have improved to the point where your services are no longer needed. She is now regularly receiving and eating meals delivered by the meals-on-wheels program. Her weight has returned to normal, and her energy level has improved. Three weeks earlier, you and Mrs. O. had discussed the progress and decided that you would conclude your relationship in one month. The meeting next week will be your last. In the space provided, write the words you would say in pointing out endings to Mrs. O.

2. You are in the midst of the next-to-last meeting with the S. family. During the past several months, many productive changes have occurred. Two sessions before, the family members indicated that they were well on their way to accomplishing their goals. At that time, you had agreed to meet three more times. Next week you will have the concluding session. In the space provided, write the words you would say in pointing out endings with the S. family.

3. Through a joint discussion two weeks earlier, you and Mrs. F. concluded that she could best complete work toward goal attainment by participating in a ten-week assertiveness training group sponsored by another community

agency. The group begins in three weeks. Next week will be your last meeting together. In the space provided, write the words you would say in pointing out endings to Mrs. F.

Progress Recording

As a professional social worker, you are legally and ethically obligated to keep records throughout all phases of practice. During the work phase, you should keep track of any revisions to the initial assessment and contract. You incorporate within the case record notes about progress toward goal achievement and include the results of evaluation procedures such as goal attainment scaling, subjective ratings, test scores, or graphs. You also record additional action steps and make note of changes to those previously established. Particularly, you record events, issues, or themes that might relate to the process of working toward goal accomplishment. In some instances, you should provide a rationale for an action you are taking or a recommendation you are making. Suppose you were to learn from an adult male client that he sometimes sexually molests his infant son. You are, of course, required by law to report this information to relevant authorities. Usually, this means a telephone call to the child-protection services division of the department of welfare or human services. Because the information has been acquired during a meeting protected by client confidentiality, you should meticulously record the data (i.e., the words the client said) that led you to conclude that the child may be at risk of abuse. You should also record what you said to the client in response. You may have informed him that you, as a professional social worker, are required by law to report this information to child-protection authorities. You should note this. You may also have indicated that you would like to continue to serve as his social worker during this time; you should record this as well. When you make the phone call to the relevant authorities, you should record the date and time, the person contacted, and what was said. Of course, unless the client provides informed consent to do so, you would refrain from sharing information about the client beyond what is needed to initiate the investigation into the possibility of child abuse.

In many settings, social workers use a problem-oriented approach to record keeping during the work phase (Burrill, 1976, pp. 67–68; Johnson, 1978, pp. 71–77; Martens & Holmstrup, 1974, pp. 554–561). The well-known SOAP format (Subjective data, Objective data, Assessment, and Plan) is commonly used within medical settings and has been widely used in social services as well. The DAR (Data, Action, Response) and APIE (Assessment, Plan, Implementation, and Evaluation) are fairly common, and there are several variations to the traditional SOAP structure. For example, SOAPIE stands for subjective, objective, assessment, plan, implementation or interventions, and evaluation. SOAPIER adds "revisions" to the format. The SOAIGP format represents another derivation (Kagle, 1991, pp. 101–104). SOAIGP stands for

- ◆ S—*supplemental* information from clients or family members
- ◆ O—your *observations* and, if applicable, those of other agency staff
- ◆ A—*activities* that you, the client, or others undertake
- ◆ I—your *impressions*, hypotheses, assessments, or evaluations
- ◆ G—current *goals*
- ◆ P—*plan* for additional activities or action steps

Within the *supplemental* category, you may include new or revised information provided by clients, family members, or other persons within the client's primary social systems. Within the *observation* section, you may describe your own observations of the person, issue, and situation. If applicable, observations of other agency staff members may also be reported. Within the *activities* category, you may summarize client tasks, worker tasks, and in-session tasks that have occurred. Within *impressions*, you may summarize your current evaluation of progress toward goal achievement and make note of your tentative impressions and hypotheses. You may also summarize results of frequency counts, subjective ratings, and test results within this section. Under *goals*, you may record goals that are the current focus of work or revise original goals. Within the *plan* section, you may make note of changes in your approach and identify additional action steps that you or your client intend to take.

For example, following an interview with Mrs. Chase, Susan Holder might prepare a SOAIGP entry for the case file as follows.

EXAMPLE

SOAIGP Entry for Meeting with Lynn Chase
February 10

- ◆ *Supplemental.* Mrs. Chase indicated that she had accomplished the action step we had identified for this week. She reported that it was a great help. She stated that she has felt in better spirits than she has for months.

   Before the meeting, Mr. Chase had telephoned to report that things are much better at home. He said, "Everybody has begun to help out at home, and we're all much happier. Thanks a lot."

- *Observations.* Mrs. Chase does indeed appear to be in much better spirits. She speaks with energy and expressiveness. Her face is animated when she talks about her family life and her gardening. When she discusses work, there is a slight change to a more "businesslike" quality.
- *Activities.* During today's meeting, Mrs. Chase and I talked at length about her childhood. On several occasions, she referred to her mother's drinking and the mixed feelings she experienced as a child when she dealt with her intoxicated mother. She sobbed when she talked of the embarrassment and rage she felt when a friend had visited while her mother was drunk and verbally abusive. She also revealed that she felt "somehow to blame" for her mother's drinking. She said, "I used to feel that if I were somehow better or less of a problem, then Mother wouldn't need to drink so much."

  I reminded Mrs. Chase that we had three more meetings together. She said that "she would miss me," but already "things were much better."
- *Impressions.* Mrs. Chase's daily logs reflect progress toward two of the goals: sleeping better and arguing less with Robert and Richard. It is my impression that the change program continues to be viable. There is no need to revise it at this time.
- *Goals.* The previously established goals remain in effect.
- *Plan.* We identified a new action step. In addition to those already identified last week, Mrs. Chase agreed to read Janet Woititz's book, *Adult Children of Alcoholics* (1983), within three weeks of today's date.

Susan Holder, BSW, MSW

The problem-oriented recording formats just described and illustrated serve many valuable functions. The SOAPIE, SOAPIER, and SOAIGP adaptations improve on the earlier SOAP system with their greater emphasis on implementation or intervention and evaluation and, in the case of SOAIGP, specific recognition of the importance of goals. To further that trend, please consider the preliminary, experimental version of a goal-focused format, tentatively called GAAP:

- *Goals.* Summarize the goals and objectives reflected in the contract.
- *Activities.* Describe the tasks, activities, and interventions undertaken by participants (e.g., social worker, client, others) during or in-between meetings in pursuit of the goals.
- *Assessment.* Report the results of assessment and evaluation processes related to effects and outcomes of activities and progress toward goal achievement.
- *Plans.* Based on the assessment and evaluation, outline plans for additional goal-related tasks and activities including, when necessary, changes to the agreed-upon goals and objectives.

Progress recordings are legal as well as professional documents. Prepare them as if they could become public knowledge—perhaps in the context of a review committee or even a legal hearing or trial. They should be organized in a coherent fashion, well-written, and legible; prepared in a timely fashion; contain descriptive or factual rather than abstract or theoretical information that pertains to the purposes and goals for work; reflect accurate, objective, unbiased reporting; reveal respect for the individual and cultural characteristics of clients and their active participation in decisions and processes; indicate the sources of information; support the reasons for decisions and actions; and reflect compliance with legal and agency policies (Kagle, 2002).

◆ EXERCISE 10-12: PROGRESS RECORDING

For these exercises, assume that you are a social worker with a family services agency. In the spaces provided, prepare progress notes for case records concerning the following client interviews.

1. On Monday of this week, you completed an interview with Mrs. O. The meeting occurred a few weeks after she had begun to receive daily hot meals through the meals-on-wheels program. For the first two weeks, she appeared to eat each of the meals that had been delivered. During the course of this meeting, however, you realized that the day's meal remained untouched. There was also evidence that she had not eaten the meals for the previous two days. You asked her about the uneaten food and she said that she hadn't been hungry. You asked whether she would eat the meal that would be delivered tomorrow. She said, "Oh, I don't know." In the space provided, prepare a progress note regarding the interview. Use the SOAIGP format.

2. Earlier today, you completed an interview with Gloria, a teenage member of the S. family. She reported that following your last meeting together, she had told her boyfriend that he would have to see his doctor and receive treatment before she would again have sex with him. She appeared to be pleased that she could report this to you. You praised her for taking that action and asked about her boyfriend's response. She said that he had left in a huff, but she thought that he might be back.

In the space provided, prepare a progress note regarding the interview. Use the SOAIGP format.

3. Earlier today, you completed a meeting with Mrs. F., her daughters, and the principal of their school. During the course of the meeting, the girls described in detail what the teenage boys had said and done to them. They talked of the boys spitting at them and calling them names that referred to their Latino heritage. The girls were able to identify the boys by name. The principal appeared to be quite taken aback by what the girls had to say. He apparently believed the girls because he said that he was indeed sorry that this had happened. Furthermore, he said that he would have a talk with the boys the very next day. He also asked the girls to tell him right away if anything like this were ever to happen again.

In the space provided, prepare a progress note regarding the interview. Use the GAAP format.

Summary

During the work and evaluation phase of social work practice, you and the client take action toward resolving the identified issues and achieving the established goals. In this process, you use both empathic skills and work phase expressive skills. Skills pertinent to the work phase include (1) rehearsing action steps, (2) reviewing action steps, (3) evaluating, (4) focusing, (5) educating, (6) advising, (7) representing, (8) responding with immediacy, (9) reframing, (10) confronting, (11) pointing out endings, and (12) progress recording.

◆ **CHAPTER 10 SUMMARY EXERCISES**

Building on the earlier meetings you had with your colleague who serves as a practice client, conduct another interview, primarily to work toward the goals identified through the contracting process. As you did previously, ensure that the interview setting is private, and once again tape-record the meeting. Using empathic and especially work-phase expressive skills, interview your colleague with a view toward helping him or her take steps toward goal attainment. Toward the conclusion of the meeting, arrange for another interview in about one week. Be sure to point out that the next meeting will be your last.

1. At the conclusion of the interview, ask your partner for feedback concerning thoughts and feelings about the experience. Ask for a candid reaction to the following questions. (a) Did you feel that I conveyed understanding and respect to you during this interview? (b) Did you think that the meeting was productive in helping you progress toward goal attainment? (c) What feedback do you have for me concerning the quality of my performance of various working and evaluating skills? (d) Did you find the experience satisfying? (e) Do you believe that you have made progress toward goal attainment? If so, what do you identify as having been most helpful to that progress? If not, what were the obstacles? Did I do anything that was not helpful to you? (f) What suggestions do you have for me concerning how the interview could have been better or more helpful for you? Summarize your partner's feedback in the following space.

2. In the following space, summarize your own reaction to the interview. How did you feel about the interview? What did you like and what did you dislike about it? Do you believe that you used all of the relevant empathic and expressive skills during the interaction? What would you do differently if you were to redo the interview? What working and evaluating skills require further practice?

3. Prepare a written progress note regarding the meeting you had with your colleague. Use the SOAIGP format described earlier. After you have completed the SOAIGP record, play the audiotape or videotape. Make notes of significant exchanges that affected the way in which you prepared your SOAIGP record; then revise it to improve its accuracy. Place the SOAIGP record in the Practice Case Record section of your Social Work Skills Learning Portfolio.

◆ CHAPTER 10 WORLD WIDE WEB EXERCISES

1. Go to the InfoTrac College Edition Web site at www.infotrac-college.com. Use your passcode to log in. Conduct a search to locate an article entitled,

"Shyness and Social Phobia: A Social Work Perspective on a Problem in Living" (Walsh, 2002). Carefully read the article and reflect on the use of various forms of psychosocial interventions such as rehearsal, practice, and repeated exposure as part of an intervention for shyness and social discomfort. In the following space, prepare a one-to-two paragraph essay in which you reflect on the implications of the article for application of the skills of rehearsing action steps, reviewing action steps, and other work phase social work skills.

2. Go to the InfoTrac College Edition Web site at www.infotrac-college.com. Use your passcode to log in. Conduct a search to locate an article entitled, "Single-Subject Designs" (Gliner, Morgan, & Harmon, 2000). Carefully read the article to become familiar with various forms of single-subject or single-case designs. In the following space, prepare a one-to-two paragraph essay in which you reflect on the implications of the article for possible use in evaluating progress toward goal attainment.

3. Go to the InfoTrac College Edition Web site at www.infotrac-college.com. Use your passcode to log in. Conduct a search to locate an article entitled "Gun Violence and Children: Factors Related to Exposure and Trauma" (Slovak, 2002). Carefully read the research article to learn about the topic. Imagine that you are serving a family that owns several handguns that are accessible to children. Use the following space to write the words you might say in using information gained from the article in applying the skills of educating and advising this family.

4. Go to the InfoTrac College Edition Web site at www.infotrac-college.com. Use your passcode to log in. Conduct a keyword search using the string "making diamonds" (include quotation marks) to locate a brief essay entitled "Making Diamonds: Helping Children Benefit from Stress" (Neal, 2002). Then conduct another search using the keywords "emotional pain reframing past" (without quotation marks) to locate a brief newspaper article entitled "You Can Heal Emotional Pain by 'Reframing' Your Past" (Hopson, Hagen, & Hopson, 1999). Read and reflect on the essay. Use the following space to summarize your thoughts about resiliency and the skill or process of reframing.

5. Go to the InfoTrac College Edition Web site at www.infotrac-college.com. Use your passcode to log in. Conduct a search to locate an article entitled "Ladies Don't: A Historical Perspective on Attitudes Toward Alcoholic Women" (Carter, 1997). Carefully read and reflect on its implication for work-phase skills. In particular, consider the pros and cons associated with the use of confrontation with women affected by alcohol misuse. Use the following space to summarize your thoughts.

6. Go to the InfoTrac College Edition Web site at www.infotrac-college.com. Use your passcode to log in. Conduct a search to locate an article entitled "Disagreements in Discharge Planning: A Normative Phenomenon" (Abramson, Donnelly, King, & Mailick, 1993). Carefully read the article and reflect on its implication for pointing-out endings. Use the following space to summarize your thoughts in a paragraph or two.

Chapter 10 Self-Appraisal

Now that you have finished this chapter and completed the exercises, please assess your proficiency in the working and evaluating skills by completing the following self-appraisal exercise.

SELF-APPRAISAL: THE WORKING AND EVALUATING SKILLS

Please respond to the following items. Your answers should help you to assess your proficiency in the working and evaluating skills. Read each statement carefully. Then, use the following four-point rating scale to indicate the degree to which you agree or disagree with each statement. Record your numerical response in the space provided.

4 = Strongly Agree

3 = Agree

2 = Disagree

1 = Strongly Disagree

_____ 1. I can effectively use the skill of rehearsing action steps.

_____ 2. I can effectively use the skill of reviewing action steps.

_____ 3. I can effectively use the skill of evaluating.

_____ 4. I can effectively use the skill of focusing.

_____ 5. I can effectively use the skill of educating.

_____ 6. I can effectively use the skill of advising.

_____ 7. I can effectively use the representing skill.

_____ 8. I can effectively use the skill of responding with immediacy.

_____ 9. I can effectively use the skill of reframing.

_____ 10. I can effectively use the skill of confronting.

_____ 11. I can effectively use the skill of pointing out endings.

_____ 12. I can effectively use the skill of progress recording.

_____ Subtotal

Note: These items are taken directly from the Social Work Skills Self-Appraisal Questionnaire contained in Appendix 3. You have responded to these items before. You may now compare your item responses to those you made on earlier occasions. You may also compare the subtotal scores. If you think you are developing greater proficiency in these skills, more recent scores should be higher than earlier.

Finally, reflect on the skills addressed in this chapter and the results of your self-appraisal. Based on your analysis, prepare a succinct one-page summary report entitled "Self-Assessment of Proficiency in the Working and Evaluating Skills." Within the report, be sure to identify those skills that you know and do well (e.g., a score of 3 or 4). Also, specify those that need further practice (e.g., scores of 2 or less) and briefly outline plans by which to achieve proficiency. When finished, include the report in your Social Work Skills Learning Portfolio.

Chapter 11

Ending

This chapter (see Box 11.1) is intended to help you develop proficiency in the *ending skills*. Social workers use these skills in concluding the working relationship productively. Although the particular form of ending may vary, several skills are important to the process. Drawing on the work of Schwartz (1971) and Kubler-Ross (1969), Shulman (1992) discusses the dynamics and describes several skills associated with the ending process. The skills presented here are derived in part from those he identifies. The social work ending skills include (1) reviewing the process, (2) final evaluating, (3) sharing ending feelings and saying goodbye, and (4) recording the closing summary.

BOX 11.1

Chapter Purpose

The purpose of this chapter is to help learners develop proficiency in the ending skills.

Goals

Following completion of this chapter, learners should be able to demonstrate proficiency in the following:

(continued)

◆ Reviewing the process
◆ Final evaluating
◆ Sharing ending feelings and saying goodbye
◆ Recording the closing summary
◆ Assessing proficiency in the ending skills

The four most common forms of concluding a relationship with a client are (1) transferral, (2) referral, (3) termination, and (4) client discontinuation. In the first three, you and the client openly discuss the ending process and jointly determine the best course of action given the circumstances. These are the preferred modes of concluding relationships with clients. The fourth form, quite common in many agency settings, is exclusively client-initiated. Often with good reason, clients may decide to stop meeting with you. They may do so by informing you during a meeting, in a telephone conversation, or even by letter. They may also discontinue without notification, perhaps by failing to attend a scheduled meeting. The ending message is communicated by their absence. In such cases (assuming you can make contact by phone or in person), it is often very useful to seek clarification from clients who have discontinued in this manner. However, you should be extremely sensitive to clients' indirect expressions during these contacts. Sometimes, in response to your inquiry, clients might say they will resume meeting with you "since you were so nice as to call," when in fact they have decided to discontinue. If you ask carefully during such contacts, you may learn something about the ways you presented yourself or how you intervened that played a role in the decision to discontinue. This information may be helpful with other clients in the future. Providing clients with an opportunity to express themselves about the service may also help them conclude the relationship in a more satisfactory manner. It may sufficiently expand their view of you, the agency, and the experience to enable them to seek services again at some point in the future.

Clients are more likely to discontinue without notification at certain times. There is an increased probability of client discontinuation whenever changes occur. Changing from a customary meeting time or relocating from one meeting place to another may lead clients to discontinue. Transferring a client to another social worker within the same agency can also be a stressful transition, which the client may resolve through discontinuation. Perhaps the most difficult of all is referring a client to another professional in a different agency. This involves many changes—a new location; another agency with at least somewhat different policies, procedures, and mission; a new meeting schedule; and, of course, a different helping professional. Many clients, understandably, cope with these numerous changes by discontinuing. Although the dynamics of transfers and referrals are similar, transfers are generally easier to manage. Referrals involve more change, and the psychosocial demands on the client are greater. Nonetheless, transfers and referrals, like termination and discontinuation, bring about a conclusion to the relationship between you and the client.

Ending a significant relationship is often a difficult and painful experience. It is certainly challenging for social workers. Concluding a relationship with a client can stimulate strong feelings of sadness, loss, and other emotions as well. For clients, the process of ending may be even more intense. By this time, clients have usually come to view you as a kind, caring, and understanding person who listened well and had their best interests at heart. Often, clients have shared personally intimate thoughts and feelings. This may lead them to feel both safe and vulnerable. They may have entrusted their secrets to you, a person with whom they may never again have contact. They may have successfully addressed a major issue, turned their lives around, or accomplished a significant goal. They may experience intense gratitude and want to express it to you—perhaps with a tangible or symbolic gift. The conclusion of the relationship may elicit a host of deep feelings. Some clients may feel intensely sad, as if they have lost a best friend, which may in fact be the case. They may feel frightened and dependent as they ask themselves, "How can I make it without you?" They may feel guilty that they did not work as hard as they might have or that they did not take as much advantage of the opportunities for change and growth as they could have. They may feel rejected by you or angry that the relationship is ending. They may think, "If you really cared about me, you wouldn't end the relationship—you must not care about me at all. You must be glad to be rid of me!" Clients may also deny or minimize feelings that lie beneath the surface of consciousness. They may present themselves as being quite ready to terminate, while actually struggling with strong feelings that they have not acknowledged or expressed. There are many manifestations of the psychological and social processes associated with ending—a transition that often provokes significant reactions from both you and your clients. Ideally, these responses are explored as part of the ending process.

Reviewing the Process

Reviewing the process is the skill of tracing what has occurred between you and the client during the time you have worked together. It is a cooperative process; each party shares in the retrospection. Usually, you begin by inviting the client to review the process from the time you first met through the present. For example, you might say, "I've been thinking about the work we've done together during these last several months. We've covered a lot of ground together, and there have been some substantial changes in you and your situation. As you think back over all that we've done together, what memories come to mind?"

Following the responses to your request, you might ask about additional thoughts and feelings and then share some of your own significant recollections. This often stimulates recall of other experiences.

◆ EXERCISE 11-1: REVIEWING THE PROCESS

For these exercises, assume that you are a social worker with a family services agency. In the spaces provided, write the words you would say in reviewing the process with each client.

1. You have been working with Mrs. O. for approximately two months. She has accomplished the goal of improving her eating and nutritional patterns. She has seen a medical doctor, who prescribed medication that has effectively controlled the spells. You both seem quite pleased about the work you have done together. This is your last meeting. In the space provided, write the words you would say in reviewing the process with Mrs. O.

2. You are in the midst of the final meeting with the S. family. During the past several months, many productive changes have occurred. In the space provided, write the words you would say in reviewing the process with the S. family.

3. This is your concluding session with Mrs. F. The school situation has dramatically improved, and Mrs. F. and her daughters are communicating in a much more satisfying way. In two weeks, Mrs. F. will begin a 10-week assertiveness training group sponsored by another community agency. In the space provided, write the words you would say in reviewing the process with Mrs. F.

Final Evaluating

In addition to reviewing the process, you also engage the client in a final evaluation of progress toward issue resolution and goal attainment. For this discussion, you may draw on the results of measurement instruments such as before-and-after test scores, graphs, and various ratings. You may also share your own subjective impressions of progress. Whatever you do share in the form of a final evaluation, be sure to seek feedback from the client about it.

As part of this process, you express your pleasure concerning the positive changes that have occurred. You credit the client for all the work that entailed, and you help the client identify issues that have not been completely resolved and goals that have been only partially achieved. Work toward such goals does not have to stop because you and your client are concluding your working relationship. The client alone, or with the support of friends and family members, may continue to take action steps toward desirable objectives. By the time they conclude the relationship with the social worker, many clients have become competent problem solvers in their own right. They are often quite capable of defining goals and identifying action steps on their own. This phenomenon, when it occurs, is enormously satisfying for social workers. When clients become effective problem solvers who are skilled at self-help, you may reasonably conclude that you have indeed helped them to help themselves. If, because of their association with you, clients acquire skills with which to address future issues, they have gained a great deal indeed.

Like most of the ending skills, *final evaluating* is a cooperative process. You and the client share your respective evaluations of progress and jointly identify areas that may require additional work. To initiate this final evaluation, you may say something such as "Let's now take a final look at where we stand in regard to progress toward the goals that we identified. One of our major goals was _____. How far do you think we have come toward achieving it?"

Goals that have been largely or completely accomplished are discussed with appropriate pleasure and satisfaction. You urge the client to experience and enjoy the sense of personal competence and self-approval that accompanies goal achievement. As areas requiring additional work are clarified, you encourage the client to plan additional action steps that can be taken after you conclude your relationship together. Of course, this discussion is not nearly as extensive or as detailed as when you and the client established action steps as part of the contracting and work processes. Rather, you encourage the client to look forward to future activities that can support continued growth and development. You may initiate this process by asking a question such as "What kinds of activities do you think might help you to continue the progress you've made so far?"

As part of the final evaluation, you may find it beneficial to seek feedback from the client about things you said or did that were helpful and things that were not. This kind of evaluation may help clients to identify behaviors they can adopt for their own future use. It may also provide an opportunity for clients to share their gratitude to you for your help. However, the primary purpose for seeking feedback about helpful and unhelpful factors is to aid you in your own professional growth and development. In a sense, you request that clients evaluate your performance as a social worker. By seeking such evaluative feedback, you may gain information about yourself that may prove useful in your work with other current and future clients. In asking for feedback, you might say, "I would appreciate it if you would tell me about those things I did that were particularly helpful to you during our work together . . . And could you also identify things I did that were not helpful?"

◆ **EXERCISE 11-2: FINAL EVALUATING**

In the spaces provided, write the words you would say to engage each client in the process of final evaluating. Prepare statements to encourage each client to identify future action steps. Finally, write the words you might say in seeking evaluative feedback from each client concerning what has been helpful and what has not.

1. You have been working with Mrs. O. for approximately two months. She has accomplished virtually all the goals that you identified together. This meet-

ing is your last. In the space provided, write the words you would say to engage Mrs. O. in the process of final evaluating.

2. You are meeting for the last time with the S. family. During the past several months, many productive changes have occurred. There is still strain among some of the family members, but they seem to be coping with it quite well. There are several indications that they are communicating much more directly and honestly with one another. The family has achieved more than half of the goals that were identified. In the space provided, write the words you would say to engage the S. family in the process of final evaluating.

3. This is your concluding session with Mrs. F. She and her daughters have made quite remarkable gains. All three seem to be quite satisfied with the

changes that have occurred. Mrs. F. is looking forward to the assertiveness training group she will join in a week or so. In the space provided, write the words you would say in initiating the process of final evaluating with Mrs. F.

Sharing Ending Feelings and Saying Goodbye

The nature and intensity of the feelings clients experience as they conclude a relationship with you vary according to their personal characteristics, the duration of service, the issue and goals, the roles and functions you served, and the degree of progress (Hess & Hess, 1999). Because ending is a significant event in the lives of most clients, you should give them an opportunity to express feelings related to the ending process.

Clients may experience several emotional responses as they end their relationship with you: anger, sadness, loss, fear, guilt, dependency, ambivalence, gratitude, and affection. Clients may hesitate to express their emotions freely at this time. If they conclude the relationship without sharing some of these feelings, they may experience a sense of incompleteness. This "unfinished" quality may impede the appropriate process of psychological separation from you and inhibit the client's movement toward increased autonomy and independence. Therefore, you should encourage clients to express their ending feelings. You may say, "We've reviewed our work together and evaluated progress, but we haven't yet shared our feelings about ending the relationship with one another. As you realize that this is our final meeting together, what emotions do you experience?"

Of course, you will also experience various feelings as you conclude your working relationships with clients. You may have spent several weeks or months with a person, a couple, a family, or a group. During your work together, a client may have shared painful emotions, discussed poignant issues, or made significant progress. Despite your professional status and commitment to an ethical code, you are also human. It is entirely understandable and appropriate that you also experience strong feelings as you end your relationships with clients. During the ending process, you may find yourself feeling guilty, inadequate, proud, satisfied, sad, angry, ambivalent, relieved, or affectionate. The kind and degree of your feelings may vary because of many factors. Like clients, you will almost always experience some kind of personal reaction during the ending phase. It is often useful to share some of these feelings. Unlike the client, however, you retain your professional responsibilities, even in ending. You cannot freely express whatever feelings you experience. You must consider the potential effects on the client. For example, suppose you feel annoyed at an adult male client because he did not work as hard toward change as you had hoped he would. You should not share these or any other such feelings unless to do so would help the client progress toward any remaining goals or aid him to conclude the relationship in a beneficial manner. Even during the final meeting, you make professional judgments about which feelings to express and how to express them. Do not simply suppress feelings that are inappropriate to share with clients. Rather, engage in the skills of self-exploration and centering (see Chapter 5) to address them in a personally and professionally effective fashion.

When they are relevant and appropriate, you may share your personal feelings about ending the relationship. For example, you might say, "When I think about the fact that we will not meet together anymore, I feel a real sense of loss. I'm really going to miss you."

Often, when you do share your feelings, clients respond by sharing additional emotions of their own. You may then reflect their feelings and perhaps share more of your own. Finally, however, you and the client complete the ending process by saying goodbye.

◆ EXERCISE 11-3: SHARING ENDING FEELINGS AND SAYING GOODBYE

In the spaces provided, write the words you would say to encourage each client to share feelings about ending. Also, prepare statements in which you share your own ending feelings with each client. As part of your own sharing, please specify those feelings that you think you might experience had you actually worked with each client. Identify those that would be appropriate to share and those that would not. Finally, note the exact words you would use in saying goodbye.

1. After working with Mrs. O. for approximately two months, you have completed your review of the process and conducted a final evaluation. You have

approximately fifteen minutes left in this very last meeting. In the space provided, write the words you would say to engage in sharing ending feelings and saying goodbye to Mrs. O.

2. You have reviewed the process and engaged in a final evaluation of progress with the S. family. In the last several minutes remaining in this final meeting, you would like to share ending feelings and say goodbye. In the space provided, write the words you would say in doing so with the S. family.

3. You are in the process of winding down your final session with Mrs. F. You have reviewed the process and engaged in a final evaluation of progress. Now

it is time to move toward closure. In the space provided, write the words you would say in sharing ending feelings and saying goodbye to Mrs. F.

Recording the Closing Summary

Following your final meeting with a client, you condense what occurred into a written closing summary. This final entry is usually somewhat more extensive than the typical progress recording. When the ending session has included a review of the process, a final evaluation, and a sharing of ending feelings, you will probably have most of what you need to complete a closing summary. Include in the final recording the following information (Wilson, 1980, pp. 119–120): (1) date of final contact; (2) your name and title as well as the name of the client; (3) beginning date of service; (4) the reason contact between you and the client was initiated; (5) the agreed-upon issues and goals for work; (6) the approach taken, the nature of the services that you provided, and the activities that you and the client undertook; (7) a summary evaluation of progress and an identification of issues and goals that remain unresolved or unaccomplished; (8) a brief assessment of the person-issue-situation as it now exists; and (9) the reason for closing the case.

You may use the following section headings to organize your closing summary:

- Process and issues
- Evaluation
- Continuing goals
- Current assessment
- Ending process

As an illustrative example, consider how social worker Susan Holder might prepare a closing summary following the final interview with Mrs. Chase:

EXAMPLE

Closing Summary: Lynn B. Chase

Process and Issues

Mrs. Lynn B. Chase and I, Susan Holder, MSW, met together today for the eighth and final time. Mrs. Chase and I first met almost three months ago. At that time, we agreed on the following issues for work: (1) frequent arguments with and feelings of irritability and anger toward son and husband; (2) stress, tension, and anxiety; (3) sleep disturbance; (4) ambivalence about job; (5) thoughts and feelings of excessive responsibility and possibly of control; and (6) role strain and possibly conflict among the roles of mother, wife, homemaker, and employee. Based on these issues, we established several related goals and developed an eight-week plan by which to approach our work together.

Evaluation

In reviewing the work process and evaluating progress, Mrs. Chase reported today that the feelings of stress and anger have decreased substantially since the time of the first contact. She also indicated that relations between her, her husband, and her son have greatly improved since the family redistributed housework responsibilities more evenly. She said that she assumes less of a caretaker role with them. She said that she now believes that they have actually benefited from the assumption of greater family and household responsibility. She stated that she now sleeps fine and rarely has a headache. Mrs. Chase reported that her job at Fox Manufacturing is now quite satisfying; she said she is glad she kept it. And she has been engaging in more playful and pleasurable activities, particularly gardening.

Mrs. Chase indicated that the single most helpful aspect of our work together was when I said to her that "doing for your husband and son may prevent them from developing their full potential."

Continuing Goals

Mrs. Chase indicated that she is still working on issues related to excessive caretaking and intends to do further reading. She reported that she might attend an ACOA meeting to see what it's like. She said that she is also considering taking an assertiveness training course.

Current Assessment

Based on the available evidence, Mrs. Chase, her son, and her husband are communicating more directly, sharing household responsibilities, and experiencing considerable satisfaction in their relationships with one another.

Robert seems to be negotiating the demands of adolescence in a constructive fashion, and Mrs. Chase has made considerable progress in reversing her long-held patterns of excessive responsibility and control.

Mrs. Chase and her family have many personal strengths that should serve them well in the future. I anticipate that Mrs. Chase will continue to grow and develop now that she has permitted herself to consider more expansive and more flexible personal and familial roles.

Ending Process

Mrs. Chase and I concluded our work together in a positive manner. She expressed her gratitude, and I shared my affection for her as well as my pleasure at the progress she has made. The case was closed in the eight-week time frame as contracted.

Susan Holder, BSW, MSW
February 27

◆ EXERCISE 11-4: RECORDING THE CLOSING SUMMARY

In the spaces provided, prepare brief closing summaries for each of the following clients. You may have to simulate some information, but your responses to earlier exercises contain most of the needed information related to issues, goals, action steps, and progress.

1. You have just completed your final meeting with Mrs. O. In the space provided, prepare a simulated closing-summary record of your work with Mrs. O.

2. You have completed the final meeting with the S. family. In the space provided, prepare a simulated closing-summary record of your work with the family.

3. You have concluded the last session with Mrs. F. In the space provided, prepare a simulated closing-summary record of your work with Mrs. F.

Chapter 11

Summary

The ending phase of social work practice provides an opportunity for you and your clients to look back on your relationship and the work you undertook together. You have a chance to evaluate overall progress and to identify directions for future work. However, concluding these working relationships can be both a joyful and a painful experience for you and your clients. Each of you may experience satisfaction concerning the progress achieved, regret about actions that might have been but were not taken, and sadness at the departure of a person who has been important. In optimum circumstances, these feelings can be explored as part of the ending process.

The particular form of ending may be transferral, referral, termination, or discontinuation. Several skills are important to the process, including (1) reviewing the process, (2) final evaluating, (3) sharing ending feelings and saying goodbye, and (4) recording the closing summary.

◆ CHAPTER 11 SUMMARY EXERCISES

Conduct a final interview with the colleague who has served as your practice client during these past several weeks. As you did previously, ensure that the interview setting is private, and once again tape-record the meeting. Using empathic, working, and especially ending skills, interview your colleague with a view toward concluding the relationship. This is your last meeting. Therefore, use the relevant ending skills of reviewing the work process, final evaluating, and sharing ending feelings and saying goodbye.

1. At the conclusion of the interview, ask your partner about his or her thoughts and feelings regarding this concluding interview. In particular, ask for feedback concerning your use of the ending skills. Because this is your last meeting together as part of this exercise, ask your partner to provide you with feedback concerning the entire five-session experience. Summarize your partner's feedback in the following space.

2. In the following space, record your own reaction to this final meeting. How did you feel about the interview? What did you like and what did you dislike about it? Do you believe that you used all the relevant empathic, expressive, and ending skills during the interaction? How well did you use the ending skills? What would you do differently if you were to redo this final interview? Which of the ending skills should you practice further?

Now reflect on the entire series of interviews. Share your overall impressions and reactions about the experience in the following space.

3. Prepare a written closing summary of your work with the colleague who served as your practice-client. After you have completed the closing summary, play the audiotape or videotape. Make note of significant exchanges that affected the way in which you prepared your record. Revise the record accordingly. Now place the closing summary in your Social Work Skills Learning Portfolio.

1. Go to the InfoTrac College Edition Web site at www.infotrac-college.com. Use your passcode to log in. Conduct a search to locate an article entitled "Ending Clinical Relationships with People with Schizophrenia" (Walsh & Meyersohn, 2001). Carefully read the article and reflect on its implication for ending processes with clients. Use the following space to summarize your thoughts in a paragraph or two.

2. Go to the InfoTrac College Edition Web site at www.infotrac-college.com. Use your passcode to log in. Conduct a search to locate an article entitled "Teaching Residents about Patient and Practice Termination in Community-Based Continuity Settings" (DeWitt & Roberts, 1995). Although the article refers to medical residents, the contents have relevance for social workers—including students in field practicum settings. Indeed, in the context of your academic or professional career, you will probably conclude relationships with clients because you are finishing a field placement or leaving a position. Carefully read the article and reflect on its implication for worker-initiated ending processes with clients. Use the following space to summarize your thoughts in a paragraph or two.

3. Go to the InfoTrac College Edition Web site at www.infotrac-college.com. Use your passcode to log in. Conduct a search to locate an article entitled "Confidentiality of Social Work Records in the Computer Age" (Gelman, Pollack, & Weiner, 1999). Read the article and consider the implications for record-keeping generally and for the preparation of closing summaries. Use the following space to summarize your thoughts in a paragraph or two.

Chapter 11 Self-Appraisal

Now that you have finished this chapter and completed the exercises, please assess your proficiency in the ending skills by completing the following self-appraisal exercise.

SELF-APPRAISAL: THE ENDING SKILLS

Please respond to the following items. Your answers should help you to assess your proficiency in the ending skills. Read each statement carefully. Then, use the following four-point rating scale to indicate the degree to which you agree or disagree with each statement. Record your numerical response in the space provided.

4 = Strongly Agree

3 = Agree

2 = Disagree

1 = Strongly Disagree

_____ 1. I can effectively use the skill of reviewing the process.
_____ 2. I can effectively use the skill of communicating a final evaluation.
_____ 3. I can effectively use the skill of sharing ending feelings and saying goodbye.
_____ 4. I can effectively use the skill of recording a closing summary.

_____ Subtotal

Note: These items are taken directly from the Social Work Skills Self-Appraisal Questionnaire contained in Appendix 3. You have responded to these items before. You may now compare your item responses to those you made on earlier occasions. You may also compare the subtotal scores. If you think you are developing greater proficiency in these skills, more recent scores should be higher than earlier.

Reflect on the skills addressed in this chapter and the results of your self-appraisal. Based on your analysis, prepare a succinct one-page summary report entitled "Self-Assessment of Proficiency in the Ending Skills." Within the report, be sure to identify those skills that you know and do well (e.g., a score of 3 or 4). Also, specify those that need further practice (e.g., scores of 2 or less) and briefly outline plans by which to achieve proficiency in them. When finished, include the report in your Social Work Skills Learning Portfolio.

◆ SUPPLEMENTAL EXERCISES: FINAL LESSONS

Congratulations! You have now reviewed all the chapters in the workbook, undertaken many, many exercises, and produced a large Social Work Skills Learning Portfolio. You have done a lot! Please acknowledge the extraordinary amount of time and effort you expended in all the various activities. You deserve a great deal of credit!

Completion of this workbook represents a kind of ending too. In a way, it resembles the ending processes that social workers and clients experience. Some of the skills you recently practiced may be adapted for this last set of exercises—the Final Lessons.

1. Using the checklist contained in Appendix 1 as a reference guide, take a few minutes to examine the contents of your portfolio. You probably have a brief essay from the first chapter, an initial readiness for social assessment report from Chapter 2, several end of chapter self-assessment of proficiency reports, description and assessment sections of your own personal case record, and a Practice Case Record based on five interviews with a colleague. Your

personal case record probably contains a genogram, eco-map, and a timeline. The Practice Case Record probably includes a DAC, a SOAIGP Progress Note, and a Closing Summary. Your portfolio contains many written products that document the extent of your learning.

The portfolio materials, however, are only a part of the story. From the time you first opened this workbook until now, you have undertaken many exercises, practice sessions, and an array of learning experiences that may not be so apparent. Reflect for a few moments about them. Consider what you have learned. Then, use the following space to note briefly the most important lessons gained from the various learning experiences.

2. Following your review of the learning process and identification of important lessons learned, conduct a final evaluation of your proficiency in the social work skills. To do so, please turn to Appendix 2 and take The Social Work Skills Practice Test once again. You completed the practice test as part of an exercise early in Chapter 2. At that point, it was part of a pre-test or baseline assessment experience. This time, it represents a part of the post-test evaluation.

After you have finished The Social Work Skills Practice Test, turn to Appendix 3 and complete it for the last time. Base your proficiency estimates on your performance on the practice test, your understanding of the material presented in the workbook, your reflections about the learning experiences, and your own lessons learned. Compare your assessment ratings on the Social Work Skills Self-Appraisal Questionnaire with those you assigned on that first time.

Using the comparative pre- and post-ratings on the Social Work Skills Self-Appraisal Questionnaire, please use the following space to identify in outline fashion those skill areas where, at this point in time, you think you need additional practice:

Appendix 1

The Social Work
Skills Learning Portfolio

Portfolios are widely used in many contexts to demonstrate talents, competence, achievement, and potential. Artists and photographers, for example, commonly maintain selections of their artistic work in portfolios. Then, when applying for jobs, bidding on a contract, applying to graduate schools or institutes, or seeking to display their work in an art gallery, they present examples of their artistic products as part of the process. Portfolios may also be used within learning contexts as well. A collection of written products, especially those that have been assessed or evaluated, can contribute to as well as reflect the depth and breadth of learning. The products you complete in undertaking the exercises contained in this workbook are especially well suited for incorporation into your own Social Work Skills Learning Portfolio.

The Social Work Skills Learning Portfolio may be handwritten, typewritten, computerized in an electronic format, or prepared using a combination of various media and formats. The portfolio should contain several completed exercises, assignments, self-assessments, and products that reflected your own learning. At various points during the learning process, "interim portfolios" may be self-assessed or submitted to someone else (e.g., a social work colleague, a professor, or a supervisor) for evaluation and feedback. A "final" portfolio may be prepared later to include a selected collection of products that have been carefully revised and reworked to reflect your very best work. Such final portfolios may be used for various purposes (e.g., as a major part of a course grade), including job interviews. Most importantly, however, they can represent a foundation for ongoing lifelong learning and skill development throughout your entire social work career.

As a first step in creating a Social Work Skills Learning Portfolio, please consider the array of products to include in your portfolio. These are derived from selected learning exercises contained in the workbook. You may use the "yes" or "no" boxes to keep track of those products you include in your portfolio.

Yes	No	
☐	☐	Chapter 1: Short Essay—Initial Reflections About the Qualities and Characteristics of Ethical and Effective Social Workers.
☐	☐	Chapter 2 (Summary Exercise 1): Report—Summary Assessment of Motivation, Readiness, and Suitability for the Profession of Social Work
☐	☐	Chapter 3: Summary Report—Self-Assessment of Proficiency in Ethical Decision-Making Skills
☐	☐	Chapter 4: Summary Report—Self-Assessment of Proficiency in the Basic Skills of Talking and Listening
☐	☐	Chapter 5: Summary Report—Self-Assessment of Proficiency in the Preparing Skills
☐	☐	Chapter 6: Summary Report—Self-Assessment of Proficiency in the Beginning Skills
☐	☐	Chapter 7: Summary Report—Self-Assessment of Proficiency in the Exploring Skills
☐	☐	Chapter 8 (Exercise 8-1): Description Section of a "Personal Case Record"
☐	☐	Chapter 8 (Exercise 8-2): Assessment Section of a "Personal Case Record"
☐	☐	Chapter 8 (Summary Exercises 3–5): Description and Assessment Sections of a "Practice Case Record"
☐	☐	Chapter 8: Summary Report—Self-Assessment of Proficiency in the Assessing Skills
☐	☐	Chapter 9 (Summary Exercise 3): Contract Section of a "Practice Case Record"
☐	☐	Chapter 9: Summary Report—Self-Assessment of Proficiency in the Contracting Skills
☐	☐	Chapter 10 (Summary Exercise 3): Progress Note (SOAIGP Format) for a "Practice Case Record"
☐	☐	Chapter 10: Summary Report—Self-Assessment of Proficiency in the Working and Evaluating Skills
☐	☐	Chapter 11: (Summary Exercise 3): Closing Summary for a "Practice Case Record"
☐	☐	Chapter 11 Summary Report—Self-Assessment of Proficiency in the Ending Skills

Appendix 2

The Social Work Skills Practice Test

Review the descriptive scenarios that precede the practice test items. Read each item carefully. Then, using a separate pad or paper, respond to each item. Number each of your responses so you can later refer back to the relevant test item. Also, record the date you took the test. You might complete this practice test again and compare your responses on one occasion with those from another.

You have been serving as a social worker in a counseling role with a voluntary client for about six months. The client has accomplished virtually all of the goals that you jointly identified during the contracting phase of work. You enjoy your visits with this client, and the client also appears to enjoy them. You have extended the time frame for work once already, and as a professional you realize that it would be unwise to do so again. You therefore suggest to the client that you meet for three more times and then conclude your working relationship. When you make this suggestion, the client pauses for a moment and then says, "That sounds about right. You have helped me a great deal, and I think I am ready to conclude this relationship with you. In gratitude for your help, however, I would very much like to invite you to join me in a terrific business opportunity. I have just bid on and won the right to open a McDonald's restaurant on that really busy highway near here. If you can come up with $500, I would like to give you a 5% share in the franchise. In one year, that share should be worth at least $20,000. Now, don't answer right away. Think about it for a week or so and then let me know when we meet next time."

1. Identify and discuss the social work values, the legal duties, and the ethical principles, if any, that might relate to this situation. If applicable, use a hierarchical ethical screen to resolve any conflicts. Then describe what you would do in this situation to behave in an ethical manner. Cite the values, ethics, and legal duties that support your action plan.

Yesterday, Mrs. Little telephoned the family service agency where you work to express her concerns that her husband (of six months) is too severe in his discipline of her 7-year-old daughter (from a previous relationship).

2. In your agency, you serve as a social worker specializing in helping couples and families. You will be talking with Mrs. Little when she visits the agency later today. Demonstrate your knowledge

of and ability to use the applicable preparing skills (*preparatory arranging, preparatory empathy, preliminary planning, preparatory self-exploration,* and *centering*) in advance of your first meeting with Mrs. Little. Be sure to label each of the skills by making a brief notation beside it.

After you have prepared for the initial meeting with Mrs. Little, the time for her appointment arrives. You walk up to her in the waiting room and escort her to your office.

3. Write the words you would say in beginning with Mrs. Little. If applicable, use the beginning skills of introducing yourself, seeking introductions, describing initial purpose and (possibly) role, orienting clients, discussing policy and ethical considerations, and seeking feedback. Label each of the skills you choose to use by making a brief notation alongside your use of the skill. If you determine that a skill would not be applicable as you begin in this situation, provide a brief rationale for omitting it.

CLIENT *(spouse of one year):* "We fight all the time about his teenage son—the one from his first marriage. My husband doesn't think I should discipline the boy at all. He doesn't want me to correct him or to punish him in any way. But, I'm around the boy much more than my husband is and I have to deal with the brat!"

4. Write the words you would say in using two forms of the skill of *asking questions* in your attempt to encourage further client exploration following this client's statement. Make your first question open-ended and the second, closed-ended.

CLIENT *(14-year-old boy):* "Sometimes I wonder whether there is something wrong with me. Girls just turn me off. But boys . . . when I'm close to a good-looking boy, I can feel myself becoming excited. Does that mean I'm gay?"

5. Write the words you would say in using the skill of *reflecting content* in your attempt to encourage further client exploration following this client's statement.

CLIENT *(14-year-old boy):* "If I am gay, what will I do? If my mother finds out, she'll be crushed. She'll feel that it's her fault somehow. I'm so scared and so worried. If my friends learn that I'm gay, what will they do?"

6. Write the words you would say in using the skill of *reflecting feelings* in your attempt to encourage further client exploration following this client's statement.

CLIENT *(21-year-old male):* "My father began to molest me when I was about 9 years old. When I think about it, I just shudder. It was so disgusting; so humiliating. Even today, whenever I think about it, I still feel dirty and damaged. My father kept doing it until I was 14. After that he'd try sometimes but I was too strong for him."

7. Write the words you would say in using the skill of *reflecting feeling and meaning* in your attempt to encourage further client exploration following this client's statement.

CLIENT *(14-year-old female in foster care):* "This family treats me like dirt. They call me names and don't let me do anything I want to do. Half the time they don't even feed me. I just hate it there!"

8. Write the words you would say in using the skill of *seeking clarification* in your attempt to encourage further client exploration following this client's statement.

CLIENT *(adult male of African ancestry):* "Sometimes it seems so phony. I grew up hearing whites call me 'boy' and 'nigger.' I was poor as dirt and sometimes I was beaten just because of the color of my skin. But I fought on through it all. I kept my pride and made it to college. I did really well too. When I graduated, a lot of the big companies wanted to meet their minority quota so I was hired right away at a good salary. I've been at this company now for five years, and I have contributed a great deal. I've been promoted twice and received raises. But, so far not one white person in the company has ever asked me to his home. Now what does that say to you?"

9. Write the words you would say in using the skill of *going beyond what is said* in your attempt to encourage further client exploration following this client's statement.

CLIENT *(17-year-old male):* "I don't know what's wrong with me. I can't get a date to save my life. Nobody will go out with me. Every girl I ask out says 'no.' I don't have any real guy friends either. I am so lonely. Even my folks hate my guts! My mother and I fight all the time, and my stepdad will have nothing to do with me. I spend most of my time alone in my room listening to music. I know I'm real depressed, but I don't know what to do about it."

10. Write the words you would say in using the skill of *partializing* in your attempt to focus the client's exploration following this client's statement.

Presume that you are a social worker in the Child Protective Services (CPS) unit of a Department of Child Welfare. Your job is to investigate allegations of child abuse and neglect and to determine if the child or children involved require protective service.

A county resident has telephoned CPS to report that she has observed severe bruises on the back and the legs of Paul K., an 8-year-old neighborhood child. The neighbor has heard loud arguments in the child's home and believes that the child has been beaten on several occasions. You are called to respond to the allegation. You drive to the neighborhood and go to the K. home, where the abuse is reported to have occurred. The door is answered by a woman who confirms that she is the child's mother, Mrs. K. After you introduce yourself by name and profession, you describe your purpose and role and outline the relevant policy and ethical factors.

Mrs. K. says, "I know why you're here—it's that damn nosy neighbor down the street. She's always butting into other people's business. She called you, didn't she?"

You respond to Mrs. K.'s expression by saying, "I'm not allowed to reveal how information regarding allegations of child abuse or neglect comes to us. My job is to investigate the reports however they occur and determine whether a child is in danger. Is that clear?"

Mrs. K. says, "Yeah. Come on in. I guess you want to see Paul." She loudly calls for Paul (who has been playing in another room).

Paul enters the room with a quizzical look on his face. Using terms he can easily understand, you introduce yourself and outline your purpose and role. You take Paul to a quiet area, well away from his mother (who abruptly goes to the kitchen). Then you say, "I'm here to make sure that you are safe from harm and to find out whether anyone might have hurt you in any way. Paul, do you understand what I am saying? Yes? Okay, then, I'd like to ask you some questions. First, who lives in this house with you?"

Paul says, "Well, my mom lives with me. And, uh uh, her boyfriend stays here a lot too." You ask, "What is he like?" Paul hesitates, looks questioningly toward the kitchen, then looks back into your eyes. It looks to you that he's afraid to say anything more. You respond by communicating your understanding about how difficult and frightening it is to be interviewed in this way.

Paul responds to your empathic feeling reflection by saying, "Yeah, it sure is." You follow that by asking, "Paul, does anyone ever hurt you?" Paul again hesitates, but then says, "Yeah. Charlie, that's my mom's boyfriend, sometimes hits me with his belt."

Paul responds to your empathic content reflection by saying, "Yeah. He and my mom get drunk and yell and hit each other. I get so scared. If I make any noise at all, Charlie starts yelling at me. Then he takes off his belt and beats me with it."

You communicate your understanding of the feeling and meaning inherent in his message. Then you ask an open-ended question concerning the nature of the beatings and the location of any bruises that might exist.

Paul responds to your question by saying, "I have bruises all over my legs and back and my bottom. It hurts real bad. Sometimes when Charlie beats me, I start to bleed. I hate him! I hate him! I wish he'd just leave and never come back."

You then ask Paul to elaborate further. He responds by saying, "Things were fine until Charlie showed up. Mom and I got along great! See, my real dad was killed in a car wreck before I was born and so it has always been just Mom and me—that is, until Charlie moved in."

11. Respond to Paul's most recent statement by using the skill of *reflecting an issue*.

After you reflect the issue, Paul says, "Yeah, that's it all right." Following that exchange, you excuse yourself from Paul and join Mrs. K in the kitchen. You indicate that you have seen severe bruises on Paul's legs, back, and buttocks. You go on to say that you will take Paul into protective custody and place him in the local Children's Home until a more complete investigation can be conducted. You indicate that the final decision about Paul's custody is in the hands of Judge Dixon, who will conduct the hearing, but before leaving with Paul, you would like to share with her your view of the problem.

12. Record the words you would say in using the skill of *identifying an issue* with Mrs. K.

After arranging for Paul to enter the Children's Home, you take time to write in the case record.

13. Outline the kinds of information that you might include in the description section of a case record as you consider organizing information concerning the K. case.

14. Outline, in general, what you might address in the assessment section of a case record as it relates to the K. case.

15. Identify what you would include in the contract section of a case record as it relates to the K. case.

16. Based on your view of an issue as described earlier, formulate a goal (any goal that reasonably follows from the issue you identified would be fine), in two ways. First, write a general goal statement. Then, write a specific goal statement.

17. Building on your view of an issue and the goal just described, identify at least one way you could evaluate progress toward goal attainment.

18. Next, in a manner that is congruent with the issue, goal, and evaluation method, formulate an action plan by which you and the client in this case might progress toward goal achievement.

Several weeks have passed. Charlie has been charged with various crimes associated with child abuse and left the K. household. (It appears he may have fled the area.) Mrs. K. has progressed from an initial state of confusion to a point where she actively participates in a counseling process with you. Indeed, she seems to find the conversations interesting and stimulating as well as helpful. Paul remains at the Children's Home, but he may be able to return home within this next week. Mrs. K. has visited him daily, and those visits have gone very well.

During one of your meetings, Mrs. K. says to you (while tears stream down her cheeks), "You know, when I was a child, my stepfather used to beat me too. He made me pull down my pants and he beat me with a razor strap. I used to cry and cry but he kept doing it, and my mother never could or would stop him. They never listened to me and nobody ever protected me. In fact, and it's strange to think about it this way, but when you came to this house to make sure that Paul was all right, that was the first time I had ever seen anybody try to protect somebody else from harm. And you are the first and only person who has ever seemed interested in me and in what I think and feel. Thank you so much for that."

19. Record the words you would say in responding to Mrs. K.'s verbal and nonverbal expression with the skill of *responding with immediacy*.

Following that exchange, you continue to explore with Mrs. K. her history of relationships with alcoholic and abusive men. It's a pattern that seems remarkably similar to the relationship she observed between her own mother and her stepfather. In the midst of this discussion, she says, "I guess I must be masochistic. I must like to be beaten and degraded. Boy, am I ever sick!"

20. Respond to the client's statement with the skill of *reframing a negative into a positive*.
21. Respond to the client's statement with the form of reframing that *personalizes the meaning*.
22. Respond to the client's statement with the form of reframing that *situationalizes the meaning*.
23. Now shift gears and respond to Mrs. K.'s expression with the skill of *confronting*.
24. Following your reframing and confrontational responses, it seems appropriate that you use the skill of *educating* in an attempt to help Mrs. K. understand how adults who were abused as children tend to behave. Write the words you might use in educating her about this topic.
25. Following your attempt to educate Mrs. K., it appears that she might benefit from some specific advice on how to be a better parent to her son Paul. Record the words you might use in *advising* her in this area.

Approximately one week goes by. Paul has returned home, and both he and his mother are delighted. In a session with the two of them, you are discussing one of the goals Mrs. K. has identified for herself: becoming a more loving parent and a better listener. You ask Paul, "How would you like your mother to show you she loves you?" Instead of answering the question, Paul grabs a ball and begins to bounce it.

26. Respond to the situation just described by using the skill of *focusing*.

Later during the visit, Paul, Mrs. K., and you are "playing a game" of drawing on large pieces of paper. With crayons, each of you draws a picture of the K. family. Interestingly, Paul's drawing reflects a mother and a child who are both large in size—that is, the child (Paul) is every bit as tall and as large as is the mother (Mrs. K.).

27. Please respond to your observation about the relative size of the mother and son by using whatever social work skill you believe to be the most applicable. Record the words you might say in using the skill. Following that, discuss the rationale for your choice.

A few more weeks go by. Paul and Mrs. K. appear to be thriving. Paul is clearly no longer in danger. You have been authorized by the court to provide no more than four additional counseling sessions.

28.   Write the words you might say to Paul and Mrs. K. in *pointing out endings*.

A month goes by. You, Paul, and Mrs. K. are meeting for the last time. Things are better than ever. They have achieved all of the identified goals and are extremely pleased with their progress. They are also grateful to you.

29.   Write the words you might say in initiating a *review of the process*.
30.   Write the words you might say in encouraging Paul and Mrs. K. to engage in a *final evaluation*.
31.   Write the words you might say in sharing ending feelings and saying goodbye.

Appendix 3

The Social Work Skills
Self-Appraisal Questionnaire

This questionnaire is intended to yield an indication of your self-appraised proficiency in the social work skills addressed in the workbook. Read each statement carefully. Then, use the following four-point rating scale to indicate the degree to which you agree or disagree with each statement. Record your numerical response in the space provided:

4 = Strongly Agree

3 = Agree

2 = Disagree

1 = Strongly Disagree

The Ethical Decision-Making Skills

_____   1. I can readily identify and describe the legal duties that apply to all helping professionals.

_____   2. I can readily identify and describe the fundamental values of the social work profession.

_____   3. I can readily summarize the principles of my social work Code of Ethics.

_____   4. I can readily identify the ethical principles and legal duties that might apply in social work contexts.

_____   5. In circumstances where two or more conflicting ethical principles or legal duties apply in social work contexts, I can determine their relative priority through the development and use of a case-specific conceptual screen.

_____   Subtotal

The Basic Interpersonal Skills of Talking and Listening

_____ 6. I can effectively use nonverbal communications and body language skills.

_____ 7. I can effectively use the talking skills.

_____ 8. I can effectively use the listening skills.

_____ 9. I can effectively use active-listening skills.

_____ Subtotal

The Preparing Skills

_____ 10. I can effectively use the preparatory reviewing skill.

_____ 11. I can effectively use the preparatory exploring skill.

_____ 12. I can effectively use the preparatory consulting skill.

_____ 13. I can effectively use the preparatory arranging skill.

_____ 14. I can effectively use the preparatory empathy skill.

_____ 15. I can effectively use the preparatory self-exploration skill.

_____ 16. I can effectively use the centering skill.

_____ 17. I can effectively use the preliminary planning and recording skills.

_____ Subtotal

The Beginning Skills

_____ 18. I can effectively use the skill of introducing myself.

_____ 19. I can effectively use the skill of seeking introductions.

_____ 20. I can effectively use the skill of describing initial purpose.

_____ 21. I can effectively use the skill of orienting clients.

_____ 22. I can effectively use the skill of discussing policy and ethical factors.

_____ 23. I can effectively use the skill of seeking feedback.

_____ Subtotal

The Exploring Skills

_____ 24. I can effectively use the skill of asking questions.

_____ 25. I can effectively use the skill of seeking clarification.

_____ 26. I can effectively use the skill of reflecting content.

_____ 27. I can effectively use the skill of reflecting feelings.

_____ 28. I can effectively use the skill of reflecting feeling and meaning.

_____ 29. I can effectively use the skill of partializing.

_____ 30. I can effectively use the skill of going beyond what is said.

_____ Subtotal

The Assessing Skills

_____ 31. I am proficient in organizing descriptive information for social work purposes.

_____ 32. I am proficient in formulating a professional quality social work assessment.

_____ Subtotal

The Contracting Skills

_____ 33. I can effectively use the skill of reflecting an issue.

_____ 34. I can effectively use the skill of identifying an issue.

_____ 35. I can effectively use the skill of clarifying issues for work.

_____ 36. I can effectively use the skill of establishing goals.

_____ 37. I can effectively use the skill of developing an action plan.

_____ 38. I can effectively use the skill of identifying action steps.

_____ 39. I can effectively use the skill of planning for evaluation.

_____ 40. I can effectively use the skill of summarizing a social work contract.

_____ Subtotal

The Working and Evaluating Skills

_____ 41. I can effectively use the skill of rehearsing action steps.

_____ 42. I can effectively use the skill of reviewing action steps.

_____ 43. I can effectively use the skill of evaluating.

_____ 44. I can effectively use the skill of focusing.

_____ 45. I can effectively use the skill of educating.

_____ 46. I can effectively use the skill of advising.

_____ 47. I can effectively use the representing skill.

_____ 48. I can effectively use the skill of responding with immediacy.

_____ 49. I can effectively use the skill of reframing.

_____ 50. I can effectively use the skill of confronting.

_____ 51. I can effectively use the skill of pointing out endings.

_____ 52. I can effectively use the skill of progress recording.

_____ Subtotal

The Ending Skills

_____ 53. I can effectively use the skill of reviewing the process.

_____ 54. I can effectively use the skill of communicating a final evaluation.

_____ 55. I can effectively use the skill of sharing ending feelings and saying goodbye.

_____ 56. I can effectively use the skill of recording a closing summary.

_____ Subtotal

_____ Total

This questionnaire provides you an indication of your self-appraised proficiency in the social work skills. Because it is based on your own beliefs about your proficiency, absolute scores are relatively unimportant. Rather, use the results as a stimulus both to ask yourself further questions concerning your competency with various skills and to develop plans by which to improve your proficiency in those skill areas that need additional study and practice. You may complete the questionnaire at various points throughout the learning process. Increased proficiency may be reflected in changing scores over time. In considering your results, please remember that a higher rating suggests a higher level of appraised proficiency.

To score the Social Work Skills Self-Appraisal Questionnaire, simply sum the total of your ratings to the 56 items. Your score should range somewhere between 56 and 224. A higher score suggests a higher level of appraised proficiency. In theory, a score of 168 (or an average of 3 on the 56 items) would indicate that, on average, you "agree" with statements suggesting that you are proficient in understanding and using the 56 skills. Please note, however, that such an average score does not necessarily indicate that you believe that you are proficient in all of the skills. You might obtain such a score by rating several items at the "4" or "strongly agree" level and an equal number at the "2" or "disagree level." Therefore, you should look carefully at your rating for each item as well as the subtotals for each skill area.

Finally, you should recognize that this questionnaire reflects your own subjective opinions. You may consciously or unconsciously overestimate or perhaps even underestimate your proficiency in these skills. Therefore, please use the results in conjunction with other evidence about your actual proficiency in the skills.

Appendix 4

Alphabetized List of Feeling Words

abandoned
abased
abashed
abdicated
abducted
abhor
abominable
abrasive
abrupt
accepted
acclaimed
accused
accustomed
achieved
acknowledged
acquiesced
acrimonious
adamant
adapted
adept
adjusted
admired
admonished
adored
adrift
adventurous
adverse

advocated
affected
affectionate
affinity
afraid
aggravated
aggressive
aggrieved
aghast
agile
agitate
aglow
agony
agonized
agreeable
aimless
alarmed
alarming
alienated
alive
alleviate
alluring
alone
aloof
altruistic
amazed
ambiguous

ambitious
ambivalent
ameliorate
amicable
amused
anemic
angelic
angry
angst
anguish
animosity
annoyed
anomie
anonymous
antagonistic
antagonized
anticipation
antsy
anxious
apathetic
apocalyptic
apologetic
appalling
appetizing
apprehensive
approachable
approving

arbitrary
arcane
archaic
ardent
ardor
arduous
argumentative
arresting
arrogant
artificial
ashamed
assailed
assaulted
assertive
assuaged
assured
astonished
astounding
attuned
attached
attentive
attracted
audacious
auspicious
aversive
awarded
awful

back-sided
backstabbed
bad
balanced
balked
bamboozled
banking
barrage
bashful
basic
battered
bawdy
beaming
beaten
beautiful
beckoning
becoming
bedazzled
bedeviled
bedraggled
befuddled
begrudging
beguiling
beholden
belittled
bellicose
belligerent
belonging
bemoan
beneficent
benign
berated
bereaved
bereft
bested
betrayed
beware
bewildered
bewitched
biased
bidden
bigoted
bitter
blah
blamed
bleary
blessed
blissful
blocked
blue
blunted
blushed
bogged-down
boggled
bolstered
bonded
bored

botched
bothered
boundless
bountiful
boxed-in
braced
branded
brave
brazen
breached
bright
brilliant
brisk
broached
broken
browbeaten
bruised
brushed-off
brutalized
bucking
buck-passing
bugged
bulldozed
bullied
buoyant
burdened
burned
burned out
busted
butchered
cakewalk
calculating
calling
callous
callow
calm
cancerous
candid
canned
capitulated
capricious
capsulated
captivated
captive
care
carefree
careful
careless
caretaking
caring
caroused
carping
cast-off
cataclysmic
catalyst
catapulted
catastrophic

catharsis
caught
caustic
cautious
celibate
cemented
censored
censured
certain
challenged
chancy
changeable
charismatic
charitable
charmed
charming
chased
chaste
cheap
cheapened
cheeky
cheered
cheerful
cheesy
cherished
chivalrous
chummy
chump
civil
clammy
clandestine
clean
cocksure
coherent
cohesive
coincidental
cold
cold-blooded
cold-shouldered
collared
collusive
combative
combustible
comfortable
come-on
coming-out
commanded
committed
compartmentalized
compassionate
compelling
compensated
competent
complacent
complementary
complete
compliant

complicated
complimented
composed
comprehensible
comprehensive
compressed
compromised
concentrating
concerned
conciliatory
conclusive
concocted
condemned
condescending
condoned
conducive
confident
confined
conflicted
congenial
congratulated
congruent
connected
conquered
conscientious
considerate
considered
consoled
consoling
conspiratorial
constant
consternation
constrained
constricted
constructive
contaminated
contemplative
contented
contentious
contributory
convenient
convinced
convincing
cool
corrected
corroborate
corrosive
cosmetic
counted
countered
courageous
courteous
covered
cowardly
cozy
crabby
crafty

craggy
crappy
credible
creepy
crestfallen
cried
cringe
critical
criticize
crooked
cross
crossed
crucified
cruddy
crummy
crushed
crystallized
curative
curious
cursed
cutoff
dangerous
debased
dejected
demeaned
demure
denigrated
depressed
detached
determined
devoted
disappointed
disapproval
disbelief
disgust
dismal
dismayed
displeased
distant
distasteful
distrust
disturbed
doubtful
dubious
ecstatic
elated
elevated
embarrassed
empty
enamored
energetic
enervated
enraged
enriched
enthusiastic
entrusted
envious

euphoric
exasperated
excited
exhausted
fantastic
fearful
fearless
ferocious
flighty
flustered
fondness
forgiveness
forgotten
forsaken
frazzled
friendly
frightened
frustrated
gagged
galvanized
gamy
garrulous
gawky
generous
genial
gentle
genuine
glad
glee
glib
gloomy
glow
glum
golden
good
graceful
graceless
gracious
grand
great
greedy
green
gregarious
grief
grim
gross
gruesome
gruff
grubby
grumpy
grungy
guarded
guilty
guiltless
gullible
gutsy
gutted

haggard
hammered
hamstrung
handcuffed
handicapped
handy
hang-dogged
hapless
happy
harassed
hard
hard-boiled
hard-edged
hardheaded
hardy
harmful
harmless
harried
hate
hated
haunting
hazardous
hazy
healthful
healthy
heartache
heartbroken
heartless
heartsick
heartwarming
helpful
helpless
hesitant
high-spirited
hoggish
hog-tied
homesick
honorable
hope
hopeful
hopeless
horny
horrendous
horrible
horrified
hostile
hot
hot-blooded
hotheaded
huffy
humble
hungry
hung up
hurried
hurt
hyped
hysterical

ice-cold
idiotic
idyllic
ignominious
ill at ease
impatient
impersonal
impetuous
impotent
impressive
impulsive
inadequate
incoherent
incompetent
incomplete
inconsiderate
indebted
indecisive
independent
indestructible
indifferent
indignant
indiscreet
indispensable
indulgent
inept
infantile
infatuated
inferior
inhibited
injurious
innocent
insane
insatiable
insolent
inspirational
intense
interested
intimate
intolerable
intolerant
intoxicated
intrusive
invincible
irate
irritable
irritated
itchy
jaded
jagged
jaundiced
jaunty
jealous
jerky
jolly
joyful
joyless

joyous
jubilant
judged
judgmental
just
keen
kind
kindhearted
kinky
kooky
laborious
lenient
light-headed
lighthearted
limited
lonely
lonesome
loss
lost
lousy
lovable
love
lovely
lovesick
love-struck
low
loyal
luckless
lucky
ludicrous
lukewarm
mad
maddening
magical
magnanimous
magnetic
magnificent
majestic
maladjusted
malaise
malicious
malignant
manic
manipulated
manipulative
martyred
masterful
mature
mean
meaningful
meaningless
mean-spirited
mediocre
meditative
melancholy
mellow
melodramatic

mercurial
methodical
mind-boggling
mindful
mindless
mischievous
miserable
mistrust
misty
misunderstood
monotonous
monstrous
monumental
moody
mortified
motivated
mournful
muddled
murky
mushy
mysterious
nasty
natural
naughty
nauseous
necessary
needful
needy
negative
neglected
neglectful
nervous
nice
noble
normal
nostalgic
nosy
noteworthy
notorious
oafish
obdurate
obedient
object
obligated
obnoxious
obscene
obstinate
obstructionist
odd
odious
offensive
onerous
optimistic
ornery
outrage
outrageous
pained

panic
panic-stricken
paranoid
passionate
passive
patchy
patient
peaceful
penalized
permissive
perplexed
persecuted
persistent
personable
pessimistic
petty
petulant
phobic
phony
picky
pitiful
pivotal
pleasing
pleasurable
plentiful
poetic
poignant
poisonous
polluted
pout
praised
praiseworthy
prejudicial
pressure
presumptuous
prickly
pride
prideful
protective
proud
prudish
pulled
pushed
put-off
puzzled
quake
qualified
qualm
quandary
quarrelsome
queasy
quizzical
radiant
radiate
radical
rage
ragged

rancor
raped
rapture
rash
raucous
raunchy
rebellious
rebuffed
recalcitrant
reckless
reclusive
refreshed
regretful
reinvigorate
rejected
rejoice
rejuvenated
relaxed
released
relentless
relieved
relish
reluctant
remorse
remorseful
remorseless
remote
renewed
repellent
repentant
reprehensible
reprimanded
reproached
repugnant
repulsive
resentful
resentment
reserved
resigned
resilient
resistant
resolute
resolved
resourceful
respectful
responsible
responsive
restful
restless
restricted
reticent
retiring
revolting
revulsion
rewarding
ridiculed
risky

rosy
rotten
rough
rude
rueful
rugged
ruined
rundown
rush
rushed
sacked
sacred
sacrificial
sacrilegious
sacrosanct
sad
saddled
safe
sanctified
sanctimonious
sanguine
satisfied
scandalized
scandalous
scapegoated
scarce
scared
scarred
scattered
scrambled
scrapped
scrawny
searching
seasoned
secure
sedated
seductive
seedy
seeking
sensational
sensitive
sensual
sentimental
serious
settled
severe
sexual
shady
shaggy
shaken
shaky
shame
shameful
shameless
sheepish
shifty
shocked

shortchanged
shunned
sick
sickening
sincere
sinful
singled-out
sinister
skeptical
sleazy
sleepless
sleepy
slick
smug
soiled
solemn
solid
sordid
sorrow
spacey
spellbound
spiritual
spiteful
splendid
split
spoiled
spooky
squeamish
stable
stalked
steady
stern
stilted
stodgy
stressed
stretched
strong
strung-out
stuck
stumped
stunned
sullen
sunk
super
supported
supportive
surly
surprised
suspicious
sympathetic
taboo
taciturn
tacky
tactful
tactless
tainted
taken

taken-in
tangled
tattered
teased
tedious
teed-off
tempted
tempting
tenacious
tender
tension
tenuous
terminal
terrible
terrific
terrified
terrorized
testy
thankful
therapeutic
thick-skinned
thin-skinned
thoughtful
thoughtless
thrashed
threatened
threatening
thrifty
thrilled
thrilling
thunderstruck
ticked
ticked-off
timid
tingle
tingling
tired
tireless
tiresome
tolerate
torment
torpid
touched
tough
toxic
tragic
tranquil
transcendent
transformed
trapped
trashed
traumatic
treacherous
tricked
tricky
triggered
tripped

triumphant
trivial
troubled
troubling
trust
tuckered
turbulent
turned-off
turned-on
twinkling
tyrannized
ubiquitous
ugly
umbrage
unabashed
unaccepted
unaccustomed
unacknowledged
unappealing
unappreciated
unashamed
unbearable
uncared-for
uncertain
unclean
uncomfortable
undaunted
undecided
understood
undesirable
undisturbed
unequal
unfaithful
unfavorable
unglued
unified
unimportant
united
unjust
unkind
unlucky
unpleasant
unproductive
unreasonable
unrelenting
unrelentless
unrepentant
unresponsive
unsafe
unselfconscious
unselfish
unstable
upbeat
uprooted
upstaged
uptight
urgent

vacant
vain
valiant
valued
vandalized
vengeful
victimized
victorious
vigilant
vigorous
vindicated
virtuous
violated
violent
vital

vitriolic
vituperative
vulnerable
wacky
wane
wanted
wanting
washed-out
washed-up
wasted
weak
weakened
well-adjusted
well-balanced
well-intentioned

well-meaning
well-rounded
wicked
wide-awake
wide-eyed
wild
wild-eyed
wily
winced
winded
wiped-out
wired
wishful
withdrawn
wobbly

wonderful
wondrous
worried
worthless
worthwhile
worthy
wounded
wretched
wrought-up
xenophobic
yielded
yielding
zealous
zestful

Appendix 5

Social Work Skills Interview Rating Form[1]

You may use this rating form as part of the process of evaluating your own or others' performance of the social work skills during interviews with clients. You may use it, for example, in rating your performance during an interview with an individual, a couple, a family, or a small group. You may also use the form to provide evaluative feedback to a colleague who is attempting to improve the quality of his or her performance.

In using the rating form, please use the following coding system:

N/A   During the course of the interview, the skill in question was not appropriate or necessary and was therefore not used, having no effect on the interview.

−3   During the course of the interview, the skill in question was used at an inappropriate time or in an unsuitable context, seriously detracting from the interview.

−2   During the course of the interview, the skill in question was attempted at an appropriate time and in a suitable context but was done so in an incompetent manner, significantly detracting from the interview.

−1   During the course of the interview, the skill in question was not used at times or in contexts when it should have been, detracting from the interview.

 0   During the course of the interview, the skill in question was used and demonstrated at a minimal level of competence. Its use did not detract from nor contribute to the interview.

+1   During the course of the interview, the skill in question was attempted at an appropriate time and in a suitable context and was generally demonstrated at a fair level of competence. Its use represented a small contribution to the interview.

+2   During the course of the interview, the skill in question was attempted at an appropriate time and in a suitable context and was generally demonstrated at a moderate level of competence. Its use represented a significant contribution to the interview.

+3   During the course of the interview, the skill in question was attempted at an appropriate

---

[1]Because this rating form is intended for the purpose of evaluating social work skills used during face-to-face interviews, skills related to ethical decision making, assessing, and recording are not included.

time and in a suitable context and was generally demonstrated at a good level of competence. Its use represented a substantial contribution to the interview.

+4   During the course of the interview, the skill in question was attempted at an appropriate time and in a suitable context and was generally demonstrated at a superior level of performance. Its use represented a major contribution to the interview.

Talking and Listening: The Basic Interpersonal Skills

1. **Speech and Language**
   Comments:

   N/A −3 −2 −1 0 +1 +2 +3 +4

2. **Body Language**
   Comments:

   N/A −3 −2 −1 0 +1 +2 +3 +4

3. **Hearing**
   Comments:

   N/A −3 −2 −1 0 +1 +2 +3 +4

4. **Observing**
   Comments:

   N/A −3 −2 −1 0 +1 +2 +3 +4

5. **Encouraging**
   Comments:

   N/A −3 −2 −1 0 +1 +2 +3 +4

6. **Remembering**
   Comments:

   N/A −3 −2 −1 0 +1 +2 +3 +4

7. **Active Listening**
   Comments:

   N/A −3 −2 −1 0 +1 +2 +3 +4

Beginning

8. **Introducing Yourself**
   Comments:

   N/A −3 −2 −1 0 +1 +2 +3 +4

9. **Seeking Introductions**
   Comments:

   N/A −3 −2 −1 0 +1 +2 +3 +4

10. **Describing Initial Purpose**

    N/A −3 −2 −1 0 +1 +2 +3 +4

Comments:

11. Orienting Clients   N/A −3 −2 −1 0 +1 +2 +3 +4
     Comments:

12. Discussing Policy   N/A −3 −2 −1 0 +1 +2 +3 +4
     and Ethical Factors
     Comments:

13. Seeking Feedback   N/A −3 −2 −1 0 +1 +2 +3 +4
     Comments:

Exploring

14. Asking Questions   N/A −3 −2 −1 0 +1 +2 +3 +4
     Comments:

15. Seeking Clarification   N/A −3 −2 −1 0 +1 +2 +3 +4
     Comments:

16. Reflecting Content   N/A −3 −2 −1 0 +1 +2 +3 +4
     Comments:

17. Reflecting Feelings   N/A −3 −2 −1 0 +1 +2 +3 +4
     Comments:

18. Reflecting Feeling and Meaning   N/A −3 −2 −1 0 +1 +2 +3 +4
     Comments:

19. Partializing   N/A −3 −2 −1 0 +1 +2 +3 +4
     Comments:

20. Going Beyond What Is Said   N/A −3 −2 −1 0 +1 +2 +3 +4
     Comments:

Contracting

21. Reflecting an Issue   N/A −3 −2 −1 0 +1 +2 +3 +4
     Comments:

22. Identifying an Issue   N/A −3 −2 −1 0 +1 +2 +3 +4

Comments:

23. Clarifying Issues for Work
    Comments:

    N/A −3 −2 −1 0 +1 +2 +3 +4

24. Establishing Goals
    Comments:

    N/A −3 −2 −1 0 +1 +2 +3 +4

25. Developing an Action Plan
    Comments:

    N/A −3 −2 −1 0 +1 +2 +3 +4

26. Identifying Action Steps
    Comments:

    N/A −3 −2 −1 0 +1 +2 +3 +4

27. Planning for Evaluation
    Comments:

    N/A −3 −2 −1 0 +1 +2 +3 +4

28. Summarizing the Contract
    Comments:

    N/A −3 −2 −1 0 +1 +2 +3 +4

Working and Evaluating

29. Rehearsing Action Steps
    Comments:

    N/A −3 −2 −1 0 +1 +2 +3 +4

30. Reviewing Action Steps
    Comments:

    N/A −3 −2 −1 0 +1 +2 +3 +4

31. Evaluating
    Comments:

    N/A −3 −2 −1 0 +1 +2 +3 +4

32. Focusing
    Comments:

    N/A −3 −2 −1 0 +1 +2 +3 +4

33. Educating
    Comments:

    N/A −3 −2 −1 0 +1 +2 +3 +4

34. Advising
    Comments:

    N/A −3 −2 −1 0 +1 +2 +3 +4

35. Representing
    Comments:

    N/A −3 −2 −1 0 +1 +2 +3 +4

36. Responding with Immediacy

    N/A −3 −2 −1 0 +1 +2 +3 +4

Comments:

37. **Reframing**   N/A −3 −2 −1 0 +1 +2 +3 +4
    Comments:

38. **Confronting**   N/A −3 −2 −1 0 +1 +2 +3 +4
    Comments:

39. **Pointing Out Endings**   N/A −3 −2 −1 0 +1 +2 +3 +4
    Comments:

Ending

40. **Reviewing the Process**   N/A −3 −2 −1 0 +1 +2 +3 +4
    Comments:

41. **Final Evaluating**   N/A −3 −2 −1 0 +1 +2 +3 +4
    Comments:

42. **Sharing Ending Feelings**   N/A −3 −2 −1 0 +1 +2 +3 +4
    and Saying Goodbye
    Comments:

References

Abramson, J. S., Donnelly, J., King, M. A., & Mailick, M. D. (1993). Disagreements in discharge planning: A normative phenomenon. *Health and Social Work, 18*(1), 57–64.

Acevedo, G., & Morales, J. (2001). Assessment with Latino/Hispanic communities. In R. Fong & S. Furuto (Eds.), *Culturally competent practice* (pp. 147–162). Boston: Allyn & Bacon.

Aguilar, I. (1972). Initial contacts with Mexican American families. *Social Work, 17*, 66–70.

Altmann, H. (1973). Effects of empathy, warmth and genuineness in the initial counseling interview. *Counselor Education and Supervision, 12*, 225–229.

Altshuler, S. J. (1999). Constructing genograms with children in care: Implications for casework practice. *Child Welfare, 78*(6), 777–790.

American Psychiatric Association. (1996). *American Psychiatric Association practice guidelines*. Washington, D.C.: Author.

American Psychiatric Association. (1997a). Practice guideline for the treatment of patients with Alzheimer's disease and other dementias of late life. *American Journal of Psychiatry, 154*(5, Supplement).

American Psychiatric Association. (1997b). *Practice guideline for the treatment of patients with schizophrenia* (Vol. 154). Washington, D.C.: Author.

American Psychiatric Association. (2000). *Diagnostic and statistical manual, fourth edition, text revision (DSM-IV-TR)*. Washington, DC: Author.

Arredondo, P. (1998). Integrating multicultural counseling competencies and universal helping conditions in culture-specific contexts. *The Counseling Psychologist, 26*(4), 592–601.

Arredondo, P., & Arciniega, G. M. (2001). Strategies and techniques for counselor training based on the multicultural counseling competencies. *Journal of Multicultural Counseling and Development, 29*(4), 263–273.

Arredondo, P., Toporek, R., Brown, S., Jones, J., Locke, D. C., Sanchez, J., et al. (1996). *Operationalization of the multicultural counseling competencies*. Alexandria, VA: Association for Multicultural Counseling and Development.

Asay, T. P., & Lambert, M. J. (1999). The empirical case for the common factors in therapy: Quantitative factors. In B. L. Duncan & M. A. Hubble (Eds.), *The heart and soul of change: What works in therapy* (pp. 23–55). Washington, DC: American Psychological Association.

Association of Social Work Boards. (2002). *ASWB home page*. Retrieved March 15, 2003, from http://www .aswb.org/

Atkins, D. M., & Patenaude, A. F. (1987). Psychosocial preparation and follow-up for pediatric bone marrow transplant patients. *American Journal of Orthopsychiatry, 57*(2), 246–252.

Austin, D. M. (1997). The profession of social work: In the second century. In M. Reisch & E. Gambrill (Eds.), *Social work in the 21st century* (pp. 376–386). Thousand Oaks, CA: Pine Forge Press.

Baer, J. S., Kivlahan, D. R., & Donovan, D. M. (2000). Combining skills training, motivational enhancement proves effective. *The Brown University Digest of Addiction Theory and Application, 19*(1), 1.

Baker, M. R., & Steiner, J. R. (1996). Solution-focused social work: Metamessages to students in higher education opportunity programs. In P. L. Ewalt, E. M. Freeman, S. A. Kirk & D. L. Poole (Eds.), *Multicultural issues in social work* (pp. 295–309). Washington DC: NASW Press.

Bandler, R., & Grinder, J. (1979). *Frogs into princes: Neuro-linguistic programming*. Moab, UT: Real People.

Bandler, R., & Grinder, J. (1982). *Reframing: Neuro-linguistic programming and the transformation of meaning*. Moab, UT: Real People.

Barker, R. L. (1995). *The social work dictionary* (3rd ed.). [CD-ROM] Washington, D.C.: National Association of Social Workers.

Bartlett, H. (1970). *The common base of social work practice*. New York: National Association of Social Workers.

Basow, S. A., & Rubenfeld, K. (2003). "Troubles talk": Effects of gender and gender-typing. *Sex Roles: A Journal of Research, 48*, 183–187.

Batson, C. D., Early, S., & Salvarani, G. (1997). Perspective taking: Imagining how another feels versus imagining how you would feel. *Personality & Social Psychology Bulletin, 23*(7), 751–759.

Beauchamp, T. L., & Childress, J. F. (1983). *Principles of biomedical ethics* (2nd ed.). New York: Oxford University Press.

Berg, I. K. (1994). *Family-based services: A solution-focused approach*. New York: W.W. Norton.

Berg, I. K., & De Jong, P. (1996). Solution-building conversations: Co-constructing a sense of competence with clients. *Families in Society, 77*, 376–391.

Berg, I. K., & Reuss, N. H. (1998). *Solutions step by step: A substance abuse treatment manual*. New York: Norton.

Berne, E. (1964). *Games people play: The psychology of human relationships*. New York: Ballantine Books.

Besharov, D. J., & Besharov, S. H. (1987). Teaching about liability. *Social Work, 32*(6), 517–522.

Beyer, B. K. (1988). *Developing a thinking skills program*. Boston: Allyn & Bacon.

Bird, M. Y. (2001). Critical values and first nation peoples. In R. Fong & S. Furuto (Eds.), *Culturally competent practice* (pp. 61–74). Boston: Allyn & Bacon.

Birdsall, B. A., & Miller, L. D. (2002). Brief counseling in the schools: A solution-focused approach for school counselors. *Counseling and Human Development, 35*(2), 1–10.

Bisman, C. D. (1999). Social work assessment: Case theory construction. *Families in Society: The Journal of Contemporary Human Services, 80*(3), 240–247.

Blount, M., Thyer, B. A., & Frye, T. (1992). Social work practice with Native Americans. In D. F. Harrison, J. S. Wodarski & B. A. Thyer (Eds.), *Cultural diversity and social work practice* (pp. 107–134). Springfield, IL: Charles C. Thomas.

Bohart, A. C., & Greenberg, L. S. (1997). Empathy and psychotherapy: An introductory overview. In A. C. Bohart & L. S. Greenberg (Eds.), *Empathy reconsidered: New directions in psychotherapy* (pp. 3–31). Washington, DC: American Psychological Association.

Bozarth, J. D. (1997). Empathy from the framework of client-centered theory and the Rogerian hypothesis. In A. C. Bohart & L. S. Greenberg (Eds.), *Empathy reconsidered: New directions in psychotherapy* (pp. 81–102). Washington, DC: American Psychological Association.

Bradford, L., Meyers, R. A. & Kane, K. A. (1999). Latino expectations of communicative competence: A focus group interview study. *Communication Quarterly, 47*(1), 98–115.

Braithwaite, D. O. (2000). *Handbook of communication and people with disabilities: Research and application*. Mahwah, NJ: Lawrence Erlbaum.

Brammer, R. (2004). *Diversity in counseling*. Pacific Grove, CA: Brooks/Cole.

Branch, W. T., & Malik, T. K. (1993). Using "windows of opportunities" in brief interviews to understand patients' concerns. *The Journal of the American Medical Association, 269*(13), 1667–1669.

Brissett-Chapman, S. (1995). Child abuse and neglect: Direct practice. In R. L. Edwards (Ed.), *Encyclopedia of social work* (19th ed., Vol. 1, pp. 353–366). Washington, DC: NASW.

Budd, R. J., & Rollnick, S. (1996). The structure of the Readiness to Change Questionnaire: A test of Prochaska & DiClemente's transtheoretical model. *British Journal of Health Psychology, 1,* 365–376.

Burchum, J. L. R. (2002). Cultural competence: An evolutionary perspective. *Nursing Forum, 37*(4), 5–15.

Burrill, G. (1976). The problem-oriented log in social casework. *Social Work, 21*(1), 67–68.

Campbell, D. (1974). *If you don't know where you're going you'll probably end up somewhere else.* Niles, IL: Argus Communications.

Campbell, J. (1972). *The hero with a thousand faces* (2nd ed.). Princeton, NJ: Princeton University Press.

Campbell, J. (1986). *The inner reaches of outer space: Metaphor as myth and as religion.* New York: Perennial Library.

Campbell, J., & Moyers, B. (1988). *The power of myth* (2nd ed.). New York: Doubleday.

Caplan, R. B., & Caplan, G. (2001). *Helping the helpers not to harm: Iatrogenic damage and community mental health.* New York: Brunner-Routledge.

Carkhuff, R. R. (1969). *Helping and human relations* (Vol. 1 & 2). New York: Holt, Rinehart and Winston.

Carkhuff, R. R. (1987). *The art of helping VI.* Amherst, MA: Human Resource Development Press.

Carkhuff, R. R., & Anthony, W. A. (1979). *The skills of helping.* Amherst, MA: Human Resource Development.

Carkhuff, R. R., & Truax, C. B. (1965). Training in counseling and psychotherapy. *Journal of Consulting Psychology, 29,* 333–336.

Carter, C. S. (1997). Ladies don't: A historical perspective on attitudes toward alcoholic women. *Affilia Journal of Women and Social Work, 12*(4), 471–485.

Cascio, T. (1998). Incorporating spirituality into social work practice: A review of what to do. *Families in Society: The Journal of Contemporary Human Services, 79*(5), 523–532.

Castex, G. M. (1996). Providing services to Hispanic/Latino populations: Profiles in diversity. In P. L. Ewalt, E. M. Freeman, S. A. Kirk & D. L. Poole (Eds.), *Multicultural issues in social work* (pp. 523–538). Washington DC: NASW Press.

Christ, W. R., Clarkin, J. F., & Hull, J. W. (1994). A high-risk screen for psychiatric discharge planning. *Health and Social Work, 19*(4), 261–270.

Chung, R. C.-Y., & Bemak, F. (2002). The relationship of culture and empathy in cross-cultural counseling. *Journal of Counseling and Development, 80*(2), 154–160.

Clark, M. (1997). Strengths-based practice: The new paradigm. *Corrections Today, 49*(2), 110–111, 165.

Clark, R. A. (1993). Men's and women's self-confidence in persuasive, comforting, and justificatory communicative tasks. *Sex Roles: A Journal of Research, 28,* 553–568.

Clemens, E. L. (1995). Multiple perceptions of discharge planning in one urban hospital. *Health and Social Work, 20*(4), 254–261.

Compton, B., & Galaway, B. (Eds.). (1989). *Social work processes* (4th ed.). Belmont, CA: Wadsworth.

Compton, B. R., & Galaway, B. (Eds.). (1994). *Social work processes* (5th ed.). Pacific Grove, CA: Brooks/Cole.

Compton, B. R., & Galaway, B. (Eds.). (1999). *Social work processes* (6th ed.). Pacific Grove, CA: Brooks/Cole.

Congress, E. P. (1994). The use of culturalgrams to assess and empower culturally diverse families. *Families in Society, 75,* 531–540.

Congress, E. P. (1999). *Social work values and ethics: Identifying and resolving ethical dilemmas.* Belmont, CA: Wadsworth.

Congress, E. P. (2000). What social workers should know about ethics: Understanding and resolving ethical dilemmas. *Advances in Social Work, 1*(1), 1–25.

Corcoran, J., & Stephenson, M. (2000). The effectiveness of solution-focused therapy with child behavior problems: A preliminary report. *Families in Society: The Journal of Contemporary Human Services, 81*(5), 468–474.

Corcoran, K., & Fischer, J. (1987). *Measures for clinical practice: A sourcebook.* New York: Free Press.

Corcoran, K., & Fischer, J. (2000a). *Measures for clinical practice: A sourcebook, Vol. 1: Couples, families, and children* (3rd ed.). New York: Free Press.

Corcoran, K., & Fischer, J. (2000b). *Measures for clinical practice: A sourcebook, Vol. 2: Adults* (3rd ed.). New York: Free Press.

Corey, G., Corey, M. S., & Callanan, P. (2003). *Issues and ethics in the helping professions* (6th ed.). Pacific Grove, CA: Brooks/Cole.

Council on Social Work Education. (2001). *Educational Policy and Accreditation Standards.* Alexandria, VA: Author.

Cournoyer, B. R. (1994). *A study of self-esteem, acceptance of others, and assertiveness among beginning MSW students*. Indianapolis: Indiana University School of Social Work.

Cournoyer, B. R. (1999). Unpublished data regarding foundation year MSW students' critical thinking and lifelong learning. Indianapolis, Indiana.

Cournoyer, B. R. (2003). Unpublished data regarding foundation year and concentration MSW students' critical thinking and lifelong learning. Indianapolis, Indiana.

Cowger, C. D. (1994). Assessing client strengths: Clinical assessment for client empowerment. *Social Work, 39*, 262–268.

Cowger, C. D. (1996). Assessment of client strengths. In D. Saleebey (Ed.), *The strengths perspective in social work practice* (2nd ed., pp. 59–73). New York: Longman.

Cox, C. B. (1996). Discharge planning for dementia patients: Factors influencing caregiver decisions and satisfaction. *Health and Social Work, 21*(2), 97–106.

Daly, A. (2001). A heuristic perspective of strengths in the African American community. In R. Fong & S. Furuto (Eds.), *Culturally competent practice* (pp. 241–254). Boston: Allyn & Bacon.

Davis, E. (2001). Evaluation skills with African American individuals and families: Three approaches. In R. Fong & S. Furuto (Eds.), *Culturally competent practice* (pp. 343–354). Boston: Allyn & Bacon.

Davis, S., & Botkin, J. (1994). The coming of knowledge-based businesses. *Harvard Business Review, 82*(September/October), 165–170.

De Jong, P., & Berg, I. K. (2001). Co-constructing cooperation with mandated clients. *Social Work, 46*(4), 361–374.

De Jong, P., & Berg, I. K. (2002). *Interviewing for solutions*. Pacific Grove, CA: Brooks/Cole.

de Shazer, S. (1988). *Clues: Investigating solutions in brief therapy*. New York: W. W. Norton.

Dean, R. G. (2001). The myth of cross-cultural competence. *Families in Society: The Journal of Contemporary Human Services, 82*(6), 623–630.

Dein, S. (1997). Mental health in a multiethnic society. *British Medical Journal, 315*(7106), 473–477.

Devore, W. (2001). "Whence came these people?" An exploration of the values and ethics of African American individuals, families, and communities. In R. Fong & S. Furuto (Eds.), *Culturally competent practice* (pp. 33–46). Boston: Allyn & Bacon.

DeWitt, T. G., & Roberts, K. B. (1995). Teaching residents about patient and practice termination in community-based continuity settings. *Archives of Pediatrics & Adolescent Medicine, 149*(12), 1367–1370.

Dilsaver, S. C. (1990). The mental status examination. *American Family Physician, 41*(5), 1489–1497.

Donahue, M. C. (1997). Empathy: Putting yourself in another person's shoes. *Current Health 2, a Weekly Reader publication, 24*(3), 22–25.

Duplass, J. A., & Ziedler, D. L. (2002). Critical thinking and logical argument. *Social Education, 66*(5), 113–127.

Edwards, R. L. (Ed.). (1995). *Encyclopedia of social work* (19th ed.). Washington, DC: NASW Press.

Edwards, R. L. (Ed.). (1997). *Encyclopedia of social work* (19th—Supplement ed.). Washington, DC: NASW Press.

Egan, G. (1982a). *Exercises in helping skills: A training manual to accompany the skilled helper* (2nd ed.). Monterey, CA: Brooks/Cole.

Egan, G. (1982b). *The skilled helper: Model, skills, and methods for effective helping* (2nd ed.). Monterey, CA: Brooks/Cole.

Epperson, D. L., Bushway, D. J., & Warman, R. E. (1983). Client self-terminations after one counseling session: Effects of problem recognition, counselor gender, and counselor experience. *Journal of Counseling Psychology, 30*, 307–315.

Erikson, E. H. (1963). *Childhood and society* (2nd ed.). New York: W. W. Norton.

Erikson, E. H. (1968). *Identity, youth and crisis* (2nd ed.). New York: W. W. Norton.

Etzioni, A. (1999). *The limits of privacy*. New York: Basic Books.

Everstine, D. S., & Everstine, L. (1983). *People in crisis: Strategic therapeutic interventions*. New York: Brunner/Mazel.

Everstine, L., Everstine, D. S., Heymann, G. M., True, D. H., Johnson, H. G., & Seiden, R. H. (1980). Privacy and confidentiality in psychotherapy. *American Psychologist, 35*, 828–840.

Fast, B., & Chapin, R. (1997). The strengths model with older adults. In D. Saleebey (Ed.), *The strengths perspective in social work practice* (2nd ed., pp. 115–132). New York: Longman.

Fey, W. F. (1955). Acceptance by others and its relation to acceptance of self and others: A revaluation. *Journal of Abnormal and Social Psychology, 30*, 274–276.

Fieldhouse, P., & Bunkowsky, L. (2002). Asphalt artisans: Creating a community eco-map on the playground. *Green Teacher, 67*, 16–19.

Fischer, J., & Corcoran, K. (1994a). *Measures for clinical practice: A sourcebook, Vol. 1: Couples, families, and children* (2nd ed.). New York: The Free Press.

Fischer, J., & Corcoran, K. (1994b). *Measures for clinical practice: A sourcebook, Vol. 2: Adults* (2nd ed.). New York: The Free Press.

Fletcher, J. F. (1966). *Situational ethics: The new morality.* Louisville, KY: Westminster John Knox Press.

Fong, R. (2001). Culturally competent social work practice: Past and present. In R. Fong & S. Furuto (Eds.), *Culturally competent practice* (pp. 1–9). Boston: Allyn & Bacon.

Fong, R. (2003). Cultural competence with Asian Americans. In D. Lum (Ed.), *Culturally competent practice: A framework for understanding diverse groups and justice issues* (2nd ed., pp. 261–281). Pacific Grove, CA: Brooks/Cole.

Fong, R., & Furuto, S. (Eds.). (2001). *Culturally competent practice.* Boston: Allyn & Bacon.

Frame, M. W. (2000). The spiritual genogram in family therapy. *Journal of Marital & Family Therapy, 26*(2), 211–216.

Franklin, J. C. (1997). Industry output and employment projections to 2006. *Monthly Labor Review* (November), 39–57.

Freeman, E. M. (1998). *Multisystem skills and interventions in school social work practice.* Washington, DC: NASW Press.

Fuller, R. W. (2002). *Somebodies and nobodies: Overcoming the abuse of rank.* Gabriola Island, BC, Canada: New Society Publishers.

Furuto, S. B. C. L., San Nicolas, R. J., Kim, G. E., & Fiaui, L. M. (2001). Interventions with Kanaka Maoli, Chamorro, and Samoan communities. In R. Fong & S. Furuto (Eds.), *Culturally competent practice* (pp. 327–342). Boston: Allyn & Bacon.

Galan, F. (2001). Intervention with Mexican American families. In R. Fong & S. Furuto (Eds.), *Culturally competent practice* (pp. 255–268). Boston: Allyn & Bacon.

Garrett, M. T., & Herring, R. D. (2001). Honoring the power of relation: Counseling native adults. *Journal of Humanistic Counseling, Education and Development, 40*(2), 139–161.

Garvin, C. (1987). *Contemporary group work* (2nd ed.). Englewood Cliffs, NJ: Prentice-Hall.

Garvin, C. (1997). *Contemporary group work* (3rd ed.). Boston: Allyn & Bacon.

Garvin, C., & Seabury, B. (1997). *Interpersonal practice in social work: Promoting competence and social justice* (2nd ed.). Boston: Allyn & Bacon.

Gelman, S. R., Pollack, D., & Weiner, A. (1999). Confidentiality of social work records in the computer age. *Social Work, 44*(3), 243–250.

General Assembly of the United Nations. (1948). *Universal declaration of human rights.* New York: Author.

Gibbs, L., & Gambrill, E. (1996). *Critical thinking for social workers: A workbook.* Thousand Oaks, CA: Pine Forge Press.

Gilbert, D. J., & Franklin, C. (2001). Developing culturally sensitive practice evaluation skills with Native American individuals and families. In R. Fong & S. Furuto (Eds.), *Culturally competent practice* (pp. 396–411). Boston: Allyn & Bacon.

Gilgun, J. F. (1999). An ecosystemic approach to assessment. In B. Compton & B. Galaway (Eds.), *Social work processes* (6th ed., pp. 66–77). Pacific Grove, CA: Brooks/Cole.

Gilligan, C. (1979). Woman's place in man's life cycle. *Harvard Educational Review, 49*(4), 431–446.

Gilligan, C. (1984). *In a different voice.* Cambridge, MA: Harvard University Press.

Gleeson, J. P., & Philbin, C. M. (1996). Preparing caseworkers for practice in kinship foster care: The supervisor's dilemma. *The Clinical Supervisor, 14*(1), 19–34.

Gliner, J. A., Morgan, G. A., & Harmon, R. J. (2000). Single-subject designs. *Journal of the American Academy of Child and Adolescent Psychiatry, 39*(10), 1327–1329.

Goldstein, H. (1987). The neglected moral link in social work practice. *Social Work, 32*, 181–186.

Good Tracks, J. (1973). Native American noninterference. *Social Work, 18*, 30–34.

Goodman, G., & Esterly, G. (1988). *The talk book: The intimate science of communicating in close relationships.* Emmaus, PA: Rodale.

Gray, J. (1992). *Men are from Mars, women are from Venus: A practical guide for improving communication and getting what you want in your relationships.* New York: HarperCollins.

Graybeal, C. (2001). Strengths-based social work assessment: Transforming the dominant paradigm. *Families in Society: The Journal of Contemporary Human Services, 82*(3), 233–242.

Greene, R. R. (Ed.). (2002). *Resiliency: An integrated approach to practice, policy, and research*. Washington, DC: NASW Press.

Hammond, D., Hepworth, D., & Smith, V. (1977). *Improving therapeutic communication*. San Francisco: Jossey-Bass.

Hansenfeld, Y. (1985). Organizational factors in service to groups. In M. Sundel, P. H. Glaser, R. Sarri & R. Vinter (Eds.), *Individual change through small groups* (2nd ed., pp. 294–309). New York: The Free Press.

Hanvey, C. P., & Philpot, T. (1994). *Practising social work*. New York: Routledge.

Hardy, K. V., & Laszloffy, T. A. (1995). The cultural genogram: Key to training culturally competent family therapists. *Journal of Marital and Family Therapy, 21*(3), 227–237.

Harrison, D. F., & Dziegielewski, S. (1992a). Social work practice with gay men, lesbian women and bisexual individuals. In D. F. Harrison, J. S. Wodarski & B. A. Thyer (Eds.), *Cultural diversity and social work practice* (pp. 135–156). Springfield, IL: Charles C. Thomas.

Harrison, D. F., & Dziegielewski, S. F. (1992b). Social work practice with the aged. In D. F. Harrison, J. S. Wodarski & B. A. Thyer (Eds.), *Cultural diversity and social work practice* (pp. 181–214). Springfield, IL: Charles C. Thomas.

Hartley, P. (1999). *Interpersonal communication*. London: Routledge.

Hartman, A., & Laird, J. (1983). *Family-centered social work practice*. New York: Free Press.

Hartman, B. L., & Wickey, J. M. (1978). The person-oriented record in treatment. *Social Work, 23*(4), 296–299.

Heart, M. Y. H. B. (2001). Culturally and historically congruent clinical social work interventions with Native clients. In R. Fong & S. Furuto (Eds.), *Culturally competent practice* (pp. 285–298). Boston: Allyn & Bacon.

Henry, S. (1981). *Group skills in social work*. Itasca, IL: F. E. Peacock.

Henry, S. (1992). *Group skills in social work* (2nd ed.). Pacific Grove, CA: Brooks/Cole.

Hepworth, D. H., Rooney, R. H., & Larsen, J. A. (2002). *Direct social work practice: Theory and skills* (6th ed.). Pacific Grove, CA: Brooks/Cole-Thomson Learning.

Herring, R. H. (1996). *Decision making with child abuse victims and their families in a pediatric setting: The use of the Hood Herring Risk Assessment Matrix (HHRAM)*. Unpublished doctoral dissertation, Howard University, Washington, DC.

Hess, H., & Hess, P. M. (1999). Termination in context. In B. Compton & B. Galaway (Eds.), *Social work processes* (6th ed., pp. 489–495). Pacific Grove, CA: Brooks/Cole.

Hill, C. E., & Gormally, J. (1977). Effect of reflection, restatement, probe, and nonverbal behaviors on client affect. *Journal of Counseling Psychology, 24*, 92–97.

Hobfoll, S. E., Jackson, A., Hobfoll, I., Pierce, C. A., & Young, S. (2002). The impact of communal-mastery versus self-mastery on emotional outcomes during stressful conditions: A prospective study of Native American women. *American Journal of Community Psychology, 30*(6), 853–871.

Hodge, D. R. (2000). Spiritual ecomaps: A new diagrammatic tool for assessing marital and family spirituality. *Journal of Marital and Family Therapy, 26*(2), 217–228.

Hodge, D. R. (2001). Spiritual genograms: A generational approach to assessing spirituality. *Families in Society, 82*(1), 35–48.

Hoffer, E. (1973). *Reflections on the human condition*. New York: Harper & Row.

Holden, G., Meenaghan, T., Anastas, J., & Metrey, G. (2002). Outcomes of social work education: The case for social work self-efficacy. *Journal of Social Work Education, 38*(1), 115–134.

Holmes, R. L. (2003). *Basic moral philosophy* (3rd ed.). Belmont, CA: Wadsworth.

Hopson, E. H., Hagen, T., & Hopson, J. L. (1999, August 16). You can heal emotional pain by "reframing" your past. *Knight Ridder/Tribune News Service*, K2265.

Hubble, M. A., Duncan, B. L., & Miller, S. D. (1999). Introduction. In B. L. Duncan & M. A. Hubble (Eds.), *The heart and soul of change: What works in therapy* (pp. 1–19). Washington, DC: American Psychological Association.

Hudson, W. (1982). *The clinical measurement package: A field manual*. Homewood, IL: Dorsey.

Hudson, W. W., & McMurtry, S. L. (1997). Comprehensive assessment in social work practice. *Research on Social Work Practice, 7*(1), 79–98.

International Federation of Social Workers. (2000). *Definition of social work*. Retrieved April 10, 2003, from http://www.ifsw.org/Publications/4.6e.pub.html

Ivey, A. E. (1971). *Microcounseling: Innovations in interview training*. Springfield, IL: Thomas.

Ivey, A. E. (1988). *Intentional interviewing and counseling: Facilitating client development* (2nd ed.). Pacific Grove, CA: Brooks/Cole.

Ivey, A. E., & Authier, J. (1978). *Microcounseling: Innovations in interviewing, counseling, psychotherapy, and psychoeducation.* Springfield, IL: Thomas.

Ivey, A. E., & Ivey, M. B. (1996). *Counseling and psychotherapy: A multicultural perspective.* Englewood Cliffs, NJ: Prentice-Hall.

Ivey, A. E., & Ivey, M. B. (2003). *Intentional interviewing and counseling: Facilitating client development in a multicultural society* (5th ed.). Pacific Grove, CA: Brooks/Cole.

Ivey, A. E., & Simek-Downing, L. (1980). *Counseling and psychotherapy: Skills, theories, and practice.* Englewood Cliffs, NJ: Prentice-Hall.

Ivey, A. E., Simek-Morgan, L., D'Andrea, M., Ivey, M. B., & D'Andrea, M. J. (2001). *Theories of counseling and psychotherapy: A multicultural perspective* (5th ed.). Boston: Allyn & Bacon.

Johnson, H. C. (1978). Integrating the problem-oriented record with a systems approach to case assessment. *Journal of Education for Social Work, 14*(3), 71–77.

Johnson, L. C. (1995). *Social work practice: A generalist approach* (5th ed.). Newton, MA: Allyn & Bacon.

Jonsen, A. R., & Toulmin, S. (1988). *The abuse of casuistry: A history of moral reasoning.* Berkeley: University of California Press.

Kadushin, A. (1983). *The social work interview* (2nd ed.). New York: Columbia University Press.

Kadushin, A., & Kadushin, G. (1997). *The social work interview: A guide for human service professionals* (4th ed.). New York: Columbia University Press.

Kagle, J. D. (1984). *Social work records.* Homewood, IL: Dorsey.

Kagle, J. D. (1991). *Social work records* (2nd ed.). Belmont, CA: Wadsworth.

Kagle, J. D. (2002). Record-keeping. In A. R. Roberts & G. J. Greene (Eds.), *Social workers' desk reference* (pp. 28–33). New York: Oxford University Press.

Kagle, J. D., & Kopels, S. (1994). Confidentiality after Tarasoff. *Health and Social Work, 19*(3), 217–223.

Kamya, H. A. (2000). Hardiness and spiritual well-being among social work students: Implications for social work education. *Journal of Social Work Education, 36*(2), 231–240.

Kanuha, V. K. (2001). Individual and family intervention skills with Asian and Pacific Island American lesbians and gay men. In R. Fong & S. Furuto (Eds.), *Culturally competent practice* (pp. 313–326). Boston: Allyn & Bacon.

Karls, J. M., & Lowery, C. T. (1997). The use of the PIE (person-in-environment) system in social work education. *Journal of Social Work Education, 33*(1), 49–59.

Karls, J. M., & Wandrei, K. E. (1992a). The person-in-environment system for classifying client problems. A new tool for more effective case management. *Journal of Case Management, 1*(3), 90–95.

Karls, J. M., & Wandrei, K. E. (1992b). PIE: A new language for social work. *Social Work, 37*(1), 80–85.

Karls, J. M., & Wandrei, K. E. (1994a). *PIE manual: Person-in-environment system: The PIE classification system for social functioning problems.* Washington, DC: NASW Press.

Karls, J. M., & Wandrei, K. E. (Eds.). (1994b). *Person-in-environment system: The PIE classification system for social functioning problems.* Washington, DC: NASW Press.

Karls, J. M., & Wandrei, K. E. (1995). Person-in-environment. In R. L. Edwards (Ed.), *Encyclopedia of social work* (19th ed., Vol. 3, pp. 1818–1827). Washington, DC: NASW Press.

Karpman, S. B. (1968). Fairy tales and script drama analysis. *Transactional Analysis Bulletin, 7*(26), 39–43.

Karpman, S. B. (1971). Options. *Transactional Analysis Journal, 1*(1), 79–87.

Kaufman, L., & Jones, R. L. (2003, May 23). Report finds flaws in inquiries on foster abuse in New Jersey. *The New York Times.*

Keefe, T. (1976). Empathy: The critical skill. *Social Work, 21,* 10–14.

Keiley, M. K., Dolbin, M., Hill, J., Karuppaswamy, N., Liu, T., Natrajan, R., et al. (2002). The cultural genogram: Experiences from within a marriage and family therapy training program. *Journal of Marital & Family Therapy, 28*(2), 165–178.

Keith-Lucas, A. (1972). *The giving and taking of help.* Chapel Hill: University of North Carolina Press.

Kinnier, R. T., Kernes, J. L., & Dautheribes, T. M. (2000). A short list of universal moral values. *Counseling and Values, 45*(1), 4–16.

Kiresuk, T., & Sherman, R. E. (1968). Goal attainment scaling: A general method for evaluating comprehensive community health programs. *Community Mental Health Journal, 4,* 443–453.

Kisthardt, W. E. (1997). The strengths model of case management: Principles and helping functions. In D. Saleebey (Ed.), *The strengths perspective in social work practice* (2nd ed., pp. 97–114). New York: Longman.

Kitchener, K. S. (2000). *Foundations of ethical practice, research, and teaching in psychology.* Mahwah, NJ: Lawrence Erlbaum.

Kitchens, J. M. (1994). Does this patient have an alcohol problem? *Journal of the American Medical Association, 272*(22), 1782–1788.

Koocher, G. P., & Keith-Spiegel, P. (1990). *Children, ethics, and the law: Professional issues and cases.* Lincoln: University of Nebraska Press.

Kovacs, P. J., & Bronstein, L. R. (1999). Preparation for oncology settings: What hospice social workers say they need. *Health and Social Work, 24*(1), 57–64.

Krill, D. F. (1986). *The beat worker: Humanizing social work & psychotherapy practice.* Lanham, MD: University Press of America.

Kubler-Ross, E. (1969). *On death and dying.* New York: Macmillan.

Kutchins, H. (1991). The fiduciary relationship: The legal basis for social workers' responsibilities to clients. *Social Work, 36*(2), 106–114.

LaFountain, R. M., & Garner, N. E. (1996). Solution-focused counseling groups: The results are in. *Journal for Specialists in Group Work, 21,* 128–143.

LaFromboise, T. D. (1992). An interpersonal analysis of affinity, clarification, and helpful responses with American Indians. *Professional Psychology: Research and Practice, 23,* 281–286.

Lambert, M. J. (1976). *The effects of psychotherapy.* New York: Human Sciences Press.

Lambert, M. J. (1982). Relation of helping skills to treatment outcome. In E. K. Marshall & P. D. Kurtz (Eds.), *Interpersonal helping skills: A guide to training methods, programs, and resources* (pp. 26–53). San Francisco: Jossey-Bass.

Lambert, M. J. (Ed.). (1983). *A guide to psychotherapy and patient relationships.* Homewood, IL: Dow Jones-Irwin.

Lambert, M. J. (1992). Implications of outcome research for psychotherapy integration. In J. C. Norcross & M. R. Goldfried (Eds.), *Handbook of psychotherapy integration* (pp. 94–129). New York: Basic Books.

Lambert, M. J. (Ed.). (2003). *Bergin and Garfield's handbook of psychotherapy and behavior change* (5th ed.). Hoboken, NJ: Wiley.

Lambert, M. J., & Bergin, A. E. (1994). The effectiveness of psychotherapy. In A. E. Bergin & S. L. Garfield (Eds.), *Handbook of psychotherapy and behavior change* (4th ed., pp. 143–189). New York: Wiley.

Lambert, M. J., & Cattani-Thompson, K. (1996). Current findings regarding the effectiveness of counseling: Implications for practice. *Journal of Counseling and Development, 74,* 601–608.

Lambert, M. J., Christensen, E. R., & DeJulio, S. S. (Eds.). (1983). *The assessment of psychotherapy outcome.* New York: Wiley.

Lambert, R. G., & Lambert, M. J. (1984). The effects of role preparation for psychotherapy on immigrant clients seeking mental health services in Hawaii. *Journal of Community Psychology, 12*(3), 263–275.

Lang, S. S. (2002). Social support networks trump number of parents. *Human Ecology, 30*(4), 24.

Lawsuit seeks discharge treatment-planning at NYC jails. (1999). *Mental Health Weekly, 9*(34), 1.

Lazarus, A. (1984). *In the mind's eye: The power of imagery for personal enrichment.* New York: Guilford.

Leaper, C. (1991). Influence and involvement in children's discourse: Age, gender, and partner effects. *Child Development, 62,* 797–811.

Lee, M. Y. (1997). A study of solution-focused brief family therapy: Outcomes and issues. *The American Journal of Family Therapy, 25,* 3–17.

Leigh, J. W. (1998). *Communicating for cultural competence.* Needham Heights, MA: Allyn & Bacon.

Leung, P., & Cheung, M. (2001). Competencies in practice evaluations with Asian American individuals and families. In R. Fong & S. Furuto (Eds.), *Culturally competent practice* (pp. 426–437). Boston: Allyn & Bacon.

Lewis, R., & Ho, M. (1975). Social work with Native Americans. *Social Work, 20,* 379–382.

Lie, G.-Y., & Lowery, C. T. (2003). Cultural competence with women of color. In D. Lum (Ed.), *Culturally competent practice: A framework for understanding diverse groups and justice issues* (2nd ed., pp. 282–308). Pacific Grove, CA: Brooks/Cole.

Lifton, D. E., Seay, S., & Bushko, A. (2000). Can student "hardiness" serve as an indicator of likely persistence to graduation? Baseline results from a longitudinal study. *Academic Exchange Quarterly, 4*(2), 73–81.

Linhorst, D. M., Hamilton, G., Young, E., & Eckert, A. (2002). Opportunities and barriers to empowering people with severe mental illness through participation in treatment planning. *Social Work, 47*(4), 425–434.

Lipchik, E. (2002). *Beyond technique in solution-focused therapy.* New York: Guilford Press.

Liu, W. M., & Clay, D. L. (2002). Multicultural counseling competencies: Guidelines in working with children and adolescents. *Journal of Mental Health Counseling, 24*(2), 177–187.

Loewenberg, F. M., Dolgoff, R., & Harrington, D. (2000). *Ethical decisions for social work practice* (6th ed.). Itasca, IL: F. E. Peacock.

MacKenzie, M. (1999). A brief solution-focused practice model. In B. Compton & B. Galaway (Eds.), *Social work processes* (3rd ed., pp. 314–319). Pacific Grove, CA: Brooks/Cole.

Maddi, S. R., Wadhwa, P., & Haier, R. J. (1996). Relationship of hardiness to alcohol and drug use in adolescents. *American Journal of Drug and Alcohol Abuse, 22*(2), 247–258.

Maluccio, A. (1979). *Learning from clients: Interpersonal helping as viewed by clients and social workers.* New York: The Free Press.

Marsh, J. C. (2002). Learning from clients. *Social Work, 47*(4), 341–344.

Marshall, E. K., Charping, J. W., & Bell, W. J. (1979). Interpersonal skills training: A review of the research. *Social Work Research and Abstracts, 15,* 10–16.

Marshall, E. K., Kurtz, P. D., & Associates. (1982). *Interpersonal helping skills: A guide to training methods, programs, and resources.* San Francisco: Jossey-Bass.

Martens, W. M., & Holmstrup, E. (1974). Problem-oriented recording. *Social Casework, 55*(9), 554–561.

Masten, A. S. (1994). Resilience in individual development: Successful adaptation despite risk and adversity. In M. C. Wang & E. W. Gordon (Eds.), *Education resilience in inner-city America: Challenges and prospects* (pp. 3–25). Hillsdale, NJ: Lawrence Erlbaum.

Mattaini, M. A. (1990). Contextual behavior analysis in the assessment process. *Families in Society, 2,* 425–444.

Mattaini, M. A. (1995). Visualizing practice with children and families. *Early Child Development and Care, 106,* 59–74.

Mattison, M. (2000). Ethical decision making: The person in the process. *Social Work, 45*(3), 201–212.

McGoldrick, M., & Gerson, R. (1985). *Genograms in family assessment.* New York: Norton.

McGoldrick, M., Gerson, R., & Shellenberger, S. (1999). *Genograms: Assessment and interventions* (2nd ed.). New York: Norton.

McMillen, J. C., & Groze, V. (1994). Using placement genograms in child welfare practice. *Child Welfare, 73*(4), 307–318.

McPeck, J. E. (1990). *Teaching critical thinking: Dialogue and dialectic.* New York: Routledge.

McRoy, R. (2003). Cultural competence with African Americans. In D. Lum (Ed.), *Culturally competent practice: A framework for understanding diverse groups and justice issues* (2nd ed., pp. 217–237). Pacific Grove, CA: Brooks/Cole.

McWhirter, D. A., & Bible, J. D. (1992). *Privacy as a constitutional right: Sex, drugs, and the right to life.* New York: Quorum Books.

Metcalf, L. (1995). *Counseling toward solutions: A practical solution-focused program for working with students, teachers, and parents.* West Nyack, NY: The Center for Applied Research in Education.

Meyer, C. H. (1993). *Assessment in social work practice.* New York: Columbia University Press.

Meyer, C. H. (1995). Assessment. In R. L. Edwards (Ed.), *Encyclopedia of social work* (19th ed., Vol. 1, pp. 260–270). Washington, DC: NASW Press.

Middleman, R. R., & Goldberg, G. G. (1990). *Skills for direct practice in social work.* New York: Columbia University Press.

Mihesuah, D. A. (1996). *American Indians: Stereotypes and realities.* Atlanta, GA: Clarity Press.

Miller, M., & Lago, D. (1990). The well-being of older women: The importance of pet and human relations. *Anthrozooes, 3*(4), 245–252.

Miller, S. D., Hubble, M. A., & Duncan, B. L. (Eds.). (1996). *Handbook of solution-focused brief therapy.* San Francisco: Jossey-Bass.

Miller, W. R., & Rollnick, S. (1991). *Motivational interviewing: Preparing people to change addictive behavior.* New York: Guilford Press.

Miller, W. R., & Rollnick, S. (2002). *Motivational interviewing: Preparing people for change* (2nd ed.). New York: Guilford Press.

Mindess, A. (1999). *Reading between the signs: Intercultural communication for sign language interpreters.* Yarmouth, ME: Intercultural Press.

Morales, A. T., & Sheafor, B. W. (1998). *Social work: A profession of many faces* (8th ed.). Boston: Allyn & Bacon.

Morone, J. A. (2003). *Hellfire nation: The politics of sin in American history.* New Haven, CT: Yale University Press.

Morrow-Howell, N., Chadiha, L. A., Proctor, E. K., Hourd-Bryant, M., & Dore, P. (1996). Racial differences in discharge planning. *Health and Social Work, 21*(2), 131–139.

Mulac, A., Erlandson, K. T., Farra, W. J., Hallett, J. S., Molloy, J. L., & Prescott, M. E. (1998). "Uh-huh. What's that all about?" Differing interpretations of conversational backchannels and questions as sources of miscommunication across gender boundaries. *Communication Research, 25*, 641–668.

Mulac, A., Bradac, J. J., & Gibbons, P. (2001). Empirical support or the gender-as-culture hypothesis: An intercultural analysis of male/female language differences. *Human Communication Research, 27*, 121–152.

Myers, J. E. B. (1992). *Legal issues in child abuse and neglect.* Newbury Park, CA: Sage Publications.

Nadler, M. K., & Nadler, L. B. (2001). The roles of sex, empathy, and credibility in out-of-class communication between faculty and students. *Women's Studies in Communication, 24*(2), 241–262.

Nassar-McMillan, S. C. (2003). Counseling Arab Americans: Counselors' call for advocacy and social justice. *Counseling and Human Development, 35*(5), 1–12.

NASW National Committee on Racial and Ethnic Diversity. (2001). *NASW standards for cultural competence in social work practice.* Retrieved May 15, 2003, 2003, from http://www.socialworkers.org/sections/credentials/cultural_comp.asp

The NASW National Council on the Practice of Clinical Social Work. (1996). *Evaluation and treatment of adults with the possibility of recovered memories of childhood sexual abuse.* Washington, D.C.: National Association of Social Workers.

National Association of Social Workers. (1981a). *NASW standards for social work practice in child protection* (rev. ed.). Silver Spring, MD: Author.

National Association of Social Workers. (1981b). *NASW standards for the classification of social work practice.* Silver Spring, MD: Author.

National Association of Social Workers. (1981c). *NASW working statement on the purpose of social work.* Silver Spring, MD: Author.

National Association of Social Workers. (1984). *NASW standards and guidelines for social work case management for the functionally impaired* (rev. ed.). Silver Spring, MD: Author.

National Association of Social Workers. (1987). *NASW standards for social work in health care settings* (rev. ed.). Washington, DC: Author.

National Association of Social Workers. (1989). *NASW standards for the practice of clinical social work* (rev. ed.). Washington, DC: Author.

National Association of Social Workers. (1999). *Code of ethics of the National Association of Social Workers.* Retrieved April 10, 2003, from http://www.socialworkers.org/pubs/code/code.asp

National Association of Social Workers. (2001). *NASW procedures for professional review* (4th ed.). Washington, DC: Author.

National Association of Social Workers. (2002a). *NASW standards for school social work services.* Washington, DC: Author.

National Association of Social Workers. (2002b). *NASW standards for social work case management* (rev. ed.). Washington, DC: Author.

National Association of Social Workers. (2003a). *NASW standards for the practice of social work with adolescents [draft]* (rev. ed.). Washington, DC: Author.

National Association of Social Workers. (2003b). *Standards for social work services in long-term care facilities* (rev. ed.). Washington, DC: Author.

Neal, J. (2002, March–April). Making diamonds: Helping children benefit from stress. *Natural Life*, 20.

Negroni-Rodriguez, L. K., & Morales, J. (2001). Individual and family assessment skills with Latino/Hispanic Americans. In R. Fong & S. Furuto (Eds.), *Culturally competent practice* (pp. 132–146). Boston: Allyn & Bacon.

Nelson, S. H., McCoy, G. F., Stetter, M., & Vanderwagen, W. C. (1992). An overview of mental health services for American-Indians and Alaska natives in the 1990s. *Hospital and Community Psychiatry, 43* 257–261.

Norman, E. (Ed.). (2000). *Resiliency enhancement: Putting the strengths perspective into social work practice.* New York: Columbia University Press.

Office for Civil Rights. (2003, May). *Summary of the HIPAA privacy rule.* United States Department of Health and Human Services.

O'Hanlon, W. H. (2003). *A guide to inclusive therapy: 26 methods of respectful resistance-dissolving therapy.* New York: W.W. Norton.

O'Hanlon, W. H., & Weiner-Davis, M. (1989). *In search of solutions: A new direction in psychotherapy.* New York: W.W. Norton.

Oktay, J. S., Steinwachs, D. M., Mamon, J., Bone, L. R., & Fahey, M. (1992). Evaluating social work discharge planning services for elderly people: Access, complexity, and outcome. *Health and Social Work, 17*(4), 239–298.

O'Neill, P. (1998). *Negotiating consent in psychotherapy.* New York: New York University Press.

O'Reilly, B. K. (1995). The Social Support Appraisals Scale: Construct validation for psychiatric patients. *Journal of Clinical Psychology, 51*(1), 37–42.

Patterson, M. M. (1998). Child abuse: Assessment and intervention. *Orthopaedic Nursing, 17*(1), 49–58.

Paul, R. (1993). *Critical thinking: What every person needs to survive in a rapidly changing world* (3rd ed.). Santa Rosa, CA: Foundation for Critical Thinking.

Payne, K. E. (2001). *Different but equal: Communication between the sexes.* Westport, CT: Praeger.

Pedersen, P. (1981). *Developing interculturally skilled counselors (DISC). Final report to the National Institute of Mental Health.* Honolulu: University of Hawaii.

Pedersen, P. (2000a). *A handbook for developing multicultural awareness.* Alexandria, VA: American Counseling Association.

Pedersen, P. (2000b). *Hidden messages in culture-centered counseling: A triad training model.* Thousand Oaks, CA: Sage Publications.

Pedersen, P. (2002). *Counseling across cultures.* Thousand Oaks, CA: Sage Publications.

Pedersen, P. (2003). *Multicultural counseling in schools: Practice handbook.* Boston: Allyn & Bacon.

Pedersen, P. B., & Ivey, A. (1993). *Culture-centered counseling and interviewing skills: A practical guide.* Westport, CT: Praeger.

Pekarik, G. (1988). The relationship of counselor identification of client problem description to continuance in a behavioral weight loss program. *Journal of Counseling Psychology, 35,* 66–70.

Pekarik, G. (1991). Relationship of expected and actual treatment duration for child and adult clients. *Journal of Child Clinical Psychology, 20,* 121–125.

Peled, E., Eisikovits, Z., Enosh, G., & Winstok, Z. (2000). Choice and empowerment for battered women who stay: Toward a constructivist model. *Social Work, 45*(1), 9–25.

Perlman, H. H. (1957). *Social casework: A problem-solving process.* Chicago: University of Chicago Press.

Perlman, H. H. (1979). *Relationship: The heart of helping people.* Chicago: University of Chicago Press.

Peters, S. (2003, January). HHS releases FAQs about medical privacy rule. *Clinical Psychiatry News, 31*(1), 71.

Phillips, H. U. (1957). *Essentials of social group work skill.* New York: Association Press.

Pinderhughes, E. (1979). Teaching empathy in cross-cultural social work. *Social Work, 24,* 312–316.

Ponterotto, J. G., & Casas, J. M. (1991). *Handbook of racial-ethnic minority counseling research.* Springfield, IL: Charles C Thomas.

Pope-Davis, D., Heesacker, M., Coleman, H. L. K., Liu, W. M., & Toporek, R. L. (2003). *Handbook of multicultural competencies in counseling and psychology.* Thousand Oaks, CA: Sage.

Prochaska, J. M. (2000). Transtheoretical model for assessing organizational change: A study of family service agencies' movement to time-limited therapy. *Families in Society: The Journal of Contemporary Human Services, 81*(1), 76–84.

Prochaska, J. O. (1999). How do people change, and how can we change to help many more people? In B. L. Duncan & M. A. Hubble (Eds.), *The heart and soul of change: What works in therapy* (pp. 227–255). Washington, DC: American Psychological Association.

Prochaska, J. O., & DiClemente, C. C. (1982). Transtheoretical therapy: Toward a more integrative model of change. *Psychotherapy: Theory, Research & Practice, 19,* 276–288.

Prochaska, J. O., Norcross, J. C., & DiClemente, C. C. (1994). *Changing for good: A revolutionary six-stage program for overcoming bad habits and moving your life positively forward.* New York: Avon.

Proctor, E. K., Morrow-Howell, N., & Kaplan, S. J. (1996). Implementation of discharge plans for chronically ill elders discharged home. *Health and Social Work, 21*(1), 30–40.

Rapp, C. A. (1998). *The strengths model: Case management with people suffering from severe and persistent mental illness.* New York: Oxford University Press.

Rapp, R. (1997). The strengths perspective and persons with substance abuse problems. In D. Saleebey (Ed.), *The strengths perspective in social work practice* (2nd ed., pp. 77–96). New York: Longman.

Reamer, F. G. (1994). *Social work malpractice and liability.* New York: Columbia University Press.

Reamer, F. G. (1995a). Ethics and values. In R. L. Edwards (Ed.), *Encyclopedia of social work* (19th ed., Vol. 1, pp. 893–902). Washington, DC: NASW Press.

Reamer, F. G. (1995b). Malpractice claims against social workers: First facts. *Social Work, 40*(5), 595–601.

Reamer, F. G. (1997). Ethical standards in social work: The NASW Code of Ethics. In R. L. Edwards (Ed.), *Encyclopedia of social work, 1997 Supplement* (19th rev ed., Vol. Supplement). Washington, DC: NASW Press.

Reamer, F. G. (1998a). *Ethical standards in social work: A critical review of the NASW Code of Ethics.* Washington, DC: NASW Press.

Reamer, F. G. (1998b). The evolution of social work ethics (Special Centennial Issue). *Social Work, 43*(6), 488–498.

Reamer, F. G. (2000). The social work ethics audit: A risk-management strategy. *Social Work, 45*(4), 355–366.

Reamer, F. G., & Conrad, S. A. P. (1995). *Professional choices: Ethics at work* [Video]. Washington, DC: NASW Press.

Recent cases. (2001). Recent cases: Evidence—Sixth Circuit holds that Tarasoff disclosures do not vitiate psychotherapist-patient privilege—*United States v. Hayes*, 227 F.3d 578 (6th Cir. 2000). *Harvard Law Review, 114*(7), 2194–2200.

Reeves, D. (1997). Consultation and development plans: Preparation and implementation of the advisory group process. *Community Development Journal, 32*(4), 332–341.

Regan, J. J., Alderson, A., & Regan, W. M. (2002). Health care providers' duty to warn. *Southern Medical Journal, 95*(12), 1396–1400.

Reid, W. J. (1992). *Task strategies: An empirical approach to social work.* New York: Columbia University Press.

Reid, W. J. (2002). Knowledge for direct social work practice: An analysis of trends. *Social Service Review, 76*(1), 6–33.

Rhodes, M. (1986). *Ethical dilemmas in social work practice.* London: Routledge & Kegan Paul.

Richmond, M. E. (1944). *Social diagnosis.* New York: The Free Press. First published in 1917.

Ripple, L. (1955). Motivation, capacity, and opportunity as related to the use of casework service: Plan of study. *Social Service Review, 29*, 172–193.

Ripple, L., & Alexander, E. (1956). Motivation, capacity, and opportunity as related to the use of casework service: Nature of client's problem. *Social Service Review, 30*, 38–54.

Ripple, L., Alexander, E., & Polemis, B. W. (1964). *Motivation, capacity, and opportunity: Studies in casework theory and practice.* Chicago: University of Chicago School of Social Service Administration.

Rogers, C. R. (1951). *Client centered therapy.* New York: Houghton Mifflin.

Rogers, C. R. (1957). The necessary and sufficient conditions of psychotherapeutic personality change. *Journal of Consulting Psychology, 21*, 95–103.

Rogers, C. R. (1961). *On becoming a person.* Boston: Houghton Mifflin.

Rogers, C. R. (1975). Empathic: An unappreciated way of being. *Counseling Psychologist, 5*, 2–10.

Rogers, J. R., Lewis, M. M., & Subich, L. M. (2002). Validity of the Suicide Assessment Checklist in an emergency crisis center. *Journal of Counseling and Development, 80*(4), 493–502.

Rollnick, S. (2002). A motivational interviewing perspective on resistance in psychotherapy. *Journal of Clinical Psychology, 58*(2), 185–193.

Rollnick, S., & Miller, W. R. (1995). What is motivational interviewing? *Behavioural and Cognitive Psychotherapy, 23*, 325–334.

Rose, S. M. (2000). Reflections on empowerment-based practice. *Social Work, 45*(5), 403–412.

Rosenbaum, M. (1980). A schedule for assessing self-control behaviors: Preliminary findings. *Behavior Therapy, 11*, 109–121.

Rosenzweig, S. (1936). Some implicit common factors in diverse methods of psychotherapy. *American Journal of Orthopsychiatry, 6*, 412–415.

Roysircar, G. (2003). *Multicultural counseling competencies 2003: Association for Multicultural Counseling and Development.* Alexandria, VA: American Counseling Association.

Saleebey, D. (Ed.). (1997). *The strengths perspective in social work practice* (2nd ed.). New York: Longman.

Saleebey, D. (1999). The strengths perspective: Principles and practices. In B. Compton & B. Galaway (Eds.), *Social work processes* (6th ed., pp. 14–23). Pacific Grove, CA: Brooks/Cole.

Saleebey, D. (2001). The Diagnostic Strengths Manual? *Social Work, 46*(2), 183–187.

Saleebey, D. (Ed.). (2002). *The strengths perspective in social work practice* (3rd ed.). Boston: Allyn & Bacon.

Saltzman, A., & Proch, K. (1990). *Law in social work practice.* Chicago: Nelson-Hall.

Samantrai, K. (2004). *Culturally competent public child welfare practice.* Pacific Grove, CA: Brooks/Cole.

Sar, B. K. (2000). Preparation for adoptive parenthood with a special-needs child: Role of agency preparation tasks. *Adoption Quarterly, 3*(4), 63–80.

Satir, V. (1972). *Peoplemaking.* Palo Alto, CA: Science and Behavior Books.

Saulnier, C. F. (2002). Deciding who to see: Lesbians discuss their preferences in health and mental health care providers. *Social Work, 47*(4), 355–364.

Schon, D. A. (1990). *Educating the reflective practitioner: Toward a new design for teaching and learning in the professions.* New York: John Wiley & Sons.

Schwartz, W. (1971). On the use of groups in social work practice. In W. Schwartz & S. Zalba (Eds.), *The practice of group work* (pp. 3–24). New York: Columbia University Press.

Schwartz, W. (1976). Between client and system: The mediating function. In R. R. Roberts & H. Northen (Eds.), *Theories of social work with groups* (pp. 188–190). New York: Columbia University Press.

Sellman, J. D., Sullivan, P. F., Dore, C. M., Adamson, S. J., & MacEwan, I. (2001). A randomized controlled trial of Motivational Enhancement Therapy (MET) for mild to moderate alcohol dependence. *Journal of Studies on Alcohol, 62*(3), 389–396.

Shulman, L. (1984). *The skills of helping individuals and groups* (2nd ed.). Itasca, IL: F. E. Peacock.

Shulman, L. (1992). *The skills of helping individuals, families, and groups* (3rd ed.). Itasca, IL: F. E. Peacock.

Shulman, L. (1999). *The skills of helping individuals, families, groups, and communities* (4th ed.). Itasca, IL: F. E. Peacock.

Shuman, A. L., & Shapiro, J. P. (2002). The effects of preparing parents for child psychotherapy on accuracy of expectations and treatment attendance. *Community Mental Health Journal, 38*(1), 3–16.

Shutiva, C. (1994). Native American culture and communication through humor. In A. Gonzalez, M. Houston, & V. Chen (Eds.), *Our voices: Essays in culture, ethnicity, and communication, an intercultural anthology* (pp. 117–121). Los Angeles: Roxbury.

Silvestri, G. T. (1997). Occupation employment projections to 2006. *Monthly Labor Review* (November), 58–83.

Sinha, S. P., Nayyar, P., & Sinha, S. P. (2002). Social support and self-control as variables in attitude toward life and perceived control among older people in India. *Journal of Social Psychology, 42*(4), 527–541.

Slovak, K. (2002). Gun violence and children: Factors related to exposure and trauma. *Health and Social Work, 27*(2), 104–112.

Smalley, R. E. (1967). *Theory for social work practice.* New York: Columbia University Press.

Spath, P. (2002). Improve your discharge planning effectiveness; patient and caregiver involvement is key. *Hospital Peer Review, 27*(6), 84–87.

Staff. (2003a, May 11). Correcting the record: Times reporter who resigned leaves long trail of deception. *New York Times,* A1.

Staff. (2003b, May 11). Witnesses and documents unveil deceptions in a reporter's work. *New York Times,* A26.

Sternbach, J. (2000). Lessons learned about working with men: A prison memoir. *Social Work, 45*(5), 413–423.

Stotland, E. (2003). Empathy. In W. E. Craighead & C. B. Nemeroff (Eds.), *The Corsini encyclopedia of psychology and behavioral science* (3rd ed.). New York: Wiley.

Stotland, E., Mathews, K., Sherman, S., Hansson, R., & Richardson, B. (1978). *Fantasy, empathy, and helping.* Beverly Hills, CA: Sage.

Strom-Gottfried, K. J. (1999). Professional boundaries: An analysis of violations by social workers. *Families in Society, 80*(5), 439–450.

Strom-Gottfried, K. J. (2000a). Ensuring ethical practice: An examination of NASW code violations, 1986–97. *Social Work, 45*(3), 251–261.

Strom-Gottfried, K. J. (2000b). Ethical vulnerability in social work education: An analysis of NASW complaints. *Journal of Social Work Education, 36*(2), 241–252.

Strom-Gottfried, K. J. (2003). Understanding adjudication: Origins, targets, and outcomes of ethics complaints. *Social Work, 48*(1), 85–95.

Sue, D. W. (1977). Counseling the culturally different: A conceptual analysis. *Personnel and Guidance Journal, 55,* 422–425.

Sue, D. W., & Arredondo, P. (1992). Multicultural counseling competencies and standards: A call to the profession. *Journal of Counseling & Development, 70*(4), 477–487.

Sue, D. W., Carter, R. T., Casas, J. M., Fouad, N. A., Ivey, A. E., Jensen, M., et al. (Eds.). (1998). *Multicultural counseling competencies: Individual and organizational development.* Thousand Oaks, CA: Sage.

Sue, D. W., & Sue, D. (1999). *Counseling the culturally different: Theory and practice* (3rd ed.). New York: Wiley.

Sutton, C. T., & Nose, M. (1996). American Indian families: An overview. In M. McGoldrick, J. Giordano, & J. K. Pears (Eds.), *Ethnicity and family therapy* (pp. 31–44). New York: Guilford.

Tannen, D. (1990). *You just don't understand: Women and men in conversation.* New York: Morrow.

Tannen, D. (1994). *Talking from 9 to 5: How women's and men's conversational styles affect who gets heard, who gets credit, and what gets done at work.* New York: Morrow.

Thyer, B. A., & Wodarski, J. S. (Eds.). (1998). *Handbook of empirical social work practice* (Vol. 1). New York: John Wiley & Sons.

Tingley, J. C. (2001). *The power of indirect influence.* New York: AMACOM Books.

Toffler, A. (1983). *The third wave.* New York: Bantam.

Tolson, E. R., Reid, W. J., & Garvin, C. D. (1994). *Generalist practice: A task-centered approach.* New York: Columbia University Press.

Toulmin, S. (1981). The tyranny of principles. *Hastings Center Report, 11*(6), 31–39.

Truax, D. B., & Carkhuff, R. R. (1967). *Toward effective counseling and psychotherapy: Training and practice.* Chicago & New York: Aldine Atherton.

Turner, R. J., & Marino, F. (1994). Social support and social structure: A descriptive epidemiology. *Journal of Health of Social Behavior, 35,* 193–212.

Tuzman, L., & Cohen, A. (1992). Clinical decision making for discharge planning in a changing psychiatric environment. *Health and Social Work, 17*(4), 299–307.

U.S. Census Bureau Population Division Population Projections Branch. (2002, August 2). *Projects of the resident population by race, Hispanic origin, and nativity: Middle series, 1999 to 2100 (NP-T5).* Retrieved May 20, 2003, from http://www.census.gov/population/www/projections/natsum-T5.html

United States Government. (2002, May). *International Classification of Diseases, Tenth Revision, Clinical Modification (ICD-10-CM) [Pre-Release Draft].* Washington, DC: Author.

United States v. Hayes. (6th Cir. 2000). 227 F.3d 578.

VandeCreek, L., & Knapp, S. (1993). *Tarasoff and beyond: Legal and clinical considerations in the treatment of life-endangering patients* (rev. ed.). Sarasota, FL: Professional Resource Press.

VandeCreek, L., & Knapp, S. (2001). *Tarasoff and beyond: Legal and clinical considerations in the treatment of life-endangering patients* (3rd ed.). Sarasota, FL: Professional Resource Press.

Vass, A. A. (1996). *Social work competences: Core knowledge, values and skills.* Thousand Oaks, CA: Sage.

Vaux, A., Phillips, J., Holly, L., Thompson, B., Williams, D., & Stewart, D. (1986). The Social Support Appraisals (SSA) Scale: Studies of reliability and validity. *American Journal of Community Psychology, 14,* 195–219.

Villa, R. F. (2001). Social work evaluation with Mexican Americans. In R. Fong & S. Furuto (Eds.), *Culturally competent practice* (pp. 370–383). Boston: Allyn & Bacon.

Vinter, R. D. (1963). Analysis of treatment organizations. *Social Work, 8,* 3–15.

Walsh, F. (2003). Family resilience: A framework for clinical practice. *Family Process, 42*(1), 1–18.

Walsh, J. (2002). Shyness and social phobia: A social work perspective on a problem in living. *Health and Social Work, 27*(2), 137–144.

Walsh, J., & Meyersohn, K. (2001). Ending clinical relationships with people with schizophrenia. *Health and Social Work, 26*(3), 188–195.

Walters, K. L., Longres, J. F., Han, C., & Icard, L. D. (2003). Cultural competence with gay and lesbian persons of color. In D. Lum (Ed.), *Culturally competent practice: A framework for understanding diverse groups and justice issues* (2nd ed., pp. 310–342). Pacific Grove, CA: Brooks/Cole.

Walz, T., & Ritchie, H. (2000). Gandhian principles in social work practice: Ethics revisited. *Social Work, 45*(3), 213–222.

Wamback, K. G., & Harrison, D. F. (1992). Social work practice with women. In D. F. Harrison, J. S. Wodarski & B. A. Thyer (Eds.), *Cultural diversity and social work practice* (pp. 157–180). Springfield, IL: Charles C. Thomas.

Weaver, H. N. (2003). Cultural competence with First Nations peoples. In D. Lum (Ed.), *Culturally competent practice: A framework for understanding diverse groups and justice issues* (2nd ed., pp. 197–216). Pacific Grove, CA: Brooks/Cole.

Wegscheider-Cruse, S. (1985). *Choice-making.* Pompano Beach, FL: Health Communications.

Weinberger, J. (1993). Common factors in psychotherapy. In G. Stricker & J. R. Gold (Eds.), *Comprehensive handbook of psychotherapy integration* (pp. 43–58). New York: Plenum.

Weinberger, J. (1995). Common factors aren't so common: The common factors dilemma. *Clinical Psychology: Science and Practice, 2,* 45–69.

Weinberger, J. (2003). Common factors. In W. E. Craighead & C. B. Nemeroff (Eds.), *The Corsini encyclopedia of psychology and behavioral science*. New York: John Wiley & Sons.

Westbrooks, K. L., & Starks, S. H. (2001). Strengths perspective inherent in cultural empowerment: A tool for assessment with African American individuals and families. In R. Fong & S. Furuto (Eds.), *Culturally competent practice* (pp. 101–118). Boston: Allyn & Bacon.

Whitfield, K. E., & Wiggins, S. (2003). The influence of social support and health on everyday problem solving in adult African Americans. *Experimental Aging Research, 29*(1), 1–13.

Wierzbicki, M., & Pekarik, G. (1993). A meta-analysis of psychotherapy dropout. *Professional Psychology Research and Practice, 24*, 190–195.

Williams, J. B. W. (1994). PIE research issues. In J. M. Karls & K. E. Wandrei (Eds.), *Person-In-Environment (PIE) System: The PIE classification system for social functioning problems* (pp. 197–202). Washington, DC: NASW Press.

Williams, J. B. W. (1995). Diagnostic and statistical manual of mental disorders. In R. L. Edwards (Ed.), *Encyclopedia of social work* (19th ed., Vol. 1, pp. 729–739). Washington, DC: NASW Press.

Williams, J. B. W., & Ell, K. (Eds.). (1998). *Advances in mental health research: Implications for practice*. Washington, DC: NASW Press.

Williams, J. B. W., Karls, J. M., & Wandrei, K. E. (1989). The Person-in-Environment (PIE) system for describing problems of social functioning. *Hospital and Community Psychiatry, 40*(11), 1125–1127.

Wilson, S. J. (1980). *Recording: Guidelines for social workers*. New York: Free Press.

Wodarski, J. S. (1992a). Social work practice with African Americans. In D. F. Harrison, J. S. Wodarski & B. A. Thyer (Eds.), *Cultural diversity and social work practice* (pp. 13–44). Springfield, IL: Charles C. Thomas.

Wodarski, J. S. (1992b). Social work practice with Asian Americans. In D. F. Harrison, J. S. Wodarski & B. A. Thyer (Eds.), *Cultural diversity and social work practice* (pp. 45–70). Springfield, IL: Charles C. Thomas.

Wodarski, J. S. (1992c). Social work practice with Hispanic Americans. In D. F. Harrison, J. S. Wodarski & B. A. Thyer (Eds.), *Cultural diversity and social work practice* (pp. 71–106). Springfield, IL: Charles C. Thomas.

Wodarski, J. S., & Thyer, B. A. (Eds.). (1998). *Handbook of empirical social work practice* (Vol. 2). New York: John Wiley & Sons.

Woititz, J. G. (1983). *Adult children of alcoholics*. Pompano Beach, FL: Health Communications.

Wolman, B. B. (Ed.). (1973). *Dictionary of behavioral science*. New York: Van Nostrand Reinhold.

Woodruff, P. (2001). *Reverence: Renewing a forgotten virtue*. New York: Oxford University Press.

Woody, R. H. (1997). *Legally safe mental health practice: Psycholegal questions and answers*. Madison, CT: Psychosocial Press.

World Health Organization. (1992). *International statistical classification of diseases and related health problems, 10th revision* (Vol. 1: Tabular List). Geneva, Switzerland: Author.

Yalom, I. D., Houts, P. S., Newell, G., & Rand, K. H. (1967). Preparation of patients for group therapy. A controlled study. *Archives of General Psychiatry, 17*(4), 416–427.

Yuen, F. K. O. (2002). *Family health social work practice: A knowledge and skills casebook*. New York: Haworth.

Zastrow, C. (1995). *The practice of social work* (5th ed.). Pacific Grove, CA: Brooks/Cole.

Zhang, N., & Dixon, D. N. (2001). Multiculturally responsive counseling: Effects on Asian students' ratings of counselors. *Journal of Multicultural Counseling and Development, 29*(4), 253–262.

Zimmerman, T. S., Jacobsen, R. B., MacIntyre, M., & Watson, C. (1996). Solution-focused parenting groups: An empirical study. *Journal of Systemic Therapies, 15*, 12–25.

Zuniga, M. E. (2001). Latinos: Cultural competence and ethics. In R. Fong & S. Furuto (Eds.), *Culturally competent practice* (pp. 47–60). Boston: Allyn & Bacon.

Zuniga, M. E. (2003). Cultural competence with Latino Americans. In D. Lum (Ed.), *Culturally competent practice: A framework for understanding diverse groups and justice issues* (2nd ed., pp. 238–260). Pacific Grove, CA: Brooks/Cole.

TO THE OWNER OF THIS BOOK:

I hope that you have found *The Social Work Skills Workbook*, Fourth Edition useful. So that this book can be improved in a future edition, would you take the time to complete this sheet and return it? Thank you.

School and address: _____

_____

Department: _____

Instructor's name: _____

1. What I like most about this book is: _____

_____

_____

2. What I like least about this book is: _____

_____

_____

3. My general reaction to this book is: _____

_____

_____

_____

4. The name of the course in which I used this book is: _____

_____

5. Were all of the chapters of the book assigned for you to read? _____

   If not, which ones weren't? _____

6. In the space below, or on a separate sheet of paper, please write specific suggestions for improving this book and anything else you'd care to share about your experience in using this book.

_____

_____

_____

_____

_____

_____

_____

THOMSON

BROOKS/COLE ™

BUSINESS REPLY MAIL
FIRST-CLASS MAIL   PERMIT NO. 102   MONTEREY CA

POSTAGE WILL BE PAID BY ADDRESSEE

Attn: *Social Work, Lisa Gebo*

BrooksCole/Thomson Learning
60 Garden Ct Ste 205
Monterey CA 93940-9967

OPTIONAL:

Your name: _____ Date: _____

May we quote you, either in promotion for *The Social Work Skills Workbook*, Fourth Edition, or in future publishing ventures?

Yes: _____ No: _____

Sincerely yours,

Barry Cournoyer